ANN S. FLETCHER

1947–1999

Open almost any book on international educational systems published for admissions officers by NAFSA or AACRAO over the past 20 years and you will find Ann Fletcher's fingerprints, as well as her trademarks of intelligence, commitment, and energy. Even when Ann was not the primary writer or researcher, her name most likely appears among the list of NAFSA or AACRAO members responsible for many of the valuable projects in the field of international education research. A good example is her important contribution to this handbook; see the chapter on the United States.

We dedicate A *Guide to Educational Systems Around the World* in honor of Ann's invaluable contributions to international admissions and education. It is a fitting testament to her zealous pursuit of the very best information for admissions personnel in the field of international education and to her longstanding commitment to graduate admissions. Those of us who knew her, as well as those who will know her only by her work, are indebted to her and her legacy.

Friends of Ann Fletcher
June 1999

CONTENTS

vi

vii

Not included in this publication is information on the following countries: Afghanistan, Azerbaijan, Benin, Burundi, Cambodia, Estonia, Guadeloupe, Guinea, Kazakhstan, Kyrgyzstan, Laos, Libya, Lithuania, Luxembourg, Madagascar, Martinique, Mauritania, Mauritius, Netherlands Antilles, New Caledonia, Paraguay, Reunion, Somalia, Sri Lanka, Sudan, Suriname, Tajikistan, Turkmenistan, Uganda, United Arab Emirates, and Uzbekistan

FOREWORD

At the 1997 NAFSA Fall Leadership Meeting, several members of the Admissions Section (ADSEC) National team came up with the idea of a new edition of *Handbook on the Placement of Foreign Graduate Students*, which has become known as the "Graduate Handbook." The then current edition of the handbook was published in 1990 and ADSEC team members knew of several changes since then that would not only justify a new publication, but make the production of a new edition feasible: the break-up of the Soviet Union, direct access to previously difficult-to-obtain information via the Internet, and the ability to create camera-ready copy on most computers, to name a few.

There were other changes as well. The National Council on the Evaluation of Foreign Academic Credentials (CEC) met in June 1996 and developed a new approach to assessing credentials for admission and placement in academic institutions in the United States. The new methodology is not dependent on CEC placement recommendations; instead, it evaluates components of education in another country that match (or do not match, as the case may be) components of education at the evaluator's institution or organization. In keeping with this new approach, this publication does not contain any placement recommendations.

In general, the goals for this project have been two-fold: produce an up-to-date, multi-country resource on educational credentials to be used as a basic reference by international admissions staff in the United States; and complete the project within a year.

In keeping with these goals, this edition of the handbook is designed to provide a visual overview of the structure of an educational system and the credentials or qualifications awarded at both the secondary and higher levels of education. The picture is provided by a ladder of the educational system, identifying at what point on the ladder the credentials are awarded and, where possible, giving the actual name of the credential awarded in the language of the country. In addition, grading scales and postsecondary recognition bodies are presented. Information on resources for additional information (especially web addresses) are identified.

Since most admissions officers and credential evaluators have easy access to computers and standard word processing software, it was decided that the research and writing of this publication could be done by several "volunteers." A template of what each country profile should contain was created on diskette and instructions for conducting and documenting the research written. The team agreed to complete the entire project within a year from the starting date, not as a challenge, but out of consideration that information and education in today's world changes, and sometimes changes rapidly.

Thus was born this transformation of the 1990 "Graduate Handbook." My first task in coordinating the effort on behalf on the ADSEC team was to identify someone who would compile and edit the book. Shelley Feagles of Educational Credential Evaluators, Inc. immediately came to mind as someone who would not only see this project through to fruition, but also make sure that the finished product was everything it could be. To everyone's surprise, Shelley agreed to volunteer, but only on condition that the ADSEC team provide support for recruiting volunteer authors and act as an advisory board to the publication. We agreed and began to recruit volunteer authors in early 1998. The project has stayed very much on schedule and true to our purpose thanks to Shelley's gentle but persistent reminders, skill, patience, and the tremendous effort of all of the volunteer authors in doing the research and producing their diskettes.

It is our hope that readers will find this publication a valuable tool in approaching various educational systems around the world. We also hope that the additional articles will be of assistance to those doing the evaluation of foreign academic credentials for the first time or be a helpful "snapshot" for those who are more experienced.

Timothy S. Thompson
ADSEC National Team
Coordinator/Liaison, *A Guide to Educational Systems Around the World*

ACKNOWLEDGMENTS

Many thanks to all of the volunteer authors/compilers, without whom there would be no publication. We are also indebted to Jim Frey of Educational Credential Evaluators, Inc., for his article on "Determining Credit Equivalents;" Margit Schatzman, representing the National Council on the Evaluation of Foreign Educational Credentials, for her article titled "Methodology for Credential Evaluation;" World Education Services, Inc., for permission to reprint Guy Haug's article "Capturing the Message Conveyed by Grades;" and Marybeth Mirzejewski of Educational Credential Evaluators, Inc., for her article on "Internet Research for the Foreign Credential Evaluator."

Additional thanks to Margo Ptacek of Educational Credential Evaluators, Inc., who developed the template that has served us so well, and to Dario Kenning, who, in his first week of his new job at the University of Pittsburgh, retyped what is reprinted from *World Education News & Reviews*.

ADVISORY BOARD

USER'S GUIDE

by Shelley M. Feagles, editor

The purpose of preparing *A Guide to Educational Systems Around the World* was to update the 1990 edition of the *Handbook on the Placement of Foreign Graduate Students*, colloquially known as the "Graduate Handbook." While the 1990 edition was our model, there are some noteworthy differences in this version:

1)   This publication provides lists of credentials and other data that can be used both for undergraduate and graduate admissions.

2)   "Advice for admissions officers" is intentionally not provided. We have strived to avoid all types of subjective interpretation, relying instead on objective data. The omission of an advice section goes hand-in-hand with a new methodology for credential evaluation from the National Council on the Evaluation of Foreign Educational Credentials. The new methodology is now in the process of replacing "placement recommendations." A full description of the methodology is included in this publication. Viewpoints for interpreting foreign grading and credit systems are provided in separate articles.

These two differences point to the necessity of institutions to provide an adequate budget for resources and training for undergraduate and graduate admissions personnel. This publication should be supplemented by additional written materials which describe complete foreign educational systems, including data on specific institutions, and by professional training in the theory and practice of credential evaluation.

At the end of each country compilation is a list of country-specific resources; Appendix A provides the contact information of publishers and distributors of resources on foreign educational systems and a short list of specific multi-country resources. These resources can be used as a starting point in establishing a credential evaluation library. In addition, admissions personnel should have access to the World Wide Web and learn how to use it conscientiously. Suggestions for using the Internet for research in foreign credential evaluation are provided in a supplementary article.

This publication was compiled by many authors using a standardized template and style. Although minor variations among entries do occur, the basic guidelines are explained as follows:

Educational Ladder

```
      ½   ½   ½   ½   ½   ½   ½   ½   ½   ½
1 → 6 |  7 |  8 |  9 | 10 | 11 | 12 | 13 | 14 | 15 | 16 |

          A               B   B
```

The year or half-year at which a credential is awarded is the point at which the corresponding credential letter is placed. In the example above, credential **A** is awarded after the 9th year of education. Note that the corresponding letter is placed directly below the number 9.

All normal possibilities of the total number of years of education that a credential might require are indicated on the ladder. This occurs for credential **B**, in which the credential can be awarded after either 12 or 13 total years of education. An explanation is provided in the description of the credential whenever a letter appears on the ladder more than once. There are a few cases when this multiple-listing style was not used; in these cases, there are explanatory comments.

An arrow (→) is used after a credential letter in cases where no maximum length of study for a particular program is specified, or where the study time is open-ended. For example, a doctor of philosophy degree program may require a *minimum* of three years of enrollment. The corresponding credential letter with an arrow will appear under the minimum number of total years of education required to earn the Ph.D.

Explanations About Documents

Credentials are divided into two categories: *secondary* and *postsecondary*. The decision to include the credential under one or the other category is not a subjective one--a credential is determined to be either secondary or postsecondary according to its designation in the country of origin. For example, the United Kingdom credential of General Certificate of Education, Advanced Level, is included with secondary credentials, even though it is quite common for U.S. institutions to consider postsecondary-level credit for this credential. The bottom line is that GCE-A Levels are considered to be part of the secondary sector in the United Kingdom.

Numerical endnotes, placed directly after the complete list of credentials, are used when a lengthy explanation about a credential is necessary.

Foreign Words

Foreign terms are used whenever possible, and are translated literally, in most cases. Literal translations are used to avoid subjectivity. We have attempted to be consistent with translations across languages, though readers may notice some differences between countries due to preferences indicated by the compilers. Credential evaluators and admissions personnel should always rely on official foreign-language documents, using translations only as guides.

Non-Roman Alphabets

We have provided the foreign terms for credentials in several non-Roman alphabets; namely Arabic, Cyrillic, Georgian, and Greek. For the Arabic-speaking countries of Bahrain, Iraq, Kuwait, and Qatar, the compilers did not have access to software that allowed the use of Arabic terms. Arabic was, however, used for Egypt, Jordan, Lebanon, Oman, Palestinian National Authority, Saudi Arabia, Syria, and Yemen. There are similarities in credentials awarded in these countries with credentials awarded in Bahrain, Iraq, Kuwait, and Qatar, so users could refer to the other country compilations for assistance in verifying Arabic terms.

We were not able to provide credential names in Chinese (People's Republic of China), Farsi (Iran), or Hebrew (Israel). Users should refer to other sources to verify the names of credentials in these languages. Most other countries using non-Roman alphabets for their native languages provide official educational documentation in English, such as Bangladesh, India, Japan, Korea, Pakistan, Taiwan, and Thailand. This applies to Bahrain, Iraq, Kuwait, and Qatar as well.

Grading Information

Only the most common grading scales used in each country are listed. Evaluators understand that variations in grading are common and that one should always consult the grading information that may be provided on official transcripts. Rather than making grade equivalency statements, the compilers of this volume provided information regarding grading practices within the countries, when known.

Resources for Additional Information

Three types of resources are listed: written resources, agencies providing information to those with questions on foreign educational systems or specific institutions, and Internet sources. Compilers may have used additional resources for their research, but only those resources that are readily available are listed. Internet home pages for individual institutions are not listed. Instead, compilers have noted web sites that provide links to institutional home pages.

Countries Not Represented

Information on the educational systems of most countries are included in this publication. Some countries were not included because we were not able to find a compiler for that country, or because adequate information could not be found to prepare an entry for that country. The countries not included in this publication are listed at the end of the table of contents.

METHODOLOGY FOR CREDENTIAL EVALUATION
A Tool for Evaluating Foreign Education

by Margit A. Schatzman

The National Council on the Evaluation of Foreign Educational Credential (the Council) has adopted a methodology for the evaluation of foreign educational credentials to replace its longstanding "placement recommendations." A practical example of how admissions professionals can use the new methodology to evaluate foreign credentials is offered below.

The Council

Established in 1955, the Council is an interassociational group of representatives from the following national educational associations: the American Association of Collegiate Registrars and Admissions Officers (AACRAO), the American Association of Community Colleges, the American Council on Education, the College Board, the Council of Graduate Schools, the Institute of International Education, and NAFSA: Association of International Educators (NAFSA).

The role of the Council is to provide guidelines for interpreting foreign educational credentials for the placement of holders of these credentials in U.S. educational and other institutions. It is the only body in the United States specifically organized to perform this role. The Council reviews, modifies, and approves so-called placement recommendations drafted by the authors of studies published in the World Education Series (WES) and Projects in International Education Research (PIER), the former published by AACRAO and the latter jointly by AACRAO and NAFSA.

The process followed to produce the Council's placement recommendations has generally served the U.S. admissions community well. Over the years, however, the needs of admissions officers have changed, the backgrounds of applicants have become more varied, and increased international mobility of students and scholars has focused attention on the quality and consistency of the credentials evaluation process, both in the United States and in other countries.

By 1996, it became increasingly clear that changes should be made to the placement recommendation process.

Limitations of Placement Recommendations

Specialists in the field of foreign credential evaluation have relied for decades on the Council's placement recommendations, but over the years, several limitations have become apparent.

➤ Placement recommendations have the image of being mandates rather than suggestions.

➤ Many users of the placement recommendations apply them in isolation, without consideration of specific institutional policies or supporting text information.

➤ There has been a reduction in the number of publications in which placement recommendations have appeared, accompanied by an explosion of information from other sources for which there is no practical means of developing placement recommenda-tions, such as electronic web sites.

➤ No mechanism exists for describing the rationale for controversial placement recommendations, or for discussing the differences in opinions between and among authors and Council members.

The Milwaukee Symposium

The methodology described here is based on work done in June 1996 at the "Milwaukee Symposium," a gathering of leaders and practitioners in the field of foreign credential evaluation. The original purpose of the Milwaukee Symposium was to articulate a new methodology that would be used by the Council to evaluate foreign educational credentials. A broader goal for the symposium soon developed, however. That goal was to describe a methodological approach *that could be used by individuals in the field* to evaluate credentials and to determine their relevance in the context of institutional admission and placement policies.

Other goals of the Milwaukee Symposium were:

➤ To provide transparency in the process used to evaluate credentials

➤ To promote greater consistency in the evaluation of similar credentials

➤ To consider ways in which placement recommendations could provide more information to users.

As a result of the Milwaukee Symposium, the Council resolved to adopt the methodology recommended by the Milwaukee Symposium and to encourage practitioners in the field of foreign credential evaluation to do the same.

The International Admissions Decision-Making Process

The evaluation methodology is just one part of the process of making international admissions decisions. Other steps include reviewing a completed application form, determining financial resources and English language proficiency, and the evaluation of foreign academic credentials.

Evaluation of an academic credential involves **Nine Basic Tasks**, not necessarily in this order:

1 Comparison of the applicant's biographical information and educational history statement with the credential.

2 Verification of the accuracy of the English translation of a non-English credential.

3 Determination of the authenticity of the credential.

4 Verification of the official status of the institution awarding the credential.

5 Determination of the level of the program represented by the credential.

6 Determination of the equivalency of the credential.

7 Calculation of credits or units, if applicable.

8 Calculation of grades or grade point average.

9 Determination of the suitability of the applicant to the admitting institution.

Task 1 is completed to ensure that the credential being evaluated actually belongs to the applicant.

Task 2 is completed whenever the foreign credential is not issued in English. Key words and numbers, such as dates, all grades, and names, should be checked to determine if the translation is complete. The foreign credential, not the translation, should be the primary resource in the credential evaluation.

Tasks 3, 4, 5, 7, and 8 are completed by using international admissions resources, such as WES or PIER volumes or other sources, such as institutional web sites, ministry of education publications, or this publication.

Task 6 is at the heart of the decision-making process, and it is the task addressed by the methodology presented here. The equivalency determination requires the application of a set of principles and methods to a body of knowledge about the foreign educational system of the applicant, the U.S. educational system, and the institutional policies of the admitting institution. *The equivalency determination is the credential evaluator's opportunity to exercise judgment based on this body of knowledge, principles, and methods.*

The issue of judgment is key to this process. Although the methodology described here provides a clear and logical method for evaluating credentials, the international admissions professional will likely encounter situations in which the equivalency decision can be debated.

Each international admissions professional needs to consider a number of philosophical questions when applying the methodology. Some of these are:

➤ Which characteristics of a benchmark credential are essential for me to make an equivalency determination?

➤ Must a foreign program be the same length in years as the U.S. benchmark credential in order for me to make an equivalency determination?

➤ Should I apply the same admissions criteria to foreign applicants as I do to U.S. applicants?

➤ Do institutional policies or goals override other admissions considerations?

There are no simple answers to these questions. Each admissions professional must answer them in the context of the admissions philosophy and policies of his or her institution.

How the Methodology Works

The purpose of the methodology developed at the Milwaukee Symposium is to provide a clear and logical means of making an evaluation decision. The methodology is comprised of three critical steps; however, we must begin with a list of key terms and definitions:

Comparability - Determination of degree of likeness between two foreign credentials.

Benchmark credential - An academic award that marks the point of transition from one level of education to the next higher level. These include:

High school diploma: The U.S. credential that marks the point of transition from secondary to postsecondary education.

Bachelor's degree: The U.S. credential that marks the point of transition from undergraduate postsecondary education to graduate postsecondary education.

Master's degree: The U.S. credential that marks the point of transition from the first graduate postsecondary level to the highest postsecondary level.

How the Council Will Use the Methodology

The Council will phase out placement recommendations and replace them with key Credential Profiles. The Council will use a modified version of the Milwaukee methodology to provide guidance to international admissions professionals.

Using **Step 1**, the Council will develop profiles of key characteristics of U.S. benchmark credentials, such as a high school diploma leading to admission to a non-selective U.S. institution, a high school diploma leading to admission to a selective U.S. institution, a bachelor's degree, etc.

Using **Step 2**, the Council will identify in publications key characteristics of foreign educational credentials and determine which characteristics the foreign credential has in common with the U.S. benchmark credential. Users may then add to the profile of the U.S. benchmark credential any additional characteristics that may be considered important to their institution or for the particular program of study. To complete **Step 2**, users will determine whether the foreign credential does or does not have those characteristics.

Step 3 is the user's own determination of comparability based on a comparison of the characteristics of the foreign credential and the U.S. benchmark credential. The profiles of key characteristics and the methodology will give users improved tools to make evaluation decisions that meet the needs of their institutions.

Afterword

The methodology is a work-in-progress. It was developed to provide useful information for international admissions professionals. Many suggestions for changes have already been incorporated, but suggestions for additional improvements, as well as feedback on how the methodology works in practice, are welcome. Please e-mail feedback to margit@ece.org or mail to: Margit A. Schatzman, ECE, Inc., P.O. Box 514070, Milwaukee WI 53203-3470, USA.

For more information on the Milwaukee Symposium, please see the complete report published at http://www.nafsa.org/educator/milsymp/intro.html.

The Three Steps in the Methodology for Credential Evaluation

Step 1
List key characteristics to form a profile of the benchmark credential at your institution for a specific program of study. This may include characteristics such as those listed in Tables A, B, and C, as well as characteristics *not* found in the tables but which are considered important for your institution or for the particular program of study.

Step 2
Determine characteristics to form a profile of the foreign credential being evaluated. Does the foreign credential share each key characteristic of your benchmark credential?

Step 3
Determine if there is an acceptable level of comparability between the foreign credential and your institution's requirements for a benchmark credential. Can a statement of comparability be made?

Admissions professionals may use this worksheet to organize information and apply the methodology.

METHODOLOGY FOR CREDENTIAL EVALUATION WORKSHEET

Your Benchmark Credential	Foreign Credential	
Step 1	Step 2	
Characteristic	✔ Yes	✔ No

TABLE A. Credential Profile of One Example of a U.S. High School Diploma

One or more of these characteristics may be included in a program leading to a U.S. high school diploma. Because there is a great deal of variation in U.S. high school diploma programs, not all characteristics will be present in all programs.

diploma awarded
awarded by a regionally accredited academic institution
appropriate age of student for graduation
completion of 16-21 units in a combination of subject areas
completion of units for work experience or other nonacademic work
completion of general education requirements (physical education, living skills)
completion of requirements for a specialized vocational or technical program of study
completion of units in a foreign language
completion of units in social studies
completion of units in English
completion of a unit in algebra
completion of a unit in geometry
completion of a unit in calculus
completion of university preparatory courses in laboratory science (earth science, biology, chemistry, physics)
completion of honors course(s)
completion of Advanced Placement course(s) culminating in an external examination
completion of International Baccalaureate course(s) culminating in an external examination
completion of postsecondary courses to supplement high school program
leads to admission to postsecondary education

Note: 1 unit = 1 year of study

TABLE B. Credential Profile of One Example of a U.S. Bachelor's Degree

One or more of these characteristics may be included in a program leading to a U.S. bachelor's degree. Because there is a great deal of variation in U.S. bachelor's degree programs, not all characteristics will be present in all programs.

degree awarded
awarded by a regionally accredited academic institution
standardized test required for admission
graduation from a secondary school program required for admission
completion of at least 120 semester hours (180 quarter hours)
designed to be completed in four years
completion of general education requirements
completion of major requirements
completion of elective courses
completion of introductory, core, and elective courses in major
completion of specialized and advanced courses in major
completion of upper division courses in major
completion of a substantial number of courses in major and related fields
completion of seminar work
introduction to research
completion of honors or senior thesis

TABLE C. Credential Profile of One Example of a U.S. Master's Degree

One or more of these characteristics may be included in a program leading to a U.S. master's degree. Because there is a great deal of variation in U.S. master's degree programs, not all characteristics will be present in all programs.

degree awarded
awarded by a regionally accredited academic institution
graduation from a bachelor's program required for admission
completion of at least one year of fulltime study
completion of at least 30 semester hours (45 quarter hours)
mastery of a core curriculum or prescribed program of study, including courses, seminars, and/or research
faculty adviser who approves program of study
completion of field work or practicum
completion of comprehensive examinations
mastery of a foreign language or research tool
completion of a capstone or culminating experience (thesis, research program, performance)
residency at the degree-awarding institution

CAPTURING THE MESSAGE CONVEYED BY GRADES

Interpreting Foreign Grades

by Guy Haug

Reprinted with permission from *World Education News and Reviews* 12, 2:12-17. 1997. New York: World Education Services, Inc.

Grading systems differ widely in philosophy and practice from one country to another, and the fair interpretation of foreign grades into national ones is a major issue, both for students returning after a study period abroad and for university staff required to assess the credentials of foreign applicants.

Credential evaluation, credit transfer and grade translation are among the most widely debated and highly sensitive issues in international education, and numerous approaches, solutions, models and formulas have been proposed over the years both in the United States and in Europe.

This article does not intend to propose any particular technique to resolve the issue. It pays more attention to the fundamental needs of interested stakeholders than to the technical tools currently available from professional credit evaluators. Its sole ambition is to recall a few basic rules and principles that tend to be forgotten as the job of translating foreign grades turns into an exercise in accounting or mathematics. The underlying idea in this article is that the first function of grades is to convey a message, and the real challenge in interpreting foreign grades is to render that same message in a different language.

My exposure to the issue of understanding/using foreign grades has been widespread and diversified, but mostly limited to Western Europe and North American systems. In this context, I would distinguish between three main approaches, each guided by a different underlying philosophy.

- **The Inter-university Cooperation Programs (ICPs) developed in the European Union under the ERASMUS program**

Under these exchange schemes set up freely between individual university departments, students spend a study period at a host university abroad and their academic performance there would be fully recognized as part of the degree prepared at the home institution, even though courses abroad may differ substantially from those in the home curriculum.

The basic principle is that "mutual trust and confidence" grades obtained abroad would be shown on the transcript of the home university. ICPs exchanging large numbers of students among partner universities in several EU countries have gone through an extensive learning process and developed empirical "grading scales" in the forms of charts of the "equivalent" grades at their partner universities. Their specific value is that they are often tailor-made and compare many (if not all) grading systems in use in the EU. Their main limitations are that they are applicable only to short periods of study abroad rather than to entire curricula and that they are negotiated between partner institutions (which entails that they differ substantially from each other: a German 23 or an Italian 27 are allocated widely differing foreign equivalents in, for example, the Spanish system, depending on the discipline, institution, and person in charge).

• The European Credit Transfer System (ECTS)

ECTS was developed as a pilot scheme under the first phase of the ERASMUS program of the EU and will now be gradually generalized under the new SOCRATES scheme. ECTS has paid considerable attention to the issue of grading, and has introduced a very elaborate "ECTS Grading System" required for use by participating institutions in their ECTS student exchanges.

ECTS goes beyond ICPs, in that it is a whole organized system within which consistency has been sought. The underlying philosophy is that of the equivalence of end products: while the curricula in history, physics, business or engineering may differ in every respect among national systems, the graduates (the "end product") produced by these systems are not all that different. In order to facilitate the transfer of grades between institutions, "ECTS grades" were introduced with five levels of pass and two levels of fails. They serve as a buffer (or common currency) between different national grades: the host university provides its own national grade and shows the ECTS grade next to the local grade on the student's transcript; the home university in turn uses the ECTS grade and translates it

into its national grade, which is used on the student's final transcript.

ECTS offers two distinct advantages: the system is open and can be adapted to all possible national systems (e.g., bridges with Central/Eastern European systems or U.S. grades can be added relatively easily) and it is an interpretative scale rather than a mathematical formula.

• The U.S. Credit Transfer System for Study Abroad

While credit transfer is widespread in the United States, it differs from its younger European counterparts in several important ways: traditional Junior Year Abroad programs are under the direct responsibility of the sending university, and grades are in the U.S. system in order to facilitate the transfer of credits. There are, of course, divergences from this model, especially in cases where students take regular courses taught by the host university and a wide variety of ad hoc conversation scales between national and U.S. grades are applied. In many cases, the difficulty of dealing with foreign grades is circumvented as credits are simply given on a pass/fail basis although this penalizes students in good standing by not showing their true achievement. On the other hand, this model has the virtue of a certain type of universality (it is independent of the educational environment in the host country) and the United States has developed considerable professional expertise in assessing credentials and translating grades from all over the world.

Mathematical Formulas Fail to Capture the Message

Both in Europe and in the United States, there have been numerous recent attempts to put together automatic, mathematical formulas that "calculate" foreign grades in the national grading system of the user. In my opinion, these formulas do not produce figures that are a reliable and fair reflection of the message conveyed by the original grade. Their main shortfall is that they cannot adequately deal with certain key characteristics of grading systems:

♦ Grading systems are **not linear** and are often characterized by a strongly skewed distribution of grades actually given to students. While American or Italian teachers would use the upper part of their grading scales (albeit in different ways), others (e.g., French and British) in practice hardly ever use the top 20% of their scale. For this reason, proposals based on linear formulas can produce devastating results: I recently saw the case of a German student in France who achieved a 15 (quite a good grade) which was converted into a German 25 (a rather mediocre one); on the contrary, a British student who gets a 27/30 in Italy would have every reason to be pleased if that grade were linearly calculated to correspond to a British 90/100!

♦ Many grading systems are **not continuous**, but divided into several "classes" or "categories" which correspond to broad levels of performance. This means that a small difference in numbers may conceal a substantial difference in meaning when a "class" limit is crossed: in the United Kingdom, a grade of 70 classified as "First Class" is very different from a 69 ("Second Class"), while the same small difference of 1 point is irrelevant between the grades of 54 and 55 (both "Lower Second Class").

♦ Grading differs **not only between countries**. There are, as well, marked differences in grading traditions and policies depending on the type and level of the grading institution, the field of study, or even the type of grade (final examination, mid-term, paper, or average computed from various grade items).

Taking France as an example, it is well known that grades at "*classes préparatoires*," which recruit among the best students on their way to "*Grandes Ecoles*," tend to be particularly low, with, for example, 11/20 seen as quite a strong grade, while the pass mark in France is usually an average of 10/20 calculated on all subjects. There may also be minimum pass grades per subject set at a lower level, for example, 8/20.

The distribution of grades tends to be different between certain quantitative fields (with grades distributed over the whole range) and the non-quantitative fields (where grades are more concentrated in the middle, and the upper part of the scale is seldom used). Thus, even within a given country, a grade may have a "normal," intuitive, abstract meaning which needs to be adjusted (up or downwards) depending on a whole series of factors relating both to who gave it and who interprets it.

From the above observations, my main conclusion is that foreign grades are not just **numbers** that can be calculated by applying a mathematical formula, but a **message** that needs first to be **understood** in the original system and in a second stage **interpreted** by users in their own system.

Simple mathematical formulas with their claim to universality are nothing but a fallacious over-simplification of a reality they fail to capture.

This, however, does not mean that the process of foreign grade interpretation cannot be organized in an efficient, expedient way based on a thorough effort to understand the message that [foreign grades] carry. It is possible to draw up tables ("grade equivalence chart," "grade concordance scale") that render a grade's "normal" or "average" meaning in another grading system, first on a bilateral basis and then in a more multi-lateral context. But this exercise has more to do with the complexity of human language than with mathematics. It takes more listening, modesty and flexibility rather than a doctrinal attitude and a creed in universal formulas/answers. More specifically, the drawing up of tables that can genuinely serve as a basis for interpreting foreign grades is only possible if a certain number of key considerations are observed. The remainder of the article presents six principles that could guide future developments in the area of foreign grade handling.

1. Grade interpretation is no more objective than grading

This is a key consideration: it is a fact of academic life that grades vary, often quite significantly, between institutions, subject areas, and even individual examiners in a given department at a given university. Expectations vary from course to course and from teacher to teacher… and even over time with the same teacher! Hence, grade conversion scales should not be expected to be more objective than the original grading, and international educators should not be overly sensitive about less-than-perfect conversion scales. Nor should we be overly disturbed that the diverging equivalence tables exist in various contexts of international mobility.

Grade interpretation is no more an exact, objective, universal science than grading itself.

2. Fairness is more important than accuracy

The general attitude towards grade interpretation should be guided by the desire to be fair to students rather than by a vain search for accuracy. In an area marked by subjectivity and diversity, the choice is usually between approximately right and accurately wrong.

But how can fairness be measured and indeed achieved? It seems to me that the only indicator is that the conversion table must provide grades that are in line with the home grades. My experience is that discussions about grade equivalencies are often complicated by emotional reactions where each side insists upon the highest possible foreign grades corresponding to their own grades. This attitude appears to be related to a somewhat defensive, misguided conception of academic pride and leads to a devaluation of foreign grades. Where a dominant partner in an exchange network is able to impose a biased equivalence scheme upon partner institutions, the result is that students from the dominant partner studying elsewhere see their academic performance undervalued when they return home. This can be detected when the performance of students returning from abroad appears to be out of line with either their own previous grades or with those of their classmates who stayed at home.

Structural misinterpretation of foreign grades is unlikely to be detected or corrected easily in the case of one-way mobility. In the case of reciprocal flows, the inevitable effect of a biased conversion scale is that it provides a structural bonus for students moving in one direction while it disadvantages those moving in the opposite direction. These signals are more easily detected in reciprocal exchanges, especially if they involve high levels of student traffic.

3. Grade categories/classes convey core information

In many systems, the full scale of grades is divided not only between pass and fail, but into various "classes" or "categories" corresponding to broad "quality labels" assigned to a certain bracket of numerical grades. Thus, in the United Kingdom, there are "First Class," "Second Class" (divided between upper and lower sub-classes) and "Third Class" performers, while French, German or Spanish students may be labeled in a similar way as, for example, *Passable* (Average), *Gut* (Good) or *Sobresaliente* (Outstanding).

The meaning of these labels in their own context is tainted by culture and tradition. Thus, a British "Third Class" (a pass mark, but usually given only to a relatively small number of very border-line students) is very different from a French *Passable* (a widely-used label that normally applies to the vast majority of pass grades). However tempting it may be, equating *passable* with "Third Class" because they both correspond to the lowest label of "pass grades" would fail to take into account their real meaning.

As a consequence, conversion scales should pay considerable attention to categories/classes of grades. A first priority should be to make certain that this core piece of information is correctly rendered when converting foreign grades; fine-tuning within each particular class/category is only a subordinate exercise: what matters in Britain is whether the grade is a "First" or not, not whether it is a 71 or a 72. This observation is particularly relevant when converting grades from systems using a broad numerical scale into, for example, the U.S. system which usually has only

three pass grades (or categories) corresponding to the letters A, B, and C. In the United States, a "D" may also be considered a passing grade, but not for transfer purposes.

The need to pay attention to grade classes reinforces the conclusion that linear methods, which ignore class boundaries, are nothing but fallacious and dangerous over-simplifications. They distort the original message in the same way as a word-for-word check in a bilingual dictionary: for each word there is a corresponding word in the other language, but the sequence of words thus obtained almost certainly means something different (or nothing at all) in the target language.

4. Average grades mean more than individual grades

This is very much related to the previous point: more comprehensive indicators of academic performance abroad convey a more valid message than each of their constituent grades, and should hence receive more attention in the process of interpreting foreign transcripts.

The problem is that in non-linear systems (i.e., in nearly all cases) the mechanical translation of an average grade (using an empirical equivalence chart) will not correspond to the average of the mechanically-translated individual grades from which the average grade was calculated. As a consequence, average grades should be computed in the original system before they are converted into another system. This simple mathematical reality seems confusing to many professionals in international circles. Every now and again, the vain search for a model without this bewildering characteristic brings about deceiving but reassuring proposals based on the simple but wrong assumption of linearity.

5. Reliable conversion scales are transitive

In most cases, institutions need only bilateral conversion scales for incoming/outgoing students between their own country and one or several foreign countries (e.g., a scale giving U.S. equivalencies for grades from France, Spain, Brazil, etc.). These institutions do not need to convert grades between third countries (e.g., a U.S. university does usually not need to convert Spanish into French grades). Thus, there is no incentive for them to check whether their various bilateral conversion scales are compatible and likely incompatibilities can go unnoticed for a long time.

Yet, there are a few laboratories where grade equivalence needs to be ensured in a multilateral setting and equivalence charts must work simultaneously between all pairs of countries involved. This is the case for a handful of fully integrated, multinational double degree curricula developed under ERASMUS in the European Union, where students go in all directions (e.g. between four partner universities), and their grades must be converted in a compatible way among all systems involved. The same applies in the case of ECTS, although the situation is slightly different because the common use of "ECTS grades" means in effect that all countries apply only bilateral conversion grades between their own and ECTS grades; yet, a great deal of compatibility between these bilateral scales must exist in order to allow the system to function properly.

The ultimate test of the reliability of equivalence charts is when they are transitive. Transitivity means that the following two exercises produce the same converted grade: (1) a grade from country A is converted into a grade for country B and the grade obtained for country B is converted into a grade for country C; and (2) the same grade from country A is converted directly into a grade for country C.

If, after repeating the exercise various times and in various directions, grades obtained through both calculations are identical or nearly so, then the equivalence charts used for the exercise are unlikely to contain any major structural biases. Developers of all types of grade conversion proposals (be they equivalence tables or mathematical formulas) are invited to submit their proposals to the transitivity test. Usually the results of the test are an invitation to modesty, and sometimes a clear message that the proposed chart needs to be completely reconsidered. Transitivity is of course, all the more difficult to achieve as the number of countries involved grows.

6. Grade interpretation should be done by users

The final interpretation of grades from abroad should be left to the institution that uses them as input for decision making (e.g., to award credits or accept a foreign applicant). In the absence of a universal model for grade interpretation —even for grades from a particular foreign country—this is the only way in which the autonomy of each institution can be guaranteed.

What this means in practical terms is that each institution should award grades in its own system and leave the interpretation of those grades in another system to the receiving foreign institution. This basic dual principle is not respected when the grading institution awards grades directly in the system of the using institution (not uncommon in transcripts issued outside of the United States for U.S.-bound exchange students), which in effect imposes pre-translated grades on the using institution, or when the using institution finds its hands bound by an automatic, mechanical conversion model that fails to leave room for interpretation. While conversion should preferably be based on stable tables of equivalencies, these tables only reflect the "normal" or "average" meaning of foreign grades. When there is non-numerical informa-tion available (e.g. about "grade inflation" at a given institution), the using institution should have the possibility of adjusting (but not distorting) converted grades to ensure fairness to the student. This may, of course, be misused and open the door to "impressionistic" conversions, but it fundamentally distinguishes grade interpretation from simplistic grade calculation.

In order to safeguard the principle that grades should be interpreted by users and at the same time enhance chances for the correct interpretation of grades, the sending institution should provide information about itself and its grading system. Useful information includes not only maximum and minimum grades, but also grade distribution and class boundaries.

The ECTS grading system is based on a shared code ("ECTS grades") where the encoding is the responsibility of the grading institution and the decoding is left to the using institution. Thus, even in a system based on "mutual trust and confidence" like ECTS, there is some room for interpretation rather than just an automated, numerical exercise. It is also interesting that the network of national academic recognition centers in Europe (known as NARICS and ENICs) is developing a "diploma supplement" appended to transcripts in order to facilitate the interpretation of grades by foreign users. This welcome initiative is jointly supported by the European Union, the Council of Europe and CEPES/UNESCO and should contribute to the education of both graders and grade users and thus reduce the chances that simplistic formulas are used except as a last recourse when nothing else is available.

ECTS GRADING SCALE		
ECTS Grade	Percent of successful students normally achieving the grade	Definition
A	10	EXCELLENT - outstanding performance with only minor errors
B	25	VERY GOOD - above the average standard but with some errors
C	30	GOOD - generally sound work with a number of notable errors
D	25	SATISFACTORY - fair but with significant shortcomings
E	10	SUFFICIENT - performance meets the minimum criteria
FX	-	FAIL - some more work required before the credit can be awarded
F	-	FAIL - considerable work is required

THE CHART BELOW was proposed for a particular consortium of institutions where common examination papers are double marked by home and host campus and hundreds of students are exchanged in all directions annually. It is <u>NOT</u> claimed that this system would be suited for grade conversion outside of this consortium. It neutralizes the British "Third Class" as it was set equal to minimum pass grade in other systems that do not have an equivalent notion as a British "Third."

EXAMPLE OF GRADES/CLASS EQUIVALENCES AMONG ONE CONSORTIUM

GREAT BRITAIN		FRANCE		GERMANY		SPAIN		UNITED STATES
	100-90		20.0-18.0		1.0		10.0	
	89		17.8		1.0		9.9	
	88	TRES	17.6		1.1		9.9	
	87	BIEN	17.4		1.1		9.9	
	86		17.2		1.2		9.8	A+
	85		17.0		1.2		9.8	
	84		16.8		1.3		9.7	
	83		16.6		1.3		9.7	
	82		16.4		1.3		9.6	
	81		16.2		1.4		9.6	
FIRST	80		16.0	SEHR	1.4	SOBRE-	9.5	
CLASS	79		15.8	GUT	1.5	SALIENTE	9.4	
	78		15.6		1.5		9.4	
	77		15.4		1.5		9.4	A
	76		15.2		1.5		9.3	
	75		15.0		1.6		9.3	
	74	BIEN	14.8		1.6		9.2	
	73		14.6		1.7		9.2	
	72		14.4		1.7		9.1	
	71		14.2		1.8		9.1	A-
	70		14.0		1.9		9.0	
	69		13.8		2.0		8.8	
	68		13.6		2.1		8.6	
	67		13.4		2.2		8.4	B+
UPPER	66	ASSEZ	13.2		2.3	NOTABLE	8.2	
	65	BIEN	13.0		2.4		8.0	
SECOND	64		12.8		2.5		7.8	
	63		12.6		2.6		7.6	
	62		12.4		2.7		7.4	B
CLASS	61		12.2		2.8		7.2	
	60		12.0		2.9		7.0	
	59		11.8		3.0		6.8	
	58		11.6		3.1		6.6	
LOWER	57		11.4	BEFRIEDIGEND	3.2	BUENO	6.4	B-
	56		11.2		3.3		6.2	
SECOND	55	PASSABLE	11.0		3.5		6.0	
CLASS	54		10.8	(AUSREICHEND)	3.6		5.8	
	53		10.6		3.7	APROBADO	5.6	
	52		10.4		3.8		5.4	
	51		10.2		3.9		5.2	C
THIRD CLASS	40-50		10.0		4.0		5.0	
	39		9.9		4.1		4.9	
FAIL	38	ECHEC	9.0	NICHT	4.3	SUSPENSO	4.7	F
	37		8.0	AUSREICHEND	4.5		4.5	
	35		7.0		4.9		4.0	
	30		6.0		5.0		3.5	
	25		5.0		5.1		3.0	
	20		4.0		5.3		2.5	
	15		3.0		5.5		2.0	
	10		2.0		5.7		1.5	
	5		1.0		5.9		1.0	
	0		0.0		6.0		0.0	

DETERMINING CREDIT EQUIVALENTS

by James S. Frey, Ed.D.

Credit Conversion: Theory and Practice

This paper deals with the theory and practice of determining U.S. credit equivalents for academic courses completed at a university in another country.

In this context, *university* means an officially recognized tertiary-level (postsecondary) degree-granting institution, whether or not that institution is officially called a university. Thus the term *university* will be used here to include other types of tertiary-level academic institutions, such as academy, college, conservatory, institute, polytechnic, and school.

In the United States, courses that can be credited toward the requirements for an academic degree at the university where the courses are offered are usually quantified via a system of *credits*. Hence they are called *credit courses*.

It should be noted that not every course offered by a university is a credit course. In the United States, and in many other countries, universities have a variety of missions in addition to offering degree programs. Many universities offer *adult education* courses to upgrade the knowledge and skills of persons not seeking an academic degree, and *in-service training* courses to upgrade the knowledge and skills of persons practicing a profession such as teaching.

Adult education and in-service training courses are defined as *non-credit courses* because they cannot be credited toward the requirements of an academic degree. Other types of courses that cannot be credited

toward the requirements for an academic degree at the institution where the course is offered are also defined as non-credit courses.

Why Is a Conversion Formula Needed?

It is a basic principle of applied comparative education that one year of full-time academic work at any one university is the equivalent of one year of full-time academic work at any other university.

Because universities use a variety of quantitative bookkeeping systems, it is necessary to use a conversion formula whenever a student moves from a university that uses one system of recording credits to a university that uses a different system.

Semester Hours of Credit

In the United States, a number of credit systems are in use. The most common is the *semester hour of credit*. In this paper, the semester hour of credit is used as a standard for comparing the other credit systems used in the United States, and for designing policies and procedures for calculating United States equivalent credit values for academic work completed at a university in another country.

Universities in the United States that use the semester hour of credit system usually divide the academic year into two terms called *semesters*, each usually 15 to 16 weeks in length.

Universities that use fifteen-week semesters usually require a minimum of 120 semester hours of credit for a bachelor's

20

degree (15 credits per semester for eight semesters = 120), whereas universities that use sixteen-week semesters usually require a minimum of 128 semester hours of credit for a bachelor's degree (16 credits per semester for eight semesters = 128). Thus one academic year of full-time academic work at a university in the United States usually represents a total of 30 to 32 semester hours of undergraduate credit, that is, one credit per week of the academic year.

In some academic fields, such as engineering and nursing, the minimum number of credits required for a bachelor's degree is usually at least 128 at most universities.

Semester hours of credit are calculated on the basis of a number of factors. The most important of these, but not the only factor taken into account, is the amount of formal instruction provided by a faculty member.

For a course in which lecture or discussion is the primary teaching method, students are expected to spend an average of two hours outside of the classroom preparing for each hour in the classroom. This preparation includes reading, library research, writing papers, reviewing lecture notes, and similar out-of-class pursuits. For courses in which practice is a major teaching method, more in-class time is usually required, and less out-of-class time is expected.

For one semester hour of credit, a lecture course is usually required to meet one hour per week for the entire semester.

For laboratory courses and for activity courses in physical education, credit is usually calculated on a two-for-one or three-for-one basis. That is, a laboratory course, or the laboratory portion of a lecture and laboratory course, usually requires two or three times as many hours of formal

instruction as a lecture course does for the same number of semester hours of credit.

For practice courses in fields such as studio art, instrumental music, and practice teaching, and for clinical courses in health-related fields, credit is usually calculated on a three-for-one or four-for-one basis. Thus a student will usually be required to complete three or four times as many hours in an art studio as in a lecture hall in order to receive one semester hour of credit.

Most universities in the United States that use the semester system also offer credit courses in one or more short academic terms, which might be called summer session, interim, intersession, winterim, or a variety of other names.

During short academic terms, a course must meet more frequently in order to encompass the same number of hours of formal instruction that a regular semester course would entail. For example, a one-credit lecture course that meets one hour per week for a fifteen-week semester would have to meet for five hours per week for a three-week summer session to merit one semester hour of credit. In both cases, a total of fifteen hours of formal classroom instruction is involved.

For most short academic terms, the usual full-time academic load is one credit per week of the term, which is the same ratio as that usually used for regular semesters.

Quarter Hours of Credit

Universities in the United States that use the *quarter hour of credit* system usually divide the academic year into three terms called *quarters*, each usually 10 or 11 weeks in length.

Universities that use ten-week quarters usually require a minimum of 180 quarter hours of credit for a bachelor's degree (15 credits per quarter for twelve quarters = 180), whereas universities that use eleven-week quarters usually require a minimum of 192 quarter hours of credit for a bachelor's degree (16 credits per quarter for twelve quarters = 192). Thus one academic year of full-time academic work usually represents a total of 45 to 48 quarter hours of undergraduate credit, that is, 1½ credits per week of the academic year.

If a student transfers from a quarter system university to a semester system university in the United States, the quarter hours of credit are multiplied by 2/3 to convert to semester hours of credit. For example, one academic year of 48 quarter hours of credit multiplied by 2/3 equals one academic year of 32 semester hours of credit. Both the 48 and the 32 represent one year of full-time academic work in the respective credit systems.

Similarly, if a student transfers from a semester system university to a quarter system university in the United States, the semester hours of credit are multiplied by 3/2 (1½) to convert to quarter hours of credit. For example, one academic year of 32 semester hours of credit multiplied by 3/2 equals 48 quarter hours of credit.

These multiplication formulas maintain recognition for having completed the same amount of full-time academic work at the receiving university as at the sending university, no matter which systems of quantitative academic bookkeeping the sending university and the receiving university might use.

Other U.S. Credit Systems

A wide variety of other record-keeping systems are used in the United States to quantify a student's academic work. Here are a few examples:

Antioch College uses a credit system. A total of 160 credits completed during eight study quarters (each 13 to 14 weeks in length), plus completion of six to eight non-credit co-op quarters, are required for a bachelor's degree. A university in the United States that uses the semester hour system would multiply Antioch College credits by 3/4 to convert to semester hours of credit.

Beloit College uses a credit system in which each course has the value of one credit. A total of 31 credits (slightly less than four credits per semester for eight semesters) is required for a bachelor's degree. Each course meets for four hours per week for one semester. A university in the United States that uses the semester hour system would multiply Beloit College credits by 4 to convert to semester hours of credit.

Brown University uses a course system. A total of 32 courses (four courses per semester for eight semesters) is required for a bachelor's degree. A university in the United States that uses the semester hour system would multiply Brown University courses by 4 to convert to semester hours of credit.

Coe College uses a course system. The academic year is divided into two fifteen-week terms, separated by a four-week winter term. A total of 36 courses (four courses for each of four fall and spring terms, and one course for each of four winter terms) is required for a bachelor's degree. A university that uses the semester hour system would multiply Coe College courses by 3½ or 4 to convert to semester hours of credit.

Columbia University uses a *points* system. A full academic load is 16 points per semester. A university that uses the semester hour system would treat Columbia University points as though they were called semester hours of credit.

Harvard University uses a course system. A total of 16 courses (two per semester for eight semesters) is required for a bachelor's degree. A university that uses the semester hour system would multiply Harvard University courses by 8 to convert to semester hours of credit.

Knox College uses a credit system in which each course has the value of one credit. The academic year is divided into three ten-week trimesters. A total of 36 credits (three per trimester for twelve trimesters) is required for a bachelor's degree. Each course meets for four to five hours per week for a trimester. A university that uses the semester hour system would multiply Knox College credits by 3½ or 4 to convert to semester hours of credit.

United States Credit Equivalents in Foreign Educational Systems

Universities in other countries use a wide variety of bookkeeping systems to report the quantity of academic work completed by a student. Therefore a wide variety of conversion formulas is needed to ensure that one year of full-time academic work completed at a university in another country receives recognition as the equivalent of one year of full-time academic work at a university in the United States.

The following conversion formulas can be used to calculate the semester hours of credit equivalents for academic work recorded in quantitative academic bookkeeping systems used in other countries.

These formulas are designed to be applied to one year of full-time academic work. If the data on a university grade report represents semesters or terms or some other portion of an academic year, rather than a full academic year, then the cumulative data for all parts of a full academic year must be used to identify the relevant formula.

Grade Reports that Use a Subject or Unit System

EXAMPLE 1

At some British universities, students take three subjects the first year, two subjects the second year, and one the third year. Thus the quantitative value of one subject varies, from one-third of a full-time academic load to one-half of a full-time academic load to a whole academic load. Therefore the equivalent semester hour of credit value of each subject also varies from year to year depending upon the number of subjects studied in each year.

Number of Subjects or Units per Year	Credits per Subject or Unit	Number of Subjects or Units per Year	Credits per Subject or Unit
1	32	16	2
2	16	17	2
3	10	18	1¾
4	8	19	1¾
5	6	20	1½
6	5	21	1½
7	4½	22	1½
8	4	23	1½
9	3½	24	1¼
10	3	25	1¼
11	3	26	1¼
12	2½	27	1¼
13	2½	28	1¼
14	2¼	29	1
15	2	30	1

Grade Reports that Use a Variable Maximum Grade

EXAMPLE 2

At many French universities, the maximum possible grade that can be earned in one subject varies, from 10 to 20 to 30 to 40 or more. **At many Indian universities**, it varies from 20 to 300, and beyond, with a multitude of possibilities in between. Variations in the maximum possible grade indicate variations in the quantitative value of individual subjects. Therefore the equivalent semester hour of credit value also varies from subject to subject. The maximum possible grade values can be used to determine the equivalent semester hour of credit values.

Maximum Marks (Grades) per Year	Credits per Maximum Marks (Grades)	Maximum Marks (Grades) per Year	Credits per Maximum Marks (Grades)
100	3 credits per 10 max	850	4 credits per 100 max
150	2 credits per 10 max	900	3½ credits per 100 max
200	1½ credits per 10 max	950	3¼ credits per 100 max
250	1¼ credits per 10 max	1000	3 credits per 100 max
300	1 credit per 10 max	1050	3 credits per 100 max
350	1 credit per 10 max	1100	3 credits per 100 max
400	8 credits per 100 max	1150	3 credits per 100 max
450	7 credits per 100 max	1200	2½ credits per 100 max
500	6 credits per 100 max	1250	2½ credits per 100 max
550	6 credits per 100 max	1300	2½ credits per 100 max
600	5 credits per 100 max	1350	2¼ credits per 100 max
650	5 credits per 100 max	1400	2¼ credits per 100 max
700	4½ credits per 100 max	1450	2 credits per 100 max
750	4 credits per 100 max	1500	2 credits per 100 max
800	4 credits per 100 max	1550	2 credits per 100 max

Grade Reports that Report Total Number of Hours per Week

EXAMPLE 3

Many Colombian universities report the hours per week of formal instruction in each subject. Variations in the number of hours of instruction indicate variations in the quantitative value of individual subjects. Therefore the equivalent semester hour of credit value also varies from subject to subject. The number of hours of formal instruction can be used to determine the equivalent semester hour of credit values.

Number of Hours per Week	Credits per Hour	Number of Hours per Week	Credits per Hour
10	3	25	1¼
11	3	26	1¼
12	2½	27	1¼
13	2½	28	1¼
14	2½	29	1¼
15	2	30	1
16	2	31	1
17	2	32	1
18	1¾	33	1
19	1¾	34	1
20	1½	35	1
21	1½	36	1
22	1½	37	¾
23	1½	38	¾
24	1¼	39	¾

Grade Reports that Report Total Number of Hours per Year

EXAMPLE 4

Many Chinese universities report the total number of hours of formal instruction that each subject represents for one academic year. Variations in the number of hours of instruction indicate variations in the quantitative value of individual subjects. Therefore the equivalent semester hour of credit value also varies from subject to subject. The number of hours of formal instruction can be used to determine the equivalent semester hour of credit values.

Number of Hours per Year	Credits per 100 Hours	Number of Hours per Year	Credits per 100 Hours
300	10	1050	3
350	9	1100	3
400	8	1150	3
450	7	1200	2½
500	6	1250	2½
550	6	1300	2½
600	5	1350	2¼
650	5	1400	2¼
700	4½	1450	2¼
750	4	1500	2
800	4	1550	2
850	4	1600	2
900	3½	1650	2
950	3¼	1700	2
1000	3	1750	2

Calculating Credit for Programs of Less Than One Year's Duration

In the United States, universities that require a minimum of 120 semester hours of credit to graduate from a bachelor's degree program usually use fifteen-week semesters. Universities that require a minimum of 128 semester hours of credit to graduate from a bachelor's degree program usually use sixteen-week semesters. In both cases, the usual full-time academic load is one semester hour of credit for one week of full-time enrollment.

The one-credit-per-week formula usually also applies to summer sessions and other short academic terms in the United States. For example, six semester hours of credit is usually a full-time academic load during a six-week summer session, and eight semester hours of credit is usually a full-time academic load during an eight-week summer session.

When determining the semester hours of credit equivalent for an academic program of less than one year's duration at a university in another country, it is reasonable to calculate a credit total that amounts to one credit per week of full-time enrollment. Therefore the total number of semester hours of credit assigned to any program that is less than one year in length should be less than 30 semester hours of credit, since 30 semester hours of credit is the equivalent of one full academic year in the United States.

Author's Perspective

The suggestions made in this paper are intended to be a guide for tertiary institutions in the United States that use the semester hour system of credits. Institutions that use other systems of credit need to make appropriate adjustments to these recommendations, just as they make adjustments to credit values when they review official transcripts submitted to them by applicants from United States institutions that use a credit system different from their own.

This paper reflects the experience and point of view of the author. Each educational institution has the responsibility for developing and administering its own policies for determining credit for academic work completed elsewhere. Institutions that decide to follow the recommendations that appear in this paper should do so after careful analysis of the policies that they apply to the different credit systems in the United States. It is irresponsible to blindly follow these recommendations merely because they appear in print.

It is the responsibility of each educational institution to be consistent in the develop-ment and application of administrative policies. There is no pedagogical justification for treating foreign-educated applicants more leniently or more severely than United States-educated applicants are treated.

INTERNET RESEARCH FOR FOREIGN CREDENTIAL EVALUATION

by Marybeth Mirzejewski

The World Wide Web

As a foreign credential evaluator, I think of the web as just one of the many tools I can utilize in my daily work. This article is for those who are new to "surfing the web;" it aims to provide a few tips specific to conducting research on foreign educational systems, and to list some useful web sites for doing so. This article does not pretend to teach the reader how to stroll through cyberspace. There are books and comprehensive web sites galore that provide instructions for everything from using search engines (such as *AltaVista*, *Webcrawler*, and *Yahoo!*), to creating your own web site. Two web sites to help you learn the basics of the Internet are listed below. They explain how to conduct searches, understand web addresses, bookmark favorite sites, understand what hyperlinks are, and so on.

www.learnthenet.com

Web Browsers OpenFAQ:
www.boutell.com/openfaq/browsers/

Links

One aspect of roaming through the Internet worth emphasizing is the use of *links*. A link is a highlighted word or phrase on a document which allows you to jump to another section on the web site, or to a completely new and different web site. It is through these links that many comprehensive and informative web sites can be found. It may be well worth your time to explore some of the web sites listed in this article.

What Information Do We Need?

As foreign credential evaluators, what information can we find while browsing the web? How can utilizing the Internet make our job easier? What information do we need?

A good place to find links to sources of information is the United States Network for Education Information (USNEI). Housed and managed by the National Library of Education, USNEI is primarily a web-based resource designed to provide access to information on education in the United States as well as foreign systems of education. For example, USNEI provides a link to the information provided through European Network of Information Centers (the ENIC Network). USNEI is constantly being monitored and upgraded, and as more information becomes available via the Internet, it will be a useful starting point for credential evaluators.

www.ed.gov/NLE/USNEI

Descriptions of Educational Systems

Whenever possible, it is best to use Internet information accompanied by written resources. Some web sites offer substantial, accurate information, while others may provide more ambiguous or not entirely accurate data. It is also important to ascertain the source of the information. One way is to check that the web site originated in the appropriate country; the foreign country code will be included in the web site address. For example, Australia university web sites should always end in the country code "au," or Chinese web sites in "cn." A list of the country codes appears in the following web site:

International E-mail Accessibility
www.nsrc.org/codes/country-codes.html

Some web sites describing educational systems that I have found useful are:

China Education and Research Network:
www.cernet.edu.cn

EURYDICE-Eurybase: The Information Network on Education in Europe:
www.eurydice.org

Permanent Missions to the United Nations:
www.undp.org/missions/

UNESCO-World Academic Database:
www.unesco.org/iau

Ministries of Education, Embassies, and Consulates

What if my written resources cannot tell me whether or not an institution is recognized by the proper educational authorities in its home country? Perhaps I need to know if a foreign university is authorized to award a certain academic credential. I have gotten answers to questions such as these by contacting local consulates, cultural and educational attachés at foreign embassies in Washington, D.C., and by e-mailing or faxing letters to various ministries of education throughout the world. Listed below are a few web sites that helped me get started:

The Electronic Embassy:
www.embassy.org/embassies/index.html

Foreign Consular Offices in the United States:
www.state.gov/

EURYDICE-The Information Network on Education in Europe-Contacts and Links:
www.eurydice.org/

Specific University Program Information

Let's say your admissions office library has a catalog for a foreign institution, but it is ten years old. Perhaps you are not sure of the length of study for an engineering program, or a student's grade report says "Mathematics 1" and you need to know course content. There are many web sites that provide links to the home pages (web sites) of foreign educational institutions.

Some institutions produce their web sites only in their native language; others may offer you a language choice. Some home pages may not provide you with all the academic information you need, while others give you detailed information. In addition to the numerous web sites listed in each country resources section in this publication, here are a few other web sites to bookmark:

AdmiNet-WORLD:
www.adminet.com/world

Association of International Education, Japan:
www.aiej.or.jp

Braintrack Universities Index:
www.braintrack.com

BUTEX Guide to Undergraduate Study
in the United Kingdom:
www.niss.ac.uk/education/butex/
undergrad/contents.html

College and Universities Home Pages:
www.mit.edu/:8001/people/cdemello/univ.html

EUNI-European Universities:
www.ensmp.fr/~scherer/euni/

European Council of International Schools:
www.ecis.org

German Academic Exchange Service:
www.daad.org

Higher Educational Institution Registry-HEIR:
www.siu.no/inst.nsf/searchform2

NORDEN-Higher Education in the Nordic Countries
www.abo.fi/norden/textvers/welcom_e.htm

Russian Institutions and Universities:
www.useic.ru/informika.ru/eng/
link to Databases and References

Scientific and Academic Activities of
Polish Universities:
www.sggw.waw.pl/plusnew/

State Higher Educational Institutions, Ukarine
www.polynet.lviv.ua/ukraine/education/eng

Other International Education Resources and Contacts

When you really get stuck, and you need to find an in-country specialist for your most difficult questions, or when you find yourself needing the translation of a foreign word and you have no dictionary, the information you need can often be found on the web. The following web sites provide links to online dictionaries, to international organizations, and most importantly, to international advising centers throughout the world:

AMIDEAST
www.amideast.org

Fulbright Association:
www.fulbright.org/commissions.htm

Institute of International Education
www.iie.org/iie/osoffice.htm

International Education Web Pages:
www.manitouheights.org/intled

International Research and Exchanges Board:
www.irex.org/ontheweb/index.htm

OSEAS*Europe-Internet Resources for
Educational Advising:
www.bibl.u-szeged.hu/oseas/links.html

UNESCO-European Network of Information Centers:
www.cepes.ro

United States Information Agency
www.usia.gov

The Need for Caution in Using the Web

Foreign credential evaluators must count on a variety of tools to assist them in their analysis of international academic qualifications. The internet provides an immense amount of information--some accurate, some perhaps not. It should be used in conjunction with more traditional sources of information and thorough training in the theory and principles of applied comparative education.

Country
Outlines

ALBANIA

YEARS OF EDUCATION →

```
       ½   ½   ½   ½   ½   ½   ½   ½   ½   ½   ½   ½   ½   ½   ½   ½   ½
1→6| 7 | 8 | 9 | 10| 11| 12| 13| 14| 15| 16| 17| 18| 19| 20| 21| 22| 23| 24|
     A       B   B   C           E   G G G   G   H H H   H       J→
                     D           F                 I I I   I       K→
```

CREDENTIALS OR DOCUMENTATION

Secondary

A   *Dëftesë Lirimi* (Certificate of Leaving): awarded upon completion of *shkollë tetëvjeçare/8-vjeçare* (eight-year school)
B   Title of *punëtor i kualifikuar* (qualified worker): Terminal employment credential
C   *Dëftesë Pjekurie* (Certificate of Maturity): awarded by *shkollë e mesme e pëgjithshme* (general middle school) or *shkollë profesionale* (vocational school) in one of several streams; agricultural, economics/business, foreign language, fine arts, pedagogical, physical education, technical
D   *Dëftesë Pjekurie* (Certificate of Maturity) and title of *infermiere* (nurse): awarded by a *shkollë mjekësore* (medical school); discontinued in 1993; see also credential **F**

Postsecondary

E   *Diplomë për Mësues te Ciklit te Ulët të Shkollës Tetëvjeçare* (Diploma of Teacher of the Lower Cycle of the Eight-Year School [grades 1-4]): awarded upon completion of a three-year program
F   *Diplomë* (Diploma) with *titull* (title) of *infermiere* (nurse) from a three-year, non-university higher education program: introduced in 1993; see also credential **D**
G   *Diplomë* (Diploma) with *titull* (title) requiring credential **C** for admission in the following fields:
    Four-year program in agricultural economics; agricultural engineering; business, economics; forestry; language and literature; law; music; natural sciences except mathematics, physics and chemistry; pedagogy (grades 5-8 of eight-year school); physical education; social sciences; teaching of subjects in middle school (grades 9-12); theater arts; veterinary medicine; visual arts[1]
    Four and one half-year program in agronomy[1]
    Five-year program in architecture; chemistry; engineering; mathematics; pharmacy; physics[1]
    Six-year program in medicine[2]

H *Kandidat i Shkencave* (Candidate of Sciences) awarded by the *Komisioni i Lartë i Atestimit* (Higher Attestation Commission): based on three years of supervised research and a thesis; discontinued in 1993 and replaced by credential **I** below; admission based on credential **G**

I *Diplomë e Studimeve te Thelluara* (Diploma of Advanced Studies): awarded by a higher education institution based on a three-year program of study and research concluding with a thesis; introduced in 1993; admission based on credential **G**

J *Doktor i Shkencave* (Doctor of Sciences) awarded by the *Komisioni i Lartë i Atestimit* (Higher Attestation Commission): based on a dissertation representing advanced research and publication; discontinued in 1993 and replaced by credential **K**; admission based on credential **H**

K *Doktor* (Doctor): awarded by the University of Tirana based on a dissertation representing advanced research and publication; introduced in 1993; admission based on credential **H** or **I**

1 Part-time study programs are usually one year longer than full-time studies.

2 Medicine was expanded to a six-year program beginning in the 1993-94 academic year. It was previously a five-year program.

GRADING INFORMATION

All Levels of Education

Numeric	Translation	Description
10 *dhëtë*	ten	highest grade
9 *nëntë*	nine	
8 *tetë*	eight	
7 *shtatë*	seven	
6 *gjashtë*	six	
5 *pesë*	five	lowest passing grade

- All of the grades listed above are commonly seen on grade reports. Failing grades (0 to 4) are recorded only on internal documents and do not appear on grade reports.

POSTSECONDARY INSTITUTION RECOGNITION BODY

Ministry of Higher Education and Research, Bul. Jhan d'Ark, 2, Tirana, Albania, Tel: 355-42-28371. Fax: 355-42-27975.

RESOURCES FOR ADDITIONAL INFORMATION

Koenig, Ann M. 1993. *ECE Presents: An Overview of the Educational System of Albania*. Milwaukee: Educational Credential Evaluators, Inc. www.ece.org

Ministry of Education and Science, Directorate of Higher Education, Rruga e Durresit, Nr. 23, Tirana, Albania. Tel. and Fax: 355-42-25874.

Skënderi, Arion. 1997. *Studieren und Forschen in Albanien*. Publication in the series *Studieren und Forschung in Europa* of the *Österreichischer Akademischer Austauschdienst*, Vienna. www.oead.ac.at

Internet Source:
UNESCO - World Academic Database: www.unesco.org/iau/educal.html

---

Compiler
Ann M. Koenig
International Admission Specialist
University of California, Berkeley

ALGERIA

YEARS OF EDUCATION →

```
    ½   ½   ½   ½   ½   ½   ½   ½   ½   ½   ½   ½   ½   ½   ½   ½   ½
1-6 | 7 | 8 | 9 | 10 | 11 | 12 | 13 | 14 | 15 | 16 | 17 | 18 | 19 | 20 | 21 | 22 | 23 | 24 |
        A   B C     D   G   H I   J       N       S       X   Y       Z-      a-
                    E       J K   K       O       T
                    F       K     L       P       U
                              M       Q       V
                                  R       W
```

CREDENTIALS OR DOCUMENTATION

Secondary

A *Brevet de l'École Fondamentale* (Basic School Certificate): signifies completion of compulsory education[1]

B *Certificat d'Aptitude Professionnelle* (Professional Proficiency Certificate)[2,3]

C *Certificat de Maîtrise Professionnelle* (Professionnal Mastery Certificate)[2,4]

D *Baccalauréat de l'Enseignement Secondaire, Baccalauréat de Technicien* (Secondary School Baccalaureate, Technician Baccalaureate)

E *Brevet Supérieur de Capacité* (Advanced Proficiency Certificate): a teacher training credential, requiring usually two years of study after the first year of secondary education (grade 10)

F *Diplôme d'Agent-Technique de la Santé, d'Agent-Paramédical* (Health Technician Diploma): a terminal vocational training certificate in paramedical fields requiring two years of study after credential **A**

G *Brevet de Technicien* (Technician Certificate): usually a two-year program normally requiring the level, but not necessarily the completion, of the second year of secondary education (grade 11)[2]

H *Certificat de Capacité en droit* (Proficiency Certificate in Law): a two-year program requiring the level of the third year of secondary education (grade 12, but credential **D** is not required for admission); the holder may be allowed to undertake the first year of law studies at university

Postsecondary

I *Diplôme de Technicien Supérieur* (Advanced Technician Diploma): a 30-month program requiring the level of the third year of secondary education (grade 12, but credential **D** is not required for admission)[2]

J *Diplôme de Fin d'Études des Instituts de technologie de l'Éducation* (Educational Technical Institute Diploma)[5]

K *Diplôme de Technicien Supérieur* (Advanced Technician Diploma): requires credential **D** for admission, duration of the program is 24, 30, or 36 months. This credential is issued by higher institutes or, up to 1991, the universities

L   *Diplôme de Technicien Supérieur de la Santé* (Advanced Health Technician Diploma): three-year program in paramedical fields requiring the level of the third year of secondary education (grade 12, but credential **D** is not required for admission)[2]

M   *Diplôme d'Études Universitaires Appliquées* (Applied University Studies Diploma): awarded by the universities, replaces credential **K** since 1991; a three-year program requiring credential **D** for admission

N   *Licence* (Licenciate): requires credential **D** for admission, normally awarded in humanities and social sciences

O   *Diplôme d'Études Supérieures* (Higher Studies Diploma): requires credential **D** for admission, normally awarded in scientific fields

P   *Licence d'Enseignement* (Teaching Licenciate): requires credential **D** for admission, qualifies holders to teach at secondary schools, does not lead to further education

Q   *Diplôme d'Ingénieur d'Application* (Applied Engineer Diploma): requires credential **D** for admission

R   *Diplôme de Chirurgien Dentiste* (Dentist Diploma): requires credential **D** for admission

S   *Diplôme d'Ingénieur d'État* (State Engineer Diploma): requires credential **D** for admission

T   *Diplôme de Pharmacien* (Pharmacist Diploma): five-year program requiring credential **D** for admission (it was a four-year program up to 1990)

U   *Diplôme de Médecin Vétérinaire* (Veterinarian Diploma): requires credential **D** for admission

V   *Diplôme d'Architecte* (Architect Diploma): requires credential **D** for admission

W   *Diplôme de Post-graduation Spécialisée* (Specialized Post-Graduation Diploma): requires minimum of credential **N** or **O** for admission; it's a terminal professional specialization credential

X   *Magister* (Master): requires minimum of credential **N** or **O** for admission; normally a two-year program

Y   *Diplôme de Médecin* (Diploma of Doctor in Medicine): seven-year program requiring credential **D** for admission (it was a six-year program up to 1994)

Z   *Doctorat* (Doctorate): at least three years, requires credential **X** for admission

a   *Diplôme d'Études Médicales Spécialisées* (Specialized Medicine Studies Diploma): medical specialization, requiring at least three years of training and credential **Y** for admission

[1] Awarded since approximately 1987. Previously, a *Brevet d'Études Moyennes* (Middle School Certificate) was awarded after six years of primary school and four years of lower secondary school.

[2] Awarded by the *Ministère de la Formation professionnelle* (Ministry of Vocational Training): a terminal vocational training certificate.

[3] Also referred to as a *Certificat d'Aptitude du Premier Degré/CAP* (1st level Vocational Training Certificate) or *CAP*. Since 1982, requires usually 12 months of training after credential **A**. Before 1982, it was a three to four-year program after six years of primary education.

[4] Also referred as a *Certificat d'Aptitude du Second Degré/CMP* (2nd level Vocational Training Certificate). Exists since 1982, requires usually 18 months of training after credential **A**.

[5] From 1983 to 1994: a one year-program for teachers of the first six years of *École fondamentale*, and a two-year program for teachers of the last three years of *École fondamentale*. Since 1994, both programs have been extended by a year. In all cases, credential **D** or equivalent is required for admission.

GRADING INFORMATION

Secondary

Numeric	Mention	Comment
16-20	Très Bien	Very Good
14-15	Bien	Good
12-13	Assez Bien	Fairly Good
10-11	Passable	Satisfactory/Pass
0-9	Insuffisant	Failed

- Marks of 14 or higher are rarely awarded.

Higher Education

Numeric	Mention	Comment
15-20	Très Bien	Very Good
13-14	Bien	Good
12	Assez Bien	Fairly Good
11	Passable	Satisfactory/Pass
10	Sans Mention	No Comment
0-9	Insuffisant	Failed

- Marks of 14 or higher are rarely awarded.

POSTSECONDARY INSTITUTION RECOGNITION BODY

Ministère de l'Enseignement supérieur et de la Recherche scientifique (Ministry of Higher Education and Scientific Research), 14, chemin Doudou Mokthar, Ben-Aknoun, Alger. Tel: 213-2-79-00-37. Fax: 213-2-78-31-97.

RESOURCES FOR ADDITIONAL INFORMATION

AMIDEAST. Undated (circa 1992). *Education in the Arab World*. Vol. I. Washington, D.C.: AMIDEAST.

The British Council. 1996. *International Guide to Qualifications in Education*. 4th ed. London: Mansell.

Ministère de la Formation professionnelle. 1995. *Nomenclature des branches professionnelles et spécialités de la formation professionnelle*. Alger: Direction des études et de la planification.

UNESCO. 1996. *World Guide to Higher Education*. Paris: UNESCO.

Internet Source:
UNESCO - World Academic Database: www.unesco.org/iau/educdz.html

---

Compiler
Michel Bédard
Service des Équivalences, Ministère des Relations avec les Citoyens et de l'Immigration, Gouvernement du Québec, Canada

ANGOLA

YEARS OF EDUCATION →

	½	½	½	½	½	½	½	½	½	½	½	½	½	½	½	½	½
1 → 6|	7		8		9		10		11		12		13		14		15		16		17		18		19		20		21		22		23		24	
A		B		B		C		G		G		G		G		H		H		K		K		K
						D						H		H		I		K						
						E								J		J								
						F										K								

CREDENTIALS OR DOCUMENTATION

Primary and Secondary

A *Diploma de Ensino de Base, III° Nivel* (Diploma of Basic Education, 3rd Level): represents completion of a total of eight years of primary education[1]

B *Diploma de Ensino Pre-Universitário* (Diploma of Pre-University Education): two-year or three-year program requiring credential **A** for admission

C *Diploma de Ensino Médio* (Diploma of Intermediate Education): four-year agricultural, commercial, economics, or industrial program requiring credential **A** for admission

D *Diploma de Ensino Industrial Pedagógico (Ensino Médio)* [Diploma of Industrial Pedagogical Education (Intermediate Education)]: four-year program requiring credential **A** for admission; prepares industrial arts teachers for primary schools[2,3]

E *Diploma de Ensino Normal de Educação Fisica* (Diploma of Teacher Training in Physical Education): four-year program requiring credential **A** for admission; prepares physical education teachers[2]

F *Diploma de Ensino Normal Pedagógico para o Ensino de Base (Ensino Médio)* [Diploma of Pedagogical Teacher Training for Primary Education (Intermediate Education)]: four-year program requiring credential **A** for admission[2,3]

Postsecondary

G *Bacharelato* (Baccalaureate) or *Bacharel* (Bachelor): three-year or four-year program requiring credential **B** or **C** for admission

H *Licenciatura* (Licentiate) or *Licenciado* (Licentiate): two-year program requiring credential **G** for admission

I *Licenciatura en Cíencias de Educação* (Licentiate in Education Sciences): five-year program requiring credential **C, D, E,** or **F** for admission; the fifth year involves supervised practice teaching and writing a dissertation

J *Licenciatura en Medicina* (Licentiate in Medicine): six-year program requiring credential **B** for admission

K   *Doutor* (Doctor): two-year to three-year research program requiring credential **H** or **I** for admission

1   *Diploma de Ensino de Base, I° Nivel* (Diploma of Basic Education, 1ˢᵗ Level) represents completion of four years of primary education. The *II° Nivel* represents completion of two additional years of study.

2   A minimum of two years of employment is required prior to university enrollment.

3   The *Ensino Médio* portion of the diploma title identifies the diploma as a secondary-level credential as opposed to a postsecondary level (university level) credential.

GRADING INFORMATION

Secondary and Higher Education
20 (highest) to 0 (lowest) with 10 as the minimum pass.

POSTSECONDARY INSTITUTION RECOGNITION BODY

Ministerio da Educação, Caixa Postal 1451, Luanda, Angola. Tel: 244-2-323-326. Fax: 244-2-321-592.

RESOURCES FOR ADDITIONAL INFORMATION

The British Council. 1996. *International Guide to Qualifications in Education.* 4ᵗʰ ed. London: Mansell.

Internet Source:
UNESCO - World Academic Database: www.unesco.org/iau/educao.html

---

Compiler
James S. Frey
President
Educational Credential Evaluators, Inc., Milwaukee, WI

ARGENTINA

YEARS OF EDUCATION →

CREDENTIALS OR DOCUMENTATION

Primary and Secondary

A *Certificado*[1] (Certificate): end of compulsory education until 2000
B *Certificado*[1] (Certificate): end of compulsory education after 2000
C *Bachillerato*: awarded upon completion of academic secondary education
D *Perito Mercantil:* awarded upon completion of business-oriented secondary program
E *Técnico* (Technician): awarded upon completion of secondary program with technical/vocational orientation until 2000 to train automobile mechanics, electricians, plumbers, etc.
F *Técnico* (Technician): awarded upon completion of secondary program with technical/vocational orientation after 2000 (same areas of study as above)

Postsecondary

G *Auxiliar* (Assistant): awarded after two to two and one-half years of postsecondary, non-university study; the complete title includes the area of study
H *Técnico en* (Technician in): *Técnico Universitario* (University-trained Technician), *Técnico Superior*[2] (Higher-level Technician): typically awarded after two to two and one-half years of study; the complete official title includes the area of study; this title is awarded by both postsecondary, non-university institutions and by universities; the *técnico* awarded at this level is likely to be in areas such as accounting, marketing, computer programming, etc.
I *Enfermera Universitaria* [2] (University Nurse): awarded after two and one-half to three years of university study
J *Bachiller Universitario* [2] (University *Bachiller*): typically awarded after three years of study
K *Programador, Programador Universitario* (Computer Programmer): typically awarded after three years of university study
L *Bibliotecario* [2] (Librarian): typically awarded after three years of study
M *Analísta* [2] (Analyst): awarded after three to three and one-half years of university study, most often in business or technology

N   *Maestro/a* (Teacher): teacher training degree for teachers of preschool to grade 12, generally awarded after two and one-half years of postsecondary, non-university study; this degree is generally awarded by *Institutos Nacionales* (National Institutes), *Institutos Provinciales* (Provincial Institutes), or *Institutos Superiores* (Higher Institutes); the Ministry intends to move this program to the university level within the next several years

O   *Profesor en* (Professor of): awarded after three to three and one-half years of postsecondary, non-university study or three to four and one-half years of university study; title includes area of specialization; the *Profesor* in music is a highly specialized degree and generally only qualifies holders to teach music; it is considered to be teaching certification — more than an academic credential

P   *Traductor/a* (Translator): first professional degree, generally awarded after four years of study

Q   *Licenciado/a*: university and professional degree in most fields[3], generally awarded after five years of university study although there is an increasing number of four-year *licenciatura* programs

R   *Ingeniero/a* (Engineer): first professional degree in engineering, generally awarded after five to six years of study

S   *Arquitecto/a* (Architect): first professional degree in architecture, generally awarded after five to six years of study

T   *Abogado/a* (Lawyer): first professional degree in law, generally awarded after five to six years of study

U   *Médico/a* (Doctor): first professional degree in medicine, generally awarded after five to seven years of study

V   *Especialista en* (Specialization in): practical and focused on a particular aspect of a field of study and usually one year in length after completion of a five-year university or first professional degree program

W   *Magister, Maestría* (Master): generally combines practical and academic study; usually requires a thesis and one to two years of study (usually) after completion of any of the credentials **P** through **U**

X   *Doctorado* (Doctorate): two to six years of study with dissertation generally after completion of any of the credentials **Q** through **U**; credential **W** is not necessarily required for admission

---

[1]   *Certificado* is a generic term for a certificate awarded at the end of a cycle of education and implies no specific level of education in and of itself.

[2]   Holders of this intermediate degree (if awarded by a university) are eligible to continue towards the next higher degree in the same field at the same university.

[3]   In Argentina, the first professional degree is also a license to practice a profession.

GRADING INFORMATION

Secondary

Until 1985:

Numeric	Descriptive	Translation
10	*Sobresaliente*	Outstanding
9	*Distinguido*	Very Good
8	*Muy Bueno*	Good
6-7	*Bueno*	Average
4-5	*Regular*	Passed
0-3	*Reprobado*	Failed

1986-1987:

Abbreviation	Descriptive	Transation
S	*Superó*	Excelled
A	*Alcanzó*	Passed
N	*No Alcanzó*	Did Not Pass

1988-1991:

Abbreviation	Descriptive	Transation
S	*Superó*	Excelled
AMS	*Alcanzó Muy Satisfactoriamente*	Passed Very Satisfactorily
AS	*Alcanzó Satsifactoriamente*	Passed Satisfactorily
A	*Alcanzó*	Passed
N	*No Alcanzó*	Did Not Pass

Since 1992:

Numeric	Descriptive	Translation
10	*Sobresaliente*	Outstanding
8-9	*Muy Bueno*	Very Good
7	*Bueno*	Average
6	*Aprobado*	Passed
1-5	*Reprobado*	Failed

- Grading practices vary from one school to another, but the highest grade (10 or S) is rarely awarded.

Higher Education

Numeric	Descriptive	Translation
10	*Sobresaliente*	Outstanding
8-9	*Distinguido*	Very Good
6–7	*Bueno*	Average
4–5	*Aprobado*	Passed
2–3	*Insuficiente*	Insufficient
0–1	*Reprobado*	Failed

- The entire grading scale is used, but grades of 9 and 10 are reserved for outstanding achievement. Grading practices vary from one university to another and from one department to another. Private universities tend to be more liberal with grades than public universities. Generally, a cumulative average of 6 or higher represents above average achievement. An average of 8 or higher reflects superior work.

- Universities have only recently begun to include cumulative grade-point averages on the *certificados analíticos* (transcript). Failing grades will probably not be included if the student has retaken the final examination and passed.

POSTSECONDARY INSTITUTION RECOGNITION BODY

Ministerio de Cultura y Educación (Ministry of Culture and Education). Secretariá de Politíticas Universitarias (Secretariat of University Policy). Tel: 54-1-813-3466/69. Fax: 54-1-813-1239. www.mcye.gov.ar

Since 1997 the Consejo Nacional de Evaluación y Acreditación Universitaria/ CONEAU (National Council of University Evaluation and Accreditation) oversees the external evaluations of all universities and provides authorization for the establishment of new universities. The CONEAU accredits graduate programs and some undergraduate programs where the public interest or safety needs to be protected (e.g., medicine and engineering).

Two associations of university rectors (one for public universities and one for private universities) have authority for the approval of curriculum design: the Consejo Interuniversitario Nacional/CIN (National Interuniversity Council) and the Consejo de Rectores de Universidades Privadas/CRUP (Council of Private University Rectors).

RESOURCES FOR ADDITIONAL INFORMATION

Instituto de Cultura Argentina-Norteamericana (ICANA). Educational Advising Office. Maipu 686, 1006 Buenos Aires, Argentina. E-mail: advising@erl.bcl.edu.ar

Lazara, Juan Antonio. 1996. *Guía de Estudios Universitarios y Terciarios*. Buenos Aires: Guias de Estudio Ediciones.

Ministerio de Cultura y Educación. 1998. *Guía de Carreras de Grado*. Buenos Aires: Ministerio de Cultura y Educación.

Ministerio de Cultura y Educación. 1998. *Guía de Posgrado*. Buenos Aires: Ministerio de Cultura y Educación.

Reisberg, Liz. 1993. *Argentina: A Study of the Educational System of Argentina and a Guide to the Academic Placement of Students in Educational Institutions in the United States*. Annapolis Junction, MD: PIER.

Compilers
JoBeth Brudner
Instituto de Cultura Argentina-Norteamericana (ICANA), Buenos Aires, Argentina

Liz Reisberg
International Strategies & Training, Arlington, MA

ARMENIA

YEARS OF EDUCATION →

```
       ½   ½   ½   ½   ½   ½   ½   ½   ½   ½   ½   ½   ½   ½   ½   ½   ½
1 →6| 7 | 8 | 9 | 10 | 11 | 12 | 13 | 14 | 15 | 16 | 17 | 18 | 19 | 20 | 21 | 22 | 23 | 24 |
      A       B       C       D   F   G           I       I           J→      J→
                              E   H   H
```

CREDENTIALS OR DOCUMENTATION

Secondary

A   *Teri Midgnakarg Krtutyan Vkaiakan* (Certificate of Eight Year Education/Incomplete Secondary Education)[1]

B   *Hasunutian Vkaiakan* (*Attestat*/Certificate of Maturity): signifies completion of academic secondary school; leads to postsecondary education[1]

C   *Diplom* (Diploma) from an *usumnaran* (vocational secondary school-corresponds to *tekhnikum* and *uchilishche* in the Soviet/Russian Federation system), or a *koledg* (college): requires credential **A** or **B** for admission; leads to postsecondary education at the same level as credential **B**[1, 2]

Postsecondary

D   *Bakalavri Kochum* (Bachelor's Degree or Baccalaureate): four years of study at universities, institutes, academies, or conservatories; requires credential **B** or **C** for admission[1]

E   *Diplom* (Diploma): four years of study at universities, institutes, academies, or conservatories in language or teaching; requires credential **B** or **C** for admission[1]

F   *Diplom* (Diploma): five years of study (the majority of *Diplom* programs are this length) at universities, institutes, academies, or conservatories; requires credential **B** or **C** for admission[1]

G   *Diplom* (Diploma): six years of study at universities or institutes in the field of medicine; requires credential **B** or **C** for admission[1]

H   *Magistrosi Kochum* (Master's Degree): one to two years requiring credential **D** for admission; coursework concentrates on the specialization[1]

I   *Gitutyunneri Teknatsu* (Candidate of Science): three years of study requiring credential **F**, **G**, or **H** for admission; focus of the degree is research; degree is awarded after the defense of a dissertation[1, 3]

J   *Gitutyunneri Doctor* (Doctor of Science): minimum of three years of study requiring credential **I** for admission; focus is independent research and defense of a dissertation[1, 4]

[1]   Armenian educational documents may still be issued in bilingual Armenian-Russian formats. The Russian names of credentials are **Свидетельство о восьмилетнем образовании** [*Svidetel'stvo o vosmiletnem obrazovanii*] (Certificate of Eight Year Education/Incomplete Secondary Education); **Аттестат о среднем образовании** [*Attestat o srednem obrazovanii*] (*Attestat*/Certificate of Maturity); **Диплом** [*Diplom*] (Diploma-the same for credentials **C** and **E-G**); **Бакалавр** [*Bakalavr*] (Bachelor's Degree); **Магистр** [*Magistr*] (Master's Degree); **Кандидат наук** [*Kandidat Nauk*] (Candidate of Science); **Доктор наук** [*Doktor Nauk*] (Doctor of Science).

Applies to programs in nursing, *feldsher* (medical assistant), midwifery, and preschool teaching, as well as technical fields awarding the qualification of technician or junior specialist. Entry with credential **A** usually requires a four-year program and includes general education courses for completion of secondary education; entry with credential **B** requires a two-year program.

3

Student's entering with credential **H** may complete a shorter program. This degree can be obtained at state institutions of higher education or research institutions of the Academy of Science.

4

Degree is only obtained at research institutions of the Academy of Science and the dissertation defense is carried out before the Highest Attestation Commission of the Republic of Armenia.

GRADING INFORMATION

All Levels of Education

Armenian	Russian	Transliteration	Numeric	Translation
Gerazants	Отлично	Otlichno	5	Excellent
Lav	Хорошо	Khorosho	4	Good
Bavarar	Удовлетворительно	Udovletvoritel'no	3	Satisfactory
Stugvats	Зачет	Zachet	-	Passed, Credited
Anbavarar	Неудовлетворительно	Neudovletvoritel'no	2	Poor
Tapalats	--	--	1	Failed

- The grade of *Stugvats*/**Зачет** is issued when an examination was not taken, but all requirements were met.

- Grade of 2 is considered failing, and grades of 2 and 1 are not shown on transcripts.

POSTSECONDARY INSTITUTION RECOGNITION BODY

Ministry of Education and Science, Movses Khorenatsu Street 13, Yerevan 375010. Tel: 3742-566-602. Fax: 3742-151-651.

RESOURCES FOR ADDITIONAL INFORMATION

Taylor, Ann C. M., ed. 1996. *International Handbook of Universities.* 14th ed. New York: Stockton Press.

Internet Source:
UNESCO - World Academic Database: www.unesco.org/iau/educam.html

---

Compiler
Gary Anderson, Evaluator
International Education Research Foundation, Inc., Los Angeles, CA

AUSTRALIA

YEARS OF EDUCATION →

```
      ½  ½  ½  ½  ½  ½  ½  ½  ½  ½  ½  ½  ½  ½  ½  ½  ½
1 → 6│7 │ 8 │ 9 │ 10 │ 11 │ 12 │ 13 │ 14 │ 15 │ 16 │ 17 │ 18 │ 19 │ 20 │ 21 │ 22 │ 23 │ 24 │
            A         B       D   E H  G   J   J  N
                      C           F  H  L   N
                                     I  M
                                     K
                                     L
```

CREDENTIALS OR DOCUMENTATION

Secondary

A   Year 10 secondary school certificates: Australian Capital Territory (ACT) Year 10 Certificate, New South Wales School Certificate, Northern Territory Junior Secondary Studies Certificate, Queensland Junior Certificate, Western Australia Certificate of Lower Secondary Studies

B   Year 12 secondary school certificates: Australian Capital Territory (ACT) Year 12 Certificate, New South Wales Higher School Certificate, Northern Territory Senior Secondary Studies Certificate[1], Queensland Senior Certificate, South Australian Certificate of Education, Tasmanian Certificate of Education, Victorian Certificate of Education, Western Australia Certificate of Secondary Education; all lead to postsecondary education

Postsecondary

C   Advanced certificate, higher certificate, post-certificate courses, further certificate, fellowship certificate, and diploma: awarded by a Technical and Further Education (TAFE) institution; may require credential A for admission

D   Associate Diploma: two years; credential B required for admission

E   Diploma: three years (including Diploma of Teaching); credential B required for admission

F   Ordinary or Pass Bachelor's degree: three years

G   Honours Bachelor's degree: four years

H   Graduate Certificate: credential F required for admission

I   Bachelor's degree: four years, in certain professional areas (e.g., agricultural science, engineering, law, medical science, music, optometry, regional and town planning, social work, surveying)

J   Bachelor's degree: more than four years (e.g., five years—architecture, building, dentistry, veterinary science; six years—medicine, medicine and surgery)

K   Postgraduate Diploma, Graduate Diploma, master's qualifying or preliminary year, or first year of two-year master's degree program completed by coursework: one year of study; requires credential F for admission, and depending on the institution and field of study, credential F may or may not be required to be in the same field

L   "Higher" (second) bachelor's degrees (e.g., B.Ed., B. Ed. Stud., [requires at least credential **E** or **F**], BLitt)

M   Master's degree/program: completed by coursework, coursework and thesis, or by thesis (including the MBA); requires credential **G** or **K** for admission; for professionally oriented Master's degrees, two or three years of professional experience may substitute for **G** or **K**

N   Doctor of Philosophy (Ph.D): usually two to three years after credential **G**, two years after credential **M**

[1] Northern Territory Year 12 students may also qualify for the South Australian Certificate of Education.

• The academic year in Australia is generally March to November.

GRADING INFORMATION

Secondary

Grading systems vary by state. Type of program followed and subjects completed are equally important for purposes of tertiary admission. Except for Tasmania, institutions in each state calculate a tertiary entrance score that determines rank for purposes of university admission.

Australian Capital Territory:
A =   Very High Achievement
B =   High Achievement
C =   Clearly Satisfactory
D =   Limited; Student Allowed to Continue
E =   Very Limited

South Australia:

A	20	=	Outstanding
	17-19	=	Very High
B	14-16	=	High
C	11-13	=	Competent
D	8-10	=	Marginal
E	0-7	=	Low

New South Wales (percentile bands)
Bands of achievement at every decile

Tasmania

C	(5-20% of candidature)
H	(Next 10-20%)
P	(Next 30-40%)
L	(Next 14-28%)

Northern Territory

A	20	=	Outstanding
	17-19	=	Very High
B	14-16	=	High
C	11-13	=	Competent
D	8-10	=	Marginal
E	0-7	=	Low

Victoria

A	=	80-100%
B	=	70-79%
C	=	60-69%
D	=	50-59%
E	=	40-49%
F	=	0 -39%

Queensland

VHA	=	Very High Achievement
HA	=	High Achievement
SA	=	Sound Achievement
LA	=	Limited Achievement
VLA	=	Very Limited Achievement

Western Australia

A	Top 20%
B	Next 20%
C	Next 30%
D	Next 20%
F	Remaining 10%

Postsecondary

Grading systems vary by institution. Honours degrees are classified overall according to achievement (First Class Honours, Class II, Division A, etc.) The most common grading system in individual subjects (and approximate percentages earned for each grade) is as follows:

Grade	Description	Percent Awarded These Grades
HD	High Distinction	(8-9%)
D	Distinction	(19-27%)
C	Credit	(19-30%)
P	Pass	(25-28%) Includes "Conceded/Terminating Pass"
F	Fail	(10-14%)

- Percentages of awarded grades vary by academic discipline.

- Conceded/terminating pass refers to a passing, but unsatisfactory grade.

POSTSECONDARY INSTITUTION RECOGNITION BODY

There are no statutory boards or agencies responsible for accreditation. Australian states are responsible for enacting legislation to create universities; consequently, established universities carry official legislative recognition. The Australian Vice Chancellors' Committee (AVCC) seeks to advance higher education through voluntary, cooperative, and coordinated action. The committee is nonpartisan and exists exclusively for educational purposes. Its continuing aim is to serve the best interests of the universities and, through them, the nation and higher education. The Department of Employment, Education, Training, and Youth Affairs (DEETYA) has done some quality assurance work, but its efforts do not constitute any form of accreditation.

RESOURCES FOR ADDITIONAL INFORMATION

Aldrich-Langen, Caroline. 1983. *Australia: A Study of the Educational System of Australia and a Guide to the Academic Placement of Students in Educational Institutions in the United States.* Washington, D.C.: AACRAO.

Aldrich-Langen, Caroline. 1990. *The Educational System of Australia, An Update of the 1983 World Education Series Volume.* Washington, D.C.: AACRAO.

Australian Education Office, 1601 Massachusetts Ave., NW, Washington, D.C. 20036-2273. Tel: 202 332 8285. Fax: 202 332 8304. E-mail: aeosec@cais.com.

Barr, Alyson, ed. 1994. *Commonwealth Universities Yearbook 1994.* 70th ed. Vols. 1 and 4. London: The Association of Commonwealth Universities.

Ives, Bron. 1996. *Australian Grades, Assessment and Study Loads.* Washington, D.C.: Australian Education Office.

Kirkland, Sue, ed. 1997.*Commonwealth Universities Yearbook 1997-1998* . 73rd ed. Vols. 1 and 2. London: The Association of Commonwealth Universities.

Leaving School 1990: Guide to Year 12 Certificates and Tertiary Entrance Statements in Australia. 1990. Queensland: Australasian Conference of Assessment and Certification Authorities.

Internet Sources:
Australian Education Office: www.austudies.org/aeo
Australian Vice-Chancellor's Committee: www.avcc.edu.au/
Department of Education, Training, and Youth Affairs (DEETYA): www.deet.gov.au
UNESCO – World Academic Database: www.unesco.org/iau/educau.html

---

Compiler
Caroline Aldrich-Langen, Director
Academic Advising Services
California State University, Chico

AUSTRIA

YEARS OF EDUCATION →

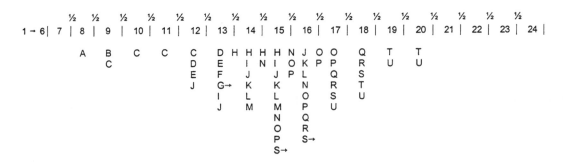

	½	½	½	½	½	½	½	½	½	½	½	½	½	½	½	½	½
1 → 6	7	8	9	10	11	12	13	14	15	16	17	18	19	20	21	22	23	24

```
        A  B  C  C  C  D  H  H  H  N  J  O  O     Q     T     T
           C           D  E  I  N  I  O  K  P  P  R  U     U
                       E  F  J     J  P  L  Q     S
                       J  G→ K     K     N  R     T
                          I  L     L     O  S     U
                          J  M     M     P  U
                                   N     Q
                                   O     R
                                   P     S→
                                   S→
```

CREDENTIALS OR DOCUMENTATION

Secondary

A *Abschlußzeugnis der Hauptschule* (Completion Certificate of Lower Secondary School): leads to further secondary education

B *Abschlußzeugnis der polytechnischen Schule* (Completion Certificate of Polytechnical School): pre-vocational course leading to apprenticeship or employment

C *Abschlußzeugnis einer berufsbildenden mittleren Schule* (Completion Certificate of Intermediate Vocational School): vocational qualification with access to employment after a one to four-year course of study[1]

D *Reifezeugnis* (Maturity Certificate), commonly known as *Matura*; *Reifeprüfungszeugnis* (Maturity Examination Certificate), *Externistenreifezeugnis* (External Maturity Examination Certificate): gives access to postsecondary education[2]

E *Reife- und Befähigungsprüfungszeugnis* (Maturity and Qualification Examination Certificate): teacher qualification for nursery school teachers and educational assistants; leads to employment or gives access to postsecondary education

F *Reife- und Diplomprüfung* (Maturity and Diploma Examination) awarded upon completion of a *Berufsbildende höhere Schule* (Higher Vocational School): *Reifeprüfung* gives access to postsecondary education and the *Diplomprüfung* grants a professional/vocational title

G *Berufsreifeprüfung* (Vocational Maturity Examination): gives access to postsecondary education[3]

H *Reifeprüfungszeugnis* (Maturity Examination Certificate) from a *Kolleg* (College): supplementary program of three or four semesters of secondary-level higher vocational training for holders of credential **D** in a different field, commonly referred to as the "*zweite Matura*" (second Maturity Examination); leads to employment or gives access to postsecondary education

50

Postsecondary

I *Diplom-Sozialarbeiter* (Certified Social Worker): six-semester program (four semesters prior to 1989) at an *Akademie für Sozialarbeit* (Academy for Social Work); requires credential **D** for admission

J *Lehramtsprüfungszeugnis* (Teaching Examination Certificate) or *Zeugnis über die Lehramtsprüfung* (Teaching Examination Certificate) from a *Berufspädogogische Akademie* (Vocational Pedagogical Academy): one to three years of vocational teacher training; requires credential **D** for admission

K *Diplom* (Diploma) with professional title in a medical technician specialty: two to three years of paramedical training in audiology technology, dietetics, eye care technology, medical laboratory technology, occupational therapy, physical therapy, radiology technology, or speech therapy; requires credential **D** for admission

L *Zeugnis über die Lehramtsprüfung für Volksschule, Hauptschule, Sonderschule,* or *polytechnicsche Lehrgänge* (Certificates for Teaching Examinations for primary, lower secondary, special education, or pre-vocational schools): three years (two years prior to 1988) of training at a *Pädogogische Akademie* (Pedagogical Academy); requires credential **D** for admission

M *Abschlußzeugnis* (Completion Certificate) from a *Schule für Ehe- und Familienberater* (School for Marriage and Family Counselors), *Lehranstalt für Familientherapie* (Institute for Family Therapy), or *Lehranstalt für Ehe- und Familienberater* (Institute for Marriage and Family Counselors): part-time program of three and one-half years (approximately equivalent to a full-time program of two years); requires credential **D** and mature-age (27-40, typically), for admission

N *Akademisch Geprüfter* _____ (Academically Certified [professional title]) (e.g. *Datentechniker* [Computer Engineer], *Kirchenmusiker* [Church Musician], *Konzertsänger* [Concert Singer], *Musiktherapeut* [Music Therapist], *Opernsänger* [Opera Singer], *Übersetzer* [Translator], *Versicherungsmathematiker* [Actuary]): awarded upon completion of a *Kurzstudium* (short-course of study), usually two and one-half or three years; requires credential **D** for admission

O *Magister (FH)* (Master [Fachhochschule (Technical College)]): six to eight semester practically oriented program in business and other fields; requires credential **D** or a relevant vocational qualification for admission[4]

P *Diplom-Ingenieur (FH)* (Graduate Engineer [Fachhochschule (Technical College)]): six to eight semester practically oriented program in engineering and technology subjects; requires credential **D** or a relevant vocational qualification for admission[4]

Q *Magister* (Master): university credential awarded after studies of a legal minimum of four or five years; requires credential **D** for admission

R *Diplom-Ingenieur* (Graduate Engineer): university credential awarded after studies of a legal minimum of four or five years; requires credential **D** for admission

S *Diplom* (Diploma), *Diplomzeugnis* (Diploma Certificate), *Reifezeugnis* (Maturity Certificate), *Lehrbefähigungszeugnis* (Teaching Qualification Certificate) from a fine arts college (prior to 1983): university-level fine arts curriculum of four to eight years; requires age 15-17 or credential **D** for admission[5]

T *Diplomierter* _____ (Graduate [title]) [e.g., *Wirtschaftstechniker* (Business Technician) or *Umwelttechniker* (Environmental Engineer)]: academic title awarded after a minimum study duration of two years; requires credential **R** for admission

U *Doktor* (Doctor): university credential awarded after studies of a minimum of two to four semesters; requires credential **Q** or **R** for admission

[1] Awarded by a *Haushaltungsschule* (Domestic Science School) (one year); *Forstliche Bundesfachschule* (Intermediate Forestry School) (one year); *Landwirtschaftliche Fachschule* (Intermediate Agricultural School) (two semesters-four years); *Fachschule für Sozialberufe* (Intermediate School for Social Occupations, such as family assistance, social services, marriage and family guidance, elder/handicapped care, pre-nursing) (one to three years); *Büroschule* (Office School); *Büropraxislehrgang* (Practical Office Training); *Lehrgang für Büroberufe* (Course for Office Occupations); *Schule für Datenverarbeitungs-Kaufleute* (School for Occupations in Data Processing) (one to three years); *Büro- und Verwaltungsschule* (Intermediate School for Office and Administrative Work) (two-year); *Hauswirtschaftsschule* (Domestic Science School) (two years); *Handelsschule* (Intermediate Commercial School) (three years); *Fachschule für wirtschaftliche Berufe* (Intermediate School for Domestic-Science Occupations) (three years); *Fachschule für Mode und Bekleidungstechnik* (Intermediate School for the Fashion and Apparel Trade) (three years); *Hotelfachschule, Gastgewerbefachschule, Tourismusfachschule* (Intermediate School for Hotel Management, Catering, and Tourism Occupations) (three years); *Fachschule (technische, gewerbliche or kunstgewerbliche)* (Intermediate Industrial, Trade and Craft School) (four years).

[2] Awarded after a total of 12-13 years of education by *Allgemeinbildende höhere Schulen* (General Secondary Schools) of the following types: *Gymnasium* (Latin-based General Secondary School); *Realgymnasium* (Standard General Secondary School); *Wirtschaftskundliches Realgymnasium* (Home-Economics-oriented General Secondary School); *Oberstufenrealgymnasium* (Specialized General Secondary School); *Aufbau- und Aufbaurealgymnasium* (Bridge-type Language-oriented and Science-oriented General Secondary School); *Gymnasium und Realgymnasium für Berufstätige* (General Secondary School for Employed Persons); *Höhere Internatsschule* (General Secondary Boarding School); *Werkschulheim* (Crafts-oriented General Secondary School). Also awarded after a total of 13 years of education by *Berufsbildende höhere Schulen* (Higher Vocational Schools) of the following types: *Höhere technische und gewerbliche Lehranstalt* (Higher Industrial and Trade School); *Höhere Lehranstalt für Mode und Bekleidungstechnik* (Higher School for the Fashion and Apparel Industry); *Höhere Lehranstalt für Tourismus/Fremdenverkehrsberufe* (Higher School for Tourism and Catering Occupations), *Handelsakademie* (Higher Commercial School); *Höhere Lehranstalt für wirtschaftliche Berufe* (Higher Domestic-Science School); *Höhere land- und forstwirtschaftliche Lehranstalten* (Higher Agricultural and Forestry Schools); *Bildungsanstalt für Kindergarten- und Sozialpädogogik* (Higher School for Kindergarten and Social Education).

[3] Implemented in September 1997. Created to facilitate access from vocational to academic education, it is an external examination that consists of two parts: the first part may be taken at age 17 by graduates of a three-year credential **C** program, the second part may be taken at age 19.

[4] Created in 1993 by the Fachhochschul-Studiengesetz (Technical College Studies Act). Courses last six to eight semesters (including one practical semester) and are offered either full-time or "berufsbegleitend" (evening and weekend courses for working persons). Graduates may enter doctoral studies at Austrian universities, but these are structured two semesters longer than for graduates of universities.

[5] Age 15 required for majors in instrumental music for programs lasting a minimum of eight years. Credential **D** required for majors in architecture, interior architecture, music theater direction, music theory, performance arts direction, and secondary teacher education. These majors require a minimum of age 17 with the programs lasting four to seven years. Except for the programs in architecture and teaching, these qualifications do not grant access to doctoral studies.

GRADING INFORMATION

Individual and comprehensive grades are awarded at all levels of education. Individual grades are awarded after coursework is completed or after one part of a multi-part examination. Comprehensive grades, which are awarded for examinations that consist of several parts, combine several individual grades according to a legally defined formula.

Individual Grades:

Numeric	Description	Translation
1	*Sehr Gut*	Very Good
2	*Gut*	Good
3	*Befriedigend*	Satisfactory
4	*Genügend*	Sufficient
5	*Nicht Genügend*	Insufficient, Fail

Comprehensive Grades:

Description	Translation	Definition
Mit Ausgezeichnetem Erfolg Bestanden	Passed With High Distinction	At least half of the individual grades are *sehr gut* and all remaining grades are *gut*
Mit Gutem Erfolg Bestanden*	Passed With Distinction	No individual grades lower than *befriedigend* and at least an equal number of *sehr gut* and *befriedigend* grades exist
Bestanden	Passed	Each individual grade is at least *genügend,* but conditions necessary for the higher comprehensive grade do not exist
Nicht Bestanden	Not Passed	At least one individual grade of *nicht genügend* exists

*awarded only at secondary school level

POSTSECONDARY INSTITUTION RECOGNITION BODIES

Bundesministerium für Wissenschaft und Verkehr (Federal Ministry for Science and Transportation). Abteilung VIII/A/5, Referat a. Rosengasse 2-6. A-1014 Vienna. Tel: 43-1-53-2071-33.

Fachhochschulrat (Fachhochschule accreditation agency), Geschäftsstelle. Liechtensteinstraße 22. A-1090 Vienna. Tel: 43-1-3195034-0. Fax:43-1-3195034-30.

RESOURCES FOR ADDITIONAL INFORMATION

Bundesministerium für Arbeit und Soziales, Bundesministerium für Unterricht und kulturelle Angelegenheiten. 1996. *Bildung und Berufsbildung: Österreich im Überblick.*
Vienna.

Bundesministerium für Unterricht und kulturelle Angelegenheiten. 1996. *Bildungswege in Österreich.* Vienna.

Bundesministerium für Unterricht und Kunst. 1990. *Education in Austria.* Vienna.

Bundesministerium für Wissenschaft und Verkehr, Bundesministerium für Unterricht und kulturelle Angelegenheiten, Bundesgeschäftsstelle des Arbeitsmarktservice. Published annually. *Universitäten/Hochschulen: Studium & Beruf.* Vienna.

Bundesministerium für Wissenschaft und Verkehr, Fachhochschul-Konferenz, Fachhochschulrat. 1998. *Fachhochschulen in Austria.* Vienna.

Lukas, Karen. 1987. *Austria: A Study of the Educational System of Austria and A Guide to the Academic Placement of Students in Educational Institutions of the United States.* Washington, D.C.: AACRAO.

Internet Sources:
Bundesministerium für Unterricht und kulturelle Angelegenheiten: www.bmuk.gv.at
Austrian Universities: www.austriaculture.net/AustrUnis36.html
Studying at Austrian Universities: www.bmwf.gv.at/3uniwes/index.htm

---

Compiler
LesLee M. Stedman
University of Puget Sound

BAHAMAS

YEARS OF EDUCATION →

```
      ½    ½    ½    ½    ½    ½    ½    ½    ½    ½    ½    ½    ½    ½    ½    ½    ½
1 → 6│ 7 │ 8 │ 9 │ 10 │ 11 │ 12 │ 13 │ 14 │ 15 │ 16 │ 17 │ 18 │ 19 │ 20 │ 21 │ 22 │ 23 │ 24 │
         A         B     E E D   F           H
                   C         F
                             G
```

CREDENTIALS OR DOCUMENTATION

Secondary

A   Bahamas Junior Certificate: external examinations taken upon completion of junior high school
B   Bahamas General Certificate of Secondary Education or General Certificate of Education, Ordinary Level, administered by the University of London: external examinations taken upon completion of senior high school; two-year program based on credential **A**
C   High School Diploma
D   General Certificate of Education, Advanced Level, administered by the University of London: two-year program based on credential **B**; leads to University of the West Indies bachelor degree programs[1]

Postsecondary

E   Certificates awarded by the Bahamas Hotel Training College, College of the Bahamas, and the Bahamas Technical and Vocational Institute, and in a variety of vocational/technical areas: programs generally require one to one and one-half years of study; admission based on credential **B** or **C**
F   Associate Degree awarded by the College of the Bahamas: two- and three-year programs are offered in the fields of Business and Administrative Studies, Humanities, Natural Sciences, Nursing and Health Sciences, Social Sciences and Technology; admission based on credential **B** or **C**; the two-year program also leads to credential **D**
G   Diploma in Hotel and Catering Operations awarded by the Bahamas Hotel Training College: two-year program based on credential **B** or **C**
H   Bachelor of Science: three-year programs in Hotel Management and Tourism Management; degrees are awarded by the University of the West Indies[1] in collaboration with the College of the Bahamas; admission based on credential **D**

---

[1]   Additional information on education in the Caribbean Region, of which Bahamas is part, can be found under the chapter titled *Commonwealth Caribbean Region* in this publication.

GRADING INFORMATION

Secondary (see credential **C**)

Letter	Percentage
A	80-100
B	70 -79
C	60-69
D	50 -59
E	below 50 (failing)

Bahamas General Certificate of Secondary Education (see credential **B**) grades range from A - G. There is no failing grade. The higher the level of the grade, the higher the level of proficiency. A minimum grade of C is necessary to gain admission to bachelor degree programs.

Higher Education

Letter	Point
A	4.0
B	3.0
C	2.0
D	1.0
F	0.0

POSTSECONDARY INSTITUTION RECOGNITION BODY

Ministry of Education and Training: P.O. Box N-3913, Nassau. Tel: 809-322-81403. Fax: 809-322-8491.

RESOURCES FOR ADDITIONAL INFORMATION

UNESCO - World Academic Database: www.unesco.org/iau/educbs.html

---

Compiler
Judi Marino
Director of Admissions
Florida Institute of Technology, Melbourne

BAHRAIN

YEARS OF EDUCATION →

```
    ½   ½   ½   ½   ½   ½   ½   ½   ½   ½   ½   ½   ½   ½   ½   ½   ½
1 →6| 7 | 8 | 9 | 10| 11| 12| 13| 14| 15| 16| 17| 18| 19| 20| 21| 22| 23| 24|
             A     A C C D D F G   H I K           N
                   B D D   E         J L
                                       M
```

CREDENTIALS OR DOCUMENTATION

Secondary

A   Secondary school certificate/diploma from a religious institute
B   Secondary School Certificate [Shahaadat itmaam al-diraasa al-thaanawiya al-aamma] and passing the "tawjihi" examination

Postsecondary

C   Orientation courses at the University of Bahrain: one or two semesters of study requiring credential **B** for admission
D   External examinations administered by the Business and Technology Education Council (BTEC) and the City and Guilds of London Institute (CGLI) conducted at Bahrain Training Institute: three months to two years requiring credential **B** for admission
E   Diploma (University of Bahrain) in accounting, associate business, associate engineering, commercial studies, population and statistical studies, and technical studies: two years of study requiring credential **B** for admission
F   Medical secretary program (College of Health Sciences): five semesters of study requiring credential **B** for admission
G   Associate degree (College of Health Sciences): three years of study requiring credential **B** for admission
H   Maternal and Child Health Nurse (College of Health Sciences): one year of study requiring credential **G** for admission
I   Diploma (College of Health Sciences) in community health nursing, health science education, midwifery, and psychiatric nursing: three semesters of study requiring credential **G** for admission
J   Bachelor of... Arts, Education, Physical Education, and Science: four years of study requiring credential **B** for admission
K   Certificate in Arabic and Islamic Studies: one year of study requiring credential **J** for admission
L   Postgraduate Diploma in Education (University of Bahrain): one year of study requiring credential **J** for admission
M   Master of Education in Science Education: one year of study requiring credential **J** for admission
N   Degree of Medical Doctor (Arabian Gulf University): seven years of study requiring credential **B** for admission

GRADING INFORMATION

Secondary

Percentage	Description
80-100	Excellent
70-79	Very Good
60-69	Good
50-59	Average
40-49	Below Average
Below 40	Fail

Postsecondary

Letter	Percentage	Description		Other abbreviations:
A	90-100	Excellent	I	Incomplete
B	80-89	Good or Very Good	IF	Incomplete or Failed
C	70-79	Fair or Good	W	Withdrew
D	60-69	Weak or Fair	P	Pass
F	Below 59	Failing		No grade reported

Arabian Gulf University
Cumulative Averages:

Points	Description
4.5-5.0	Excellent
4.0-4.4	Very Good
3.5-3.9	Good
3.0-3.4	Pass
Less than 3.0	Fail

Grading for Individual Courses

Letter	Percentage	Points	Description
A	90-100	5	Excellent
B	80-89	4	Very Good
C	70-79	3	Good
D	60-69	2	Pass
F	Less than 60	1	Fail

College of Health Sciences

Letter	Percentage	Point
A	90-100	4.00
A-	87-89	3.67
B+	84-86	3.33
B	80-83	3.00
B-	77-79	2.67
C+	74-76	2.33
C	70-73	2.00
C-	67-69	1.67
D+	64-66	1.33
D	60-63	1.00
F	0-59	0.00

Hotel and Catering Training Centre

Percentage	Description
90-100	Excellent
66-89	Very Good
50-65	Good
0-49	Fail

University of Bahrain, Faculty of Engineering

Letter	Percentage
A	90-100
A-	87-89
B+	84-86
B	80-83
B-	77-79
C+	74-76
C	70-73
C-	67-69
D+	64-66
D	60-63
F	0-59

POSTSECONDARY INSTITUTION RECOGNITION BODY

Ministry of Education, P.O. Box 43, Manama Bahrain. Tel: 973 680 071.
Fax: 973 630 161. Telex: 9094 tarbia bn.

Other ministries are responsible for recognition in the case of some specialized institutions.

RESOURCES FOR ADDITIONAL INFORMATION

Johnson, J. K., ed. 1984. *The Admission and Academic Placement of Students from: Bahrain, Oman, Qatar, United Arab Emirates, Yemen Arab Republic.* Washington, D.C.: Joint Committee on Workshops.

Nucho, Leslie S. Undated (circa 1992). *Education in the Arab World.* Vol. 1. Washington, D.C.: AMIDEAST.

Internet Source:
UNESCO – World Academic Database: www.unesco.org/educbh.html

Compilers
Bridget Canty, Manager
University of Houston

Kirven McKissic, Office Assistant
University of Houston

BANGLADESH

YEARS OF EDUCATION →

```
      ½   ½   ½   ½   ½   ½   ½   ½   ½   ½   ½   ½   ½   ½   ½   ½   ½
1 → 6| 7 | 8 | 9 | 10| 11| 12| 13| 14| 15| 16| 17| 18| 19| 20| 21| 22| 23| 24|
              A       B   E   F I J   M   M X U X d  d  c  d  d  d  f  f  f  f
                      C       G   K   N   U   Y a       d     e
                      D       H   L   O   V   Z
                                      P   W   a
                                      Q       b
                                      R
                                      S
                                      T
```

CREDENTIALS OR DOCUMENTATION

Secondary

A   Secondary School Certificate awarded by the Boards of Intermediate and Secondary Education

B   Higher Secondary Certificate awarded by the Boards of Intermediate and Secondary Education

C   Certificate in Secretarial Sciences

D   Diplomas in the fields of commerce, leather technology, and printing technology

E   Diploma in the fields of agriculture, architectural engineering, ceramic technology, chemical and food technology, civil engineering, electrical engineering, electronics engineering, marine engineering, mechanical engineering, power technology, and surveying: three-year program based on credential **A**

F   Diploma in Nursing and Midwifery, or Senior Certificate in Nursing and Midwifery, awarded by the Bangladesh Nurses Council: hospital schools of nursing programs which are 40% theoretical and 60% practical; four years of study consisting of three years of nursing and one year of midwifery training; admission requires credential **A**

Postsecondary

G   Associate degree in the field of nursing awarded by private universities: two-year program requiring credential **B** for admission

H   Bachelor's degree in the fields of arts (pass), commerce (pass), home economics (pass), leather technology, social sciences (pass), textile technology, and nursing (post-credential **F**), awarded by public universities: two-year programs requiring credential **B** or equivalent for admission[1]

I   Bachelor of Arts (Pass) degree awarded by private universities: signifies completion of a two and one-half-year program requiring credential **B** for admission

J   Bachelor's degree in the fields of arts (honours), business studies (honours), commerce (honours), fine arts (honours), home economics (honours), laws (honours), pharmacy (honours), nursing science, science (honours), and social sciences (honours) awarded by public universities: three-year programs requiring credential **B** or equivalent for admission[1]

60

K Bachelor of Fine Arts awarded by public universities: five-year program requiring credential **A** for admission

L Bachelor's degree in the field of education: one-year program requiring credential **G** for admission

M Bachelor's degree in the fields of agricultural economics (honours), agriculture (honours), animal husbandry (honours), engineering, fisheries (honours), homeopathic medicine, and law (honours), awarded by public universities: four-year programs requiring credentials **B** or **E** for admission[1]

N Doctor of Veterinary Medicine: four-year program requiring credential **B** for admission

O Bachelor's degree in the fields of arts (honours), business administration, computer science, economics, English, environmental studies, nursing, pharmacy, science (honours), and social sciences completed at private universities: four-year programs requiring credential **B** or equivalent for admission[1]

P Bachelor's degree in the fields of business administration, pharmacy, and science (honours) awarded by the University of Khulna: four-year programs requiring credential **B** or equivalent for admission[1]

Q Bachelor's degree in the field of law: two-year program requiring credential **G** for admission

R Master's degree in the fields of arts, commerce, science, and social sciences: two-year program requiring credential **G** for admission, or a one-year program requiring credential **J** for admission

S Master's degree in the fields of business administration, business studies, fine arts, and statistics: one-year program requiring credential **J** for admission

T Master's degree in the field of education: one-year program requiring credential **L** for admission

U Bachelor's degree in the fields of architecture, Ayurvedic medicine, dental surgery, medicine and surgery (Bachelor of Medicine and Bachelor of Surgery/M.B.B.S.), and Unani medicine: five-year programs requiring credential **B** or **E** for admission[1]

V Master's degree in the fields of agricultural economics, agricultural engineering, agricultural extension education, animal husbandry, fisheries, or veterinary medicine: one-year programs requiring credential **M** or **N** for admission

W Master's degree in the fields of arts, economics, or science awarded by private universities: one-year program requiring credential **O** for admission

X Master's degree in the fields of architecture and engineering: one and one-half-year programs requiring credential **M** or **U** for admission

Y Master's degree in the fields of agricultural statistics and urban and regional planning: two-year programs requiring credential **M** for admission

Z Master of Laws: two-year program requiring credential **Q** for admission

a Master of Business Administration: two or two and one-half-year program completed at a private institution; credential **O** required for admission

b Master of Philosophy: two-year program requiring credential **R, S,** or **T** for admission

c Master of Science (Cardiology) and Master of Science (Ophthalmology): three-year programs requiring credential **U** for admission

d Doctor of Philosophy: two or three-year program requiring credentials **V, W, X, Y,** or **b** for admission

e Doctor of Laws: three-year program requiring credential **Z** for admission

f Doctor of Literature and Doctor of Science: three-year programs requiring credential **d** for admission

GRADING INFORMATION

Secondary

Division	Percentage
First	60.0 to 100
Second	45.0 to 59.9
Third	33.0 to 44.9

Higher Education

Agricultural Universities:

Class	Percentage
First	60.0 to 100
Second	45.0 to 59.9

- Minimum pass for each paper is 40%.

Engineering Universities:

Class	Percetage
Honours	75.0 to 100
First	60.0 to 74.9
Second	45.0 to 59.9

Bangladesh Institute of Technology, Dhaka:

Grade	Percentage
A+	80 to 100
A	75 to 79
B+	70 to 74
B	60 to 69
C+	50 to 59
C	45 to 49
D+	40 to 44
D	35 to 39
F	0 to 34

Bangladesh University of Engineering and Technology:

Class	Percentage
First Class (Honours)	75 to 100
First Class	60 to 74
Second Class	50 to 59

- Minimum pass for each paper is 40%.

Universities of Dhaka, Chittagong, Jahangirnagar, Rajshahi; National University, and Islamic University:

Division	Percentage
First	60.0 to 100
Second	45.0 to 59.9
Third	36.0 to 49.9
Pass	33.0 to 35.0

- M.B.B.S. degree programs: minimum pass for each paper is 50%.

62

POSTSECONDARY INSTITUTION RECOGNITION BODY

Ministry of Education. 1, Sonargaon Road (Plashi-Nilkhet), Dhaka. 1205. Tel: 88-02-863420.Telex: 88-02-86342.

The Universities Grants Commission (UGC) advises the Ministry of Education on issues of higher education, and allocates funding to the universities. UGC. Sher-e-Bangla Nagar, Dhaka. 1207. Tel: 880-2-812629. Fax: 880-2-863420.

RESOURCES FOR ADDITIONAL INFORMATION

Bangladesh Bureau of Educational Information and Statistics (BANBEIS). 1997. *Education System of Bangladesh*. Dhaka: Ministry of Education.

Barr, Alyson, ed. 1994.*Commonwealth Universities Yearbook 1994.* 70th ed. Vol. 1. London: The Association of Commonwealth Universities.

National Office of Overseas Skills Recognition. 1992. *Country Education Profiles: Bangladesh.* Canberra: Australian Government Publishing Service.

Nursing in the World Editorial Committee. 1993. *Nursing in the World: The Facts, Needs, and Prospects.* 3rd ed. Tokyo: The International Nursing Foundation of Japan.

Internet Sources:
Hopper, Richard. 1997. "A Case Study in Private Postsecondary Education." *International Educator* VII, 1.
    www.nafsa.org/publications/ie/fall97_winter98/hopper.html
UNESCO - World Academic Database: www. unesco.org/iau/educbd.html

---

Compiler
Bonnie Rosenthal
World Education Services, Inc., New York, NY

BELARUS

YEARS OF EDUCATION →

```
     ½    ½    ½    ½    ½    ½    ½    ½    ½    ½    ½    ½    ½    ½    ½    ½    ½
1→6│ 7 │ 8 │ 9 │ 10 │ 11 │ 12 │ 13 │ 14 │ 15 │ 16 │ 17 │ 18 │ 19 │ 20 │ 21 │ 22 │ 23 │ 24 │
        A         B    C    C    D    E    E    E    H    I    I    I
                  C    D    D              F    G    I
                                          H
```

CREDENTIALS OR DOCUMENTATION

Credentials are issued bilingually in Belarussian and Russian. The Belarrussian terminology is provided here, as it is the primary language used in Belarus. For information pertaining to Russian terminology of credentials, refer to the section on the Russian Federation in this publication.

Secondary

A **Пасведчанне аб базавай адукацыі** [*Pasvedchanne ab bazavaj adukatsyi*] (Certificate of Basic Education) awarded by a **Агульнаадукацыйная школа** [*Agul'naadukatsyjnaja shkola*] (General Education School): signifies completion of compulsory education

B **Атэстат аб агульнай сярэдняй адукацыі** [*Atestat ab agul'naj sjarednjaj adukatsyi*] (Certificate of Completion of General Secondary Education) awarded by a **Агульнаадукацыйная школа** [*Agul'naadukatsyjnaja shkola*] (General Education School), **Гімназія** [*Gimnazija*] (Gymnasium), **Ліцэй** [**Litsej**] (Lycée): two years requiring credential **A** for admission; signifies completion of general secondary education

C **Дыплом аб пачатковай прафесіянальнай адукацыі** [*Dyplom ab pachatkovaj prafesijanal'naj adukatsyi*] (Diploma of Beginning Occupational Education) awarded by a **Прафесійна-тэхнічнае вучылішча** [*Prafesijna-tekhnichnae vychylishcha*] (Occupational Technical School): either two to four years requiring credential **A** for admission (two-year program does not signify completion of secondary education, three- to four-year program signifies completion of general secondary and beginning occupational education); or, one to two years requiring credential **B** for admission[1]

Postsecondary

D **Дыплом аб сярэдняй прафесійнай адукацыі** [*Dyplom ab sjarednjaj prafesijnaj adukatsyi*] (Diploma of Intermediate Occupational Education) awarded by a **Сярэдняя спецыяльная навучальная ўстанова: Тэхнікум, Вучылішча** [*Sjarednjaja spetsyjal'naja navuchal'naja ustanova: Tekhnikum, Vuchylishcha*] (Institution of Intermediate Occupational Education: Technical College, Lower-Division College): either two to three years requiring credential **B** for admission; or three to four years (signifies completion of combined general secondary and intermediate occupational education) requiring credential **A** for admission[2]

64

E **Дыплом аб вышэйшай адукацыі** [*Dyplom ab vyshejshaj adukatsyi*] (Diploma of Higher Education) awarded by a **Вышэйшая навучальная ўстанова: Вышэйшае вучылішча, Інстытут, Акадэмія, Універсітэт** [*Vyshejshaja navuchal'naja ustanova: Vyshejshaje vychylishcha, Instytut, Akademija, Universitet*] (Institution of Higher Education: Upper-Division College, Institute, Academy, University): four to five years (six years in case of Medicine) requiring credential **B** or **D** for admission; signifies completion of occupational education[3]

F **Дыплом бакалаўра** [*Dyplom bakalawra*] (Bachelor's Diploma) awarded by a **Вышэйшая навучальная ўстанова: Вышэйшае вучылішча, Інстытут, Акадэмія, Універсітэт** [*Vyshejshaja navuchal'naja ustanova: Vyshejshaje vychylishcha, Instytut, Akademija, Universitet*] (Institution of Higher Education: Upper-Division College, Institute, Academy, University): five years requiring credential **B** or **D** for admission; signifies completion of academic and scientific education[4]

G **Дыплом спецыяліста з паглыбленнай падрыхтоўкай** [*Dyplom spetsyjalista z paglyblennaj padrykhtowkaj*] (Diploma of Advanced Occupational Studies) awarded by a **Вышэйшая навучальная ўстанова: Акадэмія, Універсітэт** [*Vyshejshaja navuchal'naja ustanova: Akademija. Universitet*] (Institution of Higher Education: Academy, University): one year requiring credential **E** (five-year programs only) for admission; signifies completion of advanced occupational education [5]

H **Дыплом магістра** [*Dyplom magistra*] (Master's Diploma) awarded by a **Вышэйшая навучальная ўстанова: Акадэмія, Універсітэт** [*Vyshejshaja navuchal'naja ustanova: Akademija, Universitet*] (Institution of Higher Education: Academy, University): one to two years requiring credential **F** for admission; signifies completion of academic and scientific education[4]

I **Дыплом кандыдата навук** [*Dyplom kandydata navuk*] (Candidate of Sciences Diploma) awarded through the **Вышэйшая Атэстацыйная Камісія** [*Vyshejshaja Atestatsyjnaja Kamisija*] (National Higher Certification Board): three years requiring credential **E or H** for admission; signifies completion of academic and scientific education[4]

---

[1] ***Beginning Occupational Education***: An instructional program preparing individuals to apply technical knowledge and skills to create products or provide services.

[2] ***Intermediate Occupational Education***: An instructional program preparing individuals to apply basic scientific principles and technical skills to support a professional.

[3] ***Occupational Education***: An instructional program preparing individuals to apply scientific principles to solve practical problems for the benefit of society.

[4] ***Academic and Scientific Education***: An instructional program preparing individuals to apply scientific principles to solve theoretical problems for scientific advancement or other social benefit.

[5] ***Advanced Occupational Education***: An instructional program preparing individuals to apply scientific principles to solve practical and theoretical problems for the benefit of society.

GRADING INFORMATION

Secondary

Numeric	Description	Transliteration	Translation
5	выдатна	*Vydatna*	Excellent
4	добра	*Dobra*	Good
3	здавальняюча	*Zdaval'njajucha*	Satisfactory
2	нездавальняюча	*Nezdaval'njajucha*	Unsatisfactory

Postsecondary

Description	Transliteration	Translation
выдатна	*Vydatna*	Excellent
добра	*Dobra*	Good
здавальняюча	*Zdaval'njajucha*	Satisfactory
нездавальняюча	*Nezdaval'njajucha*	Unsatisfactory
залик	*Zalik*	Complete

- The grades of 2 and **нездавальняюча** [*nezdaval'njajucha*] are not passing grades.

- The grade of **залик** [*zalik*] (complete) is a passing grade for all courses requiring more than one semester of study (the final grade obtained in the sequence retroactively applies to previous parts of the course), for all elective courses, and for laboratory and practical courses.

POSTSECONDARY INSTITUTION RECOGNITION BODIES

Ministry of Higher Education, Republic of Belarus, 9 Sovetskaja Street, City of Minsk 220002, Republic of Belarus. Tel: 375-172-274-736. Fax: 375-172-208-483.

National Higher Certification Board, Republic of Belarus, 66 F. Skaryny Avenue, City of Minsk 220072, Republic of Belarus. Tel: 375-172-842-816.

RESOURCES FOR ADDITIONAL INFORMATION

National Institute of Higher Education. *1998. Higher Education in Belarus: General Description.* Minsk: Belarus State University.

Internet Source
UNESCO - World Academic Database: www.unesco.org/iau/educby.html

---

Compilers:
Sergei Vetokhin
Vice-President
National Institute of Higher Education, Republic of Belarus

Yuri Akimov
Head of the Department of Accreditation and Recognition of Foreign Credentials
Ministry of General and Professional Education, Russian Federation

Edward Golovatch
Director of the Department of Eastern Europe and the former Soviet Union
Globe Language Services, Inc., New York, NY

BELGIUM

YEARS OF EDUCATION →

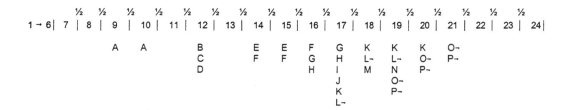

		½	½	½	½	½	½	½	½	½	½	½	½	½	½	½	½
1 → 6|	7	8	9	10	11	12	13	14	15	16	17	18	19	20	21	22	23	24|

```
            A    A           B         E    E    F    G    K    K    K    O-
                             C              F    F    G    H    L-   L-   O-   P-
                             D                        H    I    M    N    P-
                                                      J         O-
                                                      K         P-
                                                      L-
```

CREDENTIALS OR DOCUMENTATION

Secondary

A *Certificat d'Enseignement Secondaire Inférieur/Getuigschrift van Lager Secundair Onderwijs/Abschlußzeugnis der Unterstufe des Sekundarunterrichts* (Certificate of Lower Secondary Education): awarded to students in the general, technical, and artistic streams after grade nine and to students in vocational streams after grade ten

B *Certificat d'Enseignement Secondaire Supérieur/Getuigschrift van Hoger Secundair Onderwijs/Abschlußzeugnis der Oberstufe des Sekundarunterrichts* (Certificate of Higher Secondary Education)

C *Diplôme d'Enseignement Technique Secondaire Supérieur/Diploma Hoger Secundaire Technisch Onderwijs* (Diploma of Higher Secondary Technical Education)

D *Diplôme d'Aptitude à Accéder à l'Enseignement Supérieur/Bekwaamheidsdiploma dat Toegang Verleert tot het Hoger Onderwijs* (Diploma of Qualification Giving Access to Higher Education)

Postsecondary

E *Candidat/Kandidaat* (Candidate): programs in most fields require two years of study; programs in medicine and veterinary medicine require three years of study

F *Gradué(e)/Gegradueerde* (Graduate): programs require three or four years of study; prior to 1990-91, some programs required two years of study

G *Licence/Licentiaat* (Licentiate): programs require two or three years of study after credential **E**

H *Ingénieur/Ingenieur* (Engineer): programs require two or three years of study after credential **E**

I *Pharmicien/Apotheker* (Pharmacist)

J *Licence en Sciences Dentaires/Licentie in de Tandheelkunde* [now called *Tandarts*] (Licentiate in Dentistry)

K *Certificat Complémentaire/Aanvullend Getuigschrift* (Complementary Certificate), *Certificat de Spécialisation/Getuigschrift van Specialisatie* (Certificate of Specialization), *Licence Spéciale/Speciale Licentie* or *Bijzondere Licentie* (Special Licentiate), *Licence Complémentaire* (Complementary Licence), *Diplôme Spéciale* (Special Diploma), *Diplôme Avancé* (Advanced Diploma), *Maîtrise/Master* (Master): complementary credentials requiring one to three years of study after **G, H, I**, and **J**[1]

L *Doctorat/Doctoraat* (Doctorate): requires a minimum of one to two years of study after credentials **G, H, I**, and **J**

M *Doctorat en Médecine Véterinaire/Kandidatuur in de Diergeneeskundige Wetenschappen* (Doctor in Veterinary Medicine)

N *Docteur en Médecine, Chirurgie et Accouchements/Doctor in de Genees-, Heel- en Verloskunde* (Doctor in Medicine, Surgery, and Obstetrics)

O *Agrégation de l'Enseignement Supérieur/Aggregatie voor het Hoger Onderwijs* (Higher Education Teaching Credential): requires a minimum of two years of study after credential **L**; one major dissertation and three minor theses must be prepared; required for university teaching; rarely awarded

P *Doctorat Spéciale/Speciaal Doctoraat* (Special Doctorate): requires a minimum of two years of study after credential **L**; one major dissertation and three minor theses must be prepared; required for university teaching; rarely awarded

[1] Complementary credentials are known by a variety of names. The list provided in credential **K** represents just the most common variations. They represent completion of a program of specialized coursework.

GRADING INFORMATION

Secondary and Postsecondary

Scale One: 0-20; minimum pass is 10 or 50%

Numeric	Percent	Description	Translation
18-20	90-100	*Avec la plus Grande Distinction/ Met Grootste Onderscheiding*	With the Highest Distinction
16-17	80- 89	*Avec Grande Distinction/ Met Grote Onderscheiding*	With Great Distinction
14-15	70- 79	*Avec Distinction/ Met Onderscheiding*	With Distinction
10-13	50- 69	*Suffisant/Avec Satisfaction/ Met Voldoening*	Sufficient/With Satisfaction
0-9	0- 49	*Ajourné*	Failed

Scale Two: 0-20; minimum pass is 12 or 60%

Numerical	Percent	Description	Translation
16-20	80-100	*Avec Grande Distinction/ Met Grote Onderscheiding*	With Great Distinction
14-15	70- 79	*Avec Distinction/ Met Onderscheiding*	With Distinction
12-13	60- 69	*Suffisant/Avec Satisfaction Met Voldoening*	Sufficient/With Satisfaction
0-11	0- 59	*Ajourné*	Failed

- Grades received in individual courses that are lower than the minimum grade required for passing may be condoned as passes if the overall yearly grade average is at least the minimum percentage required for passing (i.e., 50% in the case of Scale One and 60% in the case of Scale Two.) Such grades are unsatisfactory but passing.

POSTSECONDARY INSTITUTION RECOGNITION BODIES

Belgium is legally divided by its constitution into three cultural-linguistic communities: French, Flemish, and German. Each community is responsible for education within its borders.

- Flemish community: *Ministerie van de Vlaamse Gemeenschap, Departement Onderwijs*, Rijksadministratief Centrum, Arcadengebouw, 1010 Brussels, Belgium. Tel: 02-210-51-1. Fax: 02-210-53-72. www.ond.vlaanderen.be

- French community: *Gouvernement de la Communauté Française*, Place Surlet de Chokier 15/17, 1000 Brussels, Belgium. Tel: 32-2-221-88-1. www.fgov.be

- German community: *Regierung der Deutschsprachigen Gemeinschaft.* www.dgov.be

RESOURCES FOR ADDITIONAL INFORMATION

Centrum voor Informatie en Documentatie. 1992. "Educational Developments in Belgium." Report for UNESCO prepared by the Ministerie van de Vlaamse Gemeenschap, Departement Onderwijs. Brussels, Belgium.

Fletcher, Ann. 1985. *Belgium: A Study of the Educational System of Belgium and a Guide to the Academic Placement of Students in Educational Institutions of the United States.* Washington, D.C.: AACRAO.

National Office of Overseas Skills Recognition. 1992. *Country Education Profiles: Belgium.* Canberra: Australian Government Publishing Service.

Philippart, A. 1995. "Belgium." *International Encyclopedia of National Systems of Education.* 2nd ed. Ed. T. Neville Postlethwaite. Oxford: Elsevier Science Ltd.

Van Resandt, Anita Wijnaendts, ed. 1991. "Belgium." *A Guide to Higher Education Systems and Qualifications in the European Community.* London: Kogan Page.

Internet Sources:
EURYDICE-Eurybase-Flemish, French, and German Communities:
www.eurydice.org/

Compiler
Kristin M. Zanetti, Senior Evaluator
Educational Credential Evaluators, Inc., Milwaukee, WI

BOLIVIA

YEARS OF EDUCATION →

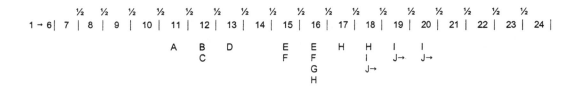

```
      ½   ½   ½   ½   ½   ½   ½   ½   ½   ½   ½   ½   ½   ½   ½   ½   ½
1 → 6| 7 | 8 | 9 | 10 | 11 | 12 | 13 | 14 | 15 | 16 | 17 | 18 | 19 | 20 | 21 | 22 | 23 | 24 |
                   A   B   D           E   E   H   H   I   I
                       C               F   F       I   J→  J→
                                       G       I   J→
                                       H
```

CREDENTIALS OR DOCUMENTATION

Secondary

A   Titles of *Secretária Comercial* (Commercial Secretary), *Técnico Medio Administrativo* (Middle-Level Administrative Technician) and *Técnico Medio Comercial* (Middle-Level Commercial Technician): awarded after 11 years of education (vocational track)

B   Titles of *Técnico Medio* (Middle-Level Technician), *Técnico Agropecuario a Nivel Medio* (Middle-Level Agricultural Technician), *Perito de Aduanas* (Customs Expert), *Perito de Administración* (Administration Expert) and *Contador* (Accountant): awarded after 12 years of education (vocational track)

C   *Bachiller en Humanidades* (Bachelor in the Humanities): awarded after 12 years of education (academic track)

D   Title of *Contador General* (General Accountant): awarded after one additional year of education (vocational track); admission based on credential **B**

Postsecondary

E   *Título de Maestra Normal* (Title of Normal Teacher): for primary school teachers awarded by an *escuela normal integrada* (integrated teacher-training college) or university requiring credential **C** for admission; both three- and four-year programs exist; see also credential **G**

F   Title of *Técnico Superior* (Advanced-Level Technician) and professional titles of *Contador* (Accountant) and *Secretario Comercial-Cajero* (Commercial Secretary): awarded by an *escuela superior* (advanced school), *instituto superior* (advanced institute) or a university after three to four years of specialized study; admission based on credential **B** or **C**

G   *Título de Maestra Normal* (Title of Normal Teacher): for secondary school teachers awarded by an *escuela normal integrada* (integrated teacher-training college) or university requiring credential **C** for admission; see also credential **E**

H   Title of *Licenciado* (Licentiate): awarded by a university or specialized higher institute after four to six years of study; the *Título en Provisión Nacional* (National Professional Title) is awarded after completion of the *Licenciatura* and upon examination

I   *Maestría* or title of *Magister* (Master): awarded by a university after two years of study; admission based on credential **H**; credential is professionally-oriented and generally does not require completion of a thesis

J   *Doctorado* or title of *Doctor* (Doctoral degree): awarded by a university following a program of study, research and preparation and defense of a thesis; requires credential **H** (including professional title) for admission

- The academic year in Bolivia is March to December.

GRADING INFORMATION

All Levels of Education Before 1969:

Numeric	Description	Translation
7	*Excelente*	Excellent
6	*Muy Bueno*	Very Good
5	*Bueno*	Good
4	*Regular*	Average
3	*Deficiente*	Deficient
2	*Malo*	Poor
1	*Pésimo*	Very Poor

- On the above scale, 3.6 is considered to be the minimum passing grade.

All Levels of Education 1969-1972:

Numeric	Description	Translation
5	*Excelente*	Excellent
4	*Muy Bueno*	Very Good
3	*Regular*	Average
2	*Deficiente*	Deficient
1	*Malo*	Poor

- On the above scale, 2.6 is considered to be the minimum passing grade.

Secondary Since 1972:

Numeric	Description	Translation
7	*Excelente*	Excellent
6	*Muy Bueno*	Very Good
5	*Bueno*	Good
4	*Regular*	Average
3	*Deficiente*	Deficient
2	*Malo*	Poor
1	*Pésimo*	Very Poor

- On the above scale, 3.6 is considered to be the minimum passing grade.

Higher Education Since 1972:

Numeric	Description	Translation
90-100	*Sobresaliente*	Outstanding
77-89	*Distinguido*	Distinguished
64-76	*Bueno*	Good
51-63	*Suficiente*	Adequate
0-50	*Reprobado*	Fail

POSTSECONDARY INSTITUTION RECOGNITION BODY

Ministerio de Desarollo Humano, Secretaria Nacional de Educación. Avenida Arce 2408, La Paz. Tel: 591-2-37-1311. Fax: 591-2-37-8756.

RESOURCES FOR ADDITIONAL INFORMATION

Aldrich-Langen, Caroline, ed. 1978. *The Admission and Academic Placement of Students from Selected South American Countries: Bolivia, Brazil, Paraguay, Uruguay*. Washington, D.C.: Joint Committee on Workshops.

National Office of Overseas Skills Recognition. 1993. *Country Education Profiles: Bolivia*. Canberra: Australian Government Publishing Service.

Internet Source:
UNESCO-World Academic Database: www.unesco.org/iau/educbo.html

---

Compiler
Nadia Awad
Graduate Admissions Officer
University of California, Berkeley

BOTSWANA

YEARS OF EDUCATION →

```
       ½    ½    ½    ½    ½    ½    ½    ½    ½    ½    ½    ½    ½    ½    ½    ½    ½
1→6|  7  | 8 | 9 | 10 | 11 | 12 | 13 | 14 | 15 | 16 | 17 | 18 | 19 | 20 | 21 | 22 | 23 | 24 |
      A         B    B    D    C    E    F    H    I  J  K    L
                               D         G
```

CREDENTIALS OR DOCUMENTATION

Primary and Secondary

A   Primary School Leaving Certificate
B   Junior Certificate: two years after credential **A** through 1995, three years since 1996
C   School Certificate
D   Primary Teachers' Certificate: two-year program requiring credential **B** for admission

Postsecondary

E   Certificate in the fields of Library Studies and Statistics: one-year programs requiring credential **C** for admission
F   Certificate in the fields of Accounting and Business Studies: two-year, part-time programs requiring credential **C** for admission
G   Diploma in the fields of Adult Education, Library Studies, Secondary Education, and Statistics: two-year programs requiring credential **C** for admission
H   Diploma in Accounting and Business Studies: one-year, part-time program requiring credential **F** for admission
I   Bachelor's degree in the fields of Arts, Commerce, Education, and Science: four-year programs requiring credential **C** for admission[1]
J   Bachelor of Laws: four and one-half year program requiring credential **C** for admission[2]
K   Postgraduate Diploma in Education: one-year program requiring credential **I** for admission
L   Master's degree in the fields of Arts, Education, and Science: two-year programs requiring credential **I** for admission

[1]   Part I refers to years one and two; part II refers to years three and four

[2]   Part I refers to years one and two; part II refers to years three and four; part III refers to year five

GRADING INFORMATION

Secondary

Numeric	Description
1	Excellent
2	Good
3-6	Credit
7-8	Pass
9	Fail

Higher Education

Individual Subjects: Overall Results:

Letter	Percentage	Description	Class
A	80-100	Outstanding	1st Class
B	70-79	Very Good	2nd Class, 1st Division
C	60-69	Good	2nd Class, 2nd Division
D	50-59	Pass	Pass
E	40-49	Fail	Fail
F	0-39	Fail	Fail

- The grade of E is failing, but a supplementary examination may be taken.

POSTSECONDARY INSTITUTION RECOGNITION BODY

Ministry of Education, Private Mail Bag 005, Gaborone. Tel: 267-31-360-0400. Fax: 267-31-360-0458.

RESOURCES FOR ADDITIONAL INFORMATION

The British Council. 1996. *International Guide to Qualifications in Education.* 4th ed. London: Mansell.

Cameron, John, and Paul Hurst, eds. 1985. *International Handbook of Education Systems.* Vol. II. Chichester, England: John Wiley & Sons.

Internet Source:
UNESCO - World Academic Database: www.unesco.org/iau/educbw.html

---

Compiler
James S. Frey
President
Educational Credential Evaluators, Inc., Milwaukee, WI

BRAZIL

YEARS OF EDUCATION →

```
      ½   ½   ½   ½   ½   ½   ½   ½   ½   ½   ½   ½   ½   ½   ½   ½   ½
1 → 6| 7 | 8 | 9 | 10| 11| 12| 13| 14| 15| 16| 17| 18 |19 | 20| 21| 22| 23| 24
         A              B   C           H   H   I   I   K   L→   N→  N→
                        C   E               I   I   J   J→  L→   M→
                        D   F               J   K   K   M→  N→
                        E                   K   L→  L→  N→
                        G                   L→  M→  M→
                                            M→      N→
```

CREDENTIALS OR DOCUMENTATION

Secondary

A *Certificado de Conclusão de Primeiro Grau* (Elementary Education Conclusion Certificate): signifies completion of eight years of compulsory education

B *Certificado de Habilitação Basica* (Basic Professional Training Certificate): awarded by a secondary school

C *Certificado de Conclusão de Segundo Grau* (Secondary Education Conclusion Certificate): awarded by a secondary school

D *Certificado de Auxiliar Técnico* (Technical Assistant Certificate): awarded by a secondary school

E *Diploma de Técnico de Segundo Grau* (Secondary Education Technician Diploma): awarded by a secondary school

F *Diploma de Professor do Ensino de Primeiro Grau* (Elementary Education Instruction Teacher Diploma)/*Diploma de Professor de Primeiro Grau* (Elementary Education Teacher Diploma)[1] : awarded by a secondary school

G *Certificado de Professor Primário* (Elementary School Teacher Certificate)/*Diploma de Professor Primário* (Elementary School Teacher Diploma)[2] : awarded by an *escola normal* (normal school) or any other secondary school

Postsecondary

H *Licenciatura de Primeiro Grau* (Elementary School Licentiate) or *Licenciatura Curta* (Short Licentiate) awarded by *universidades* (universities), *escolas isolades* (isolated schools), *faculdades* (faculties), or *federaçoes de escolas* (school federations): signifies completion of a three-year program requiring any credential **B** through **G**, plus an entrance examination, for admission[3]

I *Licenciatura Plena* (Full Licentiate) awarded by *universidades*, *escolas isolades*, *faculdades*, or *federaçoes de escolas*: signifies completion of a three to five-year program requiring any credential **B** through **G**, plus an entrance examination, for admission, offered in fields which pertain to secondary or tertiary level teaching

J *Bacharelado* (Bachelor) awarded by *universidades*, *escolas isolades*, *faculdades*, or *federaçoes de escolas*: signifies completion of a four to five-year program requiring any credential **B** through **G**, plus an entrance examination, for admission[4]

K *Título Profissional* (Professional Title) awarded by *universidades*, *escolas isolades*, *faculdades*, or *federaçoes de escolas*: signifies completion of a four- to six-year

75

program requiring any credential **B** through **G**, plus an entrance examination, for admission

L   *Mestre* (Master) awarded by *universidades, escolas isolades, faculdades,* or *federaçoes de escolas*: signifies completion of a one-year program (minimum) requiring credentials **I, J,** or **K** for admission[5]

M   *Sensu lato* (wide sense) certificate awarded by *universidades, escolas isolades, faculdades,* or *federaçoes de escolas*: signifies completion of a program (length varies) requiring credentials **I, J,** or **K** for admission[5]

N   *Doutor* (Doctor) awarded by *universidades, escolas isolades, faculdades,* or *federaçoes de escolas*: signifies completion of a two-year program (minimum) requiring credential **L** for admission

[1] Qualifies holder to teach grades 1 – 6 of *primeiro grau.*

[2] Qualifies holder to teach grades 1 – 4 of *primeiro grau.*

[3] Qualifies holder to teach grades 5 – 8 of *primeiro grau.*

[4] The *Bacharel* and the *Licenciado* are often awarded simultaneously. The *Bacharel* is awarded in the specific subject field, while the *Licenciado* is awarded in education or pedagogical studies.

[5] *Pos-graduação* (graduate) education can be either *sensu stricto* (strict sense) or *sensu lato* (wide sense). *Sensu stricto* programs lead to the degrees of *mestre* or *doutor* and *sensu lato* programs (referring to any post-bachelor's specialization course) lead to a certificate, but Brazilian universities do not generally grant credit for such courses.

GRADING INFORMATION

Secondary

Description	Translation	Abbreviation	Numeric
Superior superior	Superior	SS	9.0-10.0
Média superior	Above Average	MS	7.0-8.9
Média média	Average	MM	5.0-6.9
Média inferior	Below Average	MI	3.0-4.9
Inferior inferior	Inferior	II	0.0-2.9
Sem rendimento	No Results; Fail		
Crédito concedido	Credit Granted		

Postsecondary

Description	Translation	Numeric
Excelente	Excellent	9.0-10.0
Bom	Good	7.0-8.9
Regular	Average	5.0-6.9
Insuficiente	Insufficient	3.0-4.9
Deficiente	Deficient	0.0-2.9

Description	Translation	Grade
Excelente	Excellent	A
Bom	Good	B
Regular	Average	C
Insuficiente	Below Average	D

- Each university is autonomous in determining its grading scale.

- The grading scale used by a university is often, but not always, indicated on the official transcript.

POSTSECONDARY INSTITUTION RECOGNITION BODY

Ministério da Educação e do Desporto/MEC (Ministry of Education and Sport), Esplanada dos Ministérios, Bloco L, Brasilia, DF, Brazil. Tel: 5561-214-8520 & 5561-214-8434. Fax: 5561-224-3618.

RESOURCES FOR ADDITIONAL INFORMATION

Aldrich-Langen, Caroline, ed. 1978. *The Admission and Placement of Students from Selected South American Countries: Bolivia, Brazil, Paraguay, and Uruguay.* Washington, D.C.: Joint Committee on Workshops.

International Education Research Foundation, Inc. 1986. *The Country Index.* Vol. 1, revised ed. Alhambra, CA: Frank Severy Publishing.

Kurian, George Thomas, ed. 1988. *World Education Encyclopedia.* Vol. 1. New York: Facts on File Publications.

National Office of Overseas Skills Recognition. 1993. *Country Education Profiles: Brazil.* Canberra: Australian Government Publishing Office.

Internet Source:
UNESCO – World Academic Database: www.unesco.org/iau/educbr.html

---

Compilers
Holly O'Neill-West, Senior Evaluator
Eva Schein, Evaluator
International Education Research Foundation, Inc., Los Angeles, CA

BULGARIA

YEARS OF EDUCATION →

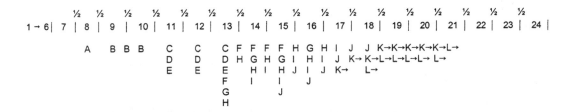

	½	½	½	½	½	½	½	½	½	½	½	½	½	½	½	½	½
1→6	7	8	9	10	11	12	13	14	15	16	17	18	19	20	21	22	23	24	

```
            A   B  B  B     C     C     C  F  F  F  H  G  H  I  J   J  K→K→K→K→K→L→
                           D     D     D  H  G  H  G  I  H  I  J   J  K→ K→L→L→L→L→ L→
                           E     E     E  H  I  H  J  I  J  J  K→      L→
                                       F  I  I     J
                                       G     J
                                       H
```

CREDENTIALS OR DOCUMENTATION

Secondary

A **Свидетелство за Завършено Осново Образование** [*Svidetelstvo za Zavarsheno Osnovno Obrazovanie*] (Certificate of Completed Primary Education)

B **Свидетелство** [Svidetelstvo] (Certificate): awarded upon completion of a program at a professional technical school; pre-1980 document

C **Свидетелство за Зрелост** [*Svidetelstvo za Zrelost*] (Certificate of Maturity): awarded upon completion of a program at a unified or general polytechnical school, secondary professional vocational or technical school, or foreign language or fine arts polytechnical school; pre-1980 document

D **Диплома за Завършено Средно Образование** [*Diploma za Zavarsheno Sredno Obrazovanie*] (Diploma of Completed Secondary Education): awarded upon completion of a program at a unified or general polytechnical school, secondary professional technical school, or technical vocational school, all with compulsory technical training in grades 11-12; issued between 1980-1992; three to five years after credential **A**

E **Диплома за Средно Образование** [*Diploma za Sredno Obrazovanie*] (Diploma of Secondary Education): awarded upon completion of a program at a general secondary school, secondary professional technical school, or technical vocational school; post-1990 document; three to five years after credential **A**

F **Удостоверение за Полувисше Техническа Практика** [*Udostoverenie za Poluvissha Tekhnicheska Praktika*] (Certificate of Semi-Higher Technician Qualification): awarded upon completion of a program at a technical vocational school; requires credential **C**, **D**, or **E** from a technical secondary school for admission

G **Диплома** [*Diploma*]: awarded by the Ministry of National Health upon completion of a two- to three-year program at a secondary-level allied health institute; requires credential **C**, **D**, or **E** for admission; awarded from 1960-76, and 1980-90

Postsecondary[1]

H **Диплома за Завършено Полувисше Образование** [*Diploma za Zavarsheno Poluvisshe Obrazovanie*] (Diploma of Completed Semi-Higher Education): awarded upon completion of a two- to three and one-half-year program at a tertiary allied health institute, or technical vocational institute; requires credential **C**, **D**, or **E** for admission (Diplomas in the allied health fields were awarded from 1976-80, and from 1990 to the present.)

I **Свидетелство за Полувисше Образование и Учителска Правоспособност** [*Svidetelstvo za Poluvisshe Obrazovanie i Uchitelska Pravosposobnost*] (Certificate of Semi-Higher Education and Teacher Qualification): awarded upon completion of a three- to three and one-half year program at a pedagogical institute; requires credential **C**, **D**, or **E** for admission

J **Диплома за Завършено Висше Образование** [*Diploma za Zavarsheno Visshe Obrazovanie*] (Diploma of Completed Higher Education): awarded upon completion of a four-, four and one-half-, or five-year program at a tertiary specialized institute or academy, pedagogical institute, or university; requires credential **C**, **D**, or **E** for admission

K **Диплома за Кандидат на Науките** [*Diploma za Kandidat na Naukite*] (Diploma of Candidate of Sciences), or **Диплома за Кандидат на** _____ (field): awarded by the Higher Attestation Committee upon completion of a program at least three years in length at a tertiary specialized institute or academy, university, or research institute; requires credential **I** for admission

L **Диплома за Доктор на Науките** [*Diploma za Doktor na Naukite*] (Diploma of Doctor of Sciences): awarded by the Higher Attestation Committee upon completion of a program at least three years in length; requires credential **J** for admission

[1] The Higher Education Act of 1995 proposed a new degree structure in higher education, including a three-year specialization program, a four-year program leading to a Bachelor's degree, a five-year program (or one-year cap program after the Bachelor's degree) leading to a Master's degree, and a three-year program after the Master's degree leading to a Doctorate degree. According to information from the Ministry, these new documents will probably be issued in 2000 at the earliest.

GRADING INFORMATION

Secondary and Postsecondary

Numeric	Description	Transliteration	Translation
6	**отличен**	*Otlichen*	Excellent
5	**много добър**	*Mnogo Dobar*	Very Good
4	**добър**	*Dobar*	Good
3	**среден**	*Sreden*	Average
2	**слаб**	*Slab*	Poor
	зачита се	*Zachita Se*	Credited
	взет	*Vzet*	Taken

- Since 1996 many institutions have issued diplomas in booklets that are larger (roughly 5 X 8 ½ inches in size) than those previously issued (roughly 4 - 4½ X 6 - 6½ inches in size).

- The National Evaluation and Accreditation Agency was organized in 1996 to begin the implementation of a national accreditation program for postsecondary institutions in order to provide quality assurance.

POSTSECONDARY INSTITUTION RECOGNITION BODY

Ministry of Education, Science and Technology (formerly the Ministry of Education, Science and Culture, and the Ministry of Education and Science). Bul. Knjaz Dondukov 2, Sofia 1000 Bulgaria. Tel: 359-2-802537. Fax: 359-2-880600 or 359-2-871289.

The Ministry of Health oversees programs in dentistry, medicine, and allied health fields.

RESOURCES FOR ADDITIONAL INFORMATION

Ismail, Margery. 1995. *Bulgaria: A Workshop Report on the Educational System and Guide to the Academic Placement of Students in Educational Institutions in the United States.* Annapolis Junction, MD: PIER.

Ministry of Education, Science and Technology, Bulgaria, 1996. "Higher Education Act 1995."

National Office of Overseas Skills Recognition. 1992. *Country Education Profiles: Bulgaria.* Canberra: Australian Government Publishing Service.

Internet Sources:
Tempus at Work: www.etf.eu.int/etfweb.nsf/pages/tempbulgaria
UNESCO - CEPES (European Centre for Higher Education): www.cepes.ro
    [click on Academic Recognition and Mobility, click on ENICS in PHARE countries, click on Bulgaria, click on System of National Education]
UNESCO - World Academic Database: www.unesco.org/iau/educbg.html

---

Compiler
Jane Yahr Shepard
Evaluator
Educational Credential Evaluators, Inc., Milwaukee, WI

BURKINA FASO

YEARS OF EDUCATION →

```
        ½   ½   ½   ½   ½   ½   ½   ½   ½   ½   ½   ½   ½   ½   ½   ½   ½
1 → 6│ 7 │ 8 │ 9 │ 10 │ 11 │ 12 │ 13 │ 14 │ 15 │ 16 │ 17 │ 18 │ 19 │ 20 │ 21 │ 22 │ 23 │ 24 │
              A   C       D       F   I   K   L   N   P
              B           E       G   J       M   O   Q
                                  H
```

CREDENTIALS OR DOCUMENTATION

Secondary

A *Brevet d'Etudes du Premier Cycle* (Certificate of First Cycle Studies)
B *Certificat d'Aptitude Professionelle* (Certificate of Professional Aptitude)
C *Brevet d'Études Professionelles* (Certificate of Professional Studies)
D *Diplôme de Bachelier de l'Enseignement du Second Degré* (Diploma of Bachelor of Secondary Education)
E *Baccalauréat de Technicien/Diplôme de Bachelier de Technicien* (Baccalaureate of Technician/Diploma of Bachelor of Technician)

Postsecondary

F *Diplôme* (Diploma), awarded upon completion of two years of vocational studies: requires credential **D** or **E** for admission
G *Diplôme d'Études Universitaires Générales* (Diploma of General University Studies): requires credential **D** for admission
H *Diplôme Universitaire de Technologie* (University Diploma of Technology): requires credential **C** for admission
I *Licence* (License)
J *Diplôme d'Ingénieur des Techniques du Développment Rural* (Diploma of Engineer of Rural Development Techniques)
K *Maîtrise* (Master)
L *Diplôme d'Études Approfondies* (Diploma of Advanced Studies)
M *Diplôme d'Études Supérieures Spécialisées* (Diploma of Higher Specialized Studies)
N *Diplôme d'Ingénieur* (Diploma of Engineer)
O *Doctorat en Médecine* (Doctorate in Medicine)
P *Doctorat de Troisième Cycle* (Third Cycle Doctorate)
Q *Doctorat d'État* (State Doctor)

GRADING INFORMATION

All Levels of Education

Numeric	Description	Translation
16 - 20	*Très Bien*	Very Good
14 - 15	*Bien*	Good
12 - 13	*Assez Bien*	Good Enough
10 - 11	*Passable*	Pass
0 - 20		

- A minimum overall grade of 10 is required to pass; however, individual subjects may be passed with grades lower than 10.

POSTSECONDARY INSTITUTION RECOGNITION BODY

Ministère des Enseignements Secondaire, Supérieur et la Recherche Scientifique B.P. 7046, Ouagadougou 03, Burkina Faso.

RESOURCES FOR ADDITIONAL INFORMATION

Mboungou-Mayengbe, D., ed. 1988. *Directory of African Universities*. 5th ed. Association of African Universities.

Internet Source:
UNESCO-World Academic Database: www.unesco.org/iau/educbf.html

---

Compiler
Margaret L. Wenger
Senior Evaluator
Educational Credential Evaluators, Inc., Milwaukee, WI

CAMEROON

YEARS OF EDUCATION →

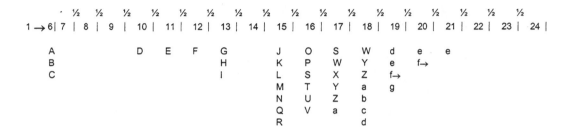

```
       ·   ½   ½   ½   ½   ½   ½   ½   ½   ½   ½   ½   ½   ½   ½   ½   ½   ½
1 → 6| 7 | 8 | 9 | 10| 11| 12| 13| 14| 15| 16| 17| 18| 19| 20| 21| 22| 23| 24|

       A           D   E   F   G       J   O   S   W   d   e   e
       B                       H       K   P   W   Y   e   f→
       C                       I       L   S   X   Z   f→
                                       M   T   Y   a   g
                                       N   U   Z   b
                                       Q   V   a   c
                                       R           d
```

CREDENTIALS OR DOCUMENTATION

Secondary

A   *Certificat d'Etudes Primaires Elementaires/CEPE* (Certificate of Primary Elementary Studies): awarded upon completion of six years of elementary/primary education in francophone schools

B   Common Entrance Examination

C   First School Leaving Certificate in anglophone schools

D   *Brevet d'Etudes du Premier Cycle/BEPC* (Certificate of First Cycle Studies)

E   General Certificate of Education/GCE, Ordinary Level, for students in the anglophone school system: administered by the Cameroon Ministry of Education since 1984; previously administered by the University of London; signifies completion of Forms I-V

F   *Certificat de Probation* (Certificate of Probation)

G   *Baccalauréat de l'Enseignement Secondaire/BAC* (Baccalaureate of Secondary Education): awarded upon completion of three years of upper secondary education in francophone schools

H   *Baccalauréat de Technicien/BAC-T* (Technician Baccalaureate): awarded upon completion of three years of upper secondary technical education in francophone schools

I   General Certificate of Education/GCE Advanced Level: awarded upon completion of two years of upper secondary education in anglophone schools

Postsecondary

J   *Capacite en Droit et Sciences Economiques* (Certificate of Aptitude in Law and Economic Sciences): terminal credential

K   *Certificat d'Etudes Générales de Droit et Sciences Economiques/CEG* (Certificate of General Studies in Law and Economic Sciences)

L   *Diplôme d'Etudes Littéraires Générales/DELG* (Diploma of General Literary Studies)

M   *Diplôme d'Etudes Scientifiques Générales/DESG* (Diploma of General Scientific Studies)

N *Diplôme d'Etudes Scientifiques Générales Agronomiques/DESG* (Diploma of Studies in General Agronomic Sciences)

O *Diplôme de Professorat des Collèges d'Enseignement Général* (Diploma of Teacher in Colleges of General Education)

P *Diplôme de Professorat des Collèges d'Enseignement* (Diploma of Teacher in Colleges of Education): prepares for teaching at the lower-secondary level in technical high schools

Q *Brevet d'Administration* (Certificate in Administration)

R *Diplôme en Soins Infirmiers Supérieures* (Diploma of Advanced Nursing)

S *Licence* (Licentiate) in Arts and Sciences: one year of study beyond any credential **L** through **Q**; two years of study in law and economic sciences beyond credential **K**

T *Diplôme de Technicien de la Santé* (Diploma of Health Technician): trains medical and pharmaceutical technicians

U *Diplôme d'Ingénieur de Travaux* (Diploma of Site Engineer): awarded by the *Universite de Yaoundé* and the *Ecole Nationale Supérieure de Travaux Publiques*

V *Diplôme Supérieure de Journalisme* (Advanced Diploma in Journalism): awarded after three years of study (two at the *Ecole Supérieur Internationale de Journalisme de Yaoundé* and one at the *Institut Français de Presse*)

W *Diplôme d'Etudes Supérieures/DES* (Diploma of Advanced Studies): one year of study in literature, languages, mathematics, sciences, or social sciences beyond credential **S**

X *Diplôme d'Ingénieur Agronome* (Diploma of Agronomy Engineer): two years of study beyond credential **N**

Y *Certificat d'Aptitude au Professorat de l'Enseignement Secondaire/CAPES* (Certificate of Teacher of Secondary Education): two years beyond credential **L, M,** or **O**; or one year beyond credential **S**

Z *Diplôme d'Administration des Entreprises* (Diploma of Business Administration): one year beyond credential **S**

a *Certificat d'Aptitude au Professorat de l'Enseignement Technique/CAPET* (Certificate of Teacher of Technical Education): one year beyond credential **S**; prepares students for teaching at the upper secondary level in technical high schools

b *Diplôme d'Ingénieur de Conception* (Diploma of Design Engineer): three years beyond credential **M** or five years beyond credential **G, H,** or **I**; awarded by the *Ecole Supérieure Polytechnique*

c *Diplôme de l'Institut des Relations Internationales du Cameroun/ Diplôme d'IRIC* (Diploma of the Institute of International Relations of Cameroon): two years beyond credential **S**

d *Maîtrise* (Master): two years of study beyond credential **S**

e *Doctorat de Troisiéme Cycle* (Third Cycle Doctorate): one to two years of study with thesis; admission based on credential **d**

f *Doctorat d'Etat* (State Doctorate): requires submission of a thesis; admission based on credential **d**

g *Doctorat en Medicine* (Doctor of Medicine): six years of medical education beyond credential **G** or **I**

GRADING INFORMATION

Secondary Anglophone System:
GCE Ordinary Level: Five passing grades A (highest) to E (lowest). Failed subjects are "ungraded."

Secondary and Postsecondary Francophone System:

Numeric	Interpretation	Translation
16-20	*Très Bien*	Very Good/Excellent
14-15	*Bien*	Good
12-13	*Assez Bien*	Good Enough
10-11	*Passable*	Pass
0-9	*Echec*	Fail

- A minimum overall grade of 10 is required to pass; however, individual subjects may be passed with grades lower than 10.

POSTSECONDARY INSTITUTION RECOGNITION BODY

Ministère de l'Enseignement Supérieur, B.P. 1457, Yaoundé, Cameroon. Tel. 237 23-1407.

Other ministries are responsible for institutional administration in the case of some specialized fields, such as in agriculture, health, post and telecommunications, forestry, and public works.

RESOURCES FOR ADDITIONAL INFORMATION

Foreign Educational Credentials Required for Consideration of Admission to Universities and Colleges in the United States. 4th ed. 1994. Washington, D.C.: AACRAO.

International Guide to Qualifications in Education. 3rd ed. 1996. National Academic Recognition Information Center for the United Kingdom. London: Mansell.

International Handbook of Universities. 14th ed. 1996. London: International Association of Universities.

The World of Learning. 39th ed. 1989. London: Europa.

World List of Universities and Other Institutions of Higher Education. 21st ed. 1997. London: International Association of Universities.

Internet Source:
UNESCO – World Academic Database: www.unesco.org/iau/educcm.html

---

Compiler
Jasmin Saidi
Academic Credentials Evaluation Institute, Inc.
Beverly Hills, CA

CANADA

YEARS OF EDUCATION →

```
       ½   ½   ½   ½   ½   ½   ½   ½   ½   ½   ½   ½   ½   ½   ½   ½   ½
1 → 6│ 7 │ 8 │ 9 │ 10 │ 11 │ 12 │ 13 │ 14 │ 15 │ 16 │ 17 │ 18 │ 19 │ 20 │ 21 │ 22 │ 23 │ 24 │
                   A    B    D    F    H    J    K    K    L~
                   D    C    F    H    I
                        D    G
                        E
```

CREDENTIALS OR DOCUMENTATION

Secondary

A *Diplôme d'Études Secondaires* (Diploma of Secondary Studies) [Quebec]: gives admission to *collèges d'études générales et professionnelles* (colleges of general and vocational studies); does not give admission to universities in Quebec or in the other provinces and territories

B General or Advanced High School Diploma [Alberta], Secondary School Graduation Diploma [British Columbia], Diploma or Transcript confirming completion of Grade 12 [Manitoba], *Certificat de Fin d'Études Secondaires*/Graduation Certificate [New Brunswick], Provincial High School Graduation Diploma [Newfoundland], Senior Secondary School Graduation Diploma [Northwest Territories], High School Completion Certificate [Nova Scotia], High School Graduation Certificate [Prince Edward Island], Record of High School Standing confirming Grade 12 or Division IV Standing [Saskatchewan], Transcript confirming completion of British Columbia graduation requirements [Yukon Territory]: secondary school completion document; gives admission to postsecondary institutions in the respective province or territory

C Ontario Secondary School Diploma: Ontario secondary school completion credential awarded after 12 years of primary/secondary education; gives admission to colleges of applied arts and technology in Ontario

D Ontario Academic Courses (OACs): completed at Ontario secondary schools; may be completed during grades 10, 11, 12, or an additional (thirteenth) year of primary/secondary education; credential **C** plus six OACs gives admission to Ontario universities

Postsecondary

E *Certificat d'Études Collégiales* [Quebec] awarded by *collèges d'études général et professionnelles* (colleges of general and vocational studies): a vocational credential; gives admission to further study at *collèges d'études général et professionnelles*; does not give admission to Quebec universities

F *Diplôme d'Études Collégiales* [Quebec] awarded by *collèges d'études général et professionnelles* (colleges of general and vocational studies) upon completion of a two- or three-year program: required for admission to universities in Quebec

G Certificate awarded by a college, community college, or college of applied arts and technology [all provinces except Quebec]

H Diploma or Associate's degree or diploma awarded upon completion of a two- or three-year program at a college, community college, or college of applied arts and technology [all provinces except Quebec]

I Bachelor's degree, usually designated "General," "Three-Year," "Ordinary," or "Pass" [Manitoba, Ontario, Saskatchewan][1]

J Bachelor's degree, sometimes designated "Honours," "Four-Year," or "Advanced"[1]

K Master's degree: admission requires credential **J** or credential **I** plus completion of an additional year of university study which is sometimes referred to as a "qualifying year"[1]

L Doctorate degree: admission usually requires credential **K**[1]

---

[1] Applies to all provinces, except for the Northwest Territories or Yukon Territory where there are no universities.

GRADING INFORMATION

Secondary

Alberta

Numerical	Description
80-100	Excellent
65-79	Good
50-64	Satisfactory
40-49	Poor
0-39	Fail

British Columbia

Letter	Numerical	Description
A	86-100	Excellent
B	73-85	Good
C	60-72	Satisfactory
P	50-59	Poor
F	0-49	Fail

Manitoba, Ontario, Saskatchewan

Numerical	Description
80-100	Excellent
70-79	Good
56-69	Satisfactory
50-55	Poor
0-49	Fail

Northwest Territories

Letter	Numerical	Description
A	80-100	Excellent
B	65-79	Good
C	50-64	Satisfactory
D	0-49	Fail

Quebec

Numerical	Description
90-100	Excellent
80-89	Good
70-79	Satisfactory
60-69	Poor
0-59	Fail

Yukon Territory

Letter	Numerical	Description
A	86-100	Excellent
B	73-85	Good
C	60-72	Satisfactory
P	50-59	Poor
F	0-49	Fail

- In New Brunswick, Newfoundland, Nova Scotia, and Prince Edward Island, nonstandardized numerical scales of 0-100 are used. Often 50 is the lowest passing grade.

Postsecondary

- There is no standard system of grading used by all Canadian postsecondary institutions.
- Most postsecondary institutions use some variant of an alphabetical (A, B, C, D, F) or numerical (0-100) grading scale.
- The grading system used by the postsecondary institution is usually described on the back of its official transcripts, or on a supplementary sheet which accompanies the transcript.
- Course catalogs published by postsecondary institutions usually include information on the grading system.
- The registrar's office of the institution concerned can provide additional information regarding grading scales and grading practices.

POSTSECONDARY INSTITUTION RECOGNITION BODIES

- Provincial ministries of education (see "Resources for Additional Information," below)
- Association of Universities and Colleges of Canada (AUCC), 350 Albert Street, Suite 600, Ottawa, Ontario K1R 1B1, Canada. Tel: 613-563-1236. Fax: 613-563-9745. www.aucc.ca
- Association of Canadian Community Colleges (ACCC), 200 - 1223 rue Michael St. N., Ottawa, Ontario K1J 7T2, Canada. Tel: 613-746-2222. Fax: 613-746-6721. www.accc.ca
- Provincial charter or legislative act

RESOURCES FOR ADDITIONAL INFORMATION

Association of Canadian Community Colleges. 1992. *The ACCC Directory of Canadian Colleges and Institutes.* Concord, Ontario: Irwin Publishers.

Association of Commonwealth Universities. 1997. *The Commonwealth Universities Yearbook.* New York: Stockton Press.

Association of International Universities. 1996. *The International Handbook of Universities.* 14th ed. New York: Stockton Press.

Association of Universities and Colleges of Canada. 1996. *The Directory of Canadian Universities.* 31st ed. 1996-97. Ottawa: Association of Universities and Colleges of Canada.

Association of Universities and Colleges of Canada. 1997. *Universities Telephone Directory.* Ottawa: Association of Universities and Colleges of Canada.

Frey, James S., ed. 1989. *The Admission and Placement of Students from Canada.* Annapolis Junction, MD: PIER.

Southam Business Communications. 1996. *The Directory of Canadian Schools.* Don Mills, Ontario: Southam Business Communications.

Internet Sources:
Alberta Education: ednet.edc.gov.ab.ca/
Alberta Transfer Guide: www.aecd.gov.ab.ca/acat/taars
Association of Canadian Community Colleges (ACCC): www.accc.ca/
Association of Universities and Colleges of Canada (AUCC): www.aucc.ca
British Columbia Council on Admissions and Transfer: www.islandnet.com/bccat
British Columbia Ministry of Education, Skills, and Training: www.educ.gov.bc.ca/
Canadian Education on the Web: www.oise.utoronto.ca/~mpress/eduweb.html
Council of Ministers of Education, Canada (CMEC): www.cmec.ca
New Brunswick Dept. of Education: inter.gov.nb.ca/education/
Newfoundland Dept. of Education and Training: www.gov.nf.ca/edu/
Northwest Territories Dept. of Education, Culture, and Employment: siksik.learnnet.nt.ca/
Nova Scotia Dept. of Education: www.ednet.ns.ca/
Ontario Ministry of Education and Training: www.edu.gov.on.ca/
    E-mail: public.inquiries@edu.gov.on.ca
Prince Edward Island Dept. of Education: www.gov.pe.ca/educ/
    E-mail: education@gov.pe.ca
Québec Ministère de l'Éducation: www.meq.gouv.qc.ca/
Saskatchewan Dept. of Education: www.sasked.gov.sk.ca/
School Finder: www.schoolfinder.com
Yukon Dept. of Education: www.yesnet.yk.ca

Compiler
Kristin M. Zanetti
Senior Evaluator
Educational Credential Evaluators, Inc., Milwaukee, WI

CENTRAL AFRICAN REPUBLIC

YEARS OF EDUCATION →

```
      ½   ½   ½   ½   ½   ½   ½   ½   ½   ½   ½   ½   ½   ½   ½   ½   ½
1 → 6| 7 | 8 | 9 | 10 | 11 | 12 | 13 | 14 | 15 | 16 | 17 | 18 | 19 | 20 | 21 | 22 | 23 | 24 |
              A       B   C       D   F   K           P
                              E   G   L
                                  H   M
                                  I   N
                                  J   O
```

CREDENTIALS OR DOCUMENTATION

Secondary

A *Brevet Élementaire du Premier Cycle/BEPC* (First Cycle Elementary Certificate)
B *Certificat d'Aptitude Pédagogique* (Pedagogical Proficiency Certificate): two years; requires credential **A** for admission; holders may teach at primary schools[1]
C *Diplôme de Bachelier l'Enseignement du Second Degré, Baccalauréat Technique* (Diploma of Secondary School Bachelor, Technical Baccalaurate)
D *Certificat de Capacité en Droit* (Proficiency Certificate in Law): two years[2]

Postsecondary

E *Diplôme d'Études Universitaires Générales/DEUG, Diplôme d'Études Universitaires Scientifiques/DUES, Diplôme d'Études Universitaires Littéraires/DUEL, Diplôme d'Études Juridiques Générales/DEJG, Diplôme d'Études Économiques Générales/DEEG* (University Diploma of General, Scientific, Arts, Law, Economics): requires credential **C** for admission
F *Diplôme d'État pour Assistantes sociales/Infirmiers/Sages femmes* (State Diploma in Social Work, Nursing, Midwifery): a three-year professionnal qualification requiring the level of the last year of secondary school (grade 13, but credential **C** is not required for admission)
G *Licence* (Licenciate): requires credential **E** for admission
H *Diplôme Supérieur de Gestion/DSG* (Higher Diploma in Management): requires credential **C** for admission
I *Diplôme d'Ingénieur en Constructions, Mines, Géologie* (Engineer Diploma in Building, Mines, Geology): requires credential **C** for admission
J *Certificat d'Aptitude Professionnelle à l'Enseignement dans les Collèges d'Enseignement Général/CAP/GEG* (Certificate of Professional Qualification in Schools of General Studies): requires credential **C** for admission; holders may teach at the *collèges* (lower secondary schools: grades 7 to 10)
K *Diplôme de Technicien Supérieur de la Santé* (Advanced Health Technician Diploma): a four-year professionnal qualification requiring the level of the last year of secondary school (grade 13, but credential **C** is not required for admission)
L *Diplôme d'État de Technicien d'Assainissement* (State Diploma for Sanitary Technicians): requires credential **C** for admission

M *Diplôme d'Ingénieur Agricole* (Diploma of Agricultural Engineer): requires credential **C** for admission

N *Certificat d'Aptitude Professionnelle au Professorat de l'Enseignement Secondaire* (Higher Secondary School Teaching Professional Proficiency Certificate): requires credential **C** for admission, holders may teach at the *lycées* (higher secondary schools: grades 11 to 13)

O *Maitrise* (Master): requires credential **G** for admission

P *Doctorat en Médecine* (Doctor of Medecine): requires credential **C** for admission

[1] The *Rapport National sur le Développement de l'Éducation en République Centrafricaine* states that primary school teachers are trained in a two-year program requiring credential **C** for admission. It does not state the name of the diploma awarded and the institution is referred to as the *ENI de Bambari*.

[2] Examination, usually for students who did not pass credential **C** but who had reached the last year of secondary education (grade 13). Holders of this certificate who had an average of 12/20 or more are eligible for admission to the first year of the *Diplôme d'Études Juridiques Générales/DEJG*.

GRADING INFORMATION

All levels of Education

Numeric	Mention	Transaltion
17-20	Très Bien	Very Good
14-16	Bien	Good
12-13	Assez Bien	Fairly Good
10-11	Passable	Satisfactory
0-9	Ajourné	Fail

- Marks of 14 or higher are rarely awarded.

POSTSECONDARY INSTITUTION RECOGNITION BODY

Ministère de l'Éducation nationale (Ministry of Education), B.P. 1583, Bangui.
Tel: 236 61 43 00. Fax: 236 61 64 94.

RESOURCES FOR ADDITIONAL INFORMATION

Bretherick, Dona. 1995. *Central African Republic: a Country Guide Report from the AACRAO-AID Project.* Washington, D.C.: AACRAO.

The British Council. 1996. *International Guide to Qualifications in Education.* 4th ed. London: Mansell.

Ministère des Enseignements, de la Coordination des Recherches et de la Technologie, and Commission Nationale Centrafricaine pour l'UNSECO. 1994. "Rapport national sur le Développement de l'Éducation en République Centrafricaine." Report presented to the 44th Session of the International Conference on Education, Bangui, République Centrafricaine.

UNESCO. 1996. *World Guide to Higher Education*. Paris: UNESCO.

Internet Source:
UNESCO - World Academic Database: www.unesco.org/iau/educcf.html

---

Compiler
Michel Bédard
Service des Équivalences, Ministère des Relations avec les Citoyens et de l'Immigration, Gouvernement du Québec, Canada

CHAD

	½	½	½	½	½	½	½	½	½	½	½	½	½	½	½	½	½
1 → 6	7	8	9	10	11	12	13	14	15	16	17	18	19	20	21	22	23	24
	A				C		E		G		I		I					
	B				D		F		H		J							

CREDENTIALS OR DOCUMENTATION

Secondary

A *Brevet d'Études du Premier Cycle* (Certificate of First Cycle Studies)
B *Certificat d'Aptitude Professionnelle* (Certificate of Professional Aptitude)
C *Baccalauréat* (Baccalaureate): leads to postsecondary education
D *Baccalauréat Technique* (Technical Baccalaureate): leads to postsecondary education

Postsecondary

E *Diplôme Universitaire*[1] (University Diploma)
F *Certificat d'Aptitude Pédagogique pour Collèges d'Enseignement Générales/CAPCEG* (Certificate of Pedagogic Aptitude for Lower Secondary Schools)
G *Licence* (License)
H *Diplôme d'Ingénieur* (Diploma of Engineer)
I *Maîtrise* (Master): one or two years following credential **G**
J *Certificat d'Aptitude Pédagogique pour l'Enseignement aux Lycées/CAPEL* (Certificate of Pedagogic Aptitude for Upper Secondary Schools): either one year after credential **G** or two years after credential **F**

---

[1] *Diplôme Universitaire de Science/DUS* (University Diploma of Science), *Diplôme Universitaire de Lettres Modernes/DULMO* (University Diploma of Modern Literature), *Diplôme Universitaire des Sciences Juridiques, Économiques et de Gestion/DUSJEG* (University Diploma of Legal Sciences, Economics, and Management), *Diplôme d'Études Universitaires Générales/DEUG* (Diploma of General University Studies).

93

GRADING INFORMATION

Secondary and Postsecondary Education

Numeric	Description	Translation
16 - 20	*Très Bien*	Very Good
14 - 15	*Bien*	Good
12 - 13	*Assez Bien*	Good Enough
10 - 11	*Passable*	Pass
0 - 20	*Ajourné*	Fail

- A minimum overall grade of 10 is required to pass; however, individual subjects may be passed with grades lower than 10.

POSTSECONDARY INSTITUTION RECOGNITION BODY

Ministère de l'Éducation Nationale; BP 731; N'Djamena; Chad

RESOURCES FOR ADDITIONAL INFORMATION

Mboungou-Mayengúe, D., ed. 1988. *Directory of African Universities.* 5th ed. Association of African Universities.

Sevigny, Joseph A. 1995. *Chad: A Country Guide Series Report from the AACRAO-AID Project.* Washington, D.C.: AACRAO.

Internet Source:
UNESCO-World Academic Database: www.unesco.org/iau/eductd.html

---

Compiler
Margaret L. Wenger
Senior Evaluator
Educational Credential Evaluators, Inc., Milwaukee, WI

CHILE

```
      ½   ½   ½   ½   ½   ½   ½   ½   ½   ½   ½   ½   ½   ½   ½   ½   ½
1 → 6|  7 | 8 | 9 | 10 | 11 | 12 | 13 | 14 | 15 | 16 | 17 | 18 | 19 | 20 | 21 | 22 | 23 | 24 |
        A           B       C   D   F   G   G   G   I→   I→
                            D   E   G   H→  H→
                                E
                                F
```

CREDENTIALS OR DOCUMENTATION

Secondary

A *Licencia de Educación Básica* (License of Basic Education), awarded by an *Escuela* (School): signifies completion of compulsory education

B *Licencia de Educación Media* (License of Middle Education), awarded by a *Colegio* (Private High School) or a *Liceo* (Public High School)

Postsecondary

C *Bachillerato en...* (Baccalaureate in...) *Ciencias* (Sciences) or *Humanidades y Ciencias Sociales* (Humanities and Social Sciences): awarded by an *Universidad* (University)

D *Título Técnico de Nivel Superior en...* (Advanced-Level Technician Title in...) *Administración de Negocios* (Business Administration), *Diseño Gráfico* (Graphic Design), *or Telecomunicaciones* (Telecommunications): requires four to six semesters; principally awarded by a *Centro de Formación Técnica* (Technical Training Center), but also by an *Instituto Profesional* (Professional Institute) or *Universidad* (University)

E *Licenciado en Educación Pre-Escolar (Parvularia)* [or] *Educación Básica* (Licentiate in Preschool or Basic [grades one through eight] Education): three-year program being phased out; awarded by an *Universidad* (University)

F *Título Profesional* (Professional Title) as a graduate in *Administración* (Administration), *Agricultura* (Agriculture), *Arte* (Art), *Ciencias* (Sciences), *Comercio* (Business), *Ciencias Sociales* (Social Sciences), *Educación Parvularia* (Preschool Education), *Humanidades* (Humanities), or *Tecnología* (Technology): requires six to eight semesters; awarded by an *Instituto Profesional* (Professional Institute) or *Universidad* (University)

G *Licenciado en...* (Licentiate in...) *Arquitectura* (Architecture), *Bioquímica* (Biochemistry), *Ciencias Jurídicas* (Law), *Educación* (Education), *Farmacia* (Pharmacy), *Filosofía* (Philosophy), *Historia* (History), *Lenguas* (Language/Linguistics), *Ingeniería* (Engineering), *Medicina* (Medicine), *Medicina Veterinaria* (Veterinary Medicine), *Odontología* (Dentistry), *Periodismo* (Journalism), *Psicología* (Psychology): requires four to seven years; awarded by an *Universidad* (University)[1]

95

H   *Magister* (Master's Degree): usually two or more years requiring credential **F** or **G** for admission; awarded by an *Universidad* (University)

I   *Doctorado* (Doctorate): usually three or more years requiring credential **H** for admission; awarded by an *Universidad* (University)

[1]   Generally, fields not requiring a professional license require four years of study, and licensed professions, such as engineering and medicine, require five or more years.

GRADING INFORMATION

All Levels of Education

Numeric	Description	Translation
6-7	*Muy Bueno*	Very Good
5-5.9	*Bueno*	Good
4-4.9	*Suficiente*	Sufficient
0-3.9	*Insuficiente*	Insufficient

- The grade of seven is rarely, if ever, awarded.

SECONDARY AND POSTSECONDARY INSTITUTION RECOGNITION BODY

Ministerio de Educación (Ministry of Education), Alameda 1371, Santiago, Chile
Tel: 011-562-699-10-15. Fax: 011-562-699-79-84.

RESOURCES FOR ADDITIONAL INFORMATION

The British Council. 1991. *International Guide to Qualifications in Education*. 3rd ed. London: Mansell.

Consejo Superior de Educacion. 1998. *Directorio de Instituciones de Educación Superior en Chile -- 1998*. Santiago: Ministry of Education.

Nunez, Ivan. 1993. *Sistemas educativos nacionales: Chile*. Santiago: Ministry of Education.

Persico, Maria. 1997. *Acreditación en Chile*. Santiago: Corporacion de Promocion Universitaria.

Internet Source:
UNESCO - World Academic Database: www.unesco.org/iau/educcl.html

---

Compiler
George Fletcher, Ed.D.
President
Globe Language Services, Inc., New York, NY

YEARS OF EDUCATION →

1 → 6	½ 7	½ 8	½ 9	½ 10	½ 11	½ 12	½ 13	½ 14	½ 15	½ 16	½ 17	½ 18	½ 19	½ 20	½ 21	½ 22	½ 23	24
A						B C	D	D	D	E	E	E	E F G K	F G	H→G G I J K	G I J	J K K	K

CREDENTIALS OR DOCUMENTATION

Secondary

A   Graduation Certificate awarded by junior (lower) middle school

B   Graduation Certificate awarded by senior (upper) middle school: may be academic or vocationally (agricultural, specialized, or vocational) oriented[1]

C   Unified National University Entrance Examinations: most graduates of senior (upper) middle school programs seeking postsecondary education take these examinations.

Postsecondary

D   Completion Certificate: awarded by postsecondary institutions[2] upon completion of programs requiring three months to three semesters of study; admission based on credential **B** or **C**

E   Graduation Certificate: awarded by postsecondary institutions[2] upon completion of programs requiring two to four years of study; admission based on credential **B** or **C**

F   Bachelor's degree in...Agriculture, Arts, Economics, Education, Engineering, History, Law, Military Studies, Nursing, Philosophy, or Science: awarded by colleges and universities upon completion of four- to five-year programs; admission based on credential **B** or **C**

G   Bachelor's degree in Medicine: programs range from four to seven years; these may be awarded in the areas of basic medical science, dentistry, medicine, pharmacy, public health, and traditional Chinese medicine or pharmacy; admission based on credential **B** or **C**; see also credential **J**

H   Postgraduate Class Graduation Certificate: awarded by colleges and universities upon completion of usually at least one and one-half years of study; admission generally based on credential **F** plus the National Postgraduate Entrance Examination (NPEE)

I   Master's degree: awarded by colleges and universities upon completion of a two- or three-year program; admission generally based on credential **F** plus the National Postgraduate Entrance Examination (NPEE)

J   Doctor of Medicine: awarded by Peking Union Medical College upon completion of an eight-year program, and by Shanghai Second Medical University upon completion of a six-year program; see also credential **G**

K   Doctoral degree: awarded by colleges and universities upon completion of a two- or three-year program based on credential **I**, or a three- or four-year program based on credential **F**

[1]   Most academic programs require three years of senior middle school study. Programs of a vocational nature may also be three years in length, though two- and four-year programs do exist.

[2]   Postsecondary institutions include colleges, radio and television universities, spare-time universities, specialized schools (also known as junior or specialized colleges), universities, vocational universities, or worker's colleges.

GRADING INFORMATION

All Levels of Education

Letter	Percentage	Description
A	90-100	Excellent
B	80-89	Good
C	70-79	Average or Fair
D	60-69	Pass or Satisfactory
F	0-59	Unsatisfactory or Fail

Letter	Percentage	Description
A	85-100	Excellent
B	75-84	Good
C	60-74	Average or Fair
D or F	0-59	Unsatisfactory or Fail

- Some subjects are graded on a pass or fail basis, such as optional courses and physical education courses.

POSTSECONDARY INSTITUTION RECOGNITION BODY

State Education Commission, 35 Damucang Hutong, Xidan, Beijing 100816.
Tel: 86-10-6609 6649. Fax: 86-10-6601 7912.

RESOURCES FOR ADDITIONAL INFORMATION

Chinese Education Association for International Exchange, compilers. 1994. *Chinese Universities and Colleges.* 2nd ed. Beijing: Higher Education Press.

Feagles, Shelley M. 1992. *ECE Presents: A Guide to Evaluating Educational Credentials from China.* Milwaukee: Educational Credential Evaluators, Inc.

Paver, William, and Yiping Wan. 1992. *Postsecondary Institutions of the People's Republic of China: A Comprehensive Guide to Institutions of Higher Education in China.* Annapolis Junction, MD: PIER.

Surowski, David, ed. Unpublished, circa 1999. The People's Republic of China: A Workshop Report on the Educational System and Guide to the Academic Placement of Students in Educational Institutions in the United States. Contact PIER Publications (see Appendix A) for information on this book's availability.

Wu, Yenbo, and Jizhu Zhang. 1994. *NAFSA Working Paper #48: Update on PRC Higher Education Institutions Accredited by the State Education System*. Washington D.C.: NAFSA

Internet Source:
UNESCO - World Academic Database: www.unesco.org/iau/educcn.html

---

Compiler
Shelley M. Feagles
Senior Evaluator
Educational Credential Evaluators, Inc., Milwaukee, WI

CHINA, REPUBLIC OF (TAIWAN)

YEARS OF EDUCATION →

1→6	7	8	9	10	11	12	13	14	15	16	17	18	19	20	21	22	23	24
	½	½	½	½	½	½	½	½	½	½	½	½	½	½	½	½	½	
			A			B		D	F	G	G	I	J→	L→	K	K	L→	L→
						C		E			H	J→	K			L→		
											J→		L→					

CREDENTIALS OR DOCUMENTATION

Secondary

A Certificate of Graduation and Transcript of Academic Record awarded by a junior high school: signifies completion of nine-year compulsory education

B Certificate of Graduation and Transcript of Academic Record awarded by a senior high school

C Certificate of Graduation and Transcript of Academic Record awarded by a senior vocational high school

Postsecondary

D Certificate of Graduation and Transcript of Academic Record awarded by a junior college: signifies completion of a two-year program requiring credential **C** for admission

E Certificate of Graduation and Transcript of Academic Record awarded by a junior college: signifies completion of a five-year program requiring credential **A** for admission

F Certificate of Graduation and Transcript of Academic Record awarded by a junior college: signifies completion of a three-year program requiring credential **B** for admission

G Bachelor's degree: signifies completion of a four-year program requiring credential **B** or **C** for admission (programs are five years in length for veterinary medicine and sometimes five years in length for fine arts, architecture, law, and pharmacy)

H Bachelor's degree awarded by a normal university: signifies completion of four years of academic work plus one year of practice teaching requiring credential **B** or **C** for admission

I Doctor of Dental Surgery (previously known as Bachelor of Dental Surgery): signifies completion of a six-year dentistry program requiring credential **B** or **C** for admission

J Master's degree: signifies completion of a program requiring credential **G, H,** or **I** for admission [1]

K Doctor of Medicine (previously known as Bachelor of Medicine): signifies completion of a seven-year program requiring credential **B** or **C** for admission or a five-year program requiring credential **G** for admission

L   Doctor of Philosophy degree: signifies completion of a program requiring credential **J** for admission or credential **K** plus two years of work experience for admission [2]

[1]   Programs can range from one to four years in length. Students can be admitted with credential **F** if accompanied by two years of appropriate work experience or credential **D** or **E** if accompanied by three years of appropriate work experience. Total years of education may vary depending on the length of the program and how the student was admitted to the program.

[2]   Programs can range from two to seven years in length. Provisions for exceptional admission exist. Total years of education may vary depending on the length of the program and how the student was admitted to this or prior programs.

GRADING INFORMATION

Secondary

Letter	Percentage
A	80-100
B	70-79
C	60-69
D	50-59
E	Less than 50

- 100 is the highest grade, and 60 is the lowest passing grade. Students can advance and graduate with individual grades lower than 60.

Higher Education

Letter	Percentage
A	80-100
B	70-79
C	60-69
D	50-59
E or F	0-49

- Even though the letter grade D is assigned to the 50-59 range, the minimum passing score is 60.
- The minimum passing score for graduate students is 70.
- Some institutions assign the letter grade D to the 0-59 range.
- Some institutions issue plus (+) and minus (-) modifiers with the letter grades A and B.
- Some institutions divide the passing range of 60-100 into four passing letter grades (A, B, C, and D).
- Some institutions divide the passing range of 60-100 into sub-ranges other than those indicated in the above grading scale (e.g., A = 85-100; B = 70-84; C = 60-69).
- Usually, the particular grading scale used by an institution is specified on the Transcript of Academic Record.

POSTSECONDARY INSTITUTION RECOGNITION BODY

Ministry of Education, 5 Chung Shan South Road, Taipei 10040, Taiwan, R.O.C.
Tel: 886-2-351-3111. Fax: 886-2-396-6803.

RESOURCES FOR ADDITIONAL INFORMATION

Bureau of International Cultural and Educational Relations, compilers. 1995. *Higher Education in the Republic of China: A Guide for Foreign Students*. Taipei: Ministry of Education

Bureau of Statistics, compilers. Taiwan, R.O.C. 1997. *Education in the Republic of China*. Taipei: Ministry of Education.

Kennedy, Patrick J. 1977. *The Republic of China (Taiwan): A Study of the Educational System of the Republic of China and a Guide to the Academic Placement of Students in Educational Institutions of the United States*. Washington D.C.: AACRAO.

Internet Source:
UNESCO - World Academic Database: www.unesco.org/iau/eductw.html

---

Compiler
Jason A. Wessel
Evaluator
Educational Credential Evaluators, Inc., Milwaukee, WI

COLOMBIA

YEARS OF EDUCATION →

	½	½	½	½	½	½	½	½	½	½	½	½	½	½	½	½	½
1 → 6|	7		8		9		10		11		12		13		14		15		16		17		18		19		20		21		22		23		24	

```
                        A           B  B  C  C  D      D      E      E      F
                                                       E      F      F      H-
                                                       G             G
```

CREDENTIALS OR DOCUMENTATION

Secondary

A *Bachiller* (Bachelor): awarded upon completion of six years of secondary education; the basic requirement for admission to postsecondary education; curricular tracks include academic, classical arts, commercial, industrial, and social studies

Postsecondary

B *Técnico Profesional Intermedio* (Intermediate Professional Technician): two or two and one-half years of study

C *Tecnólogo en _____* (Technologist in ____): three or three and one-half years of study

D *Licenciado* (Licentiate): four to five years of study[1]

E *Doctor en Medicina/Médico* (Physician), *Médico Cirujano* (Surgeon): five to seven years of medical studies[1]

F *Especialista* (Specialist): one year, usually in the field of medicine or dentistry, requiring credential **E** for admission

G *Magister/Maestría* (Master's degree): usually two years of research with thesis requiring credential **D** for admission

H *Doctor* (Doctoral degree): usually four years of research and dissertation requiring credential **D** for admission; or, two years requiring credential **G** for admission[2]

[1] For comparable degrees of four or more years of duration see *Colombia*. 1984. AACRAO. pp. 38-40.

[2] Not to be confused with the title of *Doctor* awarded prior to 1980 and considered comparable to credential **D**.

GRADING INFORMATION

Secondary

Numeric	Description
10.00 - 8.8	Extremely high, rarely awarded
8.7 - 7.6	Excellent
7.5 - 6.5	Good
6.4 - 6.0	Sufficient, Average
5.9 - 0.0	Failure

- 10 is the highest grade and 6 is the lowest passing grade and is sufficient for promotion.

Postsecondary Education

Numeric	Description
4.6 - 5.00	Extremely high, rarely awarded
4.0 - 4.59	Excellent
3.5 - 3.99	Good
3.0 - 3.49	Sufficient, Average
0.0 - 2.99	Failure

- 3.0 is the minimum passing grade and is sufficient for promotion.
- 3.5 is the minimum passing grade for most graduate programs.

POSTSECONDARY INSTITUTION RECOGNITION BODY

Instituto Colombiano para el Fomento de la Educación Superior (ICFES), Apartado Aéreo 6319, Santafé de Bogotá, D.C., Colombia. Tel: 91-281-9311, 91-334-2162, 91-283-6778. Fax: 91-286-8016, 91-286-8064.

RESOURCES FOR ADDITIONAL INFORMATION

Asociación Colombiana de Universidades (ASCUN), Apartado Aereo 012300, Santafé de Bogota, D.C., Colombia. Tel: 57-1-218-5127. Fax: 57-1-218-5098.
E-mail: Asocolun@uniandes.edu.co

Ministerio de Educación Nacional, Apartado Aereo 077983, Bogota, Colombia. Tel: 57-1-222-3311. Fax: 57-1-222-4578.

Wellington, Stanley. 1984. *Colombia: A Study of the Educational System of Colombia and a Guide to the Academic Placement of Students from Colombia in Educational Institutions of the United States.* Washington, D.C.: AACRAO.

Internet Sources:
Instituto Colombiano para el Fomento de la Educación Superior: www.icfes.gov.co
UNESCO - World Academic Database: www.unesco.org/iau/educco.html

Compiler
Freda Clement-Willis
Associate Director
Josef Silny & Associates, Inc., International Education Consultants, Coral Gables, FL

COMMONWEALTH CARIBBEAN REGION

This entry includes the countries of: Anguilla, Antigua & Barbuda, Barbados, Belize, Bermuda, British Virgin Islands, Cayman Islands, Dominica, Grenada, Guyana, Jamaica, Montserrat, St. Christopher-Nevis, St. Lucia, St. Vincent & the Grenadines, Trinidad & Tobago, and Turks & Caicos Islands. The high level of cooperation between many of these countries in matters of mutual interest, including education, and the similarity of many aspects of the educational systems of these countries make a regional treatment possible and advantageous.

YEARS OF EDUCATION →

```
       ½   ½   ½   ½   ½   ½   ½   ½   ½   ½   ½   ½   ½   ½   ½   ½   ½
1 → 6| 7 | 8 | 9 | 10| 11| 12| 13| 14| 15| 16| 17| 18| 19| 20| 21| 22| 23| 24|
           A   A   A   D   E   J       L       M   N
                       B   F   G   K
                       C       H
                               I
```

CREDENTIALS OR DOCUMENTATION

Secondary

A Jamaica School Certificate: can be awarded after a total of 9, 10, or 11 years of education

B Secondary Education Certificate awarded by the Caribbean Examinations Council (CXC)

C Secondary School Certificate awarded by the Jamaica Ministry of Education

D Bermuda Secondary School Certificate

E General Certificate of Education, Advanced Level, awarded by various examination boards, including the University of Cambridge Local Examinations Syndicate (UCLES) and the University of London: two-year program following credential **B**

Postsecondary

F Certificates awarded by a variety of non-university postsecondary institutions: admission varies, but often credential **B** or equivalent is required[1]

G Diplomas awarded by a variety of non-university postsecondary institutions: admission varies, but often credential **B** or equivalent is required[1]

H Associate degree awarded by a variety of non-university postsecondary institutions: signifies completion of two years of academic work requiring credential **B** for admission[1]

I Certificate in teaching awarded by teachers' colleges: represents completion of two years of academic work plus one year of non-academic internship requiring credential **B** or equivalent for admission

J Diploma in teaching awarded by teachers' colleges: represents completion of three years of academic work requiring credential **B** or equivalent for admission

K Diploma in nursing awarded by schools of nursing: represents completion of a three-year hospital school of nursing program requiring credential **B** or equivalent for admission

L Bachelor's degree: a three-year program requiring credential **E** for admission, or a four-year program requiring credential **B** for admission

M Master's degree: generally a two-year program requiring credential **L** for admission

N Doctor of Philosophy degree: generally a three-year program requiring credential **L** for admission, or a one-year program requiring credential **M** for admission

¹ Numerous non-degree-granting postsecondary institutions are in operation. These institutions offer certificate, diploma, and associate programs. In addition, many provide preparation for examinations of extra-regional examinations bodies such as the City and Guilds of London Institute.

- The University of the West Indies is a regional institution with campuses in Jamaica, Trinidad, and Barbados. In addition, there are university centers in most non-campus countries. The countries served by the university are: Antigua and Barbuda, Bahamas, Barbados, Belize, British Virgin Islands, Cayman Islands, St. Vincent and the Grenadines, Trinidad and Tobago. Guyana participates in the Faculty of Law.

- Nonregional degree-granting postsecondary institutions include: the University College Belize; the University of Technology, Jamaica; and the University of Guyana.

GRADING INFORMATION

Secondary

<u>Caribbean Examinations Council</u>: until June 1998

Grade	Description
1	comprehensive working knowledge of the syllabus
2	working knowledge of most aspects of the syllabus
3	working knowledge of some aspects of the syllabus
4	limited knowledge of a few aspects of the syllabus
5	insufficient evidence on which to base a judgement

<u>Caribbean Examinations Council</u>: since June 1998

Grade	Description
1	comprehensive grasp of the key concepts, knowledge, skill, and competencies required by the syllabus
2	good grasp of the key concepts, knowledge, skill, and competencies required by the syllabus
3	fairly good grasp of the key concepts, knowledge, skill, and competencies required by the syllabus
4	moderate grasp of the key concepts, knowledge, skill, and competencies required by the syllabus
5	limited grasp of the key concepts, knowledge, skill, and competencies required by the syllabus
6	very limited grasp of the key concepts, knowledge, skill, and competencies required by the syllabus

- The Caribbean Examinations Council (CXC) was established in 1972 to provide secondary examinations for students in the region. Participating countries include: Belize, British Virgin Islands, Dominica, Grenada, Guyana, Jamaica, Montserrat, St. Kitts & Nevis, St. Lucia, St. Vincent and the Grenadines, Trinidad & Tobago, and Turks and Caicos Islands.

Higher Education

University of the West Indies

Grade	% Equivalent	Description
A	70-100	First Class Honours
B+	60-69	Upper Second Class Honours
B	50-59	Lower Second Class Honours
C	40-49	Pass
Fail	0-39	Fail

POSTSECONDARY INSTITUTION RECOGNITION BODIES

Association of Caribbean Tertiary Institutions (ACTI), c/o Barbados Community College, Howell Cross Road, St. Michael, Barbados. Tel: 246-426-3186. Fax: 246-429-5935. E-mail: nholder@caribsurf.com

University Council of Jamaica (UCJ), 6B Oxford Road, Kingston 5, Jamaica. Tel: 876-929-7299, 876-906-8012. Fax/Voice: 876-929-7312. E-mail: ucjlonde@infochan.com

RESOURCES FOR ADDITIONAL INFORMATION

The British Council. 1996. *International Guide to Qualifications in Education.* 4th ed. London: Mansell.

Postlethwaite, T. Neville, ed. 1995. *International Encyclopedia of National Systems of Education.* 2nd ed. Cambridge: Cambridge University Press.

Compiler
Margit A. Schatzman
Vice President
Educational Credential Evaluators, Inc., Milwaukee, WI

CONGO

YEARS OF EDUCATION →

```
        ½   ½   ½   ½   ½   ½   ½   ½   ½   ½   ½   ½   ½   ½   ½   ½   ½
1→6|  7 | 8 | 9 | 10| 11| 12| 13| 14| 15| 16| 17| 18| 19| 20| 21| 22| 23| 24|
                 A           B       D   H   J   K   L   M~
                             C       E   I   G   G
                                     F   G
                                     G
```

CREDENTIALS OR DOCUMENTATION

Secondary

A *Brevet d'Études du Premier Cycle/BEPC* (Certificate of First Cycle Studies)
B *Baccalauréat* (Baccalaureate): leads to postsecondary education
C *Baccalauréat Technique* (Technical Baccalaureate): leads to postsecondary education

Postsecondary

D *Diplôme Universitaire d'Études Littéraires/DUEL* (University Diploma of Literary Studies)/*Diplôme Universitaire d'Études Scientifiques/DUES* (University Diploma of Scientific Studies): requires credential **B** for admission
E *Brevet de Technicien Supérieur de Secrétariat* (Certificate of Higher Technician of Secretarial Skills): requires credential **B** or **C** for admission
F *Capacité en Droit* (Capacity in Law): based on completion of secondary education, but this program does not require the *baccalauréat* (credential **B** or **C**) for admission
G *Diplôme d'Ingénieur* (Diploma of Engineer): two to five years after the *baccalauréat* (credential **B** or **C**)
H *Licence* (Licentiate): one year beyond credential **D**
I *Licence en Sciences de la Santé pour les Infirmiers* (Licentiate in Health Sciences for Nurses): three years beyond credential **B**
J *Maîtrise* (Master): one year beyond credential **H**
K *Diplôme d'Études Supérieures/DES* (Diploma of Higher Studies): one year beyond credential **J**, or two years beyond credential **H**
L *Docteur en Médecine* (Doctor in Medicine): six years beyond credential **B**
M *Doctorat* (Doctorate): two or more years beyond credential **K**

GRADING INFORMATION

Secondary and Postsecondary Education

Numeric	Description	Translation
16 - 20	*Très Bien*	Very Good
14 - 15	*Bien*	Good
12 - 13	*Assez Bien*	Good Enough
10 - 11	*Passable*	Pass
0 - 9	*Ajourné*	Fail

- A minimum overall grade of 10 is required to pass; however, individual subjects may be passed with grades lower than 10.

POSTSECONDARY INSTITUTION RECOGNITION BODY

Ministère de l'Enseignement Supérieur et Technique; BP 14557; Brazzaville; Congo.

RESOURCES USED AND SOURCES OF ADDITIONAL INFORMATION

Mboungou-Mayengúe, D., ed. 1988. *Directory of African Universities*. 5th ed. Association of African Universities.

Internet Source:
UNESCO-World Academic Database: www.unesco.org/iau/educcg.html

---

Compiler
Margaret L. Wenger
Senior Evaluator
Educational Credential Evaluators, Inc., Milwaukee, WI

CONGO, DEMOCRATIC REPUBLIC OF

Formerly known as Zaire

YEARS OF EDUCATION →

```
        ½   ½   ½    ½    ½    ½    ½    ½    ½    ½    ½    ½    ½    ½    ½    ½    ½    ½
1 – 6|  7 |  8 |  9 | 10 | 11 | 12 | 13 | 14 | 15 | 16 | 17 | 18 | 19 | 20 | 21 | 22 | 23 | 24 |

   A        B         C    C    E    G              H         K    Q    T         U    V–
                      D         F                   I         L    R    U
                                                    J         M    S
                                                              N
                                                              O
                                                              P
```

CREDENTIALS OR DOCUMENTATION

Secondary

A *Certificat d'Études Primaires* (Certificate of Primary Studies)

B *Diplôme de Fin d'Études Secondaires* (End of Secondary Studies Diploma): discontinued in 1986

C *Brevet d'Aptitude Professionnelle* (Professional Proficiency Certificate): a four- or five-year program requiring credential **A** for admission

D *Brevet d'Instituteurs* (Teacher Certificate): requires credential **A** for admission

E *Diplôme d'État de l'Enseignement Secondaire* (Secondary School State Diploma): awarded after a State examination (*Examen d'État*) and six years of secondary education

F *Diplôme d'Instituteurs* (Teacher Diploma): requires credential **A** for admission

G *Certificat de Propédeutique* (Preparatory Year Certificate)[1]

Postsecondary

H *Diplôme, Grade de Graduat* ('Graduate' Diploma): requires credential **E** for admission[2]

I *Diplôme d'Ingénieur Technicien* (Technician-Engineer Diploma): requires credential **E** for admission

J *Diplôme de Gradué en Pédagogie Appliquée* (Graduate Diploma in Applied Pedagogy): requires credential **E** for admission

K *Diplôme de Licence* (Licentiate Diploma): requires credential **H** for admission

L *Diplôme de Licencié en Pédagogie Appliquée* (Licenciate in Applied Pedagogy Diploma): requires credential **H** for admission

M *Diplôme d'Architecte* (Architect Diploma): requires credential **H** for admission

N *Diplôme d'Ingénieur* (Engineer Diploma): requires credential **H** for admission

O *Diplôme de Dentiste* (Dentist Diploma): requires credential **H** for admission

P *Diplôme de Pharmacien* (Pharmacist Diploma): requires credential **H** for admission

Q *Diplôme de Docteur en Médecine* (Doctor in Medicine Diploma): requires credential **H** for admission

R *Grade de Docteur en Médecine Vétérinaire* (Degree of Doctor in Veterinary Medicine): requires credential **H** for admission

S   *Grade d'Agrégé de l'Enseignement Secondaire du Degré Supérieur* (Higher
    Secondary Teacher Diploma): requires credential **K, L, M, N, O,** or **P** for admission
T   *Diplôme d'Études Supérieures* (Higher Studies Diploma): introduced in 1989,
    requires credential **K, L, M, N, O,** or **P** for admission
U   *Diplôme de Spécialiste* (Specialist Diploma): two-year program in architecture,
    dentistry, engineering, or pharmacy, requiring credential **M, N, O,** or **P** for admission;
    or three-year program in medicine or veterinary medicine, requiring credential **Q** or **S**
    for admission
V   *Doctorat* (Doctorate): at least three years; requires credential **T** for admission

[1] One-year program requiring credential **E** for admission. This credential is required to enroll in the first year
of some engineering programs, and in a few other programs. Other names are: *Certificat de
Prépolytechnique, Certificat de Préparatoire.*

[2] Before the mid-1970s, this credential was awarded after a two-year program.

GRADING INFORMATION

Secondary

Percentage	Description
50-100	Pass
0-49	Fail

Postsecondary Education

Numeric	Mention	Translation
90-100	*La Plus Grande Distinction*	Highest Distinction
80-89	*Grande Distinction*	High Distinction
70-79	*Distinction*	Distinction
50-69	*Satisfaction*	Satisfactory
0-49		

- The passing mark is 50.

- Marks of 70 or higher are rarely awarded.

POSTSECONDARY INSTITUTION RECOGNITION BODY

Ministère de l'Enseignement supérieur et universitaire et de la Recherche scientifique
(Ministry of Higher Education and Scientific Research) B.P. 5429, 67 Boulevard Tshathi,
Kishasa/Gombe. Tel: 243-12-34093.

RESOURCES FOR ADDITIONAL INFORMATION

The British Council. 1996. *International Guide to Qualifications in Education,* 4th ed. London: Mansell.

Sevigny, Joseph A. 1995. *Zaire: A Country Guide Report from the AACRAO-AID Project.* Washington, D.C.: AACRAO.

UNESCO. 1996. *World Guide to Higher Education*. Paris: UNESCO.

Internet Source:
UNESCO - World Academic Database: www.unesco.org/iau/educzr.html

---

Compiler
Michel Bédard
Service des Équivalences, Ministère des Relations avec les Citoyens et de l'Immigration, Gouvernement du Québec, Canada

COSTA RICA

	½	½	½	½	½	½	½	½	½	½	½	½	½	½	½	½	½
1 → 6	7	8	9	10	11	12	13	14	15	16	17	18	19	20	21	22	23	24

```
            A       B    C        D    D   F   H   H  J→I   J→      J→
                                  E    E   G   G   I
                                  F            I
```

CREDENTIALS OR DOCUMENTATION

Secondary

A   *Certificado conclusión de estudios de educación general básica* (Certificate of conclusion of general basic education studies): signifies completion of compulsory education

B   *Diploma de conclusión de estudios de educación diversificada* (Certificate of conclusion of diversified education studies) or *Bachillerato* (Bachelor): two-year program in academic or artistic studies; admission requires credential **A**

C   *Diploma de conclusión de estudios de educación diversificada* (Certificate of conclusion of diversified education studies) with title of *Técnico Medio en __* (Mid-level Technician in __): three-year program in agriculture, commercial, or industrial studies; admission requires credential **A**

Postsecondary

D   Title of *Técnico Superior* (Higher Technician) or *Diplomado* (Diplomate): two- to three-year program beyond credential **C**

E   Title of *Profesor* (Teacher): three-year program of study; admission based on credential **B** or **C**

F   *Bachiller Universitario* (University Bachelor): four-year program; admission based on credential **B** or **C**

G   Title of *Licenciado* (Licentiate): five-year program based on credential **B** or **C**, or one-year program based on credential **F**

H   Title of *Licenciado en medicína y cirugía* (Licentiate in medicine and surgery): six-year program; admission based on credential **B** or **C**

I   *Maestría* (Master degree): two-year program; admission based on credential **F** or **G**

J   *Doctorado Académico* (Academic Doctor): minimum of a three and one-half year program beyond credential **F** or **G**

GRADING INFORMATION

Secondary

Numerical	Description	Abbreviation	Translation
100	*Sobresaliente*	S	Excellent
80	*Notable*	N	Very Good
65	*Suficiente*	Suf	Pass
0	*Insuficiente*	I	Fail

Higher Education

Numerical	Description	Translation
95 - 100	*Excelente*	Excellent
85 - 94	*Muy Bueno*	Very Good
70 - 84	*Bueno*	Good
0 - 69	*Nota Mínima*	Minimum Pass

- A 10-point scale is also used at some institutions, with 10 being highest and 0 being lowest. The minimum passing grade is 7.

- Other terminology found on some transcripts is listed below.

Spanish	Abbreviation	Translation
Aprobado	A or AP	Pass
Convalidada	Conv.	Transfer Credit Granted
Cursado	C	Took Course
Exento	Ex or EXT	Exempt
Aplazado	F	Failed
Interrupción de Estudios	I or IT	Interruption of Studies
Incompleto	IN or INC	Incomplete
Matriculada	MA	Matriculated
No se presento a examen	NSP	Not Present at Exam
Perdido sin Derecho a Examen Extraordinario	P or PE	Lost Without a Right To Do the Extraordinary Exam
Reconcida	RE or REC	Recognized
Retiro Injustificado	RI	Unjustified Withdrawal
Retiro Justificado	RJ	Justified Withdrawal
Reprobado por Ausencias	RPA	Failed Due to Absences
Satisfactorio	S	Satisfactory

POSTSECONDARY INSTITUTION RECOGNITION BODIES

Ministerio de Educación Pública, P.O. Box Apdo 10087-1000, San Jose, Costa Rica. Tel: 506 234 220229. Fax: 506 234 552868. [Supervises primary, secondary, and parauniversities.]

Consejo Nacional Enseñanza Superior Universitaria (CONESUP), San Jose, Costa Rica. Tel: 506 233 9050. Fax: 506 233 6118. [Supervises private universities.]

Consejo Nacional de Rectores (CONARE), P.O. Box Apdo 374-2050, Curridabat. De Plaza Del Sol, 200 Sur 25 Este, San Jose, Costa Rica. Tel: 506 224 3066 Fax: 506 234 0374. [Supervises and authorizes new degree programs for state universities.]

RESOURCES FOR ADDITIONAL INFORMATION

Aldrich-Langen, Caroline and Kathleen Sellew. 1987. *The Admission and Placement of Students from Central America: Belize, Costa Rica, El Salvador, Guatemala, Honduras, Nicaragua, Panama.* Annapolis Junction, MD: PIER.

Marcus, Jane E. 1996. *Central America Update.* Annapolis Junction, MD: PIER.

National Office of Overseas Skills Recognition. 1993. *Country Education Profiles: Costa Rica.* Canberra: National Office of Overseas Skills Recognition.

Internet Source:
UNESCO - World Academic Database: www.unesco.org/iau/educcr.html

---

Compiler
Marybeth Mirzejewski
Evaluator
Educational Credential Evaluators, Inc., Milwaukee, WI

CÔTE D'IVOIRE

YEARS OF EDUCATION →

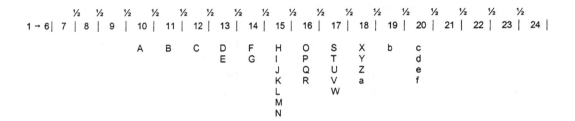

CREDENTIALS OR DOCUMENTATION

Secondary

A *Brevet d'Études du Première Cycle/BEPC* (Certificate of First Cycle Studies)
B *Certificat d'Aptitude Professionnel des Instituteurs* (Certificate of Professional Aptitude of Teachers)
C *Brevet de Technicien/BT* (Certificate of Technician)
D *Baccalauréat* (Baccalaureate)/*Diplôme de Bachelier de l'Enseignement du Second Degré* (Diploma of Bachelor of Secondary Education)
E *Diplôme d'Études Agricoles* (Diploma of Agricultural Studies)

Postsecondary

F *Certificat d'Aptitude Professionnelle des Instituteurs* (Certificate of Aptitude in the Teaching Profession): requires credential **D** for admission
G *Agent-Technique de la Statistique* (Technical Agent of Statistics): requires credential **D** for admission
H *Diplôme Universitaire* (University Diploma)[1]: requires credential **D** for admission
I *Capacité en Droit* (Capacity in Law): for students who do not hold credential **D**
J *Diplôme Universitaire de Technologie/DUT* (University Diploma of Technology): requires credential **D** for admission
K *Brevet de Technicien Supérieur/BTS* (Higher Technician Certificate): requires credential **C** or **D** for admission
L *Certificate d'Aptitude Pédagogique à l'Enseignement dans les Écoles Primaires* (Certificate of Pedagogic Aptitude in Primary Instruction): requires credential **D** for admission
M *Diplôme d'Adjoint Technique* (Diploma of Technical Assistant): requires credential **D** for admission
N *Certificat Préparatoire aux Études Comptables et Financières* (Preparatory Certificate in Accounting and Financial Studies): requires credential **D** for admission
O *Licence* (License): one year beyond credential **H**
P *Certificate d'Aptitude Pédagogique pour les Collèges d'Enseignement Général/CAP/CEG* (Certificate of Pedagogic Aptitude for Lower Secondary Schools): either three years after credential **D** or one year after credential **H**
Q *Diplôme en Pharmacie* (Diploma in Pharmacy): requires credential **D** for admission

R   *Diplôme d'Infirmier d'État* (Diploma of State Nurse)
S   *Maîtrise* (Master): one year beyond credential **O**
T   *Licence ès Sciences Economiques* (License of Economic Sciences)
U   *Diplôme d'Ingénieur* (Diploma of Engineering)
V   *Diplôme d'Agronomie Générale/DAG* (Diploma of General Agronomy)
W   *Diplôme d'Études Comptables Supérieures* (Diploma of Advanced Accounting Studies): requires credential **N** for admission
X   *Diplôme d'Études Approfondies/DEA* (Diploma of Advanced Studies): requires credential **S** for admission
Y   *Diplôme d'Études Supérieures/DES* (Diploma of Higher Studies): requires credential **S** for admission
Z   *Certificate d'Aptitude Pédagogique de l'Enseignement du Second Degré/CAPES* (Certificate of Pedagogic Aptitude for Upper Secondary Schools): requires credential **O** or **P** for admission
a   *Certificat d'Aptitude à la Profession d'Avocat* (Certificate of Aptitude in the Profession of Attorney)
b   *Doctorat de Spécialité* (Doctorate of a Specialty)
c   *Doctorat en Médecine* (Doctorate in Medicine)
d   *Doctorat d'État* (State Doctor): requires credential **X** for admission
e   *Ingénieur-Docteur* (Engineer-Doctor): requires credential **U** for admission
f   *Diplôme d'Expertise Comptable* (Diploma of Accounting Expertise): requires credential **W** for admission

[1]   *Diplôme d'Études Universitaires Générales/DEUG* (Diploma of General University Studies), *Diplôme Universitaire d'Études Littéraires/DUEL* (University Diploma of Literary Studies), *Diplôme Universitaire d'Études Scientifiques/DUES* (University Diploma of Scientific Studies)

GRADING INFORMATION

Secondary and Postsecondary Education

Numeric	Description	Translation
16 - 20	*Très Bien*	Very Good
14 - 15	*Bien*	Good
12 - 13	*Assez Bien*	Good Enough
10 - 11	*Passable*	Pass
0 - 9	*Ajourné*	Fail

- A minimum overall grade of 10 is required to pass; however, individual subjects may be passed with grades lower than 10.

POSTSECONDARY INSTITUTION RECOGNITION BODY

Ministère de l'Enseignement Supérieur; BP V24; Abidjan; Côte d'Ivoire.

RESOURCES FOR ADDITIONAL INFORMATION

Bretherick, Dona. 1995. *Côte d'Ivoire: A Country Guide Series Report from the AACRAO-AID Project.* Washington, D.C.: AACRAO.

Mboungou-Mayengúe, ed. 1988. *Directory of African Universities.* 5th ed. Association of African Universities.

Internet Source:
UNESCO-World Academic Database: www.unesco.org/iau/educci.html

---

Compiler
Margaret L. Wenger
Senior Evaluator
Educational Credential Evaluators, Inc., Milwaukee, WI

CUBA

YEARS OF EDUCATION →

```
      ½   ½   ½   ½   ½   ½   ½   ½   ½   ½   ½   ½   ½   ½   ½   ½   ½
1 → 6│ 7 │ 8 │ 9 │ 10 │ 11 │ 12 │ 13 │ 14 │ 15 │ 16 │ 17 │ 18 │ 19 │ 20 │ 21 │ 22 │ 23 │ 24 │
        A       B   B   F   E   H   I   I   J   K
                C       F               K   L→
                D       G               L→
```

CREDENTIALS OR DOCUMENTATION

Secondary

A *Estudios de Nivel Medio* (Middle Level Studies) or *Secundaria Básica* (Basic Secondary): nine years of compulsory education

B *Contador/Contador Planficador* (Bookkeeper), *Perito* (Expert), *Técnico/Técnico Medio* (Technician/Middle Technician): awarded by a *Politécnico* or *Escuela Técnica* (technical school)

C *Bachiller/Bachillerato* (Bachelor/Baccalaureate) or *Diploma de Graduado Pre-Universitario* (Pre-University Graduate Diploma)

D *Maestro de Educación Primaria*[1] (Primary School Teacher), *Profesor de Educación Física* (Physical Education Professor), *Profesor de Piano* (Professor of Piano), *Profesor de Secundaria Básica* (Professor of Basic Secondary): awarded by an *Escuela Pedagógica* (Pedagogical School)

Postsecondary

E *Profesor de Educación General Media* (Professor of General Middle Education): awarded by a *Instituto Superior Pedagógico* (Higher Pedagogical Institute); usually five years in length requiring credential **A** for admission

F *Bibliotecario Auxiliar* (Library Assistant): one- to two-year intermediate university program requiring credential **B**, **C**, or **D** for admission

G *Optometrista* (Optometrist): two-year intermediate university program requiring credential **B**, **C**, or **D** for admission

H *Hidrotécnico* (Hydrotechnician): three-year intermediate university program requiring credential **B**, **C**, or **D** for admission

I *Licenciado/Licenciatura* (Licentiate): four to five years of study requiring credential **B**, **C**, or **D** for admission; other comparable diplomas include: *Arquitecto* (Architect), *Doctor en Derecho* (Doctor of Law), *Contador Público* (Public Accountant), *Ingeniero* (Engineer), *Profesor de Nivel Secundaria Superior en* ___ (Professor of Higher Secondary Level in ___)

J *Doctor en Medicina* (Doctor of Medicine): six years of medical education requiring credential **B** for admission

K *Post Grado para Especialista* (Post-Graduate Specialist): two-year program requiring credential **I** for admission

L *Candidato a Doctor en Ciencias* (Candidate to Doctor in Sciences), *Doctor en Ciencias* (Doctor in Sciences): minimum of two years of in-depth study, research, publication, and additional dissertation requiring credential **I**, **J**, or **K** for admission

[1] *Escuela Primaria* (Primary School) in Cuba is composed of grades 1 to 6.

GRADING INFORMATION

Secondary

Numeric	Description	Translation
90 - 100	*Sobresaliente*	Excellent
80 - 89	*Aprovechado*	Average
70 - 79	*Aprobado*	Pass
0 - 69	*Suspenso, Desaprobado*	Fail

Postsecondary Education

Numeric	Description	Translation
90 - 100	*Sobresaliente*	Excellent
80 - 89	*Aprovechado*	Average
70 - 79	*Aprobado*	Pass
0 - 69	*Suspenso, Desaprobado*	Fail
90 - 100	*Sobresaliente*	Excellent
80 - 89	*Notable*	Very Good
70 - 79	*Aprovechado*	Average
60 - 69	*Aprobado*	Pass
0 - 59	*Suspenso, Desaprobado*	Fail
90 - 100	*Excelente*	Excellent
80 - 89	*Bien*	Very Good
70 - 79	*Regular*	Average
60 - 69	*Aprobado*	Pass
0 - 59	*Mal, Desaprobado*	Fail
5	*Sobresaliente*	Excellent
4	*Aprovechado*	Average
3	*Aprobado*	Pass
2, 1, 0	*Suspenso, Desaprobado*	Fail

- The particular grading scale used by an institution is sometimes specified on the *relación de notas* (transcript).

POSTSECONDARY INSTITUTION RECOGNITION BODY

Ministerio de Educación Superior, Calle 23 No. 565 esquina F. Vedado, Plaza de la Revolución, Ciudad de La Habana, La Habana, Cuba. Tel: 53-7-309383.
Fax: 53-7-333096.

RESOURCES FOR ADDITIONAL INFORMATION

Consultoría Jurídica Internacional, Calle 18 No. 120, Esquina 3a., Miramar, Ciudad Habana, Cuba.

Silny, Josef and Nancy Ortiz. 1994. *Educational System of Cuba*. Miami: JS&A Press.

U.S. Interests Section (USIS), Calzada entre L y M, Vedado, Ciudad de La Habana, Cuba. Tel: 53-7-33-3967. Fax: 53-7-33-3869. E-mail: infousis@usia.gov

Internet Sources:
UNESCO - World Academic Database: www.unesco.org/iau/eeduccu.html
U.S. Interests Section (USIS): www.usia.gov/posts/havana

Compiler
Freda Clement-Willis
Associate Director
Josef Silny & Associates, Inc., International Education Consultants, Coral Gables, FL

CYPRUS

The island of Cyprus includes two separate and distinct communities. The Greek-Cypriot community is located in the south and the Turkish-Cypriot community is located in the north. Each community has a distinct educational structure. For the purpose of clarity, each community's educational system will be dealt with separately.

South (Greek-Cypriot)

YEARS OF EDUCATION →

```
      ½   ½   ½   ½   ½   ½   ½   ½   ½   ½   ½   ½   ½   ½   ½   ½   ½
1→6| 7 | 8 | 9 | 10 | 11 | 12 | 13 | 14 | 15 | 16 | 17 | 18 | 19 | 20 | 21 | 22 | 23 | 24 |
          A            B   C   C   E   H   I   J       K
                           D   F
                               G
```

CREDENTIALS OR DOCUMENTATION

Secondary

A Απολυτηριο [Apolyterion] (Certificate of Completion) awarded upon completion of Γυμνασιον [gymnasium] (lower secondary school)

B Απολυτηριο [Apolyterion] (Certificate of Completion) awarded upon completion of Λυκειο [lykion] (upper secondary school): leads to postsecondary education

Postsecondary[1]

C Diploma from the Hotel and Catering Institute
D Diploma in Forestry from the Cyprus Forestry College
E Diploma of Technician Engineer of the Higher Technical Institute
F Diploma from the Pedagogical Academy of Cyprus (discontinued after the opening of the University of Cyprus, which now offers four-year education programs)
G Completion of a General Nurse program of the School of Nursing
H Bachelor's degree from the University of Cyprus
I Diploma in Management from the Mediterranean Institute of Management: 1 year requiring a degree from a four-year program for admission
J Master's degree: planned on being offered
K Doctorate degree: planned on being offered

[1] A number of private postsecondary institutions are in operation. Efforts to formalize their legal status are underway.

GRADING INFORMATION

Secondary

Numeric	Description
19-20	Excellent
16-18	Very Good
13-15	Average
10-12	Below Average
0-9	Fail

Postsecondary Education

Higher Technical Institute:

Percentage	Letter	Description
85-100	A	Distinction
75-84	B	Credit
65-74	C	Credit
55-64	D	Pass
50-54	E	Pass
0-49	F	Fail

University of Cyprus:

Numeric	Description
8.5-10	Excellent
6.5-8.0	Very Good
5.0-6.0	Good

POSTSECONDARY INSTITUTION RECOGNITION BODY

Accreditation Council (P.I.T.E.), Ministry of Education & Culture. 3 Gregori Afxentiou Str., Nicosia, Cyprus. Tel: 357 2 367672 (Secretary - Information). Fax: 357 2 362868. E-mail: sekap@cytanet.com.cy. Internet: www.moec.gov.cy

North (Turkish-Cypriot)

YEARS OF EDUCATION →

```
      ½   ½   ½   ½   ½   ½   ½   ½   ½   ½   ½   ½   ½   ½   ½   ½   ½
1 → 6| 7 | 8 | 9 | 10 | 11 | 12 | 13 | 14 | 15 | 16 | 17 | 18 | 19 | 20 | 21 | 22 | 23 | 24 |
          A               B       D   E   F
                          C
```

CREDENTIALS OR DOCUMENTATION

Secondary

A *Ortaokul Diplomasi* (Middle School Diploma)
B *Lise Diplomasi* (Secondary School Diploma): leads to postsecondary education
C *Diplomasi* (Diploma): awarded upon completion of a vocational technical program; leads to postsecondary education

123

Postsecondary

D   Technician Diploma
E   Diploma from Teacher Training College
F   Bachelor's degree

GRADING INFORMATION

Secondary

Numeric	Description
9-10	
7-8	
5-6	
0-4	Fail

- Grades of 3 are allowed if the overall average is 5 or more.

Postsecondary Education

Eastern Mediterranean University:

Grade	Value
A	4.00
A-	3.70
B+	3.30
B	3.00
B-	2.70
C+	2.30
C	2.00
C-	1.70
D+	1.30
D	1.00
D-	0.70
F	0.00

POSTSECONDARY INSTITUTION RECOGNITION BODY

Ministry of National Education and Culture. Lefkosa, Mersin 10, Turkey.
Tel: 392 2275032. Fax: 392 2283776.

RESOURCES FOR ADDITIONAL INFORMATION

Schatzman, Margit A. 1990. *Education on the Island of Cyprus*. Washington, D.C.: AACRAO.

Internet Source:
UNESCO - World Academic Database: www.unesco.org/iau/educcy.html

---

Compiler
Margit A. Schatzman
Vice President
Educational Credential Evaluators, Inc., Milwaukee, WI

CZECH REPUBLIC

YEARS OF EDUCATION →

		½	½	½	½	½	½	½	½	½	½	½	½	½	½	½	½
1 → 6	7	8	9	10	11	12	13	14	15	16	17	18	19	20	21	22	23	24

			A	A	B	B	B	B	C	D	H-	H-
							C	C	D	F		
							D	D	E	G		
							E	E	F	H-		
								F				
								G				

CREDENTIALS OR DOCUMENTATION

Secondary

A *Vysvědčení o Maturitní Zkoušce* (Certificate of Maturity Examination): signifies completion of secondary school; four-year programs at *gymnasia* (secondary university preparatory schools) and *střední odborné školy* (secondary technical schools); five-year programs at *střední odborná učiliště* (secondary vocational schools); a *gymnasia* graduate may enroll in a secondary technical or vocational school and receive a second *Vysvědčení o Maturitní Zkoušce*

Postsecondary

B *Bakalař* (Bachelor): two-, three-, or four-year program, either practically oriented or the first stage of a five-year university program
C *Inžynýr* (Engineer): four- or five-year program in agriculture, economics, or engineering
D *Magistr* (Master): five- or six-year program
E *Inžynýr Architekt* (Engineer Architect): five-year program in engineering for architecture or city planning
F *Doktor Medicíny* (Doctor of Medicine)
G *Doktor Veterinarni Medicíny* (Doctor of Veterinary Medicine)
H *Doktor* (Doctor): requires at least three years of study after credential C or D (total of at least seven years of postsecondary study); requires presentation and defense of a thesis as well as passing the *examen rigorosum* (rigorous examination)

GRADING INFORMATION

Secondary

Numeric	Description	Translation
1	*Výborný*	Excellent
2	*Chvalitebný*	Very Good
3	*Dobrý*	Good
4	*Dostatečný*	Satisfactory
5	*Nedostatečný*	Unsatisfactory

● *Dostatečný* (4) is the lowest passing grade.

Postsecondary

Numeric	Description	Translation
1	*Výborný*	Excellent
2	*Velmi Dobrý*	Very Good
3	*Dobrý*	Good
4	*Nedostatečný or Nevyhovél*	Unsatisfactory or Did Not Pass
-	*Zápočet*	Credit, Pass

- *Dobrý* (3) is the lowest passing grade.

- *Zápočet* is used for postsecondary courses which have been successfully completed, but for which no final exam was required. There is no numeric value assigned to *zápočet*.

POSTSECONDARY INSTITUTION RECOGNITION BODY

Ministry of Education, Karmelitská 8, 118 12 Prague 1 Czech Republic.
Tel: 42-2-5193111. Fax: 42-2-5193790.

RESOURCES FOR ADDITIONAL INFORMATION

National Office of Overseas Skills Recognition. 1992. *Country Education Profiles: Czech and Slovak Federal Republic*. Canberra: Australian Government Publishing Service.

Organisation for Economic Co-Operation and Development. 1996. *Education at a Glance*. Paris: Organisation for Economic Co-Operation and Development.

Organisation for Economic Co-Operation and Development. 1996. *Reviews of National Policies for Education: Czech Republic*. Paris: Organisation for Economic Co-Operation and Development.

Silny, Josef, Frederick Lockyear, and Edward Devlin. 1992. *The Admission and Placement of Students from the Czech and Slovak Federal Republic*. Annapolis Junction, MD: PIER.

Internet Sources:
Centre for Equivalence of Diplomas: www.csvs.cz. E-Mail: skuhrova@csvs.cz
UNESCO - World Academic Database: www.unesco.org/iau/educcz.html

---

Compiler
Margo M. Ptacek
Evaluator
Educational Credential Evaluators, Inc., Milwaukee, WI

DENMARK

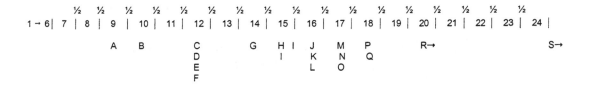

1→6	7	8	9	10	11	12	13	14	15	16	17	18	19	20	21	22	23	24
	A	B		C D E F		G	H I	J K L	M N O	P Q		R→						S→

CREDENTIALS OR DOCUMENTATION

Secondary

A *Folkeskolens Afgangsprøve* (Leaving Examination): awarded upon completion of lower secondary school; signifies completion of grade 9 and compulsory education

B *Folkeskolens Udvidede Afgangsprøve* (Extended Leaving Examination): awarded upon completion of lower secondary school; signifies completion of a supplemental grade 10 and compulsory education

C *Studentereksamen* (Student Examination): awarded upon satisfactory completion of upper secondary school; used for admission to tertiary level education

D *Højere (HF) Forberedelsesekamen* (Higher Preparatory Examination): awarded upon satisfactory completion of examinations as an alternative to the upper secondary school; used for admission to tertiary level education

E *Højere handelseksamen (HHX)* (Higher Commercial Examination): awarded upon satisfactory completion of upper secondary commercial school; used for admission to tertiary level education, particularly business programs

F *Højere teknisk eksamen (HTX)* (Higher Technical Examination): awarded upon satisfactory completion of upper secondary technical school; used for admission to tertiary level education, particularly technical and engineering programs

Postsecondary

G *Examinus Artium/Scientiarum* (Humanities/Science Examination): awarded by university; signifies completion of two years of basic studies for an upper secondary teaching qualification requiring credential **C, D, E,** or **F** for admission

H *Bachelorgraden/B.A.,B.S.*(Bachelor's degree): awarded by university; signifies completion of three-year program requiring credential **C, D, E,** or **F** for admission; used for admission to Candidate program

I *Handelsvidenskabelig afgangseksamen/HA* (Business School Leaving Diploma): awarded by university; signifies completion of three- or three and one-half year program in business requiring **C, D, E,** or **F** for admission

J *Teknikumingeniør* (Technical Engineer): awarded by university; signifies completion of four-year program in engineering requiring **C, D, E,** or **F** for admission

K *Candidatus/a philosophiae.cand.phil* (Candidate in Philosophy): awarded by university; signifies completion of a one-year program for an upper secondary teaching qualification requiring credential **H** for admission

127

L   *Candidatus/a philosophiae/cand.phil* (Candidate in Philosophy): awarded by university; signifies completion of a two-year structured university program for an upper secondary teaching qualification requiring credential **G** for admission

M   *Civilingeniør* (Engineer): awarded by university; signifies completion of five-year engineering program requiring credential **C, D, E,** or **F** or a transfer from a **J** program for admission

N   *Candidatus* (Candidate): awarded by university; signifies completion of a two-year program requiring credential **H** for admission; used for admission to doctoral level programs (**R** or **S**)

O   *Candidatus* (Candidate): awarded by university; signifies completion of a five-year program requiring credential **C, D, E,** or **F** for admission; used for admission to doctoral level programs (**R** or **S**)

P   *Candidatus* (Candidate): awarded by university; signifies completion of a six-year program in certain scientific areas, such as life sciences, requiring credential **C, D, E,** or **F** for admission; used for admission to doctoral level programs (**R** or **S**)

Q   *Magister/ra artium/ mag.art.,Magister/ra scientiarum/mag/scient.* (Master of Art/Science): awarded by university; signifies completion of a six-year program requiring **C, D, E,** or **F** for admission

R   *Ph.D.-graden/Ph.D.*(Ph.D.): awarded by university; signifies completion of a minimum of a three-year program including a dissertation requiring credential **M, N, O, P,** or **Q** for admission

S   *Doctor* (Research Doctorate): awarded by university; signifies completion of many years of independent research and published postdoctoral research

GRADING INFORMATION

Secondary

Numeric	Description
13	Exceptionally independent and excellent performance
11	Independent and excellent performance
10	Excellent but not particularly independent performance
9	Good performance, a little above average
8	Average performance
7	Mediocre performance, slightly below average
6	Somewhat hesitant but more or less satisfactory performance
5	Hesitant and not satisfactory performance
03	Very hesitant, very insufficient and unsatisfactory performance
00	Completely unacceptable performance

- The minimum passing grade is 6.
- The marks of 13 and 00 are both considered exceptional, and are used infrequently.

Postsecondary Education

Numeric	Description
13	
11	Very Good
10	

9	
8	Good
7	

6	

5	
3	Less Satisfactory
0	

- The mark of 13 is unobtainable except at The Technical University of Denmark.
- Either a total average grade of 6, or a grade of at least 6 in each subject, is required for graduation.

POSTSECONDARY INSTITUTION RECOGNITION BODY

Ministry of Education, Frederiksholms Kanal 21, København K, Danmark.
Tel: 45 33 92 50 00. Fax: 45 32 92 55 47.

Other ministries are responsible for some specialized institutions.

RESOURCES FOR ADDITIONAL INFORMATION

Danmark-Amerika Fondet and Fulbright/DAF Exchanges Project, Fiolstræde 24, 3 sal, Danmark-1171, København K. Tel: 45 33 12 82 23. Fax: 45 33 32 53 23.
E-mail: fulbdk@unidhp.uni-c.dk

Dickey, Karlene N. and Valerie A. Woolston. 1995. *Denmark: A Study of the Educational System of Denmark and Guide to the Academic Placement of Students in Educational Institutions in the United States.* Annapolis Junction, MD: PIER.

Rektorkollegiets sekretariat (Danish Rectors' Conference Secretariat),Vester Voldgade 121 A 4. sal, DK-1552 København V. Tel: 45 33 92 54 06. Fax: 45 33 92 50 75.

Internet Sources:
Danish Rectors' Conference Secretariat: www.rks.dk/90folder/engfold.htm
Higher Education in Nordic Countries: www.abo.fi/norden/textvers
Ministry of Education: www.uvm.dk
UNESCO - World Academic Database: www.unesco.org/iau/educdk.html

---

Compiler
Valerie Woolston
Director, International Education Services
University of Maryland

DOMINICAN REPUBLIC

YEARS OF EDUCATION →

```
    ½   ½   ½   ½   ½   ½   ½   ½   ½   ½   ½   ½   ½   ½   ½   ½   ½
1→6| 7 | 8 | 9 | 10| 11| 12| 13| 14| 15| 16| 17| 18| 19| 20| 21| 22| 23| 24|
                      A   D       F   F   F   F   F   G   G   H   G   G   J   L   L   L   L
                      B   E               G   G   G   K   H   M   H   H   K
                      C                           K   L   I   I   I   L   L
                                                      J   J   J       M
                                                      K   K   K
                                                      L   L   L
                                                              M
```

CREDENTIALS OR DOCUMENTATION

Secondary

A   *Bachillerato en* (specialization) [Bachelor in (specialization)]: Traditional Plan is typically a 6 + 2 + 4 program; although supposedly supplanted by the Reform Plan of 1970 (see **B**), it is still common

B   *Bachillerato en Ciencias y Letras* (Bachelor in Sciences and Letters): Reform Plan is a 6 + 4 + 2 program; implemented in 1970, but not widely accepted; this is the general academic program with the final two years of study in a specialization

C   *Bachillerato Técnico-Profesional* (Bachelor Technical-Professional): secondary school leaving certificate with a technical and/or professional emphasis

D   *Título de Maestro Normal Primario* (Title of Primary School Teacher): secondary level teacher training program that allows employment as a primary teacher or access to further teacher training

Postsecondary

E   *Enfermeras Asistentes* (Nursing Assistant): a one-year program

F   *Técnico en* (specialization) [Technician in (specialization)], *Tecnólogo en* (specialization) [Technologist in (specialization)]: usually, a two- to three-year intermediate technical program; terminal, technically oriented programs in surveying and medical technology range from three and one-half to four years; some programs allow access to credential **G** programs, others only to employment

G   *Licenciatura* (Licentiate)/*Título Profesional* (Professional Title): three- to six and one-half-year academic degree programs

H   *Ingeniero* (Engineer): five- to six and one-half-year professional degree

I   *Arquitecto* (Architect): five- to six-year professional degree

J   *Doctor en* (specialization) [Doctor of (specialization)]: five- to seven-year professional degrees in dentistry, law, medicine, pharmacy, and veterinary medicine

K   *Certificado de Postgrado* (Postgraduate Certificate): usually a one-year program beyond credential **G**; does not usually provide access to credential **L**

L   *Maestría/Magister* (Master's): one and one-half to three-year degree after credential **G**; requires a thesis or original project

M *Maestría en Administración de Negocios (*Master's in Business Administration): two-year degree after four- or five-year credential **G**

GRADING INFORMATION

Secondary

Traditional Secondary System: 0-100 with 60 as lowest passing grade. Some private schools vary the passing grade and note it on the academic transcript.

Reform Secondary System: 1-5 with 2 as lowest passing grade.

- Grades of 60 or 2 are acceptable for graduation.

Postsecondary

Individual grading scales vary from one institution to another, but the two most common are the 4.0 system with corresponding letter grades of A, B, C, D, and F, and a 100-point scale with minimum passing grade of 70 (60 in some cases). A few examples are given below:

Point	Grade	Percentage	Grade	Percentage	Description	Translation
4.0	A	90 - 100	A	96 - 100	*Sobresaliente*	Outstanding
3.0	B	80 - 89	B	86 - 95	*Muy Bueno*	Very Good
2.0	C	75 - 79	C	76 - 85	*Bueno*	Good
1.0	D	70 - 74	D	70 - 75	*Suficiente*	Sufficient
0.0	F	0 - 69	F	0 - 69	*Reprobado*	Failing

Percentage	Grade
94 - 100	A
90 - 93	A-
87 - 85	B+
80 - 83	B-
84 - 81	B
77 - 79	C+
74 - 76	C
70 - 73	C-
67 - 69	D+
64 - 66	D
60 - 63	D-
0 - 59	F

- The minimum grade required for graduation varies among institutions.

POSTSECONDARY INSTITUTION RECOGNITION BODY

Consejo Nacional de Educación Superior/CONES (National Council of Higher Education). Vicente Celestino Duarte #19, Zona Colonial, Santo Domingo, D.N., Dominican Republic. Tel: 809-688-8357.

RESOURCES FOR ADDITIONAL INFORMATION

Glover, Roy. 1998. "Higher Education in the Dominican Republic." Report to the United States Information Service. Santo Domingo, Dominican Republic.

Levy, Daniel C. 1993. "Privatization of Latin American Higher Education Reflects Worldwide Trend of Collapse of Public Monopoly in Education." *World Education News & Reviews* 7, 1:1, 21-23.

Rolwing, Kevin and Margarita Sianou, Tim Gaherty, and Liliane Bauduy. 1993. "Profiles of Selected Countries in Latin America." *World Education News & Reviews* 7, 1:9-18.

Sellew, Kathleen Troxell. 1987. *Dominican Republic.* Washington, D.C.: AACRAO.

Compiler
Patricia J. Parker
Assistant Director of Admissions
Iowa State University

ECUADOR

YEARS OF EDUCATION

	½	½	½	½	½	½	½	½	½	½	½	½	½	½	½	½	½
1 → 6| 7	8	9	10	11	12	13	14	15	16	17	18	19	20	21	22	23	24

```
                A    C    D    E         G    K    O    O    V    Y    a
                B              F         H    L    P    R    W    Z
                                         I    M    Q    S    X
                                         J    N         T    Z
                                                        U
                                                        V
```

CREDENTIALS OR DOCUMENTATION

Secondary

A *Certificado de Término de Noveno Grado* (Certificate of Completion of Ninth Grade - or the *Tercer Curso* (Third Year)

B *Técnico Auxiliar* (Assistant Technician)

C *Técnico Básico I* (Basic Technician I)

D *Técnico Básico II* (Basic Technician II)

E *Bachillerato* (Baccalaureate) or *Título de Bachiller* (Title of Bachelor): leads to postecondary education

F *Técnico Medio* (Intermediate Technician): may lead to postsecondary education in related areas

Postsecondary

G *Técnico Superior* (Higher Technician) in various technical fields

H *Asistente en Bibliotecnología* (Library Assistant)

I *Topógrafo* (Surveyor)

J *Trabajadora Social* (Social Worker)

K *Diploma de Enfermera* (Nurse's Diploma): note that the *Licenciado en Enfermería* (Licentiate in Nursing) is awarded upon completion of four-year program (see credential **O**)

L *Decorador* (Interior Decorator)

M *Auditor* (Auditor)

N *Tecnólogo* (Technologist)

O *Licenciado* (Licentiate): the length of Licentiate degrees in the same field varies between institutions — either four or five years

P *Obstetriz* (Midwife)

Q *Profesor* (Secondary School Teacher)

R *Ingeniero* (Engineer) or *Arquitecto* (Architect)

S *Médico Veterinario* (Veterinarian)

T *Doctorado en Odontología* (Doctor of Dental Medicine)

U *Contador Público* (Public Accountant)

V *Diplomado* (Diploma Holder): intermediate graduate diploma (post-credential **O**); awarded after completion of one year of a two-year credential **Z** program

W *Psicólogo* (Psychologist)

133

X   *Abogado* (Attorney)
Y   *Doctorado en Medicina* (Doctor of Medicine)
Z   *Magister, Master* (Master's degree): requires *licenciado* (credential **O**) or any professional title (credentials **P** through **U** and **W** through **Y**) for admission; awarded upon completion of a two-year program
a   *Doctorado* (Doctorate): in non-medical academic fields

GRADING INFORMATION

Secondary

Numeric	Spanish	Translation
10	*Sobresaliente*	Excellent
9	*Muy Bueno*	Very Good
8	*Bueno*	Good
7	*Regular*	Average
0-6	*Arrastre*	Failure

- Grade of *Sobresaliente* often indicates first in class, with other top students earning *muy bueno*. The minimum passing grade is 7 and is sufficient for graduation.

Postsecondary Education

Numeric	Spanish	Translation
40	*Sobresaliente*	Excellent
35-39	*Muy Bueno*	Very Good
30-34	*Bueno*	Good
24-29	*Regular*	Average
0-23	*Arrastre*	Failure

- Grade reports normally have information on the Spanish descriptions of numeric grades. Different faculties within the same university may use different numeric scales, but the Spanish descriptions of numeric grades remain constant.

POSTSECONDARY INSTITUTION RECOGNITION BODY

Consejo Nacional de Universidades y Escuelas Politécnicas (CONUEP); Dirección: 9 de Octubre N.- 624 y Carrió; Quito, Ecuador. Tel: Secretaría General 569894; Public Relations Ext. 218. Fax: 563685.

RESOURCES FOR ADDITIONAL INFORMATION

The British Council. 1991. *International Guide to Qualifications in Education*. 3rd ed. London: Mansell.

Internet Source:
UNESCO - World Academic Database: www.unesco.org/iau/educed.html

---

Compiler
David Mihalyi, Evaluator
HR Analytical Services, Inc., South Milwaukee, WI

EGYPT

YEARS OF EDUCATION →

		½	½	½	½	½	½	½	½	½	½	½	½	½	½	½	½	½
1 →6	7	8	9	10	11	12	13	14	15	16	17	18	19	20	21	22	23	24

```
                    A    F    G    J    N Q   O Q   R Z   T e   U    g    j→   l→        m→
                    B         H    L    P     P Z   T     U     d    j→   k→
                    C         I    M    Q     Q e   U     V     f    k→   l→
                    D         K         S     R     X     d     g
                    E                         U     Y     e     j→
                                              W     a     f
                                              X     b     g
                                              a     c     h
                                                    e     i→
                                                    f
```

CREDENTIALS OR DOCUMENTATION

Secondary[1]

A شهادة إتمام الدراسة الثانوية العامة (Certificate of Completion of General Secondary Education, also known as the *thaanawiya*); represents 11 years of education, awarded after passing national examination; prior to 1995, represented 12 years of education

B دبلوم المدارس الثانوية التجارية/الصناعية/الزراعية (Commercial, Industrial, or Agricultural Technical Secondary School Diploma): represents 11 years of education, awarded after passing national examination; prior to 1995, represented 12 years of education

C دبلوم المدارس الثانوية الفنية التجارية/الصناعية/الزراعية-إعداد مهني (Industrial/Agricultural Technical Secondary School Diploma in Vocational Preparation): represents 11 years of education, considered equivalent to credential B

D دبلوم التدريب المهني للقوات المصلحة (Armed Forces Vocational Training Diploma): represents 11 years of education; prior to 1995, represented 12 years of education; considered equivalent to credential B

E دبلوم المعلمين والمعلمات (Teacher's Diploma): represents 11 years of education; introduced on an experimental basis in 1988-89 to replace credential J

F شهادة إتمام الدراسة الثانوية الأزهرية (Al-Azhar secondary certificate): represents 12 years of education[2]

G دبلوم الدراسة الفنية المتقدمة التجارية/الصناعية/الزراعية (Diploma of Advanced Technical Commerical/Industrial/Agricultural Studies): represents 13 years of education; prior to 1996, represented 14 years of education[3]

H دبلوم المدارس الفنية الصناعية للمعلمين (Industrial Teacher Training School Diploma): represents 13 years of education[3]

I دبلوم الدراسات التكميلية الصناعية (Diploma of Complementary Industrial Studies): two-year program serving as a transition to the technical track for those who have completed the coursework for credential A; considered equivalent to credential B

J دبلوم المعلمين والمعلمات (Teachers' Diploma)[4]: represented 14 years of education; phased out as of 1991-92 and replaced by credential E

135

Postsecondary

K بلوم المعاهد الفنية (Technical Institute Diploma): two years, requiring credential **A** or **B**

L الدبلوم العالي في تكنولوجيا (Higher Diploma in Technology): three years, requiring credential **A** or **B** (credential **G** permits entry into second program year)

M Bachelor's degree from the Air Academy: three years, requiring credential **A** for admission (not considered equivalent to the bachelor's degrees awarded by the national universities)

N Bachelor in Naval Studies (Naval Academy); Bachelor of Civil Defense Science (Civil Defense Academy): four years, requiring credential **A** for admission[5] (graduates may pursue higher civil or military studies at the military colleges, or, under special circumstances, the national universities)

O Bachelor of Military Science (Defense Academy): five years, requiring credential **A** for admission[6]

P بكالوريوس (Bachelor's degree): four to five years, depending on the field of study; admission requires credential **A, B,** or the equivalent

Q Bachelor of Arts, Bachelor of Science: four to five and one-half years at the American University of Cairo, depending on the field of study; admission requires credential **A**

R الإجازة العليا (Bachelor's degree): four to five years at Al-Azhar University, depending on the field of study; admission requires credential **F**; credential **A** permits admission to secular faculties but requires preliminary year of religious studies

S لسانس/لسانس ممتازة (Licence; Exceptional Licence): four years in arts (including language and literature, social sciences), law, Islamic studies, education, or archaeology; requires credential **A** or **E** for admission

T بكالوريوس في الطب والجراحة (Bachelor of Medicine and Surgery): six years, requiring credential **A** or **F** for admission (licensure requires an additional year of practical training)

U دبلوم الدراسات العليا (Higher Studies Diploma): one to two years, depending on the field of study; admission requires credential **P, R,** or **S**

V شهادة في تربية–التعليم الأساسي (Certificate of Basic Education): four years, requiring credential **J** for admission; considered equivalent to credential **P** (in science and education) or **S** (in art and education)

W الدبلوم العام (General Diploma) in education or teacher training: one year, requiring four-year credential **P** or **S** for admission

X الدبلوم التطبيقي (Applied Diploma): one year in school libraries, two years in home economics; admission requires four-year credential **P** or **S**

Y دبلوم تخصص (Diploma of Specialization): two years in the field of specialization; admission requires credential **S**

Z Graduate Diploma; one to one and one-half years at the American University in Cairo in the fields of engineering, journalism and mass communications, management, or Middle East studies; admission requires credential **Q**

a الدبلوم المهني في تربية (Professional Diploma in Education): one year (including thesis) requiring four-year credential **P** or **S**, or **W** for admission

b الدبلوم الخاصة في تربية (Special Diploma in Education): one year, requiring credential **W** for admission; two years, requiring four-year credential **P** in science and education or four-year credential **S** in arts and education

c الدبلوم الخاصة لإعداد المعلم في الآداب أو في العلوم (Special teacher training diploma in arts or science): one year, requiring credential **W** for admission

d دبلوم تخصص (Diploma of Specialization): one year of medical specialization; admission requires credential **T**

e Master of Arts, Master of Business Administration, Master of Public Administration, Master of Engineering: one and one-half to two years at the American University of Cairo; admission requires credential **Q**

f ماجستير (Master's degree): two years, requiring credential **P, S,** or **T**; Master's degree in law requires two credential **U**s or one credential **U** and a thesis for admission

g درجات التخصص (Master's degree): two years, requiring credential **R** or **T**

h ماجستير في التربية (Master of Education): one year (including thesis), requiring credential **b** for admission

i ماجستير لإعداد المعلم في الآداب أو في العلوم (Master's in teacher training in arts or sciences): minimum one year (including thesis), requiring credential **c** for admission

j دكتوراه/دكتور الفلسفة (Doctorate/Ph.D.): two to five years, requiring credential **f, g, h,** or **i** for admission

k درجة العالمية (Doctorate, Ph.D.): two to five years, requiring credential **g** for admission

l دكتور في الطب والجراحة (Doctor of Medicine and Surgery): two to five years, requiring credential **f** or **g** for admission

m دكتور في العلوم (Doctor of Science, D.Sc.): at least five years after credential **j** or **k**; awarded by the Faculty of Science

[1] In 1999-2000, the sixth primary year will be reintroduced. Beginning in 2006, completion of the secondary cycle will once again represent 12 years of education.

[2] Secondary-level Islamic education is conducted under the supervision of the Ministry of Al-Azhar Affairs and is four years long (compared with the three-year general secondary cycle).

[3] Credentials **G** and **H** are awarded after a five-year secondary cycle. Depending on final scores, students are admissible to the first or second year of some technical postsecondary programs.

[4] As of 1988-89, no more students were being admitted into this program. The last class should have graduated in 1991-92.

[5] After a one-year complementary program in cooperation with Alexandria University, students are awarded a Bachelor of Engineering with a specialization in electrical engineering.

[6] Under special circumstances, credential **O** may permit admission to graduate programs in the national universities.

GRADING INFORMATION

Secondary

Percent	Remark	Translation
90–100	ممتازة	Excellent
80–89	جيد جدا	Very Good
65–79	جيد	Good
50–64	مقبول	Pass
below 50	راسب	Fail

- The above scale is for the general average only; each subject has its own minimum passing score, which may be as low as 40 out of 100.

Higher Education

Undergraduate Grading Scale A

Percent	Remark	Translation
90–100	ممتازة	Excellent
80–89	جيد جدا	Very Good
65–79	جيد	Good
50–64	مقبول	Pass
35–49	ضعيف	Weak
below 35	راسب	Fail

- Grading scale A is used in the university faculties of arts, language, Islamic studies, archaeology, commerce, economics and political science, law, and mass communications; at the Open University, the Sadat Academy, and the tourism institutes.

Undergraduate Grading Scale B

Percent	Remark	Translation
85–100	ممتازة	Excellent
75–84	جيد جدا	Very Good
65–74	جيد	Good
60–64	مقبول	Pass
30–59	ضعيف	Weak
below 30	راسب	Fail

- Grading scale B is used in the health science faculties.

Undergraduate Grading Scale C

Percent	Remark	Translation
85–100	ممتازة	Excellent
75–84	جيد جدا	Very Good
65–74	جيد	Good
50–64	مقبول	Pass
30–49	ضعيف	Weak
below 30	راسب	Fail

- Grading scale C is used in the faculties of education, engineering, fine arts, technology, social services, urban planning, and veterinary medicine.

Representative Graduate Grading Scale

Percent	Remark	Translation
90–100	ممتازة	Excellent
80–89	جيد جدا	Very Good
70–79	جيد	Good
60–69	مقبول	Pass

- Most faculties use this grading scale for graduate programs, although there are several exceptions. Among them, the Faculty of Arts and the Faculty of Law have a minimum passing score of 70.

Credit-Hour Grading Scale

Undergraduate	Graduate	Remark	Translation
3.2–4.0	3.6–4.0	ممتازة	Excellent
2.4–3.19	2.7–3.59	جيد جدا	Very Good
1.6–2.39	1.8–2.69	جيد	Good
1.0–1.59	1.0–1.79	مقبول	Pass

- The Faculty of Agriculture is among those using a credit-hour grading scale.

POSTSECONDARY INSTITUTION RECOGNITION BODY

Supreme Council of Universities; Giza, Egypt. Tel: 20-2-568-3176.
Fax: 20-2-572-8722.

RESOURCES FOR ADDITIONAL INFORMATION

National Office of Overseas Skills Recognition. 1992. *Egypt: A Comparative Study.* Canberra: Australian Government Publishing Service.

Nucho, Leslie S., ed. 1993. *Education in the Arab World. Volume I.* Washington, D.C.: AMIDEAST.

Wilcox, Lee. 1988. *Arab Republic of Egypt: A Study of the Educational System of the Arab Republic of Egypt and a Guide to the Academic Placement of Students in Educational Institutions of the United States.* Washington, D.C.: AACRAO.

Internet Sources:
Egyptian Universities Network site, with links to public university home pages:
www.frcu.eun.eg/www/universities/html/univ.html

UNESCO—World Academic Database: www.unesco.org/iau/educeg.html

---

Compilers
Maisa Galal
Unit Coordinator, Advising and Special Programs
AMIDEAST, Egypt

Leslie S. Nucho
Vice President
AMIDEAST, Washington D.C.

EL SALVADOR

YEARS OF EDUCATION →

	½	½	½	½	½	½	½	½	½	½	½	½	½	½	½	½	½
1 → 6	7	8	9	10	11	12	13	14	15	16	17	18	19	20	21	22	23	24

```
                          A           B   B       G G I  J I  K L L
                                      C   D       H H J     K
                                          E       I
                                          F
```

CREDENTIALS OR DOCUMENTATION

Secondary

A *Bachiller en __* (Bachelor in __): three-year program; admission requires completion of grade 9; programs available in various fields of study such as academic, agriculture, arts, commerce, health, industry, and vocational-technical

Postsecondary

B *Técnico en __* (Technician in __): two or three-year technical programs; admission based on credential **A**

C *Bachiller Mayor* (Higher Bachelor): two-year program offered at the *Universidad Dr. J.M. Delgado*; admission based on credential **A**

D *Profesor* (Teacher): three-year program in primary, secondary, and special education; admission based on credential **A**

E *Bibliotecario* (Librarian): three-year program in library science offered by the *Universidad de El Salvador*; admission based on credential **A**

F *Técnico Avanzado* (Advanced Technician): three-year program; admission based on credential **A**

G Title of *Licenciado* (Licentiate): five- to five and one-half-year program which is required for teaching at the university level; admission based on credential **A**

H *Ingeniero* (Engineer) or *Arquitecto* (Architect): five- to five and one-half-year programs; admission based on credential **A**

I *Doctor en Medicina* (Doctor of Medicine), *Doctor en Odontología* (Doctor of Dentistry), Title of *Cirujano Dentista* (Dental Surgeon), or Title of *Abogado* (Lawyer): five- to seven-year programs; admission based on credential **A**

J *Profesorado Universitario* (University Teacher): one-year university teaching program offered at the *Universidad Francisco Gavidia*; admission based on credential **G**

K *Maestría* (Master): two-year program beyond credential **G**

L *Doctorado* (Doctorate): one year advanced study beyond credential **K**, or three years beyond credential **G**

GRADING INFORMATION

Secondary

Numerical	Description	Translation
10	*Sobresaliente*	Excellent
9	*Muy Bueno*	Extremely Good
8	*Bastante Bueno*	Very Good
6-7	*Bueno*	Good
5	*Regular*	Pass
1-4	*Malo*	Fail

Postsecondary Education

A 10-point scale is used, with 10 being highest. Universities use a minimum pass of either 5 or 6.

POSTSECONDARY INSTITUTION RECOGNITION BODY

Ministerio de Educación y Cultura, Dirección Nacional de Educación Superior, Alameda Juan Pablo II, Plan Maestro, Centro de Gobierno, Edificio A2, San Salvador, El Salvador. Tel: 503 281 0044. Fax: 503 281 0257.

RESOURCES FOR ADDITIONAL INFORMATION

Aldrich-Langen, Caroline and Kathleen Sellew, eds. 1987. *The Admission and Placement of Students from Central America: Belize, Costa Rica, El Salvador, Guatemala, Honduras, Nicaragua, Panama*. Annapolis Junction, MD: PIER.

Marcus, Jane E. 1996. *Central America Update*. Annapolis Junction, MD: PIER.

National Office of Overseas Skills Recognition. 1993. *Country Education Profiles: El Salvador*. Canberra: Australian Government Printing Office.

Internet Source:
UNESCO - World Academic Database: www.unesco.org/iau/educsv.html

---

Compiler
Marybeth Mirzejewski
Evaluator
Educational Credential Evaluators, Inc., Milwaukee, WI

ETHIOPIA

YEARS OF EDUCATION →

```
    ½   ½   ½   ½   ½   ½   ½   ½   ½   ½   ½   ½   ½   ½   ½   ½   ½
1 → 6│ 7 │ 8 │ 9 │ 10 │ 11 │ 12 │ 13 │ 14 │ 15 │ 16 │ 17 │ 18 │ 19 │ 20 │ 21 │ 22 │ 23 │ 24 │
                         A    C    E    F    G    H    I    J→         K→   M→
                         B    D                             J→         L→
                                                                       M→
```

CREDENTIALS OR DOCUMENTATION

Secondary

A   Ethiopian School Leaving Certificate Examination (ESLCE): awarded by a comprehensive secondary school; signifies completion of the general secondary education stream

B   General Secondary Education Certificate: awarded by a comprehensive secondary school; signifies completion of the vocational secondary education stream

C   Technical Diploma: awarded by a technical school; signifies completion of the technical secondary education stream

Postsecondary

D   Teachers Certificate: awarded by a teacher training institute (TTI); signifies completion of a one-year primary school teacher training program requiring credential **B** for admission

E   Diploma: awarded by a college, university, or teacher training college (TTC); signifies completion of a two-year program requiring credential **B** for admission

F   Advanced Diploma: awarded by a college, university, or special institute; signifies completion of a three-year program in engineering fields requiring credential **B** for admission

G   Bachelor of Arts, Bachelor of Science, Bachelor of Science in Agriculture, and Bachelor of Education: awarded by a college or university; signifies completion of a four-year program requiring credential **B** for admission

H   Bachelor of Science in Engineering, Bachelor of Law, Bachelor of Science in Pharmacy, Bachelor of Science in Architecture and Town Planning: awarded by a college or university; signifies completion of a five-year program requiring credential **B** for admission

I   Doctor of Medicine and Doctor of Veterinary Medicine: awarded by a college or university; signifies completion of a six-year program requiring credential **B** for admission

J   Master of Arts, Master of Science, Master of Public Health, Master of Business Administration: awarded by a university; signifies completion of a program usually lasting at least two years; requires credential **G** or **H** for admission

K   Certificate of Specialization: awarded by a university; signifies completion of at least three years of study and a residency in a medical specialization; requires credential **I** (Doctor of Medicine) for admission

142

L   Specialization Diploma: awarded by a university; signifies completion of at least three years of study in pathology; requires credential **I** (Doctor of Medicine) for admission

M Doctor of Philosophy: awarded by a university; signifies completion of at least three years of study; requires credential **J** for admission[1]

[1] Most students admitted to a Doctor of Philosophy degree program have completed a Master's degree program. Admission directly from a Bachelor's degree program (credentials **G** and **H**) is also possible; in these cases, a minimum of five years of study is required to earn a Doctor of Philosophy degree.

GRADING INFORMATION

Secondary
50% is considered the minimum passing grade for promotion from one level to the next.

Ethiopian School Leaving Certificate Examination and Postsecondary Education

Letter	Description	Points
A	Excellent	4.0
B	Good	3.0
C	Satisfactory	2.0
D	Unsatisfactory	1.0
F	Fail	0.0

Some schools use the following scale:

Percentage	Letter
85-100	A
70-84	B
60-69	C
50-59	D
0-49	F

Addis Ababa University - Master Degree Programs:

Letter	Point
A	4.0
B+	3.5
B	3.0
C+	2.5
C	2.0
D	1.0
F	0.0
P	Pass (dissertation or thesis)

- A letter grade is awarded for each subject; the grade of C represents the minimum passing grade.

- An overall grade average of at least 2.0 is required for graduation from a Bachelor's degree program. A final cumulative grade average between 3.25 and 3.74 will garner *with Distinction*; a final cumulative GPA of 3.75 or higher will garner *with Great Distinction*.

- Diplomas awarded by Addis Ababa Commercial College will reflect the following classifications based on final cumulative GPAs: 3.25-3.49 – *with Distinction*; 3.5-3.74 – *with Great Distinction*; 3.75 or higher – *with Very Great Distinction*.

POSTSECONDARY INSTITUTION RECOGNITION BODY

Ministry of Education: Department of Higher Education, P.O. Box 30747, Addis Ababa, Ethiopia. Tel: 011-251-1-552-519. Fax: 011-251-1-550-8777.

RESOURCES FOR ADDITIONAL INFORMATION

Clark, B. and G. Neave. 1992. *The Encyclopedia of Higher Education*. Oxford: Pergammon Press.

Europa Publications Limited. 1996. *Africa South of the Sahara –1997*. 26th ed. London: Europa Publications Limited.

National Office of Overseas Skills Recognition. 1997. *Country Education Profiles: Ethiopia*. Canberra: Australian Government Printing Service.

Internet Source:
UNESCO – World Academic Database: www.unesco.org/iau/educet.html

Compiler
Joseph A. Sevigny
Director, Graduate Enrollment Services
Graduate School of Arts and Science
New York University

FINLAND

YEARS OF EDUCATION →

			½	½	½	½	½	½	½	½	½	½	½	½	½	½	½
1 → 6	7	8	9	10	11	12	13	14	15	16	17	18	19	20	21	22	23	24

```
        A              B B B C F F F F F F G I   J P O O O   R R R
                           C   C           G I I J M     Q
                           D              H     J K N
                           E              I     L
```

CREDENTIALS OR DOCUMENTATION

Secondary

A   *Peruskoulun päästötodistus* (Comprehensive School Completion Certificate): awarded by a *peruskoulu/grundskola* (comprehensive school); signifies completion of compulsory education

B   *Perustutkinto/Grundexamen* (Certificate of Vocational Qualification): awarded by an *ammatillinen oppilaitos/institut* (vocational institution); basic secondary-level vocational qualification accompanied by a descriptive title such as *Ruokapalvelujen perustutkinto/Grundexamen i matservice* (Basic Qualification in Catering Services); requires credential **A** for admission; program length is two to three years

C   *Ammattitutkinto/Yrkesexamen* (Certificate of Further Vocational Qualification): awarded by an *ammatillinen oppilaitos/institut* (vocational institution); additional vocational qualification accompanied by a descriptive title such as *Koristeveistäjän ammattitutkinto/Yrkesexamen inom finsnickare* (Further Qualification in Ornamental Wood Carving); program length is one to two years and requires credential **B** for admission

D   *Lukion päästötodistus/Dimissionsbetyg* or *Avgångsbetyg från gymnasiet* (Upper Secondary Completion Certificate): awarded by a *lukio/gymansium* (upper secondary school); three-year program requiring credential **A** for admission

E   *Ylioppilastutkintotodistus/Studentexamensbetyg* (Matriculation Examination Certificate): awarded by the national *Ylioppilastutkintolautakunta/ Studentexamensnämnd* (Matriculation Examination Board); this is the basic admission requirement for university study; it does not represent completion of additional study beyond the upper secondary completion certificate (see **D** above)

Postsecondary

F   *Teknikko/Tekniker* (Technician) or *Opistotutkinto/Institutexamen* (Postsecondary Vocational Qualification): awarded by an *ammatillinen oppilaitos/institut* (vocational institution); a postsecondary (but not university-level) vocational qualification accompanied by a descriptive title such as *Teknikko, puuala/Tekniker, träbranschen* (Technician Engineer, Wood Industry) or *Liiketalouden opistotutkinto, merkonomi/Institutexamen inom förtagsekonmi, merkonom* (Diploma in Business and Administration); in some cases, the credential will indicate a qualification title such as *Optikko/Optiker* (Diploma of Optometrist); programs are two- to four and one-half years in length and require credential **A**, **B**, or **C** for admission; programs will be discontinued after 2000

G   *Kandidaatti/Kandidat* (Candidate): awarded by an *yliopisto/universitet* (university), *korkeakoulu/högskolan* (higher school) or *akatemi/akademi* (academy); awarded in the fields of Agriculture and Forestry, Art and Design, Economics, Education, Fine Arts, Health Care, Humanities, Law, Music, Natural Sciences, Psychology, Social Sciences, Sport Sciences, Theater and Dance, and Theology; programs vary between three and four years in length and require credentials **D** and **E** for admission

H   *Farmaseutti/Farmaceut* (Dispenser): awarded by an *yliopisto/universitet* (university) or *akatemi/akademi* (academy); three-year program in Pharmacy; requires credentials **D** and **E** for admission

I   *Ammattikorkeakoulututkinto/Yrkeshögskoleexamen* (Polytechnic Degree): awarded by an *ammattikorkeakoulu [AMK]/yrkeshögskolan [YH]* (Polytechnic); four- to four and one-half years, vocational degree program requiring credentials **B**, **C**, or **D** and **E** for admission; those with credential **F** prior to admission may complete a shorter program

J   *Maisteri/Magister* (Master): awarded by an *yliopisto/universitet* (university), *korkeakoulu/högskolan* (higher school) or *akatemi/akademi* (academy); awarded in the fields of Agriculture and Forestry, Art and Design, Economics, Education, Fine Arts, Health Care, Humanities, Music, Natural Sciences, Psychology, Social Sciences, Sport Sciences, Theater and Dance, and Theology; programs vary in length from four to five years and require credentials **D** and **E** for admission, or build on credential **G** programs

K   *Arkkitehti/Arkitekt* (Degree of Architect): awarded by an *yliopisto/universitet* (university) or *korkeakoulu/högskolan* (higher school); requires credentials **D** and **E** for admission; usually a four and one-half year program

L   *Diplomi-insinööri/Diplomingenjör* (Degree of Engineer): awarded by an *yliopisto/universitet* (university), *korkeakoulu/högskolan* (higher school) or *akatemi/akademi* (academy); requires credentials **D** and **E** for admission; a four and one-half year program

M   *Proviisori/Provisor* (Pharmacist): awarded by an *yliopisto/universitet* (university); awarded in the field of Pharmacy; five-year program requiring credentials **D** and **E** for admission, or builds on credential **H**

N   *Hammaslääketieteen lisensiaatti/Odontologie licentiat* (Licentiate of Dentistry): awarded by an *yliopisto/universitet* (university); five-year program requiring credentials **D** and **E** for admission

O *Lisensiaatti/Licentiat* (Licentiate): awarded by an *yliopisto/universitet* (university), *korkeakoulu/högskolan* (higher school) or *akatemi/akademi* (academy); two-year programs in Architecture, Engineering, and Landscape Architecture, based on credential **K** or **L**; or two-year programs based on credential **J** in the fields of Agriculture and Forestry, Art and Design, Economics, Education, Health Care, Humanities, Music, Natural Sciences, Psychology, Social Sciences, Sport Sciences, Theater and Dance, and Theology

P *Eläinlääketieteen lisensiaatti/Veterinärmedicine licentiat* (Licentiate of Veterinary Medicine): awarded by an *yliopisto/universitet* (university); five and one-half-year program requiring credentials **D** and **E** for admission

Q *Lääketieteen lisensiaatti/Medicine licentiat (Licentiate of Medicine):* awarded by an *yliopisto/universitet* (university); six and one-half-year program requiring credentials **D** and **E** for admission

R *Tohtori/Doktor* (Doctorate): awarded by an *yliopisto/universitet* (university), *korkeakoulu/högskolan* (higher school) or *akatemi/akademi* (academy); awarded in all fields; program varies from two to four years in length; requires credential **G, J, N, P,** or **Q** for admission

● The number of years required to complete a program is based on the ration of 40 *opintoviikoa/studievecka* (credits) equal to one year of full-time study. The actual length of enrollment may be longer than the credits indicate, so, for example, a 120-point program might take longer to complete than the calculated three years.

GRADING INFORMATION

Secondary

Numerical	Finnish	Swedish	Translation
10	*Erinomainen*	*Utmärkta*	Excellent
9	*Kiitettävä*	*Berömliga*	Praiseworthy
8	*Hyvä*	*Goda*	Good
7	*Tyydytävä*	*Nöjaktiga*	Satisfactory
6	*Kohtalainen*	*Försvarliga*	Moderate
5	*Välttävä*	*Hjälpliga*	Adequate
4	*Hylätty*	*Icke Godkand*	Failure

Secondary-Vocational

Numerical	Finnish	Swedish	Translation
5	*Kiitettäva*	*Berömliga*	Excellent
4	*Erittäin Hyvä*	*Mycket Goda Insikter*	Very Good
3	*Hyvä*	*Goda Insikter*	Good
2	*Erittäin Tyydyttävä*	*Mycket*	Very Satisfactory
1	*Tyydyttävä*	*Nöjaktigt*	Satisfactory

Postsecondary Education

Multi-disciplinary universities:

Numerical	Finnish	Swedish	Translation
3	*Erinomaiset Tiedot (ET)*	*Utmärkta Insikter*	Excellent Notice
2	*Hyvät Tiedot (HT)*	*Goda Insikter*	Good Notice
1	*Tyydyttävät Tiedot (TT)*	*Nöjaktiga Insikter*	Satisfactory Notice
0	*Hylätty*	*Icke Godkand*	Failure

Numerical	Latin	Translation
6	*Laudatur*	Excellent
5	*Eximia Cum Laude Approbatur*	Very Good
4	*Magna Cum Laude Approbatur*	Good
3	*Cum Laude Approbatur*	Fairly Good
2	*Lubenter Approbatur*	Satisfactory
1	*Approbatur*	Fair
0	*Improbatur*	Failure

Technical universities and polytechnics:

Numerical	Finnish	Swedish	Translation
5	*Kiitettävä*	*Berömligt*	Excellent
4	*Erittäin Hyvä*	*Mycket Goda*	Very Good
3	*Hyvä*	*Goda Insikter*	Good
2	*Erittäin Tyydyttävä*	*Mycket*	Very Satisfactory
1	*Tyydyttävä*	*Nöjaktigt*	Satisfactory
0	*Hylätty*	*Icke Godkand*	Failure

POSTSECONDARY INSTITUTION RECOGNITION BODY

Ministry of Education, P.O. Box 293, FIN-00171 Helsinki. Tel: 358-9-134-171. Fax: 358-9-135-9335. www.minedu.fi/

RESOURCES FOR ADDITIONAL INFORMATION

Centre for International Mobility (CIMO), P.O. Box 343 (Hakaniemenkatu 2), FIN-00531 Helsinki. Tel: 358-9-7747-7033. Fax: 358-9-7747-7064. E-mail: cimoinfo@cimo.fi.

Ministry of Education. 1996. *Higher Education Policy in Finland.* Helsinki.

Warren, Kenneth. 1999. *ECE Presents: The Educational System of Finland.* Milwaukee: Educational Credential Evaluators, Inc.

Internet Sources:
Centre for International Mobility (CIMO): www.aka.fi
Higher Education in the Nordic Countries: www.abo.fi/norden/textvers/
UNESCO - World Academic Database: www.unesco.org/iau/educfi.html

---

Compiler
Kenneth Warren
Evaluator
Educational Credential Evaluators, Inc., Milwaukee, WI

FRANCE

YEARS OF EDUCATION →

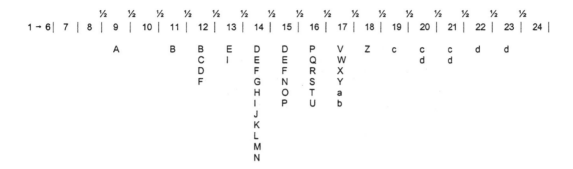

CREDENTIALS OR DOCUMENTATION

Secondary

A *Brevet des Collèges* (Certificate of Lower Secondary School): represents completion of five years of primary plus four years of secondary education

B *Brevet d'Enseignement Professionnel/BEP* (Certificate of Vocational Instruction), or *Certificat d'Aptitude Professionnelle/CAP* (Certificate of Vocational Education): two- to three-year programs of vocational education with apprenticeship; admission based on credential **A**; leads to credential **E** programs

C *Diplôme de Bachelier de l'Enseignement du Second Degré* (Diploma of Baccalaureate of Secondary Education): three years of secondary education based on credential **A**; gives access to university studies

D *Diplôme de Baccalauréat de Technicien* (Diploma of Baccalaureate of Technician): three-year program based on credential **A** or **B**; gives access to university studies at the same level as credential **C** (grade 12)

E *Baccalauréat Professionel* (Vocational Baccalaureate): two- to three-year program based on credential **B**; gives access to university studies at the same level as credential **C** (grade 12)

F *Brevet de Technicien/BT* (Certificate of Technician): three-year program based on credential **A** or **B**; leads to credential **G** or **L** programs at the same level as credential **C** (grade 12)

Postsecondary

G *Brevet de Technicien Supérieur/BTS* (Higher Technician's Certificate): two-year specialized programs in areas such as agriculture, applied science, business, engineering technology, graphic art, and health professions

H *Certificat de Fin d'Etudes Normales/CFEN* (Certificate of Completion of Teacher Training Studies): two-year program for primary school teaching based on credential **C**; discontinued in 1986

I *Class Préparatoires aux Grandes Écoles/CPGE* (Preparatory Classes for *Grandes Écoles*): usually a one-year program in business, or two years in engineering

J *Diplôme d'Etudes Universitaires Générales/DEUG* (Diploma of General University Studies): two-year first cycle program[1]

K *Diplôme d'Etudes Universitaires Professionnalises/DEUP* (Diploma of Vocational University Studies): two-year first cycle program[1]

L *Diplôme d'Etudes Universitaires Scientifiques et Techniques/DEUST* (Diploma of University Scientific and Technical Studies): usually awarded in the fields of art, sciences, and technology; two-year first cycle program[1]

M *Diplôme Universitaire de Technologie/DUT* (University Diploma in Technology): two-year first cycle program[1]

N *Diplôme d'Etat* (State Diploma) in paramedical fields: two-year programs in audioprothesist, chiropody, massage and kinesitherapy, medical laboratory technology, and radiology; three-year programs in nursing, occupational therapy, physical therapy, psychiatric nursing, rehabilitation counseling, and social service assistant

O *Licence* (Licence): one-year second cycle program[1]

P *Diplôme/Certificat de Fin d'Etudes* (Diploma/Certificate of Completion): from a private business school recognized by the state; three to four years of business study

Q *Diplôme d'Etudes Supérieures d'Instituteur* (Diploma of Higher Studies in Education): two-year program in primary school teaching, admission based on credential **J**; implemented in 1986, replacing credential **H** programs

R *Diplôme d'Etudes Supérieures Commerciales Administratives et Financières/ DESCAF* (Diploma of Higher Studies in Business, Administration, and Finance): three years of business study preceded by one year of *classe préparatoire* in business (see credential **I**)

S *Maitrise* (Master): one-year second cycle program; requires credential **O** for admission[1]

T *Maîtrise* (Master)...*des Sciences et Techniques/MST* (in Sciences and Technology), *des Sciences de Gestion/MSG* (in Business Sciences), *d'Informatique Appliquée à Gestion/MIAG* (in Computer Science Applied to Business): two-year second cycle programs; require credential **J** (or other first cycle credential) for admission[1]

U *Magistère* (Master): first awarded in 1988; three-year second-cycle program; requires credential **J** (or other first cycle credential) for admission[1]

V *Certificat d'Aptitude au Professorat de l'Enseignement Secondaire/CAPES* (Certificate of Qualification of Secondary School Teacher), *Certificat d'Aptitude au Professorat de l'Enseignement Technique/CAPET* (Certificate of Qualification of Technical Secondary Teacher): one year of academic work plus one year of teaching practice; admission based on credential **O** in teaching

W *Diplôme d'Ingénieur* (Diploma of Engineer): usually a three-year program based on credential **I, J,** or **M**

X *Diplôme d'Etat de Docteur en Chirurgie Dentaire* (State Diploma of Doctor of Dental Surgery): five-year program in dentistry

Y *Diplôme d'Etat de Docteur Veterinaire* (State Diploma of Veterinary Doctor): five-year program in veterinary medicine

Z *Diplôme d'Etat de Docteur en Pharmacie* (State Diploma of Doctor of Pharmacy): six-year program in pharmacy, formerly five years

a *Diplôme d'Etudes Supérieures Spécialisées/DESS* (Diploma of Higher Specialized Studies): one-year third cycle program requiring credential **S, T,** or **U** for admission; students enrolled in the last year of a credential **W** program may also be eligible for admission; a terminal, professionally oriented program[1]

b *Diplôme d'Etudes Approfondies/DEA* (Diploma of Advanced Studies): one-year, third cycle program requiring credential **S, T,** or **U** for admission; students enrolled in the last year of a credential **W** program may also be eligible for admission[1]

c *Doctorat* (Doctorate): three to five years of third cycle study beyond credential **S, T,** or **U**; credential **b** constitutes the first year of this program[1]

d   *Diplôme de l'Etat de Docteur en Medecine* (State Diploma of Doctor of Medicine): eight- to eleven-year program in medicine

[1]   University education is organized according to three consecutive cycles: the first cycle requires two years of university study beyond a baccalaureate (credential **C** or equivalent); the second cycle consists of an additional two or three years of study beyond the first cycle; and the third cycle consists of three to five years of further study beyond the second cycle.

GRADING INFORMATION

Secondary and Postsecondary

Numeric	Description	Translation
16 - 20	*Très Bien*	Very Good
14 - 15	*Bien*	Good
12 - 13	*Assez Bien*	Good Enough
10 - 11	*Passable*	Pass
Below 10	*Ajourné*	Fail

- Students must have an overall average (*moyenne generale*) of 10 or above to pass a complete academic year. Grades of 8 or 9, and sometimes lower, for individual courses may be considered satisfactory, as long as the overall average for the year is at least 10.

POSTSECONDARY INSTITUTION RECOGNITION BODY

Ministère de l'Education Nationale, de la Recherche et de la Technologie. 110, rue de Grenelle, 75357 Paris Cedex 07 SP. Tel: 01.55.55.10.10. Fax: 01.45.51.53.63. www.education.gouv.fr

Other ministries are responsible for recognition of some specialized institutions.

RESOURCES FOR ADDITIONAL INFORMATION

Assefa, A. Mariam. 1988. *France: A Study of the Educational System of France and a Guide to the Academic Placement of Students in Educational Institutions in the United States.* Washington D.C.: AACRAO.

L'Etudiant. 1998. *1998 ANES, L'Annuaire National de l'Enseignement Supérieur.* Paris: Groupe l'Etudiant.

Internet Source:
UNESCO - World Academic Database: www.unesco.org/iau/educfr.html

---

Compiler
Sherly M. Réjouis
International Education Consultant
Josef Silny & Associates, Inc., International Education Consultants, Coral Gables, FL

GABON

YEARS OF EDUCATION →

```
      ½   ½   ½   ½   ½   ½   ½   ½   ½   ½   ½   ½   ½   ½   ½   ½   ½
1→6|  7 | 8 | 9 | 10 | 11 | 12 | 13 | 14 | 15 | 16 | 17 | 18 | 19 | 20 | 21 | 22 | 23 | 24 |
               A              B       F   H   K   L   N   Q
                              C       G   I       M   O
                              D           J           P
                              E
```

CREDENTIALS OR DOCUMENTATION

Secondary

A   *Brevet d'Études du Premier Cycle/BEPC* (Certificate of First Cycle Studies)
B   *Baccalauréat* (Baccalaureate): leads to postsecondary education
C   *Instituteur Principal* (Principal Teacher)
D   *Baccalauréat Technique* (Technical Baccalaureate): leads to postsecondary education
E   *Certificat de Fin d'Études Secondaires* (Certificate of End of Secondary Studies); for those who complete secondary school but do not qualify for credential **B** or **D**

Postsecondary

F   *Diplôme Universitaire* (University Diploma)[1]: requires credential **B** for admission
G   *Capacité en Droit* (Capacity in Law); credential **B** or **D** is not required for admission
H   *Licence* (Licentiate)
I   *Certificate d'Aptitude Pédagogique pour les Collèges d'Enseignement Général/CAP/CEG* (Certificate of Pedagogic Aptitude for Lower Secondary Schools)
J   *Brevet de Technicien Supérieur/BTS* (Certificate of Higher Technician): requires credential **B** or **D** for admission
K   *Maîtrise* (Master)
L   *Diplôme d'Ingénieur* (Diploma of Engineer), *Ingénieur Informaticien* (Computer Technician Engineer), *Géographe Amenagiste* (Geographer Planner)
M   *Certificat d'Aptitude au Professorat de l'Enseignement Secondaire/CAPES* (Certificate of Aptitude in Secondary Teaching)
N   *Diplôme d'Administration de l'Economie et des Finances* (Diploma of Administration, Economics, and Finance): requires credential **K** for admission
O   *Diplôme d'Administrateur Civil* (Diploma of Civil Administrator)
P   *Doctorat d'État en Médecine* (State Doctorat in Medicine)
Q   *Doctorat* (Doctorate)

[1]   *Diplôme Universitaire d'Études Littéraires/DUEL* (University Diploma of Literary Studies), *Diplôme Universitaire d'Études Scientifiques/DUES* (University Diploma of Scientific Studies), *Diplôme Universitaire d'Études Juridiques/DUEJ* (University Diploma of Legal Studies), *Diplôme Universitaire d'Études Economiques/DUEE* (University Diploma of Economic Studies), *Diplôme d'Études Universitaires Générales/DEUG* (Diploma of General University Studies)

GRADING INFORMATION

Secondary and Postsecondary Education

Numeric	Description	Translation
16 - 20	Très Bien	Very Good
14 - 15	Bien	Good
12 - 13	Assez Bien	Good Enough
10 - 11	Passable	Pass
0 - 9	Ajourné	Fail

- A minimum overall grade of 10 is required to pass; however, individual subjects may be passed with grades lower than 10.

POSTSECONDARY INSTITUTION RECOGNITION BODY

Ministère de l'Enseignement Supérieur et de la Recherche Scientifique; BP 2217; Libreville; Gabon.

RESOURCES FOR ADDITIONAL INFORMATION

Mboungou-Mayengúe, D., ed. 1988. *Directory of African Universities*. 5th ed. Association of African Universities.

Internet Source:
UNESCO-World Academic Database: www.unesco.org/iau/educga.html

---

Compiler
Margaret L. Wenger
Senior Evaluator
Educational Credential Evaluators, Inc., Milwaukee, WI

GEORGIA

YEARS OF EDUCATION →

```
        ½   ½   ½   ½   ½   ½   ½   ½   ½   ½   ½   ½   ½   ½   ½   ½   ½
1 → 6│ 7 │ 8 │ 9 │ 10│ 11│ 12│ 13│ 14│ 15│ 16│ 17│ 18│ 19│ 20│ 21│ 22│ 23│ 24│
        A       B   C   C       E   E   E   F   F   H   H   H   I→
                C   D   D               F               I→  I→
                                        G
```

CREDENTIALS OR DOCUMENTATION

Secondary

A   არასრული საშუალო განათლების მოწმობა [*Arasruli sashualo ganatlebis motsmoba*] (Certificate of Basic Secondary Education): awarded by a ზოგადსაგანმანათლებლო სკოლა [*Zogadsaganmanatleblo skola*] (General Education School); signifies completion of compulsory education

B   საშუალო განათლების ატესტატი [*Sashualo ganatlebis atestati*] (Certificate of Completion, General Secondary Education): awarded by a საშუალო სკოლა [*Sashualo skola*] (General Education School), გიმნაზია [*Gimnasia*] (Gymnasium), ლიცეი [*Licei*] (Lycée); two years requiring credential **A** for admission; signifies completion of general secondary education

C   პროფესულ-ტექნიკური სასწავლებლის დიპლომი [*Prophesiul-tekhnikuri sastsavleblis diplomi*] (Diploma of Occupational Technical School): awarded by a პროეფესიულ-ტექნიკური სასწავლებლი [*Prophesiul-tekhnikuri sastsavlebli*] (Occupational Technical School); a) two to four years requiring credential **A** for admission (two year program does not signify completion of secondary education, three to four year program signifies completion of general secondary education and beginning occupational education); b) one to two years requiring credential **B** for admission

Postsecondary

D   დიპლომი [*Diplomi*] (Diploma): awarded by a ტექნიკუმი [*Tekhnikumi*] (Institution of Intermediate Occupational Education); a) two to three years requiring credential **B** for admission and b) three to four years (signifies completion of combined general secondary and intermediate occupational education) requiring credential **A** for admission

E   ბაკალავრის დიპლომი [*Bakalavris diplomi*] (Bachelor's Diploma): awarded by a უნივერსიტეტი [*Universiteti*] (University): four years requiring credential **B** or **D** for admission

F   დიპლომი [*Diplomi*] (Diploma): awarded by an ინსტიტუტი [*Instituti*] (Institute); six years requiring credential **B** or **D** for admission; offered in the fields of Medicine, Law, and Veterinary Medicine

G   მაგისტრის დიპლომი [*Magistris diplomi*] (Master's Diploma): awarded by a უნივერსიტეტი [*Universiteti*] (University): two years requiring credential **E** for admission

H მეცნიერებათა კანდიდატის დიპლომი [*Metsnierebata kandidatis diplomi*] (Candidate of Sciences Diploma) awarded through the სადისერტაწიო საბჭო [*Sadisertatsio sabtsho*] (Dissertation Board); three years requiring credential **F** or **G** for admission

I მეცნიერებათა დოქტორის დიპლომი [*Metsnierebata doctoris diplomi*] (Doctor of Sciences Diploma) awarded through the სადისერტაციო საბჭო [*Sadisertatsio Sabtsho*] (Dissertation Board); requires credential **H** for admission; signifies completion of advanced scholarly research

GRADING INFORMATION

Secondary Education

Numeric	Description	Translation
5	ფრიადი [*Priadi*]	Excellent
4	კარგი [*Kargi*]	Good
3	დამაკმაყოფილებელი [*Damakmakopilebeli*]	Satisfactory
2	არადამაკმაყოფილებელი [*Aradamakmakopilebeli*]	Unsatisfactory

Higher Education

Numeric	Description	Translation
5	ფრიადი [*Priadi*]	Excellent
4	კარგი [*Kargi*]	Good
3	დამაკმაყოფილებელი [*Damakmakopilebeli*]	Satisfactory
2	არადამაკმაყოფილებელი [*Aradamakmakopilebeli*]	Unsatisfactory
–	ჩათვლა [*Chatvla*]	Complete
–	არჩათვლა [*Archatvla*]	Incomplete

- The grade of 2 is not passing.
- The grade of ჩათვლა [*chatvla*] (complete) is passing for all courses requiring more than one semester of study (the final grade obtained in the sequence retroactively applies to previous parts of the course), for all elective courses, and for laboratory and practical courses.

POSTSECONDARY INSTITUTION RECOGNITION BODY

Ministry of Education, Republic of Georgia, 52 Uznadze Street, City of Tbilisi 380002, Republic of Georgia. Tel: 995-32-957010. Fax: 995-32-770073.

Board of Academic Experts, Republic of Georgia, 52 Rustaveli Avenue, City of Tbilisi 380008, Republic of Georgia. Tel: 995-32-999-422. Fax: 995-32-999-604.

RESOURCES FOR ADDITIONAL INFORMATION

Georgian Education Act. 1997. Tbilisi, Georgia.

Compilers
Alexandr Didebulidze
ENIC Georgia, Commission for UNESCO
Georgian Ministry of Foreign Affairs

Yuri Akimov
Head of the Department of Accreditation and Recognition of Foreign Credentials
Ministry of General and Professional Education, Russian Federation

Edward Golovatch
Geoffrey Carlson
Department of Eastern Europe and the former Soviet Union
Globe Language Services, Inc. , New York, NY

GERMANY

YEARS OF EDUCATION →

```
      ½    ½    ½    ½    ½    ½    ½    ½    ½    ½    ½    ½    ½    ½    ½
1→| 9 | 10 | 11 | 12 | 13 | 14 | 15 | 16 | 17 | 18 | 19 | 20 | 21 | 22 | 23 | 24

   A    B              G    C    F    J  M  K  P  Q  Q  Q  W  V  W  W
                            D         L  N  M  S  R  R  R     W     Y-
                            E            N  N  W  S  S  S
                            H                O     W  T  U
                            I                S        W  W
                                             W           X-
```

CREDENTIALS OR DOCUMENTATION

Secondary

Sekundar I (Secondary Level I: Lower Secondary) Credentials

A *Abschlußzeugnis* (Completion Certificate) from a *Hauptschule* (Main School)
B *Abschlußzeugnis* (Completion Certificate) from a *Realschule* (Middle School)

Sekundar II (Secondary Level II: Upper Secondary) Credentials

Terminal Vocational Credentials

C *Abschlußzeugnis* (Completion Certificate) from a vocational program at a *Berufsschule* (part-time vocational school in the "dual system") or other type of secondary vocational school
D *Prüfungszeugnis* (Examination Certificate): from an *Industrie- und Handelskammer* (Chamber of Industry and Commerce), *Handwerkerkammer* (Chamber of Skilled Trades), or other occupational regulation body; the examination certifies completion of the practical component of the "dual system" of vocational education; not an academic credential
E *Abschlußzeugnis* (Completion Certificate) and *Berufsbezeichnung* (Occupational Title) in an allied health (nursing, physical therapy, occupational therapy, etc.) or paraprofessional teaching occupation (athletic coach, gymnastics instructor, music lesson teacher, etc.)
F Title of *Staatlich Geprüfte/r* .... (State-Examined...): not an academic credential

Higher Education Admission Credentials

G *Abschlußzeugnis* (Completion Certificate) and *Fachhochschulreife* (Technical College Maturity) from a *Fachoberschule* (upper secondary specialty school): gives access to *Fachhochschule* (technical college)
H *Zeugnis der Allgemeinen Hochschulreife* (Certificate of General University Maturity): from a *Gymnasium* (university-prep secondary school), *Gymnasiale Oberstufe* (university-prep upper level); represents completion of *Abitur* examination and gives access to higher education in any field of study[1]

I   *Zeugnis der Fachgebundenen Hochschulreife* (Certificate of Subject-Restricted University Maturity): from a *Berufsgymnasium* (vocational university-prep secondary school), *Fachgymnasium* (specialty university-prep secondary school); represents completion of *Abitur* examination and gives access to higher education in specific fields of study[1]

Postsecondary

J   *Erzieher (BA)* [Educator], *Ingenieur-Assistent (BA)* [Engineer-Assistant], or *Wirtschaftsassistent (BA)* [Business Assistant] from a *Berufsakademie (BA)* (vocational academy): two calendar years[2]

K   *Diplom-Betriebswirt (BA)* [Graduate Business Administrator], *Diplom-Ingenieur (BA)* [Graduate Engineer], or *Diplom-Sozialpädagoge (BA)* [Graduate Social Pedagogist] from a *Berufsakademie (BA)* (vocational academy): three calendar years[2]

L   Credentials from various business and administration schools with the designation *Akademie* in states other than Baden-Württemberg, Berlin, Niedersachsen and Sachsen, and other private institutions supervised by business and industry; these are not academic credentials

M   *Diplom-FH* (Diploma from a *Fachhochschule* [technical college]): admission requires credential **G**; programs are seven to eight semesters long and include one or two semesters of practical training

N   Bachelor's degree from a *Fachhochschule* (technical college): admission requires credential **G**; six to eight semesters

O   Bachelor's degree from an *Universität* (university): admission requires credential **H**; six semesters

P   *Erste Juristische Staatsprüfung* (First Juridical State Examination): professional degree in law; admission requires credential **H**; seven semesters

Q   *Diplom* (Diploma), *Staatsexamen* (State Examination), *Magister Artium* (Master of Arts) or *Kirchliche Prüfung* (Ecclesiastical Examination) from an *Universität* (university), *Technische Universität/ Hochschule* (technical university) or university-level program at a *Gesamt-hochschule* (comprehensive university) or specialized *Hochschule* (non-university higher education institution); admission requires credential **H**; eight to ten semesters

R   Master's degree from an *Universität* (university): admission requires credential **H** for programs of eight to ten semesters; admission to post-bachelor's programs are four semesters long

S   *Erste Staatsprüfung für das Lehramt an .....* (First State Examination for Teaching at.... [type of school]): from an *Universität* (university) or *Pädagogische Hochschule* (pedagogical higher education institution); admission requires credential **H**; length of program varies from six to ten semesters depending on teaching level and *Land* (State)

T   *Zeugnis über die Pharmazeutische Prüfung* (Certificate of the Pharmaceutical Examination): professional degree in pharmacy; admission requires credential **H**; four and one-half years

U   *Zeugnis über die Zahnärztliche Prüfung* (Certificate of the Dental Examination): professional degree in dentistry; admission requires credential **H**; five years

V   *Zeugnis über die Ärztliche Prüfung* (Certificate of the Medical Examination): professional degree in medicine; admission requires credential **H**; six years

W   *Zertifikat* or *Zeugnis* (Certificate): confirming completion of *Aufbaustudien*, *Ergänzungsstudien*, or *Zusatzstudien* (Supplementary or Extended Studies); two to four semesters beyond any credential **M** through **V**

X *Promotionsurkunde* (Doctoral Certificate) or diploma of *Doktor der ... wissenschaften* (Doctor of ... Sciences): research degree based on dissertation and examination

Y *Habilitation* (Habilitation): required for professorship; based on scholarly publication

[1] The *Abitur* examination is given after year 13 in all of the German states except Sachsen and Mecklenburg-Vorpommern. The *Abitur* will be given after year 13 for the first time in 2002 in Mecklenburg-Vorpommern. In the state of Thüringen, the *Abitur* is given in the *Gymnasiale Oberstufe* after year 13 and in the *Gymnasium* after year 12. In addition, some states have special "condensed" programs in which the eight-year *Gymnasium* curriculum is covered in seven years and the *Abitur* examination is given after year 12.

[2] The *Berufsakademie (BA)* (Vocational Academy) in the states of Baden-Württemberg, Berlin and Niedersachsen and the *Studienkolleg* (Study College) in Sachsen are supervised by the state's education ministry in cooperation with business and industry. Admission requires the *Abitur* (credential H or I). Programs run year-round and consist of alternating blocks (10-14 weeks) of classroom instruction and practical training. The *Diplom (BA)* is legally equivalent to the *Diplom FH* (credential M) in these states. Some universities in these states may grant limited exemptions from their *Vordiplom* requirements to holders of a *Diplom BA* in the same field of study. The state of Thüringen is planning to institute *Berufsakademien* beginning in 1999.

GRADING INFORMATION

All Levels *Abitur* (credential **H**)

Numeric	Grades	Description	Translation	Interpretation in Germany (Führ 1996)
1	15, 14, 13	*Sehr Gut*	Very Good	Expectations exceeded
2	12, 11, 10	*Gut*	Good	Expectations fully met
3	9, 8, 7	*Befriedigend*	Satisfactory	Expectations met
4	6, 5, 4	*Ausreichend*	Sufficient	Expectations barely met
5	3, 2, 1	*Mangelhaft*	Deficient	Expectations not met but some basis for improvement
6	0	*Ungenügend*	Insufficient	Expectations not met and no basis for improvement

- The grade of *ausreichend* is poor, but passing. *Mangelhaft* and *ungenügend* are considered failing grades in individual subjects but the student is promoted or passed if the aggregate grade is passing.

- Many higher education institutions use gradations of or variations on the 1 to 6 numeric scale.

POSTSECONDARY INSTITUTION RECOGNITION BODY

Education and institutional recognition are regulated by state (*Land*) in the Federal Republic of Germany. Each *Land* has its own ministry of education: Baden-Württemberg, Bayern, Berlin, Brandenburg, Bremen, Hamburg, Hessen, Mecklenburg-Vorpommern, Niedersachsen, Nordrhein-Westfalen, Rheinland-Pfalz, Saarland, Sachsen, Sachsen-Anhalt, Schleswig-Holstein, Thüringen. Contact information for the ministries can be found on the Internet at *Ministerien für Wissenschaft in der BRD* (Ministries of Science in the FRG): wwwwbs.cs.tu-berlin.de/~schwartz/wiku.html.

RESOURCES FOR ADDITIONAL INFORMATION

Bildung und Wissenschaft (Education and Science). Periodical published by Inter Nationes, Bonn, Germany. Subscription available in English or German at no charge. www.inter-nationes.de

DAAD (Deutscher Akademischer Austauschdienst)/German Academic Exchange Service. *Studium in Deutschland/Study in Germany.* Series of information booklets in English and German on studies at universities, *Fachhochschulen,* and art and music schools. Kennedyallee 50, 53175 Bonn, Germany, Tel. +228-882-0, Fax +228-882-444. E-mail: postmaster@daad.de

Führ, Christoph. 1997. *The German Education System since 1945.* Bonn, Germany: Inter Nationes. (Available in German as *Deutsches Bildungswesen seit 1945.*)

Markert, Axel. 1998. "Berufsakademien: Neither here nor there?" *World Education News and Reviews* 11, 5:10-12.

National Office of Overseas Skills Recognition. 1992. *Country Education Profiles: Germany.* Canberra: Australian Government Publishing Service.

Porter, Georgeanne B. 1986. *Federal Republic of Germany: A Study of the Educational System of the Federal Republic of Germany and a Guide to the Academic Placement of Students in Educational Institutions in the United States.* Washington D.C.: AACRAO.

Internet Sources:
Berufsakademie: www.ba-bw.de
Deutsche Hochschulen (German Higher Education Institutions):
    goethe.ira.uka.de/people/felix/DeutscheHochschulen.html
German Academic Exchange Service (DAAD): www.daad.de.
Governments on the WWW, Germany: www.gksoft.com/govt/en/de.html
UNESCO-World Academic Database: www.unesco.org/iau/educde.html

---

Compiler
Ann M. Koenig
International Admission Specialist
University of California, Berkeley

GHANA

YEARS OF EDUCATION →

	½	½	½	½	½	½	½	½	½	½	½	½	½	½	½	½	½
1→6	7	8	9	10	11	12	13	14	15	16	17	18	19	20	21	22	23	24
		A	B	C	D F G H	E F G H	G H I J	G H I J K	K L	M N O P	O P Q	R S T	T→				

CREDENTIALS OR DOCUMENTATION

Secondary

A Basic Education Certificate Examination/BECE: since 1990
B Middle School Leaving Certificate/MLSC: until 1989
C West African School Certificate, General Certificate of Education-Ordinary Level/WASC,GCE-O: until 1994 for regular students and 2000 for remedial students
D Senior Secondary Certificate Examination/SSCE: since 1993; represents three years of study requiring credential **A** for admission
E Higher School Certificate, General Certificate of Education-Advanced Level/HSC,GCE-A: until 1996 for regular students and 2000 for remedial students; represents two years of study requiring credential **C** for admission

Postsecondary

F Certificates in a variety of fields awarded by universities: represents completion of one year of study requiring credential **C** or **D** for admission
G Certificates and diplomas in a variety of fields awarded by non-university postsecondary institutions: represent two or three years of study requiring credential **C** or **D** for admission
H Diplomas in a variety of fields awarded by universities: represents completion of two or three years of study requiring credential **C** or **D** for admission
I Postsecondary Teacher's Certificate A: represents three years of study requiring credential **C** or **D** for admission
J State Registered Nurse: represents three years of study requiring credential **C** or **D** for admission
K Higher National Diploma awarded by polytechnics: represents three years of study requiring credential **D** or **E** for admission
L Bachelor of Arts, Bachelor of Commerce, Bachelor of Education, Bachelor of Laws, Bachelor of Music, Bachelor of Pharmacy, Bachelor of Science: represents three years of study beyond credential **E** or four years of study beyond credential **D**
M Bachelor of Science in Engineering awarded by the University of Science and Technology: represents four years of study requiring credential **E** for admission
N Postgraduate Certificate in Education: represents completion of one year of study requiring credential **L** for admission

O Postgraduate diploma in a variety of fields awarded by universities: represents one or two years of study requiring credential **L** for admission

P Master of Arts, Master of Business Administration, Master of Laws, Master of Pharmacy, Master of Public Administration, Master of Science, Master of Social Science: represents one or two years of study requiring credential **L** for admission

Q Master of Philosophy: represents two or one year of study requiring credential **L** or **P** for admission

R Bachelor of Dental Surgery: represents six years of study beyond credential **E** or seven years of study beyond credential **D**

S Bachelor of Medicine and Bachelor of Surgery: represents six years of study beyond credential **E** or seven years of study beyond credential **D**; may also represent three years of study requiring credential **L** in Human Biology for admission

T Doctor of Philosophy: represents two or three years of study requiring credential **P** for admission

GRADING INFORMATION

Secondary

Senior Secondary Certificate Examination:

Letter	Points	Description
A	1	Passing
B	2	Passing
C	3	Passing
D	4	Passing
E	5	Passing
F	6	Failing

West African School Certificate/General Certificate of Education-Ordinary Level:

Numeric	Description
Grade 1	Excellent
Grade 2	Very Good
Grade 3	Good
Grade 4	Credit
Grade 5	Credit
Grade 6	Credit
Grade 7	Pass
Grade 8	Pass
Grade 9	Fail

Higher School Certificate, General Certificate of Education-Advanced Level:

Letter	Description
A	Excellent
B	Very Good
C	Good
D	Credit
E	Pass

Postsecondary

Universities normally note grading scale on transcripts.

POSTSECONDARY INSTITUTION RECOGNITION BODY

National Accreditation Board, Ministry of Education, POB M.28, Accra.
Tel: 233-21-665421.

RESOURCES FOR ADDITIONAL INFORMATION

The British Council. 1996. *International Guide to Qualifications in Education.* 4th ed.
London: Mansell.

Dwomoh, A. 1995. "Ghana." *International Encyclopedia of National Systems of Education.* 2nd ed. Postlethwaite, T. Neville, ed. Tarrytown, New York: Elsevier Science, Inc.

Mboungou-Mayengúe, D., ed. 1988. *Directory of African Universities.* 5th ed. Association of African Universities.

Internet Source:
UNESCO-World Academic Database: www.unesco.org/iau/eductd.html

---

Compilers
Vincent Schaff
Montclair State College, Upper Montclair, NJ

Margit A. Schatzman
Vice President
Educational Credential Evaluators, Inc., Milwaukee, WI

GREECE

YEARS OF EDUCATION →

	½	½	½	½	½	½	½	½	½	½	½	½	½	½	½	½	½
1 → 6	7	8	9	10	11	12	13	14	15	16	17	18	19	20	21	22	23	24	25

```
             A                      B                 C   E   F   H   I   I   I
                                                      D   G   G   J→  J→  J→
                                                              H
```

CREDENTIALS OR DOCUMENTATION

Secondary

A Απολυτηριο [*Apolyterio*] (Certificate of Completion) awarded by a Γυμνασιον [gymnasium] (lower secondary school): signifies completion of compulsory education

B Απολυτηριο [*Apolyterio*] (Certificate of Completion) awarded by a Λυκειο [*lyceum*] (upper secondary school)[1, 2]

Postsecondary

C Πτυχιο [*Ptychio*] (Diploma) of technical education awarded by Technological Educational Institutions/TEI[3]

D Πτυχιο [*Ptychio*] (Diploma) in the fields of Arts, Business, Communication & Mass Media, Economics, Education,[4] Humanities, Law, Management, Mathematics, Nursing,[5] Philosophy, Political Sciences, Sciences, Social Sciences, and Theology

E Πτυχιο [*Ptychio*] (Diploma) in the fields of Agriculture & Forestry, Architecture, Dentistry, Engineering, Pharmacy, and Veterinary Medicine

F Πτυχιο [*Ptychio*] (Diploma) in the field of Medicine

G Πτυχιο Μεταρτυχιακο [*Ptychio Metaptychiako*] (Diploma of Graduate Studies): one to two years requiring credential **D** for admission in the fields of Business, Communication & Mass Media, Economics, Humanities, Law, Management, Mathematics, Philosophy, Political Sciences, Sciences, Social Sciences, and Theology

H Πτυχιο Μεταρτυχιακο [*Ptychio Metaptychiako*] (Diploma of Graduate Studies) one to two years requiring credential **E** for admission in the fields of Agriculture & Forestry, Architecture, Dentistry, Engineering, Pharmacy, and Veterinary Medicine

I Διδακτορικο [*Didaktoriko*] (Doctorate): usually four or five years requiring credential **D** or **E** for admission

J Διδακτορικο [*Didaktoriko*] (Doctorate): usually two years or more requiring credential **G** or **H** for admission

[1] Lycea are divided into four types: general, classical, comprehensive, and technical/vocational. The general, classical, and comprehensive lead to university entrance. The technical/vocational may lead to entrance into a TEI.

[2] Panhellenic exams are taken nation-wide at the end of the third year of the lyceum, and are the means for admission into universities. After 1998, the Panhellenic exams, plus the grades at the lycea, will be used for university admission. Panhellenic exams are not required for admission to the TEIs.

[3] In 1983, the Technological Educational Institutions/TEI replaced the former Centers for Higher Technical and Professional Studies (KATEE). The programs are generally three and one-half years, plus one semester of practical training.

[4] Prior to 1986, pre-primary, primary, and physical education teachers were educated in specialized colleges. Since then, a university department offers this education.

[5] Nursing programs are offered by university departments and departments of health and caring of TEIs.

GRADING INFORMATION

Secondary

Numeric	Greek (upper and lower case)		Description
18.50-20	ΑΡΙΣΤΑ	αριστα	Excellent
15.5-18.4	ΛΙΑΝ ΚΑΛΩΣ	λιαν καλωs	Very Good
12.5-15.4	ΚΑΛΩΣ	καλωs	Good
10.0-12.4	ΕΠΙΤΥΧΗΣ	επιτυχηs	Pass
0.0-9.9	ΑΝΕΠΙΤΥΧΗΣ	ανεπιτυχηs	Fail

- Grades in the pass range are acceptable for graduation.

Postsecondary

Numeric	Greek (upper and lower case)		Description
8.5-10	ΑΡΙΣΤΑ	αριστα	Excellent
7.0-8.4	ΛΙΑΝ ΚΑΛΩΣ	λιαν καλωs	Very Good
5.0-6.9	ΚΑΛΩΣ	καλωs	Good
Below 5	ΑΝΕΠΙΤΥΧΗΣ	ανεπιτυχηs	Fail

- 5 is the lowest passing grade and acceptable for graduation.

- Most students receive grades of 5 or 6, and, to a lesser extent, 7. Grades of 10-8 are rarely awarded.

POSTSECONDARY INSTITUTION RECOGNITION BODY

Ministry of Education and Religious Affairs, Division of Higher Education. Mitropoleos 15, Athens 10185. Tel: +30(1) 323-1956 or 323-5200. Fax: +30(1) 322-0767 or 322-1521. www.ypepth.gr/

Although the TEIs fall under the Ministry of Education and Religious Affairs, other ministries are responsible for recognition, in the case of some specialized institutions.

RESOURCES FOR ADDITIONAL INFORMATION

Oliver, E. Eugene. 1982. *A Study of the Educational Systems of Greece and a Guide to the Academic Placement of Students from Greece in Educational Institutions in the United States.* Washington, D.C.: AACRAO.

Internet Sources:
EURYDICE Eurybase-Greece: www.eurydice.org/
The Hellenic Pedagogical Institute: www.pi-schools.gr
Technological Educational Institutions: www.teiath.gr/
UNESCO-World Academic Database: www.unesco.org/iau/edugr.html

---

Compiler
Adria L. Baker
Director, International Students and Scholars
Rice University, Houston, TX

GUATEMALA

YEARS OF EDUCATION →

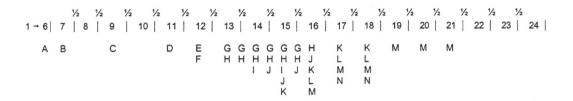

CREDENTIALS OR DOCUMENTATION

Secondary

A *Diploma* (Diploma): signifies completion of primary education
B *Auxiliar de Enfermería* (Nursing Aide)
C *Diploma* (Diploma): signifies completion of lower secondary education
D *Bachiller en Ciencias y Letras* (Bachelor in Science and Letters): signifies completion of academic upper secondary education
E *Perito en __* (Expert in __); *Secretario* en __ (Secretary in __): signifies completion of upper secondary vocational or technical studies
F *Maestro en Educación Preprimaria* (Teacher of Pre-primary Education); *Maestro de Educación Primaria Urbana* (Teacher of Urban Primary Education)

Postsecondary

G Title of *Técnico* (Technician): two- to three and one-half-year programs; admission based on credential **D**, **E**, or **F**
H Title of *Profesor* (Teacher): two- to four-year programs; admission based on credential **D**, **E**, or **F**
I Title of Enfermera (Nurse): three-year program; admission based on credential **D**, **E**, or **F**
J *Baccalaureatus* (Baccalaureate): three and one-half to four-year programs; admission based on credential **D**, **E**, or **F**
K Title of *Licenciado* (Licentiate): four- to six-year programs; admission based on credential **D**, **E**, or **F**
L Title of *Abogado* (Lawyer), *Arquitecto* (Architect), or *Ingeniero* (Engineer): five- to six-year programs; admission based on credential **D**, **E**, or **F**
M *Maestria, Magister* (Master): one to three years of study beyond credential **K**
N Title of *Cirujano Dentista* (Dental Surgeon) and *Médico y Cirujano* (Physician and Surgeon): six years of study; admission based on credential **D** or **E**

GRADING INFORMATION

Secondary
A percentage system is used, with 51% being the minimum pass in government schools, and 61% being the minimum pass in private schools.

Higher Education

Percentage	Description	Translation
91 - 100	*Excelente*	Excellent
81 - 90	*Muy Bueno*	Very Good
71 - 80	*Bueno*	Good
61 - 70	*Minimo Aceptable*	Barely Acceptable
0 - 60	*Reprobado*	Failed

Percentage	Description	Translation
80 - 100	*Excelente*	Excellent
70 - 79	*Muy Bueno*	Very Good
60 - 69	*Bueno*	Good
51 - 59	*Minimo Aceptable*	Barely Acceptable
0 - 50	*Reprobado*	Failed

POSTSECONDARY INSTITUTION RECOGNITION BODY

Ministerio de Educación, Despacho Palacio Nacional 3er Nivel, Guatemala C.A. Tel: 502 2 24202. Fax: 502 2 537386.

RESOURCES FOR ADDITIONAL INFORMATION

Aldrich-Langen, Caroline and Kathleen Sellew, eds. 1987. *The Admission and Placement of Students from Central America: Belize, Costa Rica, El Salvador, Guatemala, Honduras, Nicaragua, Panama.* Annapolis Junction, MD: PIER.

Marcus, Jane E. 1996. *Central America Update. Special Report 1996.* Annapolis Junction, MD: PIER.

National Office of Overseas Skills Recognition. 1993. *Country Education Profiles: Guatemala.* Canberra: Australian Government Publishing Service.

Internet Source:
UNESCO - World Academic Database: www.unesco.org/iau/educgt.html

---

Compiler
Marybeth Mirzejewski
Evaluator
Educational Credential Evaluators, Inc., Milwaukee, WI

HAITI

YEARS OF EDUCATION - TRADITIONAL SYSTEM →

```
         ½    ½    ½    ½    ½    ½    ½    ½    ½    ½    ½    ½    ½    ½    ½    ½
1 → 6 |  7  |  8  |  9  | 10  | 11  | 12  | 13  | 14  | 15  | 16  | 17  | 18  | 19  | 20  | 21  | 22  | 23  | 24  |

      A              B     C           D     F     J  K  L        O     P     Q     W     W     Y     Y     Y
                                       E     G                 M        P     Q     S     X     Y
                                       F                    N        Q     S     U
                                                                     R     T     V
                                                                     S     U     W
```

YEARS OF EDUCATION - REFORM SYSTEM →

```
         ½    ½    ½    ½    ½    ½    ½    ½    ½    ½    ½    ½    ½    ½    ½    ½
1 → 6 |  7  |  8  |  9  | 10  | 11  | 12  | 13  | 14  | 15  | 16  | 17  | 18  | 19  | 20  | 21  | 22  | 23  | 24  |

      A              H                 I           K  J     N     P     Q     W     W     Y     Y     Y
                                              L        O     Q     S     X     Y
                                              M        P     R     U
                                                       Q     S     V
                                                       S     T     W
                                                             U
```

CREDENTIALS OR DOCUMENTATION

Primary and Secondary - Traditional

A *Certificat d'Etudes Primaires/CAP* (Certificate of Primary Studies)

B Brevet Elementaire du Premier Cycle (Elementary Certificate of the First Cycle): three years of study beyond credential **A**

C *Brevet d'Aptitude Professional/BAP* (Certificate of Professional Aptitude): usually four years of vocational study beyond credential **A**; awarded in commercial training, accounting, and hotel management

D *Brevet Supérieur* (Advanced Certificate), or *Diplôme de Technicien* (Diploma of Technician): two years of vocational study beyond credential **C**

E *Baccalaureat I - Rhétorique* (Baccalaureate I - Rhetoric): three years of study beyond credential **B**

F *Diplome de Fin d'Etudes Normales* (Normal School Completion Diploma): three years of primary school teacher training beyond credential **B**, or one year beyond credential **E**

G *Baccalaureat II - Philosophie* (Baccalaureate II - Philosophy): one year of study beyond credential **E**; leads to postsecondary education

Secondary - Reform (partially implemented during the 1980s and 1990s):

H *Brevet d'Enseignement Fondamental* (Fundamental Instruction Certificate): three years of study beyond credential **A**

I *Baccalaureat* (Baccalaureate) awarded in either the classical, technical, or professional streams, and *Diplôme d'Enseignement Secondaire* (Diploma of Secondary Instruction) awarded by an *école normal* (normal school): three years of study beyond credential **H**; leads to postsecondary education

Postsecondary - Traditional/Reform

J *Certificat Professionnel* (Professional Certificate): two years of study requiring minimum of credential **E/I** for admission; leads to further university study

K *Diplôme de Technicien Laboratoire* (Diploma of Laboratory Technician): 15 months of study requiring credential **G/I** for admission

L *Diplôme de Technologie Médicale* (Diploma in Medical Technology): two years of study requiring credential **G/I** for admission

M *Diplôme en Sciences Comptables* (Diploma in Accounting Sciences): two years of study requiring credential **G/I** for admission

N *Diplôme d'Infirmière* (Diploma of Nurse): three years of study requiring minimum of credential **E/I** for admission

O *Certificat d'Aptitude au Professorat de l'Enseignement Secondaire/CAPES* (Certificate of Qualification of Secondary School Teacher): three years of study requiring credential **G/I** for admission; leads to further university study

P Diplôme *d'Ingénieur architecte* (Diploma of Engineer Architect): three- or four-year program requiring credential **G/I** for admission

Q *Diplôme de Fin d'Etudes* (Diploma of Completion of Studies): three to five years of study requiring credential **G/I** for admission

R *Certificat d'Infirmière Hygiéniste* (Nurse-Hygienist Certificate): one year of study requiring credential **N** for admission

S *Licence* (Licentiate): three- or four-year program in most fields; five-year program in accountancy; credential **G/I** required for admission, and leads to further university study

T *Diplôme de Pharmacien* (Diploma of Pharmacist): four years of study requiring credential **G/I** for admission

U *Diplôme d'Ingénieur* (Diploma of Engineer): four to five years of study requiring credential **G/I** for admission; leads to further university study

V *Diplôme de Chirurgien-Dentiste* (Diploma of Surgeon-Dentist): five years of study requiring credential **G/I** for admission

W *Maîtrise* (Master): two years of study requiring credential **Q** or **S** for admission

X *Diplôme de Docteur en Médecine* (Diploma of Doctor in Medicine): usually six years of medical study beyond credential **G/I**

Y *Doctorat d'Etat* (State Doctorate): two to three years of research and dissertation beyond credential **W**

GRADING INFORMATION

Secondary

Percentage	Description	Translation
70-100	*Très Bien*	Very Good
60-69	*Bien*	Good
50-59	*Passable*	Pass
0-49	*Mal*	Fail

Postsecondary

Percentage	Description	Translation
80-100	*Très Bien*	Very Good
70-79	*Bien*	Good
65-69	*Assez Bien*	Quite Good
61-64	*Passable*	Pass
50-60	*Mediocre*	Weak
30-49	*Mal*	Fail
0-29	*Nul*	Null

POSTSECONDARY INSTITUTION RECOGNITION BODY

Ministère de l'Education Nationale: 5, Rue Docteur Audain, Port-au-Prince.
Tel: 509-229731. Fax: 509-237887.

Other ministries are responsible for recognition of some specialized institutions.

RESOURCES FOR ADDITIONAL INFORMATION

Internet Source:
UNESCO - World Academic Database: www.unesco.org/iau/educht.html

---

Compiler
Sherly M. Réjouis
International Education Consultant
Josef Silny & Associates, Inc., International Education Consultants, Coral Gables, FL

HONDURAS

YEARS OF EDUCATION →

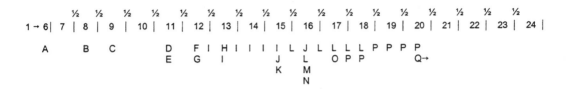

```
        ½   ½   ½   ½   ½   ½   ½   ½   ½   ½   ½   ½   ½   ½   ½   ½   ½
1 → 6|  7 | 8 | 9 | 10| 11| 12| 13| 14| 15| 16| 17| 18| 19| 20| 21| 22| 23| 24|

   A       B       C       D   F  I  H I  I  I  L  J  L  L  L  L  P  P  P  P
                           E   G     I        J     L     O  P  P        Q→
                                              K     M
                                                    N
```

CREDENTIALS OR DOCUMENTATION

Secondary

A *Certificado de Sexto Grado* (Certificate of Sixth Grade), or *Certificado Final de Estudios en Educación Primaria* (Final Certificate of Primary Education Studies): signifies completion of compulsory education

B *Auxiliar de Enfermera* (Nursing Aide) or *Enfermera Práctica* (Practical Nurse)

C *Certificado del Ciclo Común de Cultura General* (Certificate of the Common Cycle of General Education)

D *Bachiller en Ciencias y Letras* (Bachelor in Sciences and Letters): signifies completion of academic upper secondary education or the *Ciclo Diversificado* Diversified Cycle)

E *Bachiller en __* (Bachelor in __): programs offered in agriculture and business administration

F *Bachiller Técnico* (Technical Bachelor): signifies completion of technical upper secondary education

G *Maestro de Educación Primaria* (Teacher of Primary Education) or *Maestro de Educación Musical* (Teacher of Musical Education)

H *Técnico Medio* (Mid-Level Technician): four years of study beyond credential **C**

Postsecondary

I *Técnico* (Technician): one and one-half- to three-year university programs; may be terminal or may lead to further study in a technical field; admission based on credential **D** or **F**

J Title of *Profesorado* (Teacher): four-year program for secondary school teachers; admission based on credential **D**, **E**, or **G**

K *Bachiller Universitario* (University Bachelor): terminal four-year programs in agriculture, journalism, or nursing; admission based on credential **D** or **E**

L Title of *Licenciado* en __ (Licentiate in __): four and one-half- to six-year programs; admission based on credential **D**, **E**, or **G**

M Title of *Ingeniero* (Engineer) or *Arquitecto* (Architect): five-year programs; admission based on credential **D** or **E**

N Title of *Doctor en Cirugía Dental* (Doctor of Dental Surgery): five-year program beyond credential **D** or **E**

172

O   Title of *Doctor en Medicina y Cirugía* (Doctor of Medicine and Surgery): six-year program beyond credential **D** or **E**

P   *Maestría* (Master): two- or three-year program; admission based on credential **L**

Q   Diploma in *Especialidad* (Specialization): three or more years beyond credential **O**

GRADING INFORMATION

Secondary

Numerical	Description	Translation
91 - 100	*Sobresaliente*	Excellent
81 - 90	*Muy Bueno*	Very Good
61 - 80	*Bueno*	Good
41 - 60	*Aplazado*	Conditional Pass
0 - 40	*Insuficiente*	Fail

Higher Education

Numerical	Description	Translation
90 - 100	*Excelente*	Excellent
80 - 89	*Muy Bueno*	Very Good
60 - 79	*Bueno*	Good
30 - 59	*Aplazado*	Conditional Pass
0 - 29	*Insuficiente*	Fail

• The minimum pass for *Bachillerato Universitario* programs is 60; for *Licenciatura* programs it is 70; and for *Doctor* programs it is 80.

POSTSECONDARY INSTITUTION RECOGNITION BODY

Ministerio de Educación Pública, 1a Calle entre 2a y 4a Avenidas, Comayaguela, MDC. Tel: 504 227497. Fax: 504 222216.

RESOURCES FOR ADDITIONAL INFORMATION

Aldrich-Langen, Caroline and Kathleen Sellew, eds. 1987. *The Admission and Placement of Students from Central America: Belize, Costa Rica, El Salvador, Guatemala, Honduras, Nicaragua, Panama*. Annapolis Junction, MD: PIER.

Marcus, Jane E. 1996. *Central America Update.* Annapolis Junction, MD: PIER.

National Office of Overseas Skills Recognition. 1993. *Country Education Profiles: Honduras.* Canberra: Australian Government Publishing Service.

Internet Source:
UNESCO - World Academic Database. www.unesco.org/iau/educhn.html

---

Compiler
Marybeth Mirzejewski
Evaluator
Educational Credential Evaluators, Inc., Milwaukee, WI

HONG KONG

YEARS OF EDUCATION →

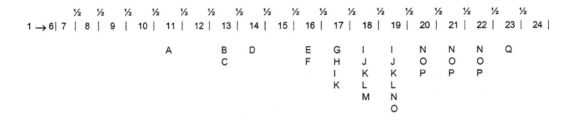

```
       ½   ½   ½   ½   ½   ½   ½   ½   ½   ½   ½   ½   ½   ½   ½   ½   ½
1 → 6| 7 | 8 | 9 | 10| 11| 12| 13| 14| 15| 16| 17| 18| 19| 20| 21| 22| 23| 24|
                A       B   D       E   G   I   I   N   N   N   Q
                        C           F   H   J   J   O   O   O
                                        I   K   K   P   P   P
                                        K   L   L
                                            M   N
                                                O
```

CREDENTIALS OR DOCUMENTATION

Secondary

A Hong Kong Certificate of Education Examination (HKCEE): awarded upon completion of six years of primary education plus five years of secondary education (Middle Five or Form V) to students who sit for the examination

B Hong Kong Advanced Supplementary Level Examination (HKASLE): students who have completed Upper Form VI are eligible to sit for these examinations

C Hong Kong Advanced Level Examination (HKALE): students who have completed Upper Form VI are eligible to sit for these examinations

Postsecondary

D Certificate in Education: one year of study beyond credential **B** or **C**

E Bachelor's degree in Arts & Sciences; Bachelor of Pharmacy; Bachelor of Education; Bachelor of Engineering; Bachelor of Laws: three years of study beyond credential **B** or **C**

F Bachelor's degree awarded by the Chinese University of Hong Kong: four years of study beyond Lower Form VI (Year 12)[1]

G Bachelor of Nursing: four years of study beyond credential **B** or **C**

H Master of Engineering: four years of study beyond credential **B** or **C**

I Postgraduate Certificate: one to two years of part-time study beyond credential **E, F,** or **G**

J Postgraduate Diploma: two years of part-time study beyond credential **E, F,** or **G**[2]

K Master's degree: one or two years of study beyond credential **E, F,** or **G**

L Master of Philosophy (MPhil): two years of study beyond credential **E, F,** or **G**

M Bachelor of Medicine and Bachelor of Surgery (MBChB): five years of study beyond credential **B** or **C**

N Doctor of Philosophy (Ph.D.): two to three years of study beyond credential **K**

O Doctor of Education (Ed.D.): two to three years of study beyond credential **K**

P   Doctor of Music: three years of study beyond credential **K**
Q   Doctor of Medicine (M.D.): five years of study beyond credential **M**

[1]   To comply with a government directive, the length of the Bachelor degree programs at the Chinese University of Hong Kong was reduced from four years to three years, admission is now based on credential **C**. This change was phased in beginning in the late 1980s.

GRADING INFORMATION

Secondary

- Hong Kong Certificate of Education Examination (HKCEE), and Hong Kong Advanced Level/Advanced Supplementary Level Examination: Six passing grades —**A** (highest) to **F** (Lowest)—are used. Failing grades are designated as **U** (unclassified).

Higher Education

- Grading scales and patterns vary by university, by faculty within a university, and by level of study.Transcripts issued by the universities provide grading scale information/legend.

- Most bachelor's degrees may be awarded with a classification that implies the quality of the student's records: First Class; Second Class, Upper; Second Class, Lower; and Third Class.

- Bachelor's degrees may be termed "honours" degrees. Honours, as compared to "ordinary" or "pass," usually refers to depth of study in a particular discipline, rather than quality of study.

POSTSECONDARY INSTITUTION RECOGNITION BODY

The Education Department. Wu Chung House, 213 Queen's Road East, Wanchari, Hong Kong. Tel: 852 2892-6192. Fax: 852 2575-7050.

RESOURCES FOR ADDITIONAL INFORMATION

National Office of Overseas Skills Recognition. 1995. *Country Education Profiles: Hong Kong.* 2nd ed. Canberra: Australian Government Publishing Service.

Saidi, Jasmin and Timothy Thompson. 1998. *The Educational System of Hong Kong.* Annapolis Junction, MD: PIER.

Internet Source:
UNESCO –World Academic Database: www.unesco.org/iau/educhk.html

Compiler
Jasmin Saidi
President
Academic Credentials Evaluation Institute, Inc., Beverly Hills, CA

HUNGARY

YEARS OF EDUCATION →

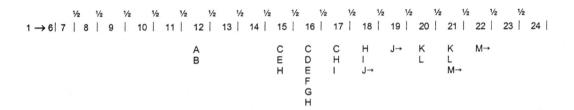

CREDENTIALS OR DOCUMENTATION

Secondary

A *Gimnáziumi Érettségi Bizonyítvány* (Secondary School Maturity Certificate), also known as *Matura*: awarded upon completion of academic secondary school; generally a four-year program following eight years of elementary and lower secondary education[1]

B *Szakközépiskolai Érettségi-Képesíto Bizonyítvány* (Technical Secondary School Maturity Certificate): awarded upon completion of technical/vocational school; generally a four-year program following eight years of elementary and lower secondary education[1]

Postsecondary

C *Oklevél* (Diploma) with professional title, such as *üzemmérnök* (production engineer): awarded by a *főiskola* (college), *akadémia* (academy), or *egyetem* (university); three- to five-year programs offered in allied health, commerce and economics, production engineering and technical fields, military and police education, political science, and state management; requires credential **A** or **B** for admission

D *Oklevél* (Diploma) awarded by a *főiskola* (college): four-year programs offered in the fields of crafts and design, drama and film, fine art, music, and physical education; requires credential **A** or **B** for admission

E *Óvónői Oklevél* (Kindergarten Teacher Diploma): three- and four-year programs offered by *óvónőképző intézetek/óvóda pedagógusi* (kindergarten teacher training colleges); requires credential **A** or **B** for admission

F *Tanítói Oklevél* (Lower Primary Teacher's Diploma): four-year program offered by a *tanitóképző főiskola/általános iskolai tanítói* (teacher training college); requires credential **A** or **B** for admission; prior to 1996, this was a three-year program

G *Tanári Oklevél* (Upper Primary Teacher's Diploma): four-year program offered by a *tanárképző főiskola/felső osztály* (teacher training college); requires credential **A** or **B** for admission

H Theological credentials: awarded by an *akadémia* (academy), *fóiskola* (college), or egyetem (university); four-, five-, and six-year programs for ministers, priests, and rabbis; three-year, non-professional programs also offered; credential **A** or **B** required for admission

I *Oklevél* (Diploma) awarded by an *egyetem* (university): most programs require five years of study, medicine requires six years of study; credential **A** or **B** required for admission

J *Egyetemi doktor* (University doctor), *müszaki doktor* (technical doctor): awarded by universities upon completion of variable length programs requiring examinations and thesis defense before a university panel; credential **I** required for admission; replaced by credential **L** after 1993

K *Kandidátus* (Candidate) awarded by the Committee of Scientific Qualifications: variable length programs, usually approximately three years, which include an in-depth knowledge of the chosen subject and a public defense of a thesis; credential **I** required for admission; replaced by credential **L** after 1993

L *Doktori Bizonyítvány* (Doctoral Certificate): awarded by an *egyetem* (university) after three years of coursework and thesis defense; credential **I** required for admission

M *Tudományok Doktorának Oklevele* (Doctor of Sciences) awarded by the Committee of Scientific Qualifications: requires extensive research and publication; credential **L** or equivalent required for admission

[1] With recent reforms some secondary programs begin after either grade 4 or grade 6, but most still follow the 8 + 4 pattern.

GRADING INFORMATION

All Levels of Education

Numeric	Description	Translation
5	*Jeles*	Excellent
4	*Jó*	Good
3	*Közepes*	Fair
2	*Elégséges*	Satisfactory
1	*Elégtelen*	Unsatisfactory

POSTSECONDARY INSTITUTION RECOGNITION BODY

Hungarian Accreditation Committee, H-1146 Budapest , Ajtósi Dürer sor 19-21. Tel: 36-1-251-2951, 36-1-344-0314. Fax: 36-1-344-0313.

RESOURCES FOR ADDITIONAL INFORMATION

Department of Scientific Affairs. 1997. *Research and Development in Hungarian Higher Education*. Budapest: Ministry of Education and Culture.

Dickey, Karlene N., and Desmond C. Bevis, eds. 1990. *The Admission and Placement of Students from the Republic of Hungary*. Annapolis Junction, MD: PIER.

Hungarian Center for Equivalence and International Mobility. 1996. *Hungarian Higher Education Qualifications*. Budapest: Ministry of Culture and Education.

National Institute of Public Education. 1997. "The Education System, Progress Within the System." *Education in Hungary*. Budapest: National Institute of Public Education. www.oki.hu/eduhun97/EduHunC.html

Internet Sources:
UNESCO World Academic Database: www.unesco.org/iau/educhu.html
OSEAS Europe-Hungarian Education: www.bibl.u-szeged.hu/oseas/HUED.html

---

Compilers
Cynthia J. Fish
CUNY Baruch College

Ildiko Ficzko
Educational Adviser, Jozsef Attila University
American Higher Education Information Center, Szeged, Hungary

ICELAND

YEARS OF EDUCATION →

```
        ½   ½   ½   ½   ½   ½   ½   ½   ½   ½   ½   ½   ½   ½   ½   ½   ½
1 → 6|  7 | 8 | 9 | 10| 11| 12| 13| 14| 15| 16| 17| 18| 19| 20| 21| 22| 23| 24|
            A               B           C   D   H   J
                                            E   I   K
                                            F   J   L-
                                            G
```

CREDENTIALS OR DOCUMENTATION

Secondary

A   Certificate confirming completion of *Grunnskoli* (Compulsory School)
B   *Stúdentspróf* (Matriculation Examination): represents four years of study requiring credential **A** for admission

Postsecondary

C   Bachelor's degrees/*Baccalaureatus Artium/Baccalaureatus Educationis/ Baccalaureatus Scientiarum*/Bachelor of Music/BA/BEd/BS/B.Mus.: represents three years of study requiring credential **B** for admission[1]

D   Bachelor's degrees/BS in Nursing, BS in Physiotherapy: represents four years of study requiring credential **B** for admission

E   Certificates in various fields (education, journalism and mass communication, school counseling, social work) awarded by the University of Iceland: represents one year of study requiring credential **C** for admission

F   Final Examination in Engineering: represents four years of study requiring credential **B** for admission

G   *Kandidatspróf/Cand. Œcon.* (business administration): represents four years of study requiring credential **B** for admission

H   *Kandidatspróf/Cand Juris* (law), *Cand. Pharm.* (pharmacy), *Cand. Theol.* (theology): represents five years of study requiring credential **B** for admission

I   *M.Paed.* in Icelandic and Education: represents two years of study requiring credential **C** for admission

J   *Meistarapróf*/MA/MS: represents two or three years of study requiring credential **C** for admission

K   *Kandidatspróf/Cand. Med. et Chir.* (medicine), *Cand. Odont.* (dentistry): represents six years of study requiring credential **B** for admission

L   *Doctorspróf/Doctor Philosophicus /dr.phil., dr.scient.*: represents dissertation based on research of an unspecified length, requiring credential **J** for admission

---

[1]   *Baccalaureatus Philologiae Islandicae/B.Ph.Isl.*, awarded by the University of Iceland, represents three years of study for foreign students

GRADING INFORMATION

Secondary

A scale of 10 (highest) to 0 (lowest) is used. Generally, an average grade of 5 is required for graduation, with individual course grades of 4 representing the minimum pass level. Prior to 1990, the minimum pass level was 3.

Postsecondary

A scale of 10 (highest) to 0 (lowest) is used. The minimum pass level is 5.

POSTSECONDARY INSTITUTION RECOGNITION BODY

Ministry of Education, Science and Culture, Solvholsgotu 4, Reykjavik, IS-101. Tel: 354-560-9500. Fax: 354-562-3068. E-mail: postur@mrn.stjr.is

RESOURCES FOR ADDITIONAL INFORMATION

The British Council. 1996. *International Guide to Qualifications in Education.* 4th ed. London: Mansell.

Lárusson, H. "Iceland." 1995. In *International Encyclopedia of National Systems of Education.* 2nd ed. Postlethwaite, T. Neville, ed. Tarrytown, NY: Elsevier Science, Ltd.

Internet Sources:
Higher Education in the Nordic Countries: www.abo.fi/norden/welcom_e.htm
UNESCO-World Academic Database: www.unesco.org/iau/eductd.html

---

Compiler
Margit A. Schatzman
Vice President
Educational Credential Evaluators, Inc., Milwaukee, WI

INDIA

YEARS OF EDUCATION →

		½	½	½	½	½	½	½	½	½	½	½	½	½	½	½	½
1→6| 7	8	9	10	11	12	13	14	15	16	17	18	19	20	21	22	23	24

```
                A        D           G    J    O    T    X
                B        E           H    K    P    U    Y→
                C        F           I    L    Q    V
                                          M    R    X
                                          N    S    W
                                          W    W
```

CREDENTIALS OR DOCUMENTATION

Secondary

A   School Leaving Certificate awarded by a State Secondary School Board
B   All India Secondary School Certificate awarded by the Central Board of Secondary Education
C   Indian Certificate of Secondary Education awarded by the Council for Indian School Certificate Examinations
D   State Higher Secondary Certificate awarded by a State Board of Higher Secondary Education
E   All India and Delhi Senior School Certificates awarded by the Central Board of Secondary Education
F   Indian School Certificate awarded by the Council for Indian School Certificate Examinations

Postsecondary

G   Bachelor of Arts
H   Bachelor of Commerce
I   Bachelor of Science
J   Bachelor of Agricultural Sciences
K   Bachelor of Dentistry
L   Bachelor of Engineering
M   Bachelor of Forestry
N   Bachelor of Pharmacy
O   Bachelor of Medicine
P   Bachelor of Veterinary Science
Q   Master of Arts: two years requiring credential of **G** for admission
R   Master of Commerce: two years requiring credential **H** for admission
S   Master of Science: two years requiring credential **I** for admission
T   Master of Agricultural Sciences: two years requiring credential **J** for admission
U   Master of Engineering: two years requiring credential **L** for admission
V   Master of Pharmacy: two years requiring credential **N** for admission

W Post Graduate Diploma: usually one or two years requiring credential **G, H, I, K, L, M,** or **N** for admission

X Master of Philosophy: usually one or two years requiring credential **Q, R,** or **S** for admission

Y Doctor of Philosophy: usually two or more years of research beyond any of credentials **Q** through **X**

GRADING INFORMATION

Secondary

State Board Examinations (credentials **A** and **D**):

Class or Division	Description
First	Excellent
Second	Good
Third	Pass

Central Board Examinations (credentials **B** and **E**):

Letter/Number	Ratio/Recipients
A1	Top 1/8 of the passed candidates
A2	Next 1/8 of the passed candidates
B1	Next 1/8 of the passed candidates
B2	Next 1/8 of the passed candidates
C1	Next 1/8 of the passed candidates
C2	Next 1/8 of the passed candidates
D1	Next 1/8 of the passed candidates
D2	Next 1/8 of the passed candidates
E	Failed candidates

Council for Indian School Certificate Examinations (credentials **C** and **F**):

Numeric	Description
1	Very Good
2	Very Good
3	Pass With Credit
4	Pass With Credit
5	Pass With Credit
6	Pass With Credit
7	Pass
8	Pass
9	Failure

• Grades in the "pass" range are acceptable for graduation.

Postsecondary Education

Most university programs in Arts, Commerce, and Science:

Class or Division	Percentage	Description
First Class/Division	60-100	Excellent
Second Class/Division	50-59	Good
Third Class/Division	35-49	Pass
--	0-34	Failure

At the Master's level, students must secure at least 40% overall marks to graduate.

- Four-point grading (4.0 to 0.0) is being adopted slowly.

POSTSECONDARY INSTITUTION RECOGNITION BODIES

The Association of Indian Universities (AIU) is the best source for listings of all recognized universities, deemed universities, and institutions of national importance. AIU, AIU House, 16 Kotla Marg, New Delhi 110 001, India. Fax: 91-11-371-5901.

Recognition of universities generally is the responsibility of the University Grants Commission (UGC). Some national universities and institutes are autonomous, however, having been established by act of Parliament. Colleges and institutes often are recognized by universities and affiliated therewith.

Recognition in the fields of technical education (applied arts and crafts, architecture, engineering, management, pharmacy, technology, and town planning) is the responsibility of the All India Council for Technical Education (AICTE). All Indian Council for Technical Education, Indira Gandhi Sports Complex, I.P. Estate, New Dehli 110 001, India.

RESOURCES FOR ADDITIONAL INFORMATION

Kallur, Ravi A. and Leo J. Sweeney. 1998. *Special Report on India*. Annapolis Junction, MD: PIER.

Internet Source:
UNESCO – World Academic Database: www.unesco.org/aiu/educin.html

---

Compiler
Ravi Kallur
Director, International Student Affairs
University of Missouri-Kansas City

INDONESIA

YEARS OF EDUCATION →

```
      ½   ½   ½   ½   ½   ½   ½   ½   ½   ½   ½   ½   ½   ½   ½   ½   ½
1 → 6| 7 | 8 | 9 | 10 | 11 | 12 | 13 | 14 | 15 | 16 | 17 | 18 | 19 | 20 | 21 | 22 | 23 | 24 |
          A               B   D   E   F   G L J M N       P P R R R       R
                          C               H   I   O Q     Q R
                                          K
```

CREDENTIALS OR DOCUMENTATION

Secondary

A   *Surat Tanda Tamat Belajar Sekolah Lanjutan Tingkat Pertama* (Certificate of Completion of Lower Secondary School) awarded by a *Sekolah Lanjutan Tingkat Pertama* (lower secondary school): signifies completion of compulsory education

B   *Surat Tanda Tamat Belajar Sekolah Menegah Unum* (Certificate of Completion of Upper Secondary School): awarded by a *Sekolah Menengah Unum* (General Academic Secondary School); signifies completion of academic secondary school

C   *Surat Tanda Tamat Belajar Sekolah Menegah Kejuruan* (Certificate of Completion of Vocational Upper Secondary School): awarded by a *Sekolah Menengah Kejuruan* (Vocational Secondary School); signifies completion of upper secondary career-oriented programs

Postsecondary

D   *Diploma I* (Diploma I): one-year program requiring credential **B** or **C** for admission

E   *Diploma II* (Diploma II): two-year program requiring credential **B** or **C** for admission

F   *Diploma III* (Diploma III): three-year program requiring credential **B** or **C** for admission

G   *Diploma IV* (Diploma IV): four-year program requiring credential **B** or **C** for admission

H   *Akta II* (Teacher Certification II): one-year program of primary or lower secondary school teacher training; requires credential **E** for admission[1]

I   *Akta III* (Teacher Certification III): one-year program of lower or upper secondary school teacher training; requires credential **F** for admission[1]

J   *Akta IV* (Teacher Certification IV): one-year program of upper secondary school teacher Training; requires credential **G** or **K** for admission[1]

K   *Sarjana strata satu* (S1) [Degree Stage 1]: four-year academic and professional degree programs, including law programs; require credential **B** for admission[2]

L   *Sarjana strata satu Farmasi* (S1) [Degree Stage 1 Pharmacy]: four and one-half-year program requiring credential **B** for admission

M   *Sarjana strata satu Kedokteran* (S1) [Degree Stage 1 Medicine]: five and one-half-year professional programs with the titles of *Kedokteran* or *Dokter* (in Medicine), *Kedokteran Gigi* (in Dentistry), and *Kedokteran Hewan* (in Veterinary Medicine); requires credential **B** for admission

N   *Magister/strata dua* (S2) [Master Stage Two]: two-year program requiring credential **K** (or other S1 degree) with a thesis for admission

O   *Magister Manajemen* (MM) [Master in Management]: 12- to 14- month program; requires credential **K** (or other S1 degree) for admission[3]

P   *Doktor (DR) strata tiga* (S3) [Doctor Stage Three]: two-year program requiring credential **N** or **O** for admission

Q   *Specialis I* (Specialist I): two-year programs in medical fields (for credential **M** graduates) and in law (credential **K**) plus appropriate professional experience

R   *Specialis II* (Specialist II): two- to three-year programs for holders of credential **N**, **O**, or **Q**, plus appropriate professional experience

1   *Akta I* programs, which required credential **D** for admission, were discontinued in 1992. *Akta* diplomas are awarded by teacher training institutes. Each program includes approximately one semester of academic coursework plus one semester of teaching practice.

2   Documentation for S1 degrees indicate the field of study, such as *Sarjana Pendidikan* (Degree in Education). The degree of *Insinyur* (Engineer), discontinued in 1990, is now referred to as the S1 degree of *Sarjana Teknik (ST)*.

3   The Master of Management degree is offered at the University of Indonesia, Bogor Institute of Agriculture, and Bandung Institute of Technology. The degree is distinguished from the Master of Business Administration (MBA) degree, which is not recognized by the Directorate General of Higher Education or by the government. MBA graduates are not eligible for admission into credential **P** programs.

GRADING INFORMATION

Secondary

Numerical	Description	Translation
10, *Sepuluh*	*Istimewa*	Excellent
9, *Sembilan*	*Sangat Baik/Baik Sekali*	Very Good
8, *Delapan*	*Baik*	Good
7, *Tujuh*	*Lebih Dari Cukup*	Above Average
6, *Enam*	*Cukup*	Average
5, *Lima*	*Hampir Cukup*	Below Average
4, *Empat*	*Kurang*	Failure
3, *Tiga*	*Kurang Sekali*	Failure
2, *Dua*	*Buruk*	Failure
1, *Satu*	*Buruk Sekali*	Failure

Postsecondary Education

<u>Prior to 1990</u>: Grading varied, including 5- 10- and 100-point scales. A 5-point scale (5 being highest) continues to be used by at least one institution (Bandung Institute of Technology). Current and previous grading information may be provided on transcripts.

<u>Since 1990</u>:

Grade	Point	Description	Translation
A	4	*Istimewa, Sangat Baik, Baik Sekali, Bagus Sekali*	Excellent
B	3	*Baik*	Good
C	2	*Cukup, Sedang*	Average, Passed With Credit
D	1	*Kurang/Lulus Bersyarat*	Poor, Passed
E/F	0	*Gagal/Tidak Lulus*	Failure

POSTSECONDARY INSTITUTION RECOGNITION BODY

Ministry of Education and Culture, Directorate General, Jl. Jenderal Sudirman, Senayan, Jakarta, 12041, Republic of Indonesia. Tel: 62-21-573-1665. Fax: 62-21-572-1243.

RESOURCES FOR ADDITIONAL INFORMATION

Aanenson, Charles. 1979. *A Study of Indonesian Education and a Guide to the Academic Placement of Students from Indonesia in Educational Institutions of the United States.* Washington, D.C.: AACRAO.

Johnson, Karin, et al. 1993. *Indonesia: A Study of the Educational System of the Republic of Indonesia and a Guide to the Academic Placement of Students in Educational Institutions in the United States.* Annapolis Junction, MD: PIER.

Internet Sources:
Indonesian Department of Education: www.pdk.go.id
UNESCO – World Academic Database: www.unesco/iau/eduid.html

Compiler
Sandra Dyson Rodríguez
SDR Educational Consultants
Foreign Educational Equivalencies, Houston, TX

IRAN

YEARS OF EDUCATION →

	½	½	½	½	½	½	½	½	½	½	½	½	½	½	½	½	½
1 →6| 7	8	9	10	11	12	13	14	15	16	17	18	19	20	21	22	23	24

```
                    A    B         C         D    D    E    E        ↦    ↦
                                                       F    H
                                                       G
```

CREDENTIALS OR DOCUMENTATION

Secondary

A *Diplome* (Diploma) also known as (Certificate of Completion of Secondary Study): awarded upon completion of 11 years of education (five years of primary school, three years of lower secondary (junior high) and two years of higher secondary (senior high)); holders of the *Diplome* cannot continue studies at the university level but may seek employment

B Pre-university Year, National Entrance Examination *(Concours)*, and personal interview to ensure that moral-ethical and religious standards are met: leads to postsecondary education

Postsecondary

C *Kardani* (Higher Diploma) (formerly known as *Foghé Diplome*): awarded by some universities, higher education institutions and technical institutions upon completion of a minimum of two years of education and 70-74 credits

D *Karshenasi* (formerly known as *Licence,* usually translated as Bachelor's degree): prior to 1964, it was awarded after three years of study; since 1964, it requires a minimum of four years of education and 140-148 credits; architecture requires five years of education

E *Karshenasi-arshad-napeyvasteh* (formerly known as *Foghé Licence,* usually translated as Master's degree); awarded upon completion of two years of study (32-36 units) by coursework and some research

F Doctor of Dentistry: six-year professional degree

G Doctor of Veterinary Medicine: six-year professional degree

H Doctor of Medicine: seven-year professional degree

I *Doctora* (Doctorate): minimum of three years, maximum of six, following credential **E**; requires completion of 60 units and a thesis

GRADING INFORMATION

Secondary

Numeric
17-20	
15-16	
12-14	
10-11	Minimum passing grade is 10
0- 9	Failure

- Total year average is calculated by adding the sum of the first term of study, the sum of the second term, and the sum of the third term June Examination grades, multiplying by two, and dividing the total by four.

Postsecondary Education

The 20-point scale (with 10 as minimum passing grade) used by secondary schools is also used by some postsecondary institutions. Other postsecondary institutions use a 20-point scale with 13 as minimum passing:

20-point scale with 13 as minimum passing
18-20	
15-17.9	
13-14.9	
below 13	Failure

POSTSECONDARY INSTITUTION RECOGNITION BODY

Ministry of Culture and Higher Education: Africa Ave, Golpham Street, #1. Tehran, Iran. Tel: 9821 204-3600. Fax: 9821 205-0338.

RESOURCES FOR ADDITIONAL INFORMATION

Department of Statistics and Information, Ministry of Culture and Higher Education, Tehran, Iran. (address above)

Internet Source:
UNESCO – World Academic Database: www.unesco.org/iau/educir.html

---

Compiler
Alan Saidi
Vice-President
Academic Credentials Evaluation Institute, Inc., Beverly Hills, CA

IRAQ

YEARS OF EDUCATION →

```
       ½   ½   ½   ½   ½   ½   ½   ½   ½   ½   ½   ½   ½   ½   ½   ½   ½
1→6| 7 | 8 | 9 | 10| 11| 12| 13| 14| 15| 16| 17| 18| 19| 20| 21| 22| 23| 24|

   A       B           C       E       G   H   I   J   J   L   L   L
                       D       F               J       K
```

CREDENTIALS OR DOCUMENTATION

Primary and Secondary

A   Primary School Certificate: signifies completion of six-year compulsory education
B   Baccalaureate Examination for the Intermediate Schools
C   Baccalaureate Examination for the Preparatory Schools: Literary Section or Scientific Section
D   Baccalaureate Examination for the Vocational Schools

Postsecondary

E   Technician Diploma: two-year program requiring credential **C** or **D** for admission
F   Diploma in Education: two-year program requiring credential **C** for admission, or a five-year program requiring credential **B** for admission
G   Bachelor's degree in the fields of Arts, Education, and Science: four-year programs requiring credential **C** for admission
H   Bachelor's degree in the fields of Architectural Engineering, Dental Surgery, Pharmacy, and Veterinary Medicine and Surgery: five-year programs requiring credential **C** for admission
I   Bachelor of Medicine, Bachelor of Surgery: six-year program requiring credential **C** for admission
J   Master's degree: one year of coursework and one year of thesis research in a program requiring credential **G, H,** or **I** for admission
K   Higher Diploma in Medicine or Surgery: two-year clinical program requiring credential **I** for admission
L   Doctor of Philosophy: one year of coursework and two years of thesis research in a program requiring credential **J** for admission

GRADING INFORMATION

Secondary

Percentage	Description
50-100	Passing
0-49	Failing

Postsecondary Education

Percentage	Description
90-100	Excellent
80-89	Very good
70-79	Good
60-69	Medium
50-59	Pass
0-49	Failure

POSTSECONDARY INSTITUTION RECOGNITION BODY

Ministry of Education and Scientific Research: P.O. Box 258, Baghdad.
Tel: 964-1-886 0000. Fax: 964-1-885 1989.

Eighteen other ministries each supervise one or more specialized university-level institutions.

RESOURCES FOR ADDITIONAL INFORMATION

Frey, James S. 1988. *Iraq: A Study of the Educational System of Iraq and a Guide to the Academic Placement of Students in Educational Institutions in the United States.* Washington, D.C.: AACRAO.

The British Council. 1996. *International Guide to Qualifications in Education.* 4th ed. London: Mansell.

Internet Source:
UNESCO - World Academic Database: www.unesco.org/iau/educiq.html

---

Compiler
James S. Frey
President
Educational Credential Evaluators, Inc., Milwaukee, WI

IRELAND

YEARS OF EDUCATION →

```
        ½   ½   ½   ½   ½   ½   ½   ½   ½   ½   ½   ½   ½   ½   ½   ½   ½
1→6| 7 | 8 | 9 | 10| 11| 12| 13| 14| 15| 16| 17| 18| 19| 20| 21| 22| 23| 24|
            A           B   B   E   E   F   H   I   J   L   L
                        C   C       F   G   I   J   K   M   M-  M-
                        D   D       G   H   K   K   L
                                    H   K   L   L
```

CREDENTIALS OR DOCUMENTATION

Secondary

A   Junior Certificate: three-year junior secondary cycle following primary education; formerly the Intermediate Certificate

B   Leaving Certificate: two-year senior secondary cycle; subjects studied at ordinary or higher level, following credential **A**; satisfies higher education admission requirements[1]

C   Leaving Certificate Vocational Program: two-year senior secondary cycle; subjects studied at ordinary or higher level, following credential **A**; satisfies higher education admission requirements to limited programs[1]

D   Leaving Certificate Applied: two-year senior secondary cycle; subjects studied at ordinary or higher level, following credential **A**; does not satisfy higher education admission requirements; formerly the Senior Certificate[1]

Postsecondary

E   National Certificate: two years of tertiary education following credential **B** or **C**

F   National Diploma: three years of tertiary education following credential **B** or **C**, or one year following credential **E**

G   Diploma in Theology: three years following credential **B**

H   Bachelor's Degree: three or four years of tertiary education following credential **B** or C, two years following credential **E**, or one year following credential **F**[2]

I   Bachelor's Degree: in the fields of architecture, dentistry, and veterinary medicine; five years of tertiary education following credential **B**

J   Bachelor's Degree: in the field of medicine, obstetrics, and surgery; completion of six years of tertiary education following credential **B**

K   Graduate Diploma: usually one year of coursework following credential **H** or **I**[3]

L   Master's Degree: usually one or two years of coursework and/or research following credential **H, I,** or **J**[4]

M   Doctor of Philosophy Degree: usually five years following credential **H** or a minimum of two years of original research following credential **L**[4]

[1]   Some students complete a transition year after the junior secondary cycle before beginning a senior secondary cycle.

[2]   Requires completion of three or four years of study at universities, with most honors degrees requiring completion of four years of study. At Regional Technical Colleges (as of 1998 re-named Institutes of Technology), the degree programs typically require completion of four years of study. Whether the programs require either three or four years of study varies between institutions.

[3]   The field of study varies, and can be undertaken on a part-time basis usually over two years. This can also be called the Higher Diploma or Postgraduate Diploma.

[4]   The length of the program varies with the admission and the field of study.

GRADING INFORMATION

Secondary

Leaving Certificate (Ordinary and Higher Level Subjects)

Percentage	Mark
85-100	A
70-84	B
55-69	C
40-54	D
25-39	E
10-24	F
0-9	No Grade

- The mark of D is considered a fully passing grade. Higher examinations are weighted and a mark of A on an Ordinary examination is equivalent to a mark of C on the Higher examination.

Postsecondary Education

National Council for Educational Awards — Certificate, Diploma, and Degree Classifications

Percentage	Description
70-100	Distinction
60-69	Merit
40-59	Pass
0-39	Fail

- The National Council for Educational Awards validates programs at the Institutes of Technology (including the former Regional Technical Colleges).

National Council for Educational Awards — Certificate, Diploma, and Degree Classifications as of 1998

Percentage	Description
70-100	Distinction
63-69	Merit Grade 1
55-62	Merit Grade 2
40-54	Pass
0-39	Fail

- This scale begins with the class of 1998, but will only be used with final awards for students beginning programs in 1998 or later.

National Council for Educational Awards — Course Grades

Percentage	Mark
80-100	A
70-79	B+
60-69	B
55-59	B-
50-54	C+
40-49	C
36-39	D
0-35	F

University Degree Classification

Percentage	Degree Classification	
70-100	I	First Class
63-69	II-I	Second Class, Upper Division
55-62	II-II	Second Class, Lower Division
50-54	III	Third Class
40-49	P	Pass
0-39	F	Fail

University Course Grades

Percentage	Mark
75-100	A
60-74	B
45-59	C
35-44	D
25-34	E (Fail)
20-24	F
0 -20	No Grade

- Scales vary between universities, as well as university colleges.

POSTSECONDARY INSTITUTION RECOGNITION BODIES

Higher Education Authority (HEA). 21 Fitzwilliam Square, Dublin 2, Ireland.
Tel: 353-1-6612748. Fax: 353-1- 6610492. www.irlgov.ie/educ

National Council for Educational Awards. 26 Mountjoy Square, Dublin 1, Ireland.
Tel: 353-1-855 6526. Fax: 353-1-855 4250.

RESOURCES FOR ADDITIONAL INFORMATION

The British Council. 1996. *International Guide to Qualifications in Education.* 4th ed.
London, England: Mansell.

Turner, Solveig and Antoinette Frederick. 1994. *Education in Ireland: Admission and
Placement of Irish Graduates.* Boston: CED Publications.

Internet Sources:
Department of Education and Science, Government of Ireland, *Brief Description of the
    Irish Education System.* Department of Education: www.irlgov.ie/educ/organisation/
EURYDICE-Eurybase: www.eurydice.org/eurybase
Irish National Information Server: *The Irish Educational System.*
    www.heanet.ie/links/irished.
UNESCO - World Academic Database: www.unesco.org/iau/educie.html

---

Compiler
Christy R. Samford
Foreign Credential Evaluator
Josef Silny & Associates, Inc., International Education Consultants, Coral Gables, FL

ISRAEL

YEARS OF EDUCATION →

```
       ½   ½   ½   ½   ½   ½   ½   ½   ½   ½   ½   ½   ½   ½   ½   ½   ½
1 → 6| 7 | 8 | 9 | 10 | 11 | 12 | 13 | 14 | 15 | 16 | 17 | 18 | 19 | 20 | 21 | 22 | 23 | 24 |

                        A    C      D    K  F      F   k  a      r  x  v→
                        B           E    R  H      W  p  b      u     w→
                                    F       I      Z     c      v→    x
                                    H       J      a     d
                                    I       K      b     e
                                    J       S      c     f
                                    L       T      d     g
                                    M       U      e     i
                                    N       V      f     m
                                    O       W      g     o
                                    P       X      h     p
                                    Q       Y      i     q
                                                   j     s
                                                   l     t
                                                   m
                                                   n
                                                   q
```

CREDENTIALS OR DOCUMENTATION

Secondary

A   *Teudat Gemer Tichonit* (Secondary School Final Diploma)
B   *Teudat Bagrut* (Matriculation Certificate): leads to postsecondary education

Postsecondary: Non-University Diplomas

C   Technician Diploma
D   *Handassai* (Practical Engineer): two to three years in architecture and engineering fields
E   Post-matriculation diplomas: usually two years, in various fields, such as hotel management, occupational therapy, and social work
F   Teacher's Certificate: two years following credential **B** or one year following credential **H** or equivalent
G   Registered Nurse

Postsecondary: University and College Degrees

H   Bachelor of Arts
I   Bachelor of Music
J   Bachelor of Fine Arts: three or four years
K   Bachelor of Law: three and one-half or four years
L   Bachelor of Medical Sciences
M   Bachelor of Occupational Therapy
N   Bachelor of Pharmacy
O   Bachelor of Social Work

195

P   Bachelor of Science
Q   Bachelor of Science in Nutrition
R   Bachelor of Science in Agriculture
S   Bachelor of Business
T   Bachelor of Dance
U   Bachelor of Design, Bachelor of Design (Fashion), and Bachelor of Design (Textile)
V   Bachelor of ...Education, Music Education, Education in Technology, Science in Technology Education
W   Bachelor of Nursing, Bachelor of Arts in Nursing, and Bachelor of Science in Nursing: four years with admission based on credential **B**; or at least two years based on credential **G**
X   Bachelor of Physiotherapy
Y   Bachelor of ...Technology, Technology and Applied Science, Technology in Industrial Management, Technology (Textile)
Z   Bachelor of Architecture
a   Post-bachelor diplomas: usually two years following credential **H** or equivalent; available in various areas including artist diploma, dietition, librarianship, qualified archivist, social work, and translation.
b   Master of Arts: two years following credential **H** or equivalent[1]
c   Master of Arts in Music: two years following credential **I**[1]
d   Master of Fine Arts: two years following credential **H** or **J**[1]
e   Master of Business Administration: two years following credential **H** or equivalent[1]
f   Master of Health Systems Management: two years following credential **H** or equivalent[1]
g   Master of Library Science: two years following credential **H**[1]
h   Master of Medical Science: two years following credential **L**[1]
i   Master of Public Health: two years following credential **H**[1]
j   Master of Science: two years following credential **P** or equivalent[1]
k   Master of Science in Agriculture: two years following credential **R**[1]
l   Master of Science in Pharmacy: two years generally following credential **N**[1]
m   Master of Social Science: two years following credential **H** or equivalent[1]
n   Master of Social Work: two years generally following credential **O**[1]
o   Master of Engineering and Master of Science in Technology: two years generally following credential **Y**[1]
p   Master of Law: two years generally following credential **K**[1]
q   Master of Music: two years generally following credential **I**[1]
r   Master of Architecture: two years generally following credential **Z**[1]
s   Doctor of Dental Medicine: six years following credential **B**[2]
t   Doctor of Veterinary Medicine: six years following credential **B**[2]
u   Doctor of Medicine: six or seven years following credential **B**[2]
x   Doctor of Philosophy: two or more years following credential **b** or **p** or equivalent, or following a credential in the "direct path" of a Doctor of Philosophy degree
w   Doctor of Science or Doctor of Science in Technology: two or more years following credential **o**
x   Doctor of Jurisprudence: two years following credential **p**

[1]   Admission to master degree programs is based on completion of a relevant bachelor's degree program.

[2]   Considered in Israel to be the equivalent of a Master of Science degree.

GRADING INFORMATION

Secondary
Teudat Bagrut (Matriculation Certificate):

Numeric	Percentage	Description
10	95-100	Excellent
9	85-94	Very Good
8	75-84	Good
7	65-74	Almost Good
6	55-64	Satisfactory
5	45-54	Almost Satisfactory
0-4	0-44	Fail, Unsatisfactory

Postsecondary: Non-University Diplomas

Percentage	Numeric	Description
95-100	10	Excellent
85-94	9	Very Good
75-84	8	Good
65-74	7	Fair, Good, Almost Good
55-64	6	Sufficient, Poor, Fair
0-54	5	Almost Insufficient, Fail, Weak
--	4	Insufficient, Fail, Weak

Postsecondary: University and College Degrees

Percentage	Description
95-100	Excellent
85-94	Very Good
75-84	Good
65-74	Fair
50-64	Pass
0-49	Fail

- Scales may vary slightly. Usually grading information is provided on transcripts.

POSTSECONDARY INSTITUTION RECOGNITION BODY

Council for Higher Education, P.O. Box 4037, Jerusalem 91040. Tel: 972-2-5679902. Fax: 972-2-5679955. (Authorizes institutions of higher education to award degrees.)

The Ministry of Education and Culture, Ministry of Labor and Social Welfare, and Ministry of Health grant licenses and endorsements to postsecondary institutions of the following types: teacher training colleges, technical colleges, and para-medical colleges.

RESOURCES FOR ADDITIONAL INFORMATION

Association of Regional Colleges in Israel. 65 Ibn Gvirol Street, Tel Aviv, Israel, 64362. Tel: 972-3-6917641. Fax: 972-3-6960117. E-mail: colleges@post.tau.ac.il

Fletcher, Ann. 1993. *Higher Education in Israel.* Annapolis Junction, MD: PIER.

Nursing in the World Editorial Committee. 1993. *Nursing in the World*. 3rd ed. Tokyo: International Nursing Foundation of Japan.

Internet Sources:
Educational Information Center, US-Israel Educational Foundation (Fulbright):
    http://studyusa.fulbright.org.il (click "Education in Israel")
UNESCO - World Academic Database: http://www.unesco.org/iau/educil.html
 Web sites listing major Israeli institutions of higher education:
    http://www.iguide.co.il/english/19.html
    http://www.ac.il

Compilers
Evelyn Levinson
Director of Educational Information Center
Fulbright Foundation in Israel, Tel Aviv

Shelley M. Feagles
Senior Evaluator
Educational Credential Evaluators, Inc., Milwaukee, WI

ITALY

YEARS OF EDUCATION →

	½	½	½	½	½	½	½	½	½	½	½	½	½	½	½	½	½		
1 →5	6	7	8	9	10	11	12	13	14	15	16	17	18	19	20	21	22	23	24|

```
                A               B   E   G       K   K   S   S   S   W   Y-
                                C   F   H       L   L   T   W   X-
                                D       I       M   P   U
                                        J       N   Q   V
                                                O   R
```

CREDENTIALS OR DOCUMENTATION

Secondary

A *Diploma di Licenza della Scuola Media* (Diploma of Graduation from Middle School): awarded by a *scuola media* (middle school); signifies completion of compulsory education

B *Diploma di Qualifica Professionale* (Diploma of Vocational Qualification): awarded by an *istituto professionale* (vocational institute); holders of this diploma are not eligible for admission to postsecondary programs on the basis of this credential alone

C *Diploma di Abilitazione all'Insegnamento nelle Scuole del Grado Preparatorio* (Diploma of Qualification to Teach in Preparatory-Level Schools): awarded by a *scuola magistrale* (teacher training school); holders of this diploma are not eligible for admission to postsecondary programs on the basis of this credential alone

D *Diploma di Maestro d'Arte* (Diploma of Master of Art): awarded by an *istituto d'arte* (institute of art); holders of this diploma are eligible for admission to *accademie di belle arti* (academies of fine arts)

E *Diploma di Maturità Magistrale* (Teacher Training Maturity Diploma): awarded by an *istituto magistrale* (teacher training institute); holders of this diploma are eligible for admission to university faculties of education and languages

F *Diploma di Maturità Artistica* (Diploma of Artistic Maturity): awarded by a *liceo artistico* (artistic lyceum); holders of this diploma are eligible for admission to *accademie di belle arti* (academies of fine arts) and university faculties of architecture

G *Diploma di Licenza Linguistica* (Linguistic Graduation Diploma): awarded by a *liceo linguistico* (linguistic lyceum); holders of this diploma are eligible for admission to *università* (universities) and other postsecondary programs

H *Diploma di Maturità* (Diploma of Maturity) from the following streams: *Arte Applicata* (Applied Arts), awarded by an *istituto d'arte* (institute of art); *Classico* (Classical), awarded by a *liceo classico* (classical lyceum); *Musicale* (Musical), awarded by a *conservatorio di musica* (music conservatory); *Professionale* (Vocational), awarded by an *istituto professionale* (vocational institute); *Scientifico* (Scientific), awarded by a *liceo scientifico* (scientific lyceum); and *Tecnico (Technical)*: awarded by an *istituto tecnico* (technical institute); holders of these diplomas are eligible for admission to *università* (universities) and other postsecondary programs

I   *Attestato di Idoneità* (Affidavit of Equivalence): awarded to holders of secondary credentials **E** and **F** who successfully complete a *corso integrativo* (integrative program); leads to admission to all faculties at universities and other postsecondary institutions

J   *Diploma di Infermiere Professionale* (Diploma of Professional Nurse): this qualification is being phased out and is being replaced by a *Diploma Universitario* (University Diploma) program in *Scienze Infermieristiche* (Nursing Sciences)

Postsecondary

K   *Diploma Universitario* (University Diploma) [referred to colloquially as *Laurea Breve* (Short Degree)]: awarded by a *università degli studi* (university), *politecnico* (polytechnic), or *istituto universitario* (university institute); requires credential **G, H,** or **I** for admission

L   *Diploma* (Diploma) awarded by a *scuola diretta a fini speciali* (school for special purposes) attached to a *università degli studi* (university), *politecnico* (polytechnic), or *istituto universitario* (university institute): requires credential **G, H,** or **I** for admission

M   *Diploma di Ostetrica* (Diploma of Midwife): awarded by a *università degli studi* (university); requires credential **J** or completion of two to three years of university-level study in medicine for admission

N   *Diploma di Infermiera Volontaria* (Diploma of Volunteer Nurse): awarded by the *Croce Rossa Italiana* (Italian Red Cross); requires credential **E, F, G,** or **H** for admission; this diploma has no legal value, and its holders may only work as volunteers

O   *Diploma di Traduttore Interprete Corrispondente in Lingue Estere* (Diploma of Translator, Interpreter, and Correspondent in Foreign Languages): awarded by a *scuola superiore per interpreti e traduttori* (higher school for interpreters and translators); requires credential **G, H,** or **I** for admission

P   *Diploma di Educazione Fisica* (Diploma of Physical Education): awarded by an *istituto superiore di educazione fisica* (higher institute of physical education); requires credential **G, H,** or **I** for admission

Q   *Diploma in Scienze Religiose* (Diploma in Religious Sciences): awarded by an *istituto superiore di scienze religiose* (higher insitute of religious sciences); requires credential **G, H,** or **I** for admission

R   *Diploma Superiore* (Higher Diploma) in the following specializations: *Interprete di Trattativa* (Interpreter of Negotiations), *Traduttore* (Translator), and *Traduttore e Interprete* (Translator and Interpreter): awarded by a *scuola superiore per interpreti e traduttori* (higher school for interpreters and translators); requires credential **G, H,** or **I** for admission

S   *Laurea di Dottore* (Degree of Doctor): awarded by a *università degli studi* (university), *politecnico* (polytechnic), or *istituto universitario* (university institute); requires credential **G, H,** or **I** for admission; programs in medicine require six years of study; programs in all other fields require four or five years of study

T   *Magistero in Scienze Religiose* (Teaching Degree in Religious Sciences): awarded by an *istituto superiore di scienze religiose* (higher insitute of religious sciences); requires credential **G, H,** or **I** for admission

U   *Diploma di Licenza* (Graduation Diploma): awarded by an *accademia di belle arti* (academy of fine arts); requires credential **D, F, G, H,** or **I** for admission

V *Diploma* (Diploma) awarded by an *istituto superiore di industrie artistiche* (higher institute of artistic industries): requires credential **F, G, H,** or **I** for admission

W Master's degree: awarded by a *università degli studi* (university), *politecnico* (polytechnic), or *istituto universitario* (university institute); one- to two-year programs usually requiring credential **S** for admission

X *Diploma di Specialista* (Diploma of Specialist): awarded by a *scuola di specializzazione* (school of specialization) attached to a *università degli studi* (university), *politecnico* (polytechnic), or *istituto universitario* (university institute); programs are two to five years in length and require credential **S** for admission

Y *Dottorato di Ricerca* (Research Doctorate): awarded by a *università degli studi* (university), *politecnico* (polytechnic), or *istituto universitario* (university institute); programs are three to four years in length and require credential **S** for admission

GRADING INFORMATION

Secondary

Numeric: Course Work	Numeric: Maturity Exam	Description
10	60	Denotes perfection; never, or almost never, awarded
9	54-59	Consistently excellent performance; capable of analysis and synthesis; rarely awarded
8	48-53	Good performance
7	42-47	Fairly good performance
6	36-41	Satisfactory performance
1-5	0-35	Unsatisfactory performance

Postsecondary

Numeric: Course Work	Numeric: Degree Exam	Description
27-30	99-110	Excellent
21-26	77-98	Good
18-20	66-76	Satisfactory
0-17	0-65	Unsatisfactory

- The designation *e lode* (with honors) may be added to a perfect score (grades of 30 on course work and 110 on degree examinations) to recognize exceptional achievement.

Other grading scales are multiples of the following basic ten-point scale:

Numeric	Description
9-10	Excellent
7-8	Good
6	Satisfactory
1-5	Unsatisfactory

POSTSECONDARY INSTITUTION RECOGNITION BODY

Ministero delle Università e della Ricerca Scientifica e Tecnologica/ MURST (Ministry of Universities and of Scientific and Technological Research). Lungotevere Thaon de Revel 76, Rome 00194, Italy. Tel: (6) 32681. Fax: (6) 32689228. http://www.murst.it

RESOURCES FOR ADDITIONAL INFORMATION

Alatri, Roberto, ed. 1994. *The Italian Higher Education System and Its Qualifications.* Rome, Italy: CIMEA della Fondazione Rui. Ministero delle Università e della Ricerca Scientifica e Tecnologica.

Capobianco, Joseph P. 1981. *Italy: A Study of the Educational System of Italy and a Guide to the Academic Placement of Students from Italy in Educational Institutions in the United States.* Washington, D.C.: AACRAO.

National Office of Overseas Skills Recognition. 1992. *Country Education Profiles: Italy.* Canberra: Australian Government Publishing Service.

Visalberghi, A. 1995. "Italy." In *International Encyclopedia of National Systems of Education.* 2nd ed. Postlethwaite, T. Neville, ed. Tarrytown, NY: Elsevier Science, Inc.

Zanetti, Kristin M. 1996. *ECE Presents: The Educational System of Italy.* Milwaukee: Educational Credential Evaluators, Inc.

Compiler
Kristin M. Zanetti
Senior Evaluator
Educational Credential Evaluators, Inc., Milwaukee, WI

JAPAN

YEARS OF EDUCATION →

```
     ½   ½   ½   ½   ½   ½   ½   ½   ½   ½   ½   ½   ½   ½   ½   ½   ½
1 → 6| 7 | 8 | 9 | 10| 11| 12| 13| 14| 15| 16| 17| 18| 19| 20| 21| 22| 23| 24|
        A           B       D F D   G       H       J→      K
                    C         E             I
```

CREDENTIALS OR DOCUMENTATION

Secondary

A *Shuryo shosho* (Certificate of Completion): awarded by a *Chugakko* (Lower Secondary School); signifies completion of compulsory education

B *Sotsugyo shosho* (Diploma of Graduation): awarded by a *Kotogakko* (Upper Secondary School)[1]

C *Shuryo shomei* (Certificate of Completion): awarded by a *Koto Senmon Gakko* (College of Technology) if study is terminated after the first three years of a five-year program

Postsecondary

D *Shuryo shosho* (Certificate of Completion; also translated as Associate Degree): awarded after two or three years at a *Tanki-daigaku* (Junior College); admission based on credential **B**

E *Sotsugyo shosho* (Diploma of Graduation; also translated as Associate Diploma): awarded after five years by a *Koto Senmon Gakko* (College of Technology); Admission based on credential **A**

F *Sotsugyo shosho* (Diploma of Graduation; also translated as Associate Diploma): awarded after five-and-one-half years by a *Koto Senmon Gakko* (College of Technology) in merchant marine studies; admission based on credential **A**

G *Gakushi-go* (Bachelor's Degree): awarded by a *Daigaku* (university) following credential **B**[2]

H *Gakushi-go* (Bachelor's Degree): awarded by a *Daigaku* (university) in the fields of Dentistry, Medicine, and Veterinary Medicine following credential **B**[2]

I *Shushi-go* (Master's Degree): awarded after two years by a *Daigaku* (university); requires credential **G** for admission[2]

J *Hakase-go* (Doctoral Degree): awarded by a *Daigaku* (university); at least two years requiring credential **I** for admission, or at least four years requiring credential **G** for admission

K *Hakase-go* (Doctoral Degree): awarded by a *Daigaku* (university) in Dentistry, Medicine, and Veterinary Medicine requiring credential **H** for admission

[1] School examination required for admission

[2] National examination and/or school examination required for admission

203

GRADING INFORMATION

Secondary
5   (highest)
4
3
2   (lowest passing)
1   (failure)

Higher Education

Percentage	Description	Translation
80-100	*Shu*	Superior
70-79	*Yu*	Excellent
60-69	*Ryo*	Good
0-59	*Fuka*	Fail

POSTSECONDARY INSTITUTION RECOGNITION BODY

Ministry of Education, Science, Sports and Culture (Monbusho), 3-2-2 Kasumigaseki, Chiyoda-ku, Tokyo 100, Japan Tel: 81-3-35814211 Fax: 81-3-35819149.

RESOURCES FOR ADDITIONAL INFORMATION

Japanese University Accreditation Association, 2-7-13 Sadohara-cho Ichigaya, Shinjuku-ku, Tokyo 162 Japan Tel: 81-3-6228-2020. Fax: 81-3-5228-2323.

Mashiko, Ellen E. 1989. *Japan: A Study of the Educational System of Japan and a Guide to the Academic Placement of Students in Educational Institutions of the United States.* Washington, D.C.: AACRAO.

Internet Sources:
Japan-US Educational Commission: www.jusec.go.jp
Ministry of Education, Science, Sports and Culture: www.monbu.go.jp
UNESCO-World Academic Database: www.unesco.org/iau/educjp.html

---

Compiler
Diane M. Roney
Executive Director
International Education Research Foundation, Los Angeles, CA

JORDAN

YEARS OF EDUCATION →

```
       ½    ½    ½    ½    ½    ½    ½    ½    ½    ½    ½    ½    ½    ½    ½    ½    ½
1 → 6 : 7 : 8 : 9 : 10 : 11 : 12 : 13 : 14 : 15 : 16 : 17 : 18 : 19 : 20 : 21 : 22 : 23 : 24 :
                    A         B    B    C    C    C    H    I    I    I    I
                                            D    E              J→
                                            F    H
                                            G
                                            H
```

CREDENTIALS OR DOCUMENTATION

Secondary

A شهادة الدراسة الثانوية العامة (General Secondary Education Certificate): awarded after passing of national examination; also known as the *tawjihi*

Postsecondary

B شهادة دبلوم كلية المجتمعة: الشهادة الجامعية المتوسطة (Community College Diploma; Intermediate University Certificate): two to three years, depending on the field of study; requires credential **A** for admission[1] (the name of the credential was changed from "Community College Diploma" to "Intermediate University Certificate" as of the 1998-99 academic year)

C بكالوريوس في الآداب: بكالوريوس في العلوم (Bachelor of Arts, Bachelor of Science): four to six years, depending on the field of study; requires credential **A** for admission

D بكالوريوس طب أسنان (Bachelor of Dental Medicine): five years, requiring credential **A** for admission

E بكالوريوس في الطب والجراحة (Bachelor of Medicine and Surgery): six years, requiring credential **A** for admission; additional one-year internship required prior to qualifying for license to practice medicine

F دبلوم (Diploma): one-year education diploma, requiring four-year credential **C** for admission

G دبلوم الدراسات العليا (Diploma of Higher Studies): one year, requiring four-year credential **C** for admission[2]

H ماجستير في الآداب: ماجستير في العلوم (Master of Arts, Master of Science): one to two years, requiring four- or five-year credential **C** for admission[3]

I ماجستير في العلوم (Master of Science) in Basic and Clinical Medicine: two to five years depending on specialty; requires credential **E** for admission

J دكتوراه في ... (Doctor of Philosophy in...): three or more years, requiring credential **H** for admission

---

[1] Three-year programs are offered in the fields of occupational therapy, radiology technology, and optometry.

[2] The University of Jordan cancelled its Diploma of Higher Studies in 1991-92. A Diploma of Higher Studies is currently awarded by Yarmouk University in the fields of Islamic studies and education.

[3] Prior to 1992-93, the University of Jordan awarded up to 15 hours of credit towards the master's degree to holders of credential **G**.

GRADING INFORMATION

Secondary

Percent	Remark	Translation
90–100	ممتاز	Excellent
80–89	جيد جدا	Very Good
70–79	جيد	Good
60–69	مقبول	Acceptable
50–59	ضعيف	Poor, Weak
0–49	راسب	Fail

Higher Education

Community college grading scale:

Percent	Remark	Translation
90–100	ممتاز	Excellent
80–89	جيد جدا	Very Good
70–79	جيد	Good
60–69	مقبول	Acceptable
50–59	ضعيف	Poor, Weak
0–49	راسب	Fail

University Grading Scale—Cumulative and Semester Averages
(suggested letter-grade equivalents are indicated by the universities themselves)

Percent	Remark	Letter grade equivalent
84–100	Excellent	A
76–83	Very Good	B
68–75	Good	C
60–67	Pass	D
0–59	Fail	F

University Grading Scale—Individual Courses
(suggested letter-grade equivalents are indicated by the universities themselves)

Percent	Remark	Letter grade equivalent
90–100	Excellent	A
80–89	Very Good	B
70–79	Good	C
60–69	Fair	D
50–59	Pass	E
0–49	Fail	F

- A grade of E designates a range considered minimally passing for individual courses but failing as an average.
- At the graduate level, students must maintain a cumulative average of at least 70–75% to remain in good standing.
- Some universities may use grading scales other than those listed above.

POSTSECONDARY INSTITUTION RECOGNITION BODY

Council of Higher Education; Amman, Jordan. Tel: 962-6-534-7671.
Fax: 962-6-533-7616.

RESOURCES FOR ADDITIONAL INFORMATION

National Office of Overseas Skills Recognition. 1992. *Jordan: A Comparative Study.*
Canberra: Australian Government Printing Service.

Nucho, Leslie S., ed. 1993. *Education in the Arab World.* Volume I. Washington, D.C.:
AMIDEAST.

Internet Source:
UNESCO—World Academic Database: www.unesco.org/iau/educjo.html

---

Compiler
Leslie S. Nucho
Vice President
AMIDEAST, Washington, D.C.

KENYA

YEARS OF EDUCATION →

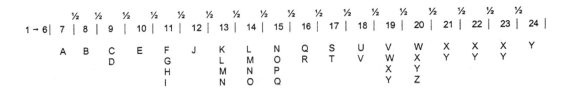

CREDENTIALS OR DOCUMENTATION

Primary and Secondary

A Kenya Preliminary Examination; Certificate of Primary Education: signifies completion of compulsory education (prior to 1985)

B Kenya Certificate of Primary Education: signifies completion of compulsory education (beginning 1985)

C Kenya Junior Secondary Examination: last administered in 1983

D Certificate of Teacher Education (P3)

E Artisan Certificate

F East African Certificate of Education; Kenya Certificate of Education

G Operative Trade Test

H Craft Certificate (prior to late 1980s)

I Certificate of Teacher Education (P2)

J Kenya Certificate of Secondary Education: first awarded in 1989

K East African Advanced Certificate of Education; Kenya Advanced Certificate of Education: last awarded in 1989

Postsecondary

L Ordinary Diploma: two-year program based on credential **F** or **J**

M Certificate of Teacher Education (P1): two-year program based on credential **F** or **J**

N Diploma in Education (S1): two-year program based on credential **K**, or three-year program based on credential **F**; discontinued in 1983

O Technician Certificate: three-year program based on credential **F** or **J**

P Craft Certificate (since the late 1980s): three-year program based on credential **J**

Q Higher Diploma: two-year program based on credential **L**

R Bachelor of... Arts, Commerce, Education, Engineering, Laws, Science, and Technology: three-year programs based on credential **K**, or four-year programs based on credential **J**

S Bachelor of... Dental Surgery, Pharmacy, and Veterinary Medicine: four-year programs based on credential **K**, or five-year programs based on credential **J**

T Bachelor of Philosophy: one-year program based on credential **R**

U   Bachelor of Architecture; Bachelor of Medicine and Bachelor of Surgery (MBBS): five-year programs based on credential **K**, or six years based on credential **J**
V   Master of... Arts, Business Administration, Education, Laws, Philosophy, Public Health, and Science: two-year programs based on credential **R** or **S**
W   Doctor of Education: two-year program based on credential **V**, or three-year program based on credential **R**; discontinued in 1980[1]
X   Doctor of Philosophy
Y   Doctor of Medicine: one to six years following MBBS[1]
Z   Master of Architecture; Master of Medicine: two-year programs based on credential **U**

[1]   In addition to the Doctor of Literature and the Doctor of Science, the Doctor of Education and the Doctor of Medicine may be awarded as honorary degrees.

GRADING INFORMATION

Secondary

East African Certificate of Education; Kenya Certificate of Education

Numeric	Description
1-2	Very Good
3-6	Pass With Credit
7-8	Pass
9	Fail

Kenya Certificate of Secondary Education

Letter	Description
A,A-	Very Good
B+,B,B-	Good
C+,C,C-,D+	Average
D,D-	Weak
E	Poor

- D- is the lowest passing grade in this scale.

East African Advanced Certificate of Education; Kenya Advanced Certificate of Education

Letter	Description
A,B,C,D,E	Principal Level Pass
O	Subsidiary Level Pass (but failed at Principal Level)
F	Fail

Higher Education

Percentage	Letter	Description
70-100	A	First Class Honours
60-69	B	Second Class Honours, Upper Division
50-59	C	Second Class Honours, Lower Division
40-49	D	Pass
0-39	E,F	Fail

POSTSECONDARY INSTITUTION RECOGNITION BODY

The Ministry of Education is responsible for academic (non-technical) education. P.O. Box 30040, Nairobi. Tel: 254-2-334-41. Fax: 254-2-214-287.

The Commission for Higher Education is responsible for the process of university accreditation. P.O. Box 54999, Nairobi. Tel: 254-2-333-315. Fax: 254-2-222-218.

The Ministry of Technical Training and Applied Technology is responsible for some non-university technical postsecondary institutions. Various other national ministries and directorates supervise training in certain applied professional areas.

RESOURCES FOR ADDITIONAL INFORMATION

Meyers, James P. 1993. *ECE Presents: The Educational System of Kenya*. Milwaukee: Educational Credential Evaluators, Inc.

Internet Source:
UNESCO - World Academic Database: www.unesco.org/iau/educke.html

---

Compiler
James P. Meyers
Senior Evaluator
Educational Credential Evaluators, Inc., Milwaukee, WI

KOREA, REPUBLIC OF

YEARS OF EDUCATION →

```
        ½   ½   ½   ½   ½   ½   ½   ½   ½   ½   ½   ½   ½   ½   ½   ½   ½
1 → 6|  7 |  8 |  9 | 10 | 11 | 12 | 13 | 14 | 15 | 16 | 17 | 18 | 19 | 20 | 21 | 22 | 23 | 24 |
           A            B           C   F   G           H →               K →
                                    D                   I
                                    E                   J
```

CREDENTIALS OR DOCUMENTATION

Secondary

A Junior high school diploma: awarded by a general or vocational high school after three years of study beyond grade six

B Senior high school diploma: awarded by a general, vocational, or special purpose high school after three years of study beyond grade nine

Postsecondary

C Junior Vocational College Certificate: awarded by a junior college after two years of vocational study; admission requires credential **A** or **B**

D Junior Technical College Certificate: awarded by a technical junior college after two years of technical study; admission requires credential **A** or **B**

E Pre-Dental or Pre-Medicine Certificate: awarded by a university after two years of study

F Diploma in Nursing: awarded by a junior college after three years of nursing study; admission requires credential **A** or **B**

G Bachelor's degree: awarded by a university or college after four years of study; admission requires credential **A** or **B**

H Master's degree: awarded by a university or college after at least two years of study; admission requires credential **G**

I Bachelor of Science in Dentistry: six-year professional program

J Bachelor of Science in Medicine: six-year professional program

K Doctor of Philosophy degree: awarded upon completion of three or more years of study

GRADING INFORMATION

Secondary
Secondary schools use a uniform grading system: A, B, C, D, E, and F, with D as the lowest passing grade.

211

Postsecondary Education

Letter	Description
A	Excellent or Superior
B	Good or Above Average
C	Fair or Average
D	Inferior But Passing
F	Failure
FA	Failure for Excessive Absences
S	Satisfactory
P	Passing
U	Unsatisfactory
INC	Incomplete
W	Withdrawal

Percentage	Letter	Point
95-100	A+	4.5
90-94	A	4.0
85-89	B+	3.5
80-84	B	3.0
75-79	C+	2.5
70-74	C	2.0
65-69	D+	1.5
60-64	D	1.0
0-59	F	0

POSTSECONDARY INSTITUTION RECOGNITION BODY

Ministry of Education, 77 Sejong-ro, Chongno-Ku, Seoul, 110, Republic of Korea.
Tel: 82 2 738-7981.

RESOURCES FOR ADDITIONAL INFORMATION

The British Council. 1987. *International Guide to Qualifications in Education*. 2nd ed. London, England: Mansell.

Gannon, Philip J. 1985. *The Republic of Korea: A Study of the Educational System of the Republic of Korea and a Guide to the Academic Placement of Students in Educational Institutions in the United States*. Washington D.C.: AACRAO.

National Office of Overseas Skills Recognition. 1991. *Country Education Profiles: Korea*. Canberra: Australian Government Publishing Service.

Internet Source:
UNESCO - World Academic Database: www.unesco.org/iau/educkr.html

Compiler
Marybeth Mirzejewski
Evaluator
Educational Credential Evaluators, Inc., Milwaukee, WI

KUWAIT

YEARS OF EDUCATION →

	½	½	½	½	½	½	½	½	½	½	½	½	½	½	½	½	½
1 → 6| 7	8	9	10	11	12	13	14	15	16	17	18	19	20	21	22	23	24

```
                    A           C C D   C E F F F   G
                    B                   E
```

CREDENTIALS OR DOCUMENTATION

Secondary

A   *Shahadat Al-Thanawiya-Al-A'ama* [Secondary School Leaving Certificate] awarded in the following areas of specialization: science or art, religious, or special education

B   Certificate in Nursing: requires completion of grade nine for admission

Postsecondary

C   Diploma awarded in: applied business studies (two years), allied health fields (two years), technological fields (two to two and one-half years), arts and education (four years), and science and education (four years); requires credential **A** for admission

D   Bachelor's degree in Police Science: requires credential **A** for admission; graduates of this program can enter the second year of the four-year law program at Kuwait University

E   Bachelor's degree: requires credential **A** for admission

F   Master's degree: awarded upon completion of a one- to one and one-half-year program; requires credential **E** for admission

G   Bachelor of Medicine degree: requires credential **A** for admission

GRADING INFORMATION

Secondary
Secondary School Leaving Certificate:

Percentage	Description
70-100	Excellent
60-69	Very Good
50-59	Good
40-49	Pass
0-39	Fail

213

Annual Examinations leading to the Secondary School Leaving Certificate:

Percentage	Description
85-100	Excellent
70-84	Very Good
60-69	Good
50-59	Pass
0-49	Fail

Postsecondary Education

Kuwait University:

Letter/Point Value	Description
A 9.00	Distinction
A- 8.00	Distinction
B+ 7.00	Very Good
B 6.00	Very Good
B- 5.00	Very Good
C+ 4.00	Good
C 3.00	Good
D+ 2.00	Satisfactory
D 1.00	Satisfactory
F 0.00	Fail

Technical Training Centers:

Percentage	Letter/Point Value	Description
90-100	A 4.00	Distinction
80-89.9	B 3.00	Very Good
70-79.9	C 2.00	Good
60-69.9	D 1.00	Pass
0-59.9	F 0.00	Poor

- Student records were not destroyed during the Gulf War.

POSTSECONDARY INSTITUTION RECOGNITION BODY

Ministry of Higher Education. P.O. Box 7, Safat Kuwait. Tel: 965-483-9452. Fax: 965-483-7601.

The Ministry of the Interior oversees programs in police science.

RESOURCES FOR ADDITIONAL INFORMATION

Safwat, Ismail. 1993. *The System of Education in Kuwait.* Annapolis Junction, MD: PIER.

Internet Source
UNESCO - World Academic Database: www.unesco.org/iau/educkw.html

---

Compiler
Jane Yahr Shepard
Evaluator
Educational Credential Evaluators, Inc., Milwaukee, WI

LATVIA

YEARS OF EDUCATION→

```
      ½   ½   ½   ½   ½   ½   ½   ½   ½   ½   ½   ½   ½   ½   ½   ½   ½
1→6| 7 | 8 | 9 | 10| 11| 12| 13| 14| 15| 16| 17| 18| 19| 20| 21| 22| 23| 24|
          A       C   C   C   E   E   F   G   H   H   K   K   K   L→
          B           D   E       F       G   H   J
                                  G       H
                                          I
```

CREDENTIALS OR DOCUMENTATION

Secondary

A *Apliecība par Pamatizglītibu* (Basic School Certificate): signifies completion of nine years of compulsory education

B *Diploms par arodpamatizglītibu* (Diploma of Basic Vocational Education): awarded upon completion of vocational instruction to those who have not earned credential **A** by age 15

C *Diploms par vidējo arodizglītibu* (Diploma of Vocational Secondary Education): two-, three-, and four-year programs requiring credential **A** for admission[1]

D *Atestāts par vispārējo vidējo izglītibu* (Certificate of General Secondary Education): three-year program following credential **A**; leads to postsecondary education

E *Diploms par vidējo speciālo izglītibu* (Diploma of Professional Secondary Education): four and five-year programs requiring credential **A** for admission, or two- and three-year programs requiring credential **D** for admission; programs can be technical and lead to the qualification of "technician," or be in the areas of arts, business, music, nursing, or pharmacy[1,2]

Postsecondary

F *Bakalaurs* (Bachelor): three- and four-year programs based on credential **D** or equivalent[3]

G *Diploms* (Diploma) leading to professional qualifications: four- to five-year professionally oriented university and university-level programs, (e.g., economist, engineer, nurse, social worker, translator/interpreter); some programs lead to credential **H** programs; admission may be based on credential **C, D,** or **E**, or may be one- to two-year programs based on credential **F**[1]

H *Magistrs* (Master): five- to six-year programs based on credential **D** or equivalent, or one- to three-year programs based on credential **F** or **G**

I *Stomatologa Grādu* (Stomatologist Degree): five-year program in dentistry based on credential **D** or equivalent

J *Ārsts Grādu* (Physician Degree): six-year program in medicine based on credential **D** or equivalent

K *Doktors* (Doctor): three to four years culminating in a thesis; admission based on credential **G, H, I** or **J**

L *Habilitēts Doktors* (Doctor): variable length, generally following credential **K**; required for full professorship at present; being phased out with the last expected to be awarded in 1999

216

[1] The four-year credential **C** programs, and the four- and five-year credential **E** programs lead to postsecondary education, though at the same level as credential **D**

[2] Programs in business, nursing, and some technical programs are being upgraded to the higher education sector.

[3] Three-year programs are considered to be an intermediate step toward credential **G**, and four-year programs are considered to represent a completed higher education program.

GRADING INFORMATION

Secondary and Postsecondary Education

Numeric	Description	Translation
10	*Izcili*	With Distinction
9	*Teicami*	Excellent
8	*Ļoti Labi*	Very Good
7	*Labi*	Good
6	*Gandrīz Labi*	Almost Good
5	*Viduvēji*	Satisfactory
4	*Gandrīz Viduvēji*	Almost Satisfactory
1-3	*Neapmierinoši*	Unsatisfactory

Traditional University Scale (being phased out)

Numeric	Description	Translation
5	*Teicami*	Excellent
4	*Labi*	Good
3	*Apmierinosi*	Satisfactory, Fair
2	*Neapmierinoši*	Unsatisfactory
1	*Loti Vaji*	Totally Unsatisfactory

POSTSECONDARY INSTITUTION RECOGNITION BODY

Ministry of Education and Science; Valnu Street 2; Riga 1050, Latvia. Tel: 3717222415. Fax: 3717213992. E-mail: izm@izm.gov.lv

RESOURCES FOR ADDITIONAL INFORMATION

Academic Information Centre-Latvian ENIC/NARIC. 1997. *Izglītība Latvijā* (Education in Latvia). Riga, Latvia: Ministry of Education and Science.

Rauhvargers, A. 1995. "Latvia's Current Educational System." *World Education News & Reviews* 8, 2:10-18.

Rauhvargers, A. and Ieva Brensone, eds. 1996. *Higher Education Institutions in Latvia.* Riga, Latvia: Academic Information Centre-Latvian ENIC, Ministry of Education.

Rauhvargers, A. and Ieva Brensone, eds. 1998. *Higher Education in Latvia 1998/99.* Riga, Latvia: Academic Information Centre-Latvian ENIC/NARIC, Ministry of Education and Science.

Internet Sources:
Ministry of Education and Science: www.iclub.lv/izm/e/head.htm
UNESCO - World Academic Database: www.unesco.org/iau/educlv.html

---

Compilers
Andrejs Rauhvargers
Director-Academic Information Centre
Ministry of Education and Science, Latvia

Jean Ringer
Associate, Global Credential Evaluators, Inc.
Owner of J.B. Ringer Credential Evaluation, Inc., College Station, TX

LEBANON

YEARS OF EDUCATION →

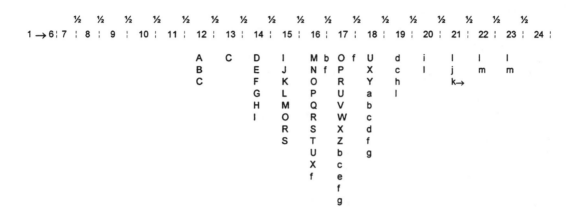

	½	½	½	½	½	½	½	½	½	½	½	½	½	½	½	½	½
1 → 6	7	8	9	10	11	12	13	14	15	16	17	18	19	20	21	22	23	24

```
                    A   C   D   I   M b  O f  U   d   i   l   l   l
                    B       E   J   N f  P    X   c   l   j   m   m
                    C       F   K   O    R    Y   h       k→
                            G   L   P    U    a   l
                            H   M   Q    V    b
                            I   O   R    W    c
                                R   S    X    d
                                S   T    Z    f
                                    U    b    g
                                    X    c
                                    f    e
                                         f
                                         g
```

CREDENTIALS OR DOCUMENTATION

Secondary

A   البكالوريا اللبنانية للتعليم الثانوي (Lebanese Baccalaureate): awarded upon passing of national examination[1]

B   *Baccalauréat technique;* البكالوريا الفنية (Technical Baccalaureate): awarded upon passing of national examination[2]

C   *Baccalauréat d'enseignement;* البكالوريا التعليمية (Teaching Baccalaureate), previously known as the First Teaching Certificate (شهادة التعليمية الأولى): three years after the intermediate-level *Brevet* (certificate representing nine years of education) or one year after credential **A**; considered equivalent to credential **A** for admission to university education programs in Lebanon

Postsecondary

D   Associate of Arts, Science, Applied Science: two years, requiring credential **A** for admission

E   *Diplôme d'études scientifiques préparatoires* (Diploma of Preparatory Scientific Studies): two years, requiring credential **A** for admission

F   *Diplôme d'études techniques de banque* (Diploma of Technical Banking Studies): two years, requiring credential **A** for admission

G   *Diplôme d'études universitaires générales/DEUG* (Diploma of General University Studies), and *Diplôme universitaire d'études et de formation pédagogique/DUEFP* (University Diploma of Pedagogical Studies and Training): two years, requiring credential **A** for admission

H   *Diplôme universitaire de technologie/DUT* (University Technology Diploma): two years, requiring credential **A** or **B** for admission

I   *Technicien supérieur,* الامتياز الفني (Higher Technician): two years when entering with credential **B**, three years when entering with credential **A**

219

J *Diplôme d'agronomie appliquée* (Diploma of Applied Agronomy): three years, requiring credential **A** for admission

K *Diplôme d'Etat Français d'infirmiers* (French State Diploma in Nursing), *Licence en soins infirmiers* (Licence in Nursing): three years; requires credential **A** for admission

L *Diplôme d'études techniques d'assurance* (Diploma of Insurance Studies): three years, requiring credential **A** for admission

M الشهادة التعليمية (Teaching Certificate): three years, requiring credential **A** or **C**

N *Diplôme d'études supérieur de banque* (Diploma of Higher Banking Studies): two years, requiring credential **F** for admission

O Bachelor of...Arts, Science, Engineering, Architecture: three to five years in American-style universities; requires credential **A** for admission[3]

P بكالوريوس (Bachelor's degree): four to five years, requiring credential **A** for admission

Q *Diplôme* (Diploma) in theater arts, audiovisual studies, agronomy engineering (*Diplôme d'ingénieur agronomie*): four years, requiring credential **A** for admission

R *Licence* (Licence): three to five years (depending on institution and field of study), requiring credential **A** or **B** (depending on field) for admission; *Licence spécialisée* (Specialized Licence), two years, requiring credential **H** for admission

S *Licence d'enseignement* (Teaching Licence): three to four years[4], requiring credential **A** or **C** for admission, two years when entering with credential **G**

T *Licence d'enseignement technique;* الإجازة التعليمية الفنية (Licence of Technical Education): four years, requiring credential **A** or **B** for admission

U *Maîtrise* (Master): four years entering with credential **A**; in some fields, one to two years, requiring three- or four-year credential **R** or four-year credential **S**

V *Diplôme* (Diploma): five years in the fields of veterinary medicine, dental surgery, and pharmacy; requires credential **A** for admission

W *Diplôme de traducteur, d'intreprète* (Translation, Interpretation Diploma): two years, requiring three-year credential **R** for admission

X *Diplôme d'études supérieures/DES* (Diploma of Higher Studies): four to six years in fine and applied arts; requires credential **A** for admission

Y *Diplôme d'études supérieures spécialisées en sciences infirmières* (Diploma of Higher Specialized Studies in Nursing): three years, requiring three-year credential **R** in nursing

Z *Diplôme d'ingénieur, d'ingenieur agronome* (Diploma of Engineering, Agronomy Engineering): three years, requiring credential **E** for admission; or five years, requiring credential **A** for admission

a *Certificat d'aptitude professionnel d'education supérieur/CAPES* (Certificate of Aptitude in Higher Education): two years, requiring four-year credential **R** for admission

b *Diplôme d'études approfondies/DEA* (Diploma of Advanced Studies): one year, requiring four-year credential **R** or **U** for admission; one and one-half to two years, requiring three-year credential **R** for admission

c *Diplôme d'études supérieures/DES;* دبلوم الدراسات العليا (Diploma of Higher Studies): one to two years, requiring four-year credential **R**, four- or five-year credential **P**, credential **U**, **V**, or **Z** for admission

d ماجستير (Master's degree): two years, requiring credential **P** for admission

e *Magistere* (Master's degree): one year, requiring four-year credential **S** for admission

f Master of Science, Arts, Architecture, Public Health: one to two years, requiring three- or four-year credential **O** for admission

g Normal Diploma: one year (18–24 credits) at American-style institutions;[3] requires credential **O** for admission

h *Diplôme en médecine générale, diplôme de docteur en médecine* (Diploma of General Medicine, Medical Doctor): seven years, requiring credential **A**

220

i *Docteur de pharmacie* (Doctor of Pharmacy): three years (including one year clinical experience), requiring credential **V** for admission

j *Docteur en médecine dentaire* (Doctor of Dental Medicine, Pharmacy): four years (including one year clinical experience), requiring credential **V** for admission

k Medical Doctor (MD) four years (plus two to four years residency), requiring four-year credential **O** for admission

l *Doctorat, Doctorat d'Etat, Doctorat es lettres, Doctorat troisième cycle* (Doctorate, State Doctorate, Doctorate in Letters, Third Cycle Doctorate): two to five years, requiring credential **b**, **c**, **f**, or **e** for admission

m *Doctorat première cycle* (First-Cycle Doctorate): 3–5 years, requiring **b** for admission

[1] Prior to 1987, credential **A** was issued in two parts, "Part I" and "Part II." Part I was eliminated in 1987.

[2] Prior to 1980, credential **B** was issued in two parts, "Part I" and "Part II." Part I was eliminated in 1980, when the cycle was reduced from four to three years.

[3] Durations indicated for bachelor's degrees are those required for students entering as freshmen. Students holding credential **A** are usually awarded 30 "advance placement" credits and enter as sophomores. The universities awarding degrees on this pattern are: The American University of Beirut, Lebanese-American University (formerly Beirut University College), Notre Dame University of Louiaze, and Haigazian University College.

[4] Credential **S** is awarded after three years at the Lebanese University's Institute of Social Sciences, and after four years at other institutions.

GRADING INFORMATION

Secondary

Score	Remark	Translation
18–20	*Excellent*, ممتاز	Excellent
15–17	*Très Bien*, جيد جدا	Very Good
12–14	*Bien*, جيد	Good
10–11	*Passable*, مقبول	Pass
0–9	*Insuffisant*, راسب	Fail

• Some private secondary schools grade on a 100-point scale.

Higher Education

Considerable variation exists in the grading scales used by postsecondary institutions in Lebanon. The two illustrations below should be used for general reference only, and not as a definitive guide to individual transcripts.

Twenty-point scale

Score	Remark
18–20.0	Excellent (*Exceptionnel*)
16–17.9	Very Good (*Très Bien*)
14–15.9	Good (*Bien*)
12–13.9	Satisfactory (*Assez Bien*)
10–11.9	Passing (*Passable*)
below 10	Fail

- Minimum passing scores for individual courses may be as low as seven in some institutions/faculties.
- The twenty-point scale is used predominantly by the French-style institutions.

Hundred-point scale

Score	Remark	Translation
90–100	*Excellent, Exceptionnel,* ممتاز	Excellent
80–89	*Très Bien,* جيد جداً	Very Good
70–79	*Bien,* جيد	Good
60–69	*Assez Bien,* مقبول/حسن	Satisfactory
50–59	*Passable,* وسط/ضعيف	Passing, Weak

- In some institutions, the minimum passing average is 60.

POSTSECONDARY INSTITUTION RECOGNITION BODY

National Council of Higher Education; Ministry of Higher Education, Starco Building, 9th Floor, Beirut, Lebanon. Tel: 961-1-373224 or 961-1-371478. Fax: 961-1-652810 or 961-1-371276.

RESOURCES FOR ADDITIONAL INFORMATION

Griff, Ernest R. 1988. *A Guide for the Evaluation of Credentials from Lebanon.* Washington, D.C.: AACRAO.

National Office of Overseas Skills Recognition. 1992. *Lebanon: A Comparative Study.* Canberra: Australian Government Publishing Service.

Nucho, Leslie S., ed. 1993. *Education in the Arab World, Volume I.* Washington, D.C.: AMIDEAST.

Internet Sources:
Embassy of Lebanon's list of universities, faculties, and phone numbers:
www.embofleb.org/lebanon.htm

UNESCO—World Academic Database: www.unesco.org/iau/educlb.html

---

Compiler
Leslie S. Nucho
Vice President
AMIDEAST, Washington, D.C.

LESOTHO

```
      ½   ½   ½   ½   ½   ½   ½   ½   ½   ½   ½   ½   ½   ½   ½   ½   ½
1→6│ 7 │ 8 │ 9 │10 │11 │12 │13 │14 │15 │16 │17 │18 │19 │20 │21 │22 │23 │24 │
     A           B         C D F   G   H   J   M   L   O   O   O
                             E         I   K   N   N
                                       J
```

CREDENTIALS OR DOCUMENTATION

Primary and Secondary

A   Standard Seven Leaving Certificate or Primary School Leaving Certificate (There is no compulsory education.)
B   Junior Certificate of Secondary Education
C   Cambridge Overseas School Certificate: awarded by the University of Cambridge Local Examinations Syndicate
D   Certificate in Agriculture: two and one-half-year program requiring credential **B** for admission
E   Certificate in Home Economics: two and one-half-year program requiring credential **B** for admission
F   Primary Teachers' Certificate: two years of courses separated by one year of practice teaching, requiring credential **B** for admission

Postsecondary

G   Diploma in Agriculture: two-year program requiring credential **C** for admission
H   Advanced Primary Teachers' Certificate: three-year program of training for primary school head teachers, requiring credential **C** for admission
I   Secondary Teachers' Certificate: three-year program of training for lower secondary school teachers, requiring credential **C** for admission
J   Bachelor of Education: four-year program requiring credential **C** for admission, or a two-year program requiring credential **F** and teaching experience for admission [1]
K   Bachelor's degree in the fields of Arts, Commerce, and Science: four-year program requiring credential **C** for admission[2]
L   Bachelor of Laws (LL.B.): two-year program (referred to as part III) requiring credential **K** for admission
M   Postgraduate Certificate in Education: one-year program requiring credential **K** for admission
N   Master's degree in the fields of Arts, Education, and Science: two-year programs requiring credential **J** or **K** for admission
O   Doctoral degree: two-year to three-year program requiring credential **N** for admission

[1]   A Concurrent Certificate of Education (CCE) is awarded with each Bachelor of Education degree.
[2]   Part I: years 1 and 2; Part II: years 3 and 4.

GRADING INFORMATION

Secondary

Numeric	Description
1	Excellent
2	Good
3-6	Credit
7-8	Pass
9	Fail

Higher Education

Individual Subjects:

Letter	Percentage	Description	Overall Results: Class
A	80-100	Excellent	1st Class
B	70-79	Very Good	2nd Class, 1st Division
C	60-69	Good	2nd Class, 2nd Division
D	50-59	Pass	Pass
E	40-49	Fail	Fail
F	0-39	Fail	Fail

- The grade of E is failing, but a supplementary examination may be taken.

POSTSECONDARY INSTITUTION RECOGNITION BODY

Ministry of Education and Manpower Development. P.O. Box 47, Maseru.
Tel: 266-315932. Fax: 266-310297.

RESOURCES FOR ADDITIONAL INFORMATION

The British Council. 1996. *International Guide to Qualifications in Education.* 4th ed.
London: Mansell.

Cameron, John, and Paul Hurst, eds. 1985. *International Handbook of Educational Systems.* Vol. II. Chichester, England: John Wiley and Sons.

Internet Source:
UNESCO - World Academic Database: www.unesco.org/iau/educls.html

---

Compiler
James S. Frey
President
Educational Credential Evaluators, Inc., Milwaukee, WI

LIBERIA

YEARS OF EDUCATION →

1 → 6	7	8	9	10	11	12	13	14	15	16	17	18	19	20	21	22	23	24
	½	½	½	½	½	½	½	½	½	½	½	½	½	½	½	½	½	

```
                      A          B B B    E    E    F    F
                                 C   C                   G
                                     D
```

CREDENTIALS OR DOCUMENTATION

Secondary

A High School Diploma: graduates interested in attending a university take the Senior School Certificate Examination administered by the West African Examinations Council

Postsecondary

B Associate's degree: requires credential **A** for admission
C Teacher's Certificate: requires credential **A** for admission
D Nursing Certificate: requires credential **A** for admission
E Bachelor's degree: requires credential **A** for admission
F Master's degree: awarded upon completion of a one- to two-year program; requires credential **E** for admission
G Bachelor of Medicine degree: requires credential **A** for admission

GRADING INFORMATION

Secondary
Percentage
90 - 100
80 - 89
73 - 79
70 - 72
0 - 69

Postsecondary
Letter/Point Value
A   4.00
B   3.00
C   2.00
D   1.00
F   0.00

- The official language in Liberia is English.

- Due to the current political situation, students may be unable to obtain academic records. Some institutions and their records have been destroyed. It is extremely difficult and sometimes impossible to verify documents.

POSTSECONDARY INSTITUTION RECOGNITION BODY

Ministry of Education. Broad Street, Monrovia Liberia. Tel: 231-1-222-654. Fax: 231-515-515.

RESOURCES FOR ADDITIONAL INFORMATION

Wise, Cynthia. 1973. *The Admission and Academic Placement of Students from Selected Sub-Saharan African Countries.* Washington D.C.: AACRAO.

Internet Source:
UNESCO - World Academic Database. www.unesco.org/iau/educlr.html

Compiler
Jane Yahr Shepard
Evaluator
Educational Credential Evaluators, Inc., Milwaukee, WI

MACAU

YEARS OF EDUCATION

```
      ½    ½    ½    ½    ½    ½    ½    ½    ½    ½    ½    ½    ½    ½    ½    ½    ½
1 → 6|  7 |  8 |  9 | 10 | 11 | 12 | 13 | 14 | 15 | 16 | 17 | 18 | 19 | 20 | 21 | 22 | 23 | 24 |
                 A          B    E    J              O    O    P    R    S→
                            C    F    K                   P    Q    S→
                            D    G    L                   Q    R
                            E    H    N                   R    S→
                                 I
                                 L
                                 M
```

CREDENTIALS OR DOCUMENTATION

Macau's schools, especially those at the primary and secondary levels, are influenced by the educational systems of Hong Kong and Great Britain, Portugal, the People's Republic of China (PRC), and the Republic of China (ROC). Credentials of a particular influence are indicated. More information on those credentials may be found under those country compilations in this publication.

Secondary

A *Certificao do Curso do Ensino Unificado* (Certificate of the General Unified Course of Study): issued until 1986; since 1986, a diploma is issued (Portugal)

B *Certidao do Curso Complementar* (Certificate of the Complementary Course): issued until 1986 (Portugal)

C Hong Kong Certificate of Education Examination (Hong Kong)

D General Certificate of Education, Ordinary Level, Examinations (Hong Kong)

E Diploma (PRC)

F *Certidao do Decimo-Segundo Ano* (Certificate of Year 12) issued until 1986; since 1986, a diploma is issued (Portugal)

G *Certificado de Fim de Estudios Secondarios* (Certificate of Secondary Studies) (Portugal)

H Hong Kong Higher Level Examination: last administered in 1992 (Hong Kong)

I Senior High School or Senior Middle School Diploma (ROC)

J Hong Kong Advanced Level Examination (Hong Kong)

K General Certificate of Education, Advanced Level Examinations (Hong Kong)

Postsecondary

L Diploma: one to two years of study based on age 18 and usually a grade 11 credential (**B, C, D,** or **E**)

M Certificate in General Studies: one year of study based on a grade 11 credential (**B, C, D,** or **E**)

N Associate degrees: two years of study based on a grade 11 credential (**B, C, D,** or **E**)

O *Bacheralato*, or Bachelor's degree: three-year programs through 1989-90, and four-year programs since 1990-91; admission based on a grade 12 credential (**E, F, G, H,** or **I**)

P *Licenciatura*, or Licenciate, in the fields of law (five-year program), and Portuguese language and culture (four-year program); admission based on a grade 12 credential (**E, F, G, H,** or **I**)

Q Post Graduate Certificates and Diplomas: one to two years of part-time study beyond credential **O** or equivalent

R *Mestrado*, or Master's degree: one or two years of study beyond credential **O** or equivalent

S *Doutoramento*, or Doctorate: awarded upon completion of research; admission based on credential **R**

GRADING INFORMATION

Secondary

Grading varies depending upon the school's influence. Pass marks range between 40% and 50%. Grades may be reported as letter or percentage. For more information, see the compilations for the influencing countries in this publication.

Higher Education

University of Macau and Macau Polytechnic:

Letter	Point	Alternative	Description
A	3.7-4.0	18-20	Superior or Very Good with Distinction, 20 w/Honors
B	2.7-3.69	16-17	Good with Distinction
C	1.7-2.69	14-15	Good
D	1.0-1.69	10-13	Satisfactory
F	0-0.99	0-9	Fail

- The Junior College and College of Continuing Education became the Polytechnic College and were incorporated into Macau Polytechnic in 1990.

- The University of East Asia (Universidade da Asia Oriental) became the Universidade de Macau or the University of Macau in 1991.

Asian International Open University and East Asia Open Institute:

Letter	Percentage	Point	Description
A	70-100	4.0	Very Good
B	60-69	3.0	Good
C	50-59	2.0	Average
D	40-49	1.0	Pass
F	0-39	0.0	Fail

- The Open College in Hong Kong became East Asia Open Institute in 1988 and then became Asia International Open University (also known as the Universidade Aberta Internacional da Asia) in 1992.

POSTSECONDARY INSTITUTION RECOGNITION BODY

Serviços de Educação e Juventude de Macau; Rua Central de Toi San, Edif. Litoral, 2°
andar, Macau.

RESOURCES FOR ADDITIONAL INFORMATION

Bray, Mark. 1992. "Colonialism, Scale and Politics: Divergence and Convergence of
Educational Development in Hong Kong and Macau." *Comparative Education Review*
36, 3: 322-342.

National Office of Overseas Skills Recognition. 1996. *Country Education Profiles:
Macau*. Canberra: Australian Government Publishing Service.

Internet Source:
UNESCO - World Academic Database: www.unesco.org/iau/educmo.html

---

Compiler
Jean Ringer
Associate, Global Credential Evaluators, Inc.
Owner of J.B. Ringer Credential Evaluation, Inc., College Station, TX

MALAWI

YEARS OF EDUCATION →

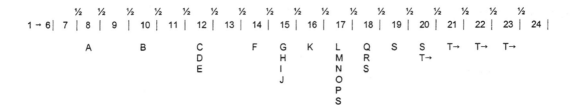

CREDENTIALS OR DOCUMENTATION

Primary and Secondary

A Primary School Leaving Certificate (There is no compulsory education.)
B Junior Certificate of Education, or Junior Secondary School Certificate
C Malawi School Certificate of Education, or Malawi General Certificate of Education
D Teachers' Certificate T3: two-year program in lower primary education requiring credential **B** for admission
E State Enrolled Nurse: two-year program requires credential **B** for admission

Postsecondary

F Teachers' Certificate T2: two-year program in upper primary education requiring credential **C** for admission
G Diploma in the fields of Agriculture, Business Studies, Engineering, Laboratory Technology, and Public Health Inspection: three-year programs requiring credential **C** for admission
H Diploma in Education, or Diploma in Secondary Teaching: three-year program requiring credential **C** for admission
I State Registered Nurse: three-year program requiring credential **C** for admission
J Medical Auxiliary: three-year program requiring credential **C** for admission
K Bachelor (Pass) degree in the fields of Arts, Public Administration, Science, & Social Science: four-year programs requiring credential **C** for admission
L Bachelor's degree in the fields of Education and Technical Education: two-year programs requiring credential **G** or **H** for admission
M Bachelor of Education: five-year program in secondary education requiring credential **C** for admission
N Bachelor's degree in the fields of Agriculture and Commerce: two-year programs requiring credential **G** for admission
O Bachelor (Honours) degree: five-year program requiring credential **C** for admission
P Bachelor of Laws: five-year program requiring credential **C** for admission
Q Bachelor of Engineering: three-year program requiring credential **G** for admission

R   University Certificate in Education: one-year program in secondary education requiring credential **L** or **M** and at least one year of teaching experience for admission

S   Master: one- to two-year programs requiring any of credentials **K** through **Q** for admission

T   Doctor of Philosophy: usually three or more years beyond credential **S**

GRADING INFORMATION

Secondary

Numeric	Description
1-2	Distinction
3-6	Credit
7-8	Pass
9	Fail

Postsecondary Education

Percentage	Description
75-100	Undoubted Distinction
70-74	Marginal Distinction
60-69	Bare Distinction, or Credit
50-59	Pass
40-49	Bare Pass
35-39	Marginal Failure
0-34	Undoubted Failure

POSTSECONDARY INSTITUTION RECOGNITION BODY

Ministry of Education: P.O. Box 328, Lilongwe 3. Tel: 265-784 800. Fax: 265-782 873.

RESOURCES FOR ADDITIONAL INFORMATION

The British Council. 1996. *International Guide to Qualifications in Education.* 4th ed. London: Mansell.

Cameron, John and Paul Hurst, eds. 1985. *International Handbook of Educational Systems.* Vol. II. Chichester, England: John Wiley and Sons.

Internet Source:
UNESCO - World Academic Database: www.unesco.org/iau/educmw.html

---

Compiler
James S. Frey
President
Educational Credential Evaluators, Inc., Milwaukee WI

MALAYSIA

YEARS OF EDUCATION →

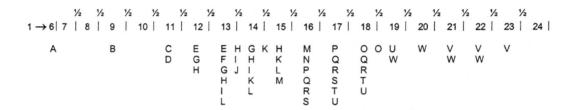

CREDENTIALS OR DOCUMENTATION

Secondary

A *Ujian Percapaian Sekolah Rendah/UPSR* (Primary School Certificate): signifies completion of primary education

B *Penilaian Menengah Rendah/PMR* (Lower Certificate of Education): signifies completion of lower secondary education; prior to 1991 Lower Certificate of Education was *Sijil Rendah Pelajaran/SPR*

C *Sijil Pelajaran Malaysia/SPM* (Malaysian Certificate of Education): signifies completion of upper secondary education

D *Sijil Pelajaran Vokesyenal Malaysia/SPVM* (Malaysian Certificate of Vocational Education): signifies completion of technical/vocational education

E *Sijil Matrikulasi* (Matriculation Certificate): requires credential **C** for admission; taken after one or two years of study; gives direct university access to students without credential **F**; primarily for *Bumiputra* (native Malay) students

F *Sijil Tinggi Persekolahan Malaysia/STPM* (Malaysian Higher School Certificate): requires credential **C** for admission; signifies completion of sixth form—pre-university academic certification and selection exam

Postsecondary

G University Certificate: requires credential **C** for admission; awarded after one to three years of study

H Diplomas awarded by technical institutes: requires credential **C** or **D** for admission; one to four years in the fields of architecture, art and design, business administration, chemistry, and many others

I *Sijil Guru* (Teacher Training Certificate): requires credential **C** for admission; signifies two, two and one-half, or three years at government teacher training center

J Polytechnic Certificate: requires credential **C** or **D** for admission; signifies completion of 27 months of study at polytechnic

K *Sijil Guru…(field)…* (Specialist Teacher Training Certificate): admission based on credential **I** and five years teaching experience; one-year program

L University Advanced Certificate: requires credential **G** for admission; one-year program

M *Sarjana Muda or Bacelor* (Bachelor's degree): awarded by a university after three years of study; requires credential **E** or **F** for admission

N   Diplomas awarded in technical institutes: three years following credential **F** in the fields of law, library science, and mass communication

O   Advanced Diplomas awarded by technical institutes: two to two and one-half years following credential **N** in fields of accounting, architecture, engineering, law, and others

P   Diploma in Education awarded by a university: one-year program requiring credential **M** for admission

Q   Certificate, Diploma, or Postgraduate Diploma awarded by a university: requires credential **M** for admission; awarded after one or two years of study

R   *Sarjana* (Master's degree): requires credential **M** for admission; awarded by a university after one or two years

S   Bachelor of Dental Surgery: four-year program requiring credential **E** or **F** for admission

T   Doctor of Veterinary Medicine/DVM: five-year program requiring credential **E** or **F** for admission

U   Bachelor of Medicine, Bachelor of Surgery/M.B.,B.S., or Doctor of Medicine/M.D.: five- or six-year program requiring credential **E** or **F** for admission

V   Master's degree in Medicine or Surgery: four-year program requiring credential **U** for admission

W   *Doktor Falsafah* (Doctor of Philosophy): requires credential **R** for admission; programs require two to five years of study

GRADING INFORMATION

Secondary Education
Sijil Pelajaran Malaysia

Numeric	Description	Certificate Symbol
1-2	Very Good	P
3-4	Pass With Credit	P
5-6	Pass With Credit	P
7-8	Pass	S
9	Fail	F

Sijil Tinggi Persekolahan Malaysia

Grade	Percentage	Description
A & B	65-100	Pass
C & D	50-64	Pass
E	40-49	Pass
R	30-39	Partial Pass
Fail		Fail

Postsecondary Education

Letter	Percentage	Description
A	70 and above	Pass With Distinction
B	60-69	Pass With High Credit
C	50-59	Pass With Credit
D	40-49	Pass
F	0-30	Fail

- Percent grading scales vary by university, by faculty within a university, and by level of study.

Degree Classification
First Class
Second Class (Upper Division)
Second Class (Lower Division)
Third Class or Pass

POSTSECONDARY INSTITUTION RECOGNITION BODY

Ministry of Education, Paras 7 Block J, Pusat Bandar Damansara, 50604 Kuala Lumpur, Malaysia. Tel: 60-3-2556812. Fax: 60-3-2555305.

RESOURCES FOR ADDITIONAL INFORMATION

Stedman, Joann. 1986. *Malaysia: A Study of the Educational System of Malaysia and a Guide to the Academic Placement of Students in Educational Institutions in the United States*. Washington, D.C.: AACRAO.

Internet Sources:
Ministry of Education: www.moe.gov.my
UNESCO – World Academic Database: www.unesco.org/iau/educmy.html

---

Compiler
Sandy Gault
University of Kansas

MALI

YEARS OF EDUCATION →

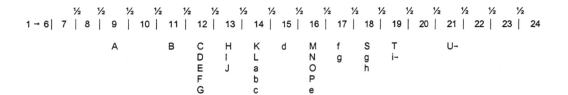

```
     ½   ½   ½   ½   ½   ½   ½   ½   ½   ½   ½   ½   ½   ½   ½   ½   ½
1 → 6│ 7 │ 8 │ 9 │ 10 │ 11 │ 12 │ 13 │ 14 │ 15 │ 16 │ 17 │ 18 │ 19 │ 20 │ 21 │ 22 │ 23 │ 24
            A       B   C   H   K   d   M   f   S   T       U-
                        D   I   L       N   g   g   i-
                        E   J   a       O       h
                        F       b       P
                        G       c       e
```

CREDENTIALS OR DOCUMENTATION

Secondary

A   *Diplôme d'Études Fondamentales* (Basic Studies Diploma)

B   *Certificat d'aptitude professionnelle* (Professional proficiency certificate): requires credential **A** for admission

C   *Baccalauréat Malien* (Malian Baccalaureate)

D   *Baccalauréat Technique* (Technical Baccalaureate)

E   *Diplôme d'Infirmier d'État* (State Nursing Diploma): requires credential **A** for admission

F   *Diplôme de Technicien de Laboratoire* (Laboratory Technician Diploma): requires credential **A** for admission

G   *Diplôme de Sage-femme d'État* (State Midwife's Diploma): requires credential **A** for admission

H   *Brevet de Technicien* (Technician Certificate): from the *École Centrale pour l'Industrie, le Commerce et l'Administration (ECICA)*; requires credential **A** for admission

I   *Diplôme de Technicien Supérieur* (Advanced Technician Diploma): from the *Institut Polytechnique rural*; requires credential **A** for admission

J   *Diplôme de Dessin et d'Arts Plastiques* (Fine Arts Diploma): from the *Institut National des Arts (INA)*; requires credential **A** for admission

Postsecondary (pre-1996) [1]

K   *Diplôme de Technicien Supérieur* (Advanced Technician Diploma): from the *École des Hautes Études Pratiques*; required credential **C** for admission (two years)

L   *Diplôme des Écoles Normales Secondaires* (Secondary Teacher-training School Diploma): required credential **C** for admission[2]

M   *Diplôme de l'École Normale Supérieure* (Higher Teacher-training School Diploma): required credential **C** for admission

N   *Diplôme de l'École Nationale d'Administration* (National School of Management Diploma): required credential **C** for admission

O   *Diplôme d'Ingénieur des Sciences Appliquées* (Engineer Diploma in Applied Sciences): from the *École Nationale d'Ingénieurs* or the *Institut Polytechnique Rural de Katibougou*; required credential **C** for admission

235

P   *Diplôme de Professeur de l'Enseignement Secondaire Technique et Professionnel* (Technical and Vocational Secondary School Teacher Diploma): from the *École National d'Ingénieurs*; required credential **C** for admission

Q   *Diplôme de Docteur en Médecine* (Doctor of Medicine Diploma): from the *École Nationale de Médecine et de Pharmacie*; a five-year program and a year of practice; required credential **C** for admission

R   *Diplôme de Docteur en Pharmacie* (Doctor of Pharmacy Diploma): from the *École Nationale de Médecine et de Pharmacie*; a five-year program and a year of practice; required credential **C** for admission

S   *Diplôme d'Études Approfondies* (Diploma of Advanced Studies): from the *Institut Supérieur pour la Formation et la Recherche Appliquée*; required credential **M, N, O, P** or equivalent for admission

T   *Diplôme de Docteur-Ingénieur ès-Sciences* (Doctorate in Engineering): from the *Institut Polytechnique Rural de Katibougou*; required credential **O** for admission

U   *Doctorat Malien* (Doctorate): from the *Institut Supérieur pour la Formation et la Recherche Appliquée*; required credential **S** for admission

Postsecondary (post-1996)[1]

a   *Diplôme d'Études Universitaires Générales (DEUG)* (Diploma of General University Studies): requires credential **C** for admission

b   *Diplôme Universitaire de Technologie (DUT)* (University Diploma in Technology): requires credential **C** for admission

c   *Diplôme de Technicien Supérieur* (Higher Technician Diploma): requires credential **C** for admission

d   *Licence* (Licentiate): requires credential **a** for admission

e   *Maîtrise* (Master): requires credential **d** for admission

f   *Diplôme d'Ingénieur* (Diploma of Engineer): requires credential **a** or equivalent for admission

g   *Diplôme d'Études Approfondies (DEA)* (Diploma of Advanced Studies): mostly a two-year program, but some one-year programs may exist; requires credential **e** or equivalent for admission

h   *Diplôme d'Études Supérieures Spécialisées (DESS)* (Diploma of Higher Specialized Studies): requires credential **e** for admission

i   *Doctorat* (Doctorate): requires credential **g** for admission[3]

[1] In 1996, the *Université du Mali* was created by the merger of the following institutions: *École Normale Supérieure, École Nationale d'Ingénieurs, Institut Polytechnique rural de Katibougou, École National d'Administration, École National de Médecine et de Pharmacie, Institut Supérieur de Formation et de Recherche Appliquée, École des Hautes Études Pratiques*. New diplomas were then introduced.

[2] Holders of this credential may teach at grades 7-9. Before 1989, the program was four years and required credential **A** for admission. Up to 1989, primary school teachers were trained in the *Instituts Pédagogiques d'Enseignement Général (IPEG)* in a two-year program requiring credential **A** for admission. Since 1989, credential **C** has been required for admission to the *IPEG*.

[3] The doctorate may be earned in two to four years at the *Institut Supérieur de Formation et de Recherche Appliquée (ISFRA)* (Higher Institute of Training and Applied Research): it may then be called a *Doctorat de Spécialité* (Specialized Doctorate). In the Faculties *(Faculté des Sciences et Techniques* -Applied Sciences- *Faculté des Lettres, des Langues, des Arts et des Sciences Humaines* -Humanities and Social Sciences- *Faculté des Sciences Juridiques et Économiques* -Law and Economics-), the Doctorate requires at least three years of preparation.

GRADING INFORMATION

Secondary and Higher Education

Numeric	*Mention*	Comment
16-20	*Très Bien*	Very Good
14-15	*Bien*	Good
12-13	*Assez Bien*	Almost Good
10-11	*Passable*	Satisfactory/Pass
8-9	*Médiocre*	Mediocre
6-7	*Faible*	Weak
3-5	*Très Faible*	Very Weak
0-2	*Nul*	Zero

- 10 is the passing mark.

- Marks of 14 or higher are rarely awarded.

POSTSECONDARY INSTITUTION RECOGNITION BODY

Ministère des enseignements secondaire, supérieur et de la recherche scientifique (Ministry of Secondary and Higher Education and Scientific Research), B.P. 2468, Bamako. Tel: 223 22 55 30. Fax: 223 22 82 97.

RESOURCES USED AND SOURCES OF ADDITIONAL INFORMATION

The British Council. 1996. *International Guide to Qualifications in Education.* 4th ed. London: Mansell.

Ministère des enseignements secondaire, supérieur et de la recherche scientifique, Ministère de l'éducation de base. 1994. "Développement de l'Éducation au Mali." Report presented for the 44th session of the Conférence Internationale sur l'Éducation. Bamako, Mali.

UNESCO. 1996. *World Guide to Higher Education*. Paris: UNESCO.

Internet Source:
UNESCO - World Academic Database: www.unesco.org/iau/educml.html

---

Compiler
Michel Bédard
Service des Équivalences, Ministère des Relations avec les Citoyens et de l'Immigration, Gouvernement du Québec, Canada

MALTA

YEARS OF EDUCATION →

```
   ½   ½   ½   ½   ½   ½   ½   ½   ½   ½   ½   ½   ½   ½   ½   ½   ½
1→6| 7 | 8 | 9 | 10| 11| 12| 13| 14| 15| 16| 17| 18| 19| 20| 21| 22| 23| 24|
                    A   C   D       I   J   K   L   K       O   R   S
                    B       E                   L   N       Q   S   V
                    C       F                   M   P       R
                            G                   P   Q       W
                            H                       T
                                                    U
```

CREDENTIALS OR DOCUMENTATION

Secondary

A General Certificate of Education Ordinary Level: signifies completion of compulsory education (prior to 1992)

B Secondary Education Certificate Examination: signifies completion of compulsory education (beginning in 1992)

C Trade School Certificate: signifies completion of a three- or four-year technical program

D General Certificate of Education Advanced Level: two-year program requiring credential **A** or **B** for admission

E Advanced Matriculation Certificate: two-year program requiring credential **A** or **B** for admission (prior to October 1997)

F Matriculation Certificate: two-year program requiring credential **A** or **B** for admission (beginning October 1997)[1]

Postsecondary

G Ordinary Technician Diploma: two-year program in mechanical or electrical engineering requiring credential **A** or **B** for admission

H Certificate or Diploma: two-year technical program requiring credential **A** or **B** for admission

I Higher Technician Diploma: two years of study in mechanical or electrical engineering requiring credential **G** for admission

J Bachelor of Arts, Bachelor of Commerce, Bachelor of Science: three-year programs requiring credential **D, E,** or **F** for admission

K Bachelor of Arts (Honours): four-year program requiring credential **D, E,** or **F** for admission; in the fields only of Accountancy, Business Management, and Public Administration, five years of study are required

L Bachelor of Dental Surgery (prior to 1990), Bachelor of Pharmacy, and Bachelor of Science in Nursing: four-year programs requiring credential **D, E,** or **F** for admission; the Bachelor of Dental Surgery beginning in 1990 requires four and one-half years of study

M Bachelor of Education (Honours): four-year program requiring credential **D, E,** or **F** for admission

N   Bachelor of Electrical Engineering (Honours) and Bachelor of Mechanical Engineering (Honours): five-year programs requiring credential **D, E,** or **F** for admission

O   Bachelor of Engineering & Architecture: six-year program requiring credential **D, E,** or **F** for admission

P   Master of Arts: one- to two-year program requiring credential **J** for admission

Q   Master of Education: one- to two-year program requiring credential **M** for admission

R   Master of Engineering: one- to two-year program requiring credential **N** for admission

S   Master of Architecture: one- to two-year program requiring credential **O** for admission

T   Master of Philosophy: two-year program requiring at least credential **J** for admission

U   Doctor of Medicine and Surgery: five-year program requiring credential **D, E,** or **F** for admission

V   Doctor of Philosophy: three-year program requiring credential **T** for admission

W   Doctor of Laws: six-year program including thesis; admission based on credential **D, E,** or **F**

---

[1]   Since October 1997, the Matriculation Certificate has been the main entry qualification at the University of Malta. It replaced the previous requirement of three General Certificate of Education Advanced Levels (credential **D**) or Advanced Matriculation Certificate (credential **E**) plus five General Certificate of Education Ordinary Levels (credential **A**) or Secondary Education Certificate (credential **B**).

GRADING INFORMATION

Secondary Education

General Certificate of Education Ordinary Level Examinations: Passing grades of 1 to 5 are used, with "F" indicating failure. Grades 1 to 5 qualify students for further study in the subject.

Secondary Education Certificate Examination: Passing grades of 1 to 7 are used, with "F" indicating failure. Grades 1 to 5 qualify students for further study in the subject.

Trade School Certificate and other Technical Certificates and Diplomas: Grades of Distinction, Credit, and Pass are used.

General Certificate of Education Advanced Level Examinations: Grades of A, B, C, D, and E indicate Principal Level passes; the grade of O indicates a Subsidiary Level pass (but failed at Principal Level), and the grade of F indicates failure.

Advanced Matriculation Certificate: The grades of A, B, C, D, and E are passing; F indicates failing.

Matriculation Certificate: Overall grade given as A, B, or C.

Higher Education

Percentage	Letter	Description
70-100	A	First Class Honours
60-69	B	Second Class Honours, Upper Division
50-59	C	Second Class Honours, Lower Division
40-49	D	Pass
0-39	E, F	Fail

- The University of Malta is the only recognized higher educational institution in Malta.

POSTSECONDARY INSTITUTION RECOGNITION BODY

Ministry of Education, Great Siege Road, Floriana - CMR 02. Tel: 356-221-401.
Fax: 356-221-634.

RESOURCES FOR ADDITIONAL INFORMATION

The British Council. 1996. *International Guide to Qualifications in Education.* 4th ed.
London: Mansell.

National Office of Overseas Skills Recognition. 1992. *Country Education Profiles: Malta.*
Canberra: Australian Government Publishing Service.

Internet Sources:
The official web site of the Maltese Government: Education Division of the Ministry of
    Education and National Culture: www.magnet.mt/home/education
UNESCO - World Academic Database: www.unesco.org/iau/educmt.html

---

Compiler
Suzanne K. Michaels
Evaluator
Educational Credential Evaluators, Inc., Milwaukee, WI

MEXICO

YEARS OF EDUCATION →

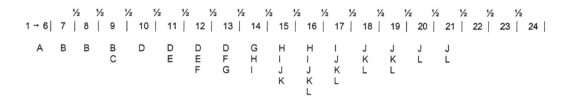

```
      ½   ½   ½   ½   ½   ½   ½   ½   ½   ½   ½   ½   ½   ½   ½   ½   ½
1→6| 7 | 8 | 9 | 10| 11| 12| 13| 14| 15| 16| 17| 18| 19| 20| 21| 22| 23| 24|

 A   B   B   B   D   D   D   D   G   H   H   I   J   J   J   J
             C           E   E   F   H   I   I   J   K   K   L   L
                             F   G   I   J   J   K   L   L
                                     K   K   L
                                     L
```

CREDENTIALS OR DOCUMENTATION

Secondary

A Certificate for *Educación Primaria* (Primary Education): signifies completion of compulsory education

B Certificate for study in artistic, commercial, secretarial, and technical fields: terminal qualifications not providing access to further study

C Certificate for *Educación Secundaria* (Secondary Education)

D Certificate for *Técnico* (Technician) and professional titles including *Enfermero(a)* (Nurse), *Secretario(a)* (Secretary), and *Trabajador(a) Social* (Social Worker): one- to four-year programs; requires credential **C** for admission[1]

E Certificate for *Bachillerato* (Baccalaureate) in the fields of Chemical & Biological Sciences, Economic & Administrative Sciences, Fine Arts, Humanities, Physical & Mathematical Sciences, and Social Sciences: two- or three-year programs; requires credential **C** for admission

F Title of *Profesor* (Teacher) or *Maestro* (Teacher) for Preschool Education, Primary Education, and Physical Education: three- or four-year programs[2]

Postsecondary

G Certificate for *Técnico* (Technician): one- and two-year programs requiring credential **E** for admission[1]

H Title of *Profesor* (Teacher) or *Maestro* (Teacher) for Preschool Education, Primary Education, and Physical Education[2]

I *Licenciado* (Licentiate): three- to five-year programs requiring credential **E** for admission[3]

J *Especialización* (Specialization): one- to four-year (mostly two-year) programs requiring credential **I** for admission

K *Maestría* (Masters): one- and two-year programs requiring credential **I** for admission

L *Doctorado* (Doctorate): two years of coursework plus dissertation, requiring credential **K**, and in some cases credential **I**, for admission

[1] Most technical qualifications are secondary level (based on credential **C**); a few are postsecondary (based on credential **E**). Because terminology on educational documents and the institution name may not clarify the level of study, supporting documentation may be required to determine level.

[2] In 1984 teacher training for preschool and primary school teachers was upgraded. Previously based on credential **C**, admission now requires credential **E**. However, this change was not implemented

uniformly in 1984, so several of these qualifications awarded into the late 1980s represent a program of study based on credential **C**. Physical education teacher training was gradually upgraded starting in 1975; previously based on credential **C**, admission now requires credential **E**.

3   Many *Licenciado* programs do not include the terminology "*Licenciado*" or "*Licenciatura*" and refer instead to the profession itself (e.g., *Ingeniero* [Engineer]). Completion of all degree requirements (such as social service, professional examination, and a thesis), in addition to the coursework, results in the award of a *Título* (Title).

GRADING INFORMATION

All Levels of Education-grading varies between institutions; common scales are noted.

Spanish	Abbreviation	Translation	Numeric	Percentage
Excelente	E	Excellent	10	100
Muy Bien	MB	Very Good	9	90-99
Bien	B	Good	8	80-89
Regular	R	Average	7	70-79
Suficiente	S	Sufficient	6	60-69
No Suficiente	N	Insufficient	5	50-59

- 6 is the minimum passing grade and is sufficient for graduation.

Spanish	Abbreviation	Translation	Numeric	Percentage
Muy Bien	MB	Very Good	9-10.00	90-100
Bien	B	Good	8-8.90	80-89
Suficiente	S	Sufficient	7-7.90	70-79
No Suficiente	N	Insufficient	6-6.90	60-69

- 7 is the minimum passing grade and is sufficient for graduation.

Spanish	Abbreviation	Translation
No Acreditada	NA	Not Passed
Acreditada	AC	Passed
Equivalencia	EQ	Equivalence (exempt)
No Derecho	ND	No Right (unable to sit for final examination due to low attendance rate or low grades)
No Presentada	NP	Not presented (did not sit for final examination)
Revalidada	REV	Revalidated (transfer credit granted)

Grade notations:		
Examen Ordinario	OR	Ordinary Examination (regularly scheduled final examination)
Examen Extraordinario	EX or EE	Extraordinary Examination (first make-up examination)
Examen a Título de suficiencia	TS	Title by way of Sufficiency Examination (second make-up examination)

POSTSECONDARY INSTITUTION RECOGNITION BODY

Programs of study, rather than the educational institutions, are subject to official academic recognition. Programs of study offered by public institutions are automatically officially recognized. A few private institutions have the status of *libre* (free), and their programs of study are officially recognized. The remainder of the private institutions must seek program recognition either through incorporation with a public institution, involving a formal arrangement for the program offering, or through receipt of official recognition by a federal or state agency or ministry of education.

RESOURCES FOR ADDITIONAL INFORMATION

Villa, Kitty M. 1982. *Mexico: A Study of the Educational System of Mexico and a Guide to the Academic Placement of Students in Educational Institutions in the United States.* Washington, D.C.: AACRAO.

National Office of Overseas Skills Recognition. 1993. *Country Education Profiles: Mexico.* Canberra: Australian Government Publishing Service.

Compiler
James P. Meyers
Senior Evaluator
Educational Credential Evaluators, Inc., Milwaukee, WI

MOLDOVA

YEARS OF EDUCATION →

```
      ½   ½   ½   ½   ½   ½   ½   ½   ½   ½   ½   ½   ½   ½   ½   ½   ½
1 → 6| 7 | 8 | 9 | 10 | 11 | 12 | 13 | 14 | 15 | 16 | 17 | 18 | 19 | 20 | 21 | 22 | 23 | 24 |

                              A C   A   B   BFE  F   G   G   G   G   G   H   L    L
                                    D   F   E F  G   H   H   H   H   H   K   M→   M→
                                        F   G   H   I   I   I   I   I   L   N→   N→
                                            I   J   J   J   J   J   M→
                                            J   K   K   K   K   K   N→
                                            L   L   L   L   L   L
                                                    M→  M→  M→  M→
                                                    N→  N→  N→
```

CREDENTIALS OR DOCUMENTATION

Secondary

A *Adeverinţă de* "specialization" (Certificate of Qualification in a Profession) or *Certificat de Studii Secundare Professionale* (Certificate of Professional Secondary School Study) awarded by a *şcoala de Meserii* (Trade School): signifies the completion of a one-year program following credential **C** or a one and one-half year program following ninth grade; leads to a qualification in a basic trade (e.g. Masonry)

B *Adeverinţă de* "specialization" (Diploma of Qualification in a Profession) or *Certificat de Studii Secundare Professionale* (Certificate of Professional Secondary School Study) plus a *Diplomă de Bacalaureat* with a specialization (Baccalaureate Diploma), awarded by a *şcoala Profesional Polivalente* (Professional Multi-Profile Secondary School): signifies completion of a two year program following credential **C** or **D**, or a four-year program following ninth grade; results in the award of a qualification in a technical profession, and the completion of secondary education

C *Atestat de Maturitate* (Maturity Certificate) or *Atestat de Studii Medii* (Certificate of Secondary Education) awarded by a *şcoala Medie de Cultură Generală* (General Secondary School): signifies the completion of an 11-year general secondary education; this credential is to be phased out by 2005

D *Diplomă de Bacalaureat* (Baccalaureate Diploma) awarded by a *Licee* (Lyceum): signifies completion of a 12-year general secondary education

E *Diplomă de Technologii* (Diploma of Technology) awarded by a *şcoala Profesional Polivalente* (Professional Multi-Profile Secondary School): signifies completion of a one-year program in a professional technical field requiring credential **B** for admission

Postsecondary

F *Diplomă de Studii Superioare Scurtă Durată* (Diploma of Higher Level Short Duration Studies) indicating specialization, awarded by *Colegii* (Colleges): signifies the completion of a two- to three-year program following credential **B**, **C**, or **D**, or a four-year program following ninth grade or credential **A**

244

G Diplomă de Studii Superioare (Diploma of Higher Studies) or Diplomă de Licență (Diploma of Licence) awarded by a university, institute, academy, or conservatory: signifies completion of a four- to five-year program in most fields; requires credential **B, C, D,** or **F** for admission

H Diplomă de Inginer (Diploma of Engineer): five- to six-year program requiring credential **B, C, D,** or **F** for admission

I Diplomă de Doctor-Stomatolog (Diploma of Doctor-Dentist): five-year program requiring credential **B, C, D,** or **F** for admission

J Diplomă de Doctor-Veterinar (Diploma of Doctor-Veterinary Surgeon): five-year program requiring credential **B, C, D,** or **F** for admission

K Diplomă de Doctor-Medic (Diploma of Doctor-Physician): six-year program requiring credential **B, C, D,** or **F** for admission

L Magistru (Master): Newer one to three-year specialized program of study requiring credential **G** for admission

M Diplomă de Doctor (Diploma of Doctor) or Doctor în științe (Doctor of Sciences): A minimum of three years of study. Focus of the program is research, with the degree being awarded after defense of a dissertation. Requires credential **G, H, I, J, K, or L** for admission

N Doctor Abilitat în "specialization" (Doctor Habilitation in a specialization) or Doctor Habilitat în științe (Doctor Habilitation of Sciences): Of no set duration, the focus of this program is research and the credential is awarded after defense of a dissertation. Requires credential **M** for admission

GRADING INFORMATION

All Levels of Education

Numeric	Moldovan	Translation
10 (zece)	Excelente	Excellent
9 (nouă)	Foarte Bine	Very Good
8 (opt)	Bine	Good
7 (șapte)	Bine	Good
7 (șase)	Satisfacătore	Satisfactory
5 (cinci)	Satisfacătore	Satisfactory
4 (patru)	Nesatisfacătore	Not Satisfactory
3 (trei)	Nesatisfacătore	Not Satisfactory
2 (doi)	Nesatisfacătore	Not Satisfactory
1 (un)	Nesatisfacătore	Not Satisfactory

- Grades of 1 to 4 are considered failing and are not normally shown on a statement of grades.

- Moldovan descriptors (Excelente, Bine, etc.) are not normally used on Moldovan transcripts but have been included here to aid grade interpretation.

POSTSECONDARY INSTITUTION RECOGNITION BODY

Ministry of Education and Science. Piaţa Marii Adunări Naţionale, nr.1, Chişinău, MD-2033. Tel: 373-2-23-33-48. Fax: 373-2-23-35-15.

RESOURCES FOR ADDITIONAL INFORMATION

Association of Teachers of Moldova, St. P. Zadnipru 1, of.20, Chişinău, 2042.

Ministry of Education and Science of the Republic of Moldova, Piaţa Marii Adunări Naţionale, nr.1, Chişinău, MD-2033.

Internet Source:
UNESCO - World Academic Database: www.unesco.org/iau/educmd.html

---

Compiler
Robert Stevenson, Assistant Administrator of Graduate Admissions
University of British Columbia, Canada

MONGOLIA

YEARS OF EDUCATION →

	½	½	½	½	½	½	½	½	½	½	½	½	½	½	½	½	½
1 →6| 7	8	9	10	11	12	13	14	15	16	17	18	19	20	21	22	23	24
	A	B		C	D		E	F	G			H→					

CREDENTIALS OR DOCUMENTATION

Secondary

A Гэрчилгээ (Certificate of Completion): awarded by primary schools; signifies completion of basic education

B Дунд Боловсролын Унэмлэх (Certificate of Incomplete Secondary Education): awarded by secondary schools; signifies completion of compulsory education

C Бурэн Дунд Боловсролын Унэмлэх (Certificate of Complete Secondary Education): awarded by the Ministry of Science, Technology, Education, and Culture; signifies completion of secondary education and leads to postsecondary education

Postsecondary

D Мэргэжлийн Унэмлэх (Certificate of a Profession): vocational credential awarded after one year of study, though credential **C** is not required for admission

E Диплом (Diploma): three-year program with admission based on credential **C**

F Бакалаврын Зэрэг (Bachelor Degree) awarded in specific fields: four-year program requiring credential **C** for admission, or one-year program beyond credential **E**

G Магистрын Зэрэг (Master Degree) awarded in specific fields: one-year program with admission based on credential **F**

H Докторын Зэрэг (Doctoral Degree): three or more years of education requiring credential **G** for admission

GRADING INFORMATION

Secondary

Percent	Letter
90-100	A
80-89	B
70-79	C
60-69	D
0-59	F

247

Higher Education

Percent	Letter	Points
90-100	A	4
80-89	B	3
70-79	C	2
60-69	D	1
0-59	F	0

POSTSECONDARY INSTITUTION RECOGNITION BODY

Ministry of Science, Technology, Education, and Culture (MOSTEC), Room #420, Government Building III, Baga Toiruu-44, Ulaanbaatar-11, Mongolia. Tel: 976-1-323589. Fax: 976-1-323158. E-mail: bmostec@magicnet.mn

RESOURCES FOR ADDITIONAL INFORMATION

Educational Law Package. 1995. Ministry of Science, Technology, Education, and Culture. (MOSTEC).

Educational Standards. 1997. MOSTEC.

New Amendments to Higher Education Law. 1998. MOSTEC.

Internet Source:
UNESCO – World Academic Database: www.unesco.org/iau/educmn.html

---

Compilers
R. Bat-Erdene
State Secretary, MOSTEC, Ulan Bator, Mongolia

J. Sukhbaatar
Executive Director
Consortium of Mongolian Management Development Institutions, Ulan Bator, Mongolia

MOROCCO

YEARS OF EDUCATION →

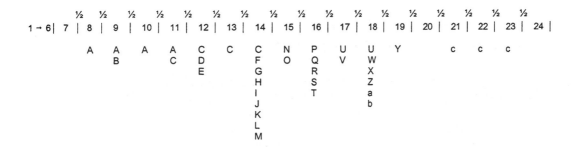

CREDENTIALS OR DOCUMENTATION

Secondary

A *Certificat de Formation Professionnelle* (Professional Training Certificate): a two-year vocational program (three-year program in agriculture) requiring grade 6, 7, or 8 for admission

B *Certificat d'Enseignement Secondaire* (Secondary Studies Certificate): awarded to sucessful students who do not wish to go to secondary schools[1]

C *Certificat de Qualification Professionnelle* (Professional Qualification Certificate): a two-year vocational program (three-year program in agriculture) requiring grade 9, 10, or 11 for admission

D *Baccalauréat de l'Enseignement Secondaire* (Secondary Education Baccalaureate): awarded after nine years of basic studies plus three years of secondary school

E *Baccalauréat de Technicien* (Technical Baccalaureate): awarded after nine years of basic studies and three years of technical secondary school

F *Diplôme de Capacité en droit* (Diploma of Proficiency in Law): a two-year program requiring the level of the last year of secondary education (grade 12, but credential **D** is not required for admission). The holder may be allowed to undertake the first year of law studies at university

Postsecondary[2]

G *Diplôme de Technicien, Diplôme d'Adjoint Technique* (Associate Technician Diploma): a two-year terminal vocational program; the admission requirement is the level of the last year of secondary education (grade 12, but credential **D** is not required)

H *Diplôme de Techicien Spécialisé, Diplôme d'Adjoint Technique Spécialisé* (Specialized Associate Technician Diploma): a two-year terminal vocational program; credential **D** is required for admission

I *Diplôme d'État d'Adjoint de Santé* (State Diploma of Heath Technician): a two-year terminal vocational program in health; the admission requirement is the last year of secondary education (grade 12, but credential **D** is not required); it was replaced around 1993 by credential **O**

249

J *Diplôme de Technicien Supérieur* (Advanced Technician Diploma): a two-year terminal vocational program; credential **D** is required for admission

K *Certificat Universitaire d'Études Littéraires/CUEL, Supérieures/CUES* (Literary, Higher University Studies Diploma): requires credential **D** for admission

L *Diplôme d'Études Universitaires Générales/DEUG, de Technologie/DEUT* (General, Technological University Studies Diploma): requires credential **D** for admission[3]

M *Diplôme Universitaire de Technologie/DUT* (Applied Sciences University Diploma): requires credential **D** for admission

N *Brevet Supérieur de Mécanicien Avion* (Advanced Technician in Airplane Mechanics): a three-year terminal vocational program; the admission requirement is the last year of secondary studies (grade 12, but credential **D** is not required)

O *Diplôme d'État Polyvalent* (General State Diploma): a three-year program in health fields, requiring credential **D** for admission; replaces credential **I** since 1993[4]

P *Licence* (Licenciate): requires credential **K** or **L** for admission

Q *Maîtrise ès Sciences Spécialisées/MSS, ès Sciences et Techniques/MST* (Master in Applied Sciences): requires credential **L** for admission

R *Diplôme d'Ingénieur d'Application* (Applied Engineering Diploma): requires credential **D** for admission

S *Diplôme de l'École Normale Supérieure* (Higher Teacher Training School Diploma): requires credential **D** for admission[5]

T *Diplôme des Écoles Nationales de Commerce et de Gestion* (National Schools of Commerce and Management Diploma): requires credential **D** for admission[6]

U *Diplôme d'Ingénieur d'État* (State Engineer Diploma): requires credential **D** for admission

V *Diplôme de Docteur en Médecine Dentaire* (Doctor of Dental Medicine Diploma): requires credential **D** for admission

W *Diplôme de Docteur Vétérinaire* (Veterinary Doctor Diploma): requires credential **D** for admission

X *Diplôme de Docteur en Pharmacie* (Doctor in Pharmacy Diploma): requires credential **D** for admission

Y *Diplôme de Docteur en Médecine* (Doctor in Medicine Diploma): requires credential **D** for admission; the program is seven years long, including a one-year internship

Z *Diplôme d'Architecte* (Architect Diploma): requires credential **D** for admission

a *Diplôme d'Études Supérieures Spécialisées/DESS* (Specialized Higher Studies Diploma): a two-year terminal program, requires credential **P, Q,** or equivalent for admission[7]

b *Diplôme d'Études Supérieures Approfondies/DESA* (Extended Higher Studies Diploma): a two-year program, requires credential **P, Q,** or equivalent for admission[8]

c *Doctorat* (Doctorate): three to five years, requires credential **b** for admission

[1] Up to 1991-92, this credential was awarded after five years of primary studies and four years of first cycle of secondary studies. Since 1991-92, it is now awarded after six years of first cycle of basic studies, and three years of second cycle of basic studies. Those nine years of basic studies are referred to as the *Enseignement Fondamental*.

[2] Around 50 private post-secondary institutions are operating in Morocco. Although highly supervised by the *Ministère de l'Enseignement supérieur, de la Formation des cadres et de la Recherche scientifique*, diplomas from these privates institutions are not recognized, and there is no equivalency with diplomas issued by public institutions. Typically, the diploma of such a private institution will include, under the name of the institution, this note: *Établissement d'Enseignement Supérieur Privé autorisé par le Ministère de l'Enseignement Supérieur, de la Formation des cadres et de la Recherche scientifique sous le numéro* (a number and a date follows).

[3] Awarded by *Facultés des Sciences et Techniques* (Sciences and Applied Sciences Faculties) of the main universities.

[4] May be called *Diplôme d'État d'Infirmier, de Kinésithérapeute, de Technicien de Laboratoire, de Technicien de Radiologie, d'Assistante Sociale*, etc.

[5] This credential may also be awarded after a two-year program requiring credential **K** or **L** for admission, or after a one-year program requiring credential **P** for admission. The credential may also be called *Diplôme de professeur de deuxième cycle*. Holders may teach at secondary level (grades 10-12).

[6] These schools were created according to a law adopted in January 1991.

[7] Since 1996, replaces the *Certificat d'Études Approfondies*, which was a one-year program requiring credential **P** for admission.

[8] Since 1996, replaces the *Diplôme d'Études Supérieures/DES*, which required two or three years of studies requiring credential **P** for admission.

GRADING INFORMATION

All Levels of Education

Numeric	Mention	Translation
16-20	*Très bien*	Very Good
14-15	*Bien*	Good
12-13	*Assez bien*	Fairly Good
10-11	*Passable*	Satisfactory/Pass
0- 9	*Insuffisant*	Failed

- 10 is the passing mark, but at the secondary level candidates with a 9 may be passed by the examination committee.

- Marks of 14 or higher are rarely awarded.

POSTSECONDARY INSTITUTION RECOGNITION BODY

Ministère de l'Enseignement supérieur et de la Formation des cadres (Ministry of Higher Education and Specialists training), B.P. 4500, Rabat-Hassan. Tel: (212) 7 774839. Fax: (212) 7 779029.

RESOURCES FOR ADDITIONAL INFORMATION

AMIDEAST. Undated, circa 1992. *Education in the Arab World*. Vol I. Washington, D.C.: AMIDEAST.

The British Council. 1996. *International Guide to Qualifications in Education*. 4th ed. London: Mansell.

251

Ministère de l'Enseignement supérieur, de la Formation des cadres et de la Recherche scientifique. 1995. *Carrières n ° 12, Guide sur les Enseignements et les Formations au Maroc.* Rabat, Morocco: Direction de la formation des cadres.

UNESCO. 1996. *World Guide to Higher Education.* Paris: UNESCO Publishing.

Internet Sources:
Ministère de l'Enseignement Supérieur, de la Formation des Cadres et de la Recherche Scientifique - *Direction de la Formation des Cadres.* www.dfc.gov.ma
UNESCO - World Academic Database: www.unesco.org/iau/educma.html

---

Compiler
Michel Bédard
Service des Équivalences, Ministère des Relations avec les Citoyens et de l'Immigration, Gouvernement du Québec, Canada

MOZAMBIQUE

YEARS OF EDUCATION →

```
         ½   ½   ½   ½   ½   ½   ½   ½   ½   ½   ½   ½   ½   ½   ½   ½   ½
1→6|  7 | 8 | 9 | 10| 11| 12| 13| 14| 15| 16| 17| 18| 19| 20| 21| 22| 23| 24|
         A   B           C   C   D   D   E   E   F   F   F
```

CREDENTIALS OR DOCUMENTATION

Secondary

A *Ensino Secundário Geral (11ª classe)* [General Secondary Education (11th class)]: awarded through 1996
B *Certificado de Habilitação es Literarias* (Certificate of Learning Competence, also translated as Secondary School Leaving Certificate): awarded since 1997

Postsecondary[1]

C *Bacharelato* (Baccalaureate) or *Bacharel* (Bachelor): three-year program requiring credential **B** for admission since 1997, or credential **A** prior to 1997
D *Licenciatura* (Licentiate) or *Licenciado* (Licentiate): five-year program requiring credential **B** for admission since 1997, or credential **A** prior to 1997, or a two-year program requiring credential **C** for admission; the final year usually involves research for a thesis
E *Licenciatura en Medicina* (Licentiate in Medicine): seven-year program requiring credential **B** for admission since 1997, or credential **A** prior to 1997

[1] Two additional degree programs are being planned: 1) *mestrado* (master) which will be a two-year program following credential **E**, and 2) a *doutoramento* (doctorate) which will be two years of research with dissertation following the *mestrado*.

GRADING INFORMATION

Secondary

Numerical	Description
19-20	Excellent
17-18	Very Good
14-16	Good
10-13	Pass
0- 9	Fail

Higher Education

Numerical	Percentage	Point	Description
18-20	90-100	5	Excellent Pass
15-17	70-89	4	Good Pass
12-14	60-69	3	Better Pass
10-11	50-59	2	Low Pass
0- 9	0-49	1	Fail

POSTSECONDARY INSTITUTION RECOGNITION BODY

Ministerio da Educação e Cultura, Caixa Postal 34, Maputo, Mozambique.
Tel: 258-1-491-158. Fax: 258-1-490-979.

RESOURCES FOR ADDITIONAL INFORMATION

The British Council. 1996. *International Guide to Qualifications in Education*. 4th ed.
London: Mansell.

Internet Source:
UNESCO - World Academic Database: www.unesco.org/iau/educmz.html

---

Compiler
James S. Frey
President
Educational Credential Evaluators, Inc., Milwaukee, WI

MYANMAR

YEARS OF EDUCATION →

```
     ½   ½   ½   ½   ½   ½   ½   ½   ½   ½   ½   ½   ½   ½   ½   ½
1 → 6│ 7 │ 8 │ 9 │ 10│ 11│ 12│ 13│ 14│ 15│ 16│ 17│ 18│ 19│ 20│ 21│ 22│ 23│ 24│
            A   B   D   C   C   F   H I J   K
                        D   E   G   J   K
                            H   K
```

CREDENTIALS OR DOCUMENTATION

Secondary

A Basic Education High School Examination in the "A" or "B" stream. The "A" Stream allows access to university-level education; the "B" stream allows access to technical and vocational programs.

Postsecondary

B Diploma in Teaching at the Primary School Level
C Diploma or Associateship: programs offered in agriculture, allied health fields, business, or technology; requires credential **A** for admission
D Diploma in Teaching at the Middle School Level: two- or three-year program; requires credential **A** for admission
E Bachelor (Pass) degree: offered in the fields of arts, commerce, computer science, economics, or science; requires credential **A** for admission
F Bachelor (Honours) degree: offered in the fields of agriculture, arts, commerce, computer science, economics, law, or science; requires credential **A** for admission
G Bachelor's degree in education: requires credential **E** for admission
H Bachelor's degree in architecture, dentistry, engineering, forestry, or veterinary science: requires credential **A** for admission
I Bachelor's degree in medicine: requires credential **E** for admission
J Master of Philosophy degree: two-year program; requires credential **E** or **F** for admission
K Master of Arts or Science degree: two- to three-year program; requires credential **E** or **F** for admission

GRADING INFORMATION

Postsecondary Education

Numeric	Description
5.0	Excellent
4.5	Excellent
4.0	Good
3.5	Good
3.0	Satisfactory
2.5	Satisfactory
2.0	Unsatisfactory
1.5	Unsatisfactory
1.0	Fail

- Many students pursue university study through distance education programs through the Institute of Economics in Yangon, the University of Rangon, and the University of Distance Education in Yangon.

- In 1989, the name of the capital city (Rangoon) was changed to Yangon when the name of the country (Burma) was changed to Myanmar. This name change appears in educational documents issued by institutions located in Yangon (Rangoon).

- Due to political unrest, higher education institutions have been closed and reopened periodically since 1988.

POSTSECONDARY INSTITUTION RECOGNITION BODY

Ministry of Education. Theinbyu Street, Yangon, Myanmar. Tel: 95-1-86704.
Fax: 95-1-85480.

The Ministry of Health oversees programs in dentistry, medicine, and allied health fields. The Ministry of Defence oversees military programs.

RESOURCES FOR ADDITIONAL INFORMATION

National Office of Overseas Skills Recognition. 1992. *Country Education Profiles: Myanmar.* Canberra: Australian Government Publishing Service.

Internet Source:
UNESCO - World Academic Database: www.unesco.org/iau/educmm.html

---

Compiler
Jane Yahr Shepard
Evaluator
Educational Credential Evaluators, Inc., Milwaukee, WI

NEPAL

	½	½	½	½	½	½	½	½	½	½	½	½	½	½	½	½	½
1→6	7	8	9	10	11	12	13	14	15	16	17	18	19	20	21	22	23	24
		A		B	C	D	E	F G	G	H I		I						

CREDENTIALS OR DOCUMENTATION

Secondary

A School Leaving Certificate (SLC): awarded by the Ministry of Education and Culture

B Proficiency Certificate: known as the Intermediate Certificate prior to 1987; awarded by Tribhuvan University

C Technician Certificate: awarded by the Mechanical Training Center in Kathmandu; admission based on credential **A**

Postsecondary

D Bachelor degree; known as Diploma through 1986; two-year program with admission based on credential **B**

E Bachelor degree: three-year programs since 1997 in the areas of agriculture, business administration, commerce, education, humanities, law, and social sciences; previously they were two-year programs; admission based on credential **B**

F Bachelor degree in engineering and forestry: four-year programs with admission based on credential **B**

G Master Degree: known as Degree (Master Level) through 1986; two-year programs after credentials **D** or **E**; awarded in the areas of animal husbandry, business administration, commerce, humanities, management, and social sciences

H Bachelor degree in medicine: six and one-half-year program based on credential **B**

I Doctor of Philosophy degree: awarded on the basis of research and thesis in a few fields; generally three years beyond credential **G**

GRADING INFORMATION

Secondary

School Leaving Certificate (SLC):

Division	Percentage
I	60.0 - 100.0
II	45.0 - 59.9
III	35.0 - 44.9

Proficiency Certificate:
Division	Percentage
I	80.0 - 100
II	65.0 - 79.9
III	50.0 - 64.9

Higher Education

Bachelor degree and Master degree:
Division	Percentage
Distinction	80 - 100
I	65 - 79
II	50 - 64
III	40 - 49

POSTSECONDARY INSTITUTION RECOGNITION BODY

Ministry of Education, Kaiser Mahal, Kantipah, Kathmandu. Tel: 977 1 418782. Fax: 977 1 412460.

RESOURCES FOR ADDITIONAL INFORMATION

The British Council. 1987. *International Guide to Qualifications in Education.* 2nd ed. London: Mansell.

Cameron, J., R. Cowen, B. Holmes, P. Hurst, and M. McLean. 1984. *International Handbook of Educational Systems.* Vol. III. London: Institute of Education, University of London.

Fulbright Commission, The American Center, Educational Advising Center, Nepal. P.O. Box 380 Gyaneswor, Kathmandu, Nepal. Tel: 977 1 414598. Fax: 977 1410881.

National Office of Overseas Skills Recognition. 1992. *Country Education Profiles: Nepal.* Canberra: National Office of Overseas Skills Recognition.

Internet Source:
UNESCO - World Academic Database: www.unesco.org/iau/educnp.html

---

Compiler
Marybeth Mirzejewski
Evaluator
Educational Credential Evaluators, Inc., Milwaukee, WI

NETHERLANDS

YEARS OF EDUCATION →

		½	½	½	½	½	½	½	½	½	½	½	½	½	½	½	½	
1 → 6	7	8	9	10	11	12	13	14	15	16	17	18	19	20	21	22	23	24

```
                    A   C   D   E   E   F   G   G   J           M→
                    B                           H   K
                                                I   L
```

CREDENTIALS OR DOCUMENTATION

Secondary

A *VBO Diploma [Voorbereidend Beroepsonderwijs]* (Preparatory Vocational Education): does not provide access to postsecondary education

B MAVO *Diploma [Middelbaar Algemeen Voortgezet Onderwijs]* (Junior General Secondary Education): does not provide access to postsecondary education

C *HAVO Diploma [Hoger Algemeen Voortgezet Onderwijs]* (Senior General Secondary Education)

D *VWO Diploma [Voorbereidend Wetenschappelijk Onderwijs]* (University Preparatory Education)

E *MBO Diploma [Middelbaar Beroepsonderwijs]* (Senior Secondary Vocational Education): three to four years, requiring credential **A** or **B** for admission

Postsecondary

F *Getuigschrift Hoger Beroepsonderwijs, (HBO)* (Higher Professional Education Degree): awarded by *hogescholen* (Universities of Professional Education); four-year program in the applied arts and sciences; credential **C, D,** or **E** required for admission

G *Doctoraal Examen* (*Doctoraal* Degree): awarded by universities; four- to five-year program in all traditional university fields [1, 2]

H *Doctoraal Examen*: awarded by Universities of Engineering and University of Agriculture; five-year program in the fields of engineering or agriculture [2]

I *Tandartsexamen*: (professional degree in dentistry); five-year program [2]

J *Artsexamen*: (professional degree in medicine); six-year program

K *Apothekersexamen*: (professional degree in pharmacy), six-year program

L *Diergeneeskundig Examen*: (professional degree in veterinary medicine); six-year program

M *Doctor* (Doctorate): completion of at least four years of research; credential **F, G,** or **H** required for admission

---

[1] The length of programs in the exact sciences (mathematics, physics, chemistry) offered by traditional universities is in the process of being extended to five years

[2] Credential **D** required for admission, or one year of *HBO* program (credential **F**)

GRADING INFORMATION

Secondary and Postsecondary Education

Numeric	Description	Translation
10	*Uitmuntend*	Excellent
9	*Zeer Goed*	Very Good
8	*Goed*	Good
7	*Ruim Voldoende*	Amply Satisfactory
6	*Voldoende*	Satisfactory
5	*Bijna Voldoende*	Almost Satisfactory
4	*Onvoldoende*	Insufficient
3	*Gering*	Low
2	*Slecht*	Bad
1	*Zeer Slecht*	Very Bad

Letter		
V	*Voldoende*	Satisfactory
O	*Onvoldoende*	Unsatisfactory

- Grades of 9 and 10 are rarely given, 6 is the lowest passing grade, and a grade of 5, though not acceptable as an average, may be passing in a single subject if other grades are high enough.

- Traditionally, less importance is placed on obtaining high grades than on obtaining passing grades.

POSTSECONDARY INSTITUTION RECOGNITION BODY

Ministry of Education, Culture, and Science, P.O. Box 25000, 2700 LZ Zoetermeer, Netherlands. Tel: 31 79 323 23 23. Fax: 31 79 323 23 20.

Other ministries are responsible for recognition in the case of some specialized institutions.

RESOURCES FOR ADDITIONAL INFORMATION

Schuler, Peter, Jessica Stannard, and Robert Warmenhoven. 1996. *The Education System of the Netherlands.* The Hague, Netherlands: Nuffic (see below) in cooperation with PIER. The book can be ordered free of charge from Nuffic: P.O.Box 29777, 2502 LT The Hague, Netherlands. Tel: 31-70-4260260. Fax: 31-70-4260399.

Internet Sources:
Dutch NARIC/ENIC Office, Nuffic (Netherlands Organisation for International Cooperation in Higher Education): www.nuffic.nl
UNESCO – World Academic Database: www.unesco.org/iau/educnl.html

---

Compiler
Jessica Stannard
Netherlands Organisation for International Cooperation in Higher Education (Nuffic)

NEW ZEALAND

YEARS OF EDUCATION →

	½	½	½	½	½	½	½	½	½	½	½	½	½	½	½	½
1→6	7	8	9	10	11	12	13	14	15	16	17	18	19	20	21	22	23	24

```
                            ←A    B    D         F    F    H    J    J    Q→   Q→
                                  C    E         G    G    I    L    P
                                                 H    J    M    Q→
                                                 I    K    N
                                                 J    L    Q→
                                                 K    N
                                                 L
```

CREDENTIALS OR DOCUMENTATION

Secondary

A   New Zealand School Certificate: awarded on a single subject basis by the New Zealand Qualifications Authority (awarded by the Department of Education prior to 1990) following passes in national examinations at the end of Form 5 (Year 11); usually five or six subjects are attempted

B   Sixth Form Certificate: awarded on a single subject basis by the New Zealand Qualifications Authority after one year of study beyond the level of credential **A**; recognized for entry to programs offered by polytechnics and colleges of education, and for provisional entrance to universities in some cases

C   University Entrance Certificate: discontinued in 1986; earned by exemption based on school records or by University Entrance Board Examination; taken at the end of Form 6 (Year 12)

D   University Entrance, Bursaries, and Scholarships Examination: final secondary school credential usually taken in Form 7 (Year 13); may provide entry into selective programs, and in some cases, exemptions from first-year university courses

E   Higher School Certificate: awarded upon satisfactory completion of Form 7 (Year 13) coursework in a minimum of three subjects; there is no examination and no subjects or grades appear on the certificate

Postsecondary

F   Diploma of Teaching: three-year college of education programs following at least credential **B**, but beginning in 1998, these programs are being replaced by credential **G** (three-year Bachelor of Teaching) programs; this credential can also be earned in a one-year program with admission based on credential **G** (in a field other than teaching)

G   Bachelor's degree: three to four years of study after credential **B** or **D**[1]

H   Bachelor of Education and Diploma of Teaching: four-year program of study after credential **B** or **D**

I   Bachelor's degree (Honours): usually one year beyond credential **G**; considered a postgraduate award in New Zealand

261

J   Master's degree: one- or two-year program requiring credential **G, H,** or **I** for admission

K   Higher Diploma of Teaching: one-year program in primary teaching requiring credential **F** (three-year diploma) for admission; offered only by colleges of education

L   Education specialist programs in various fields: usually one-year programs requiring credential **F** or **H** for admission

M   Bachelor's degree in the fields of architecture, dentistry, and veterinary medicine: five-year programs requiring credential **D** for admission

N   Advanced Diploma of Teaching: one-year program in primary teaching requiring credential **K** for admission

P   Bachelor's degree in the field of medicine: six-year program with admission based on credential **D**

Q   Doctoral degree[2]: supervised research or coursework with research; at least two years of study beyond credential **I** or **J**

[1]   The length of bachelor's degree programs (i.e., three-year programs versus four-year programs), varies between institutions and over time. Generally speaking, bachelor's degrees in arts, commerce, and sciences require three years of study, and bachelor's degrees in applied fields, such as applied sciences, design, engineering, law, medical laboratory technology, pharmacy, optometry, physiotherapy, physical education, resource and environmental planning, social work, speech therapy, and technology, require four years of study. Many variations to this pattern exist.

[2]   Higher doctoral degrees may be awarded for meritorious independent research, and honorary doctoral degrees may be awarded in recognition of significant contribution to academia, profession, or society; there are no prerequisites.

GRADING INFORMATION

Secondary

New Zealand School Certificate: assessment can be internal, external, or a combination

1969-85: School Certificate awarded for success (at least 50%) in one or more subjects, according to the scale below.

Letter	Percent
A	80-100
B	65-79
C	50-64

1986-92:

Mark	Percent
A1	80-100
A2	68-79
B1	56-67
B2	45-55
C1	31-44
C2	16-30
D	0-15

Since 1993:

Letter	Percent
A	80-100
B	65-79
C	50-64
D	30-49
E	0-29

- Until 1962: No grades were issued.

- From 1962-68: Marks of over 50% were required in four subjects, including English.

Sixth Form Certificate

Nationally monitored, internally assessed, with no public examination. Grades are allocated by schools on the basis of student achievement in each subject, on a scale from 1 (highest) to 9 (lowest), where a grade of 5 is the minimum pass. Each school works out its own procedures for the allocation of grades to subjects and students.

New Zealand University Entrance, Bursaries, and Scholarships Examinations

Performance is rated on a single subject basis.

Letter	Percent
A	66-100
B	56-65
C	46-55
D	31-45
E	0-30

- "A" Bursary: An aggregate of 300 marks or more on five subjects; for six subject candidates, the best five are aggregated.

- "B" Bursary: An aggregate of 250-299 marks.

- Since 1993, a minimum of three Cs plus the Higher School Certificate achieves university entry. Prior to 1993, the requirement was four Ds or an aggregate of 160 marks in four subjects.

Higher Education

<u>Universities</u>

Bachelor degree courses

Letter	Description
A+	High First
A	Clear First
A- A	Bare First
B+	High Second
B	Clear Second
B-	Bare Second
C+	Satisfactory Pass
C	Pass
C-	Restricted/Bare Pass
D	Failure; reasonable chance of succeeding if the course is repeated
E	Failure; little likelihood of succeeding if the course is repeated

- The grade of C- (restricted/bare pass) means that the student is credited with a pass, but may not proceed to more advanced study in that subject. Those who narrowly fail one subject, but who achieve B or higher grades in other subjects, may be given a "conceded pass."

- Certificate of Proficiency (COP) is sometimes indicated on transcripts. This designates a pass awarded in a single subject that may be outside of the requirements of a particular qualification or award.

Bachelor (Honours) Degree Classifications

Classification	Letter
First Class	A
Second Class (Division I)	A-/B+
Second Class (Division II)	B/B-
Third Class	C+

<u>Polytechnics</u>: either scale may be used

Letter	Percent		Letter	Description
A+	85-100		A	Pass With Credit
A	80-84		B	Good Pass
A-	75-79		C	Pass
B+	70-74		D	Marginal Fail
B	65-69		E, F	Fail
B-	60-64			
C+	55-59			
C	50-54 - minimum pass level			
D	45-49			
E	40-44			
F	0-39			

<u>Colleges of Education</u>: Each college uses its own grading system. The most common is the use of grades A to E, where A, B, and C are passing, and D and E are failing.

POSTSECONDARY INSTITUTION RECOGNITION BODIES

Universities: New Zealand Vice-Chancellor's Committee, P.O. Box: 11-915, 94 Dixon Street (11th floor), Wellington. Tel: 64-4-3818500. Fax: 64-4-3818501.

Non-University Institutions: For further information regarding qualifications and awarding, and academic institutions, enquiries may be directed to the Qualifications Evaluation Service, New Zealand Qualifications Authority. P.O. Box 160, Wellington. Tel: 64-4-8023000. Fax: 64-4-8023401.

RESOURCES FOR ADDITIONAL INFORMATION

The British Council. 1996. *International Guide to Qualifications in Education.* 4th ed. London: Mansell.

National Office of Overseas Skills Recognition. 1995. *Country Education Profiles: New Zealand.* 2nd ed. Canberra: Australian Government Publishing Service.

Internet Sources:
Ministry of Education: www.minedu.govt.nz
New Zealand Qualifications Authority: www.nzqa.govt.nz
UNESCO - World Academic Database: unesco.org/iau/educnz.html

Compiler
Pam Vaughan-Jones, Qualifications Evaluator
Qualifications Evaluation Service, New Zealand Qualifications Authority, Wellington, New Zealand

NICARAGUA

YEARS OF EDUCATION →

```
       ½   ½   ½   ½   ½   ½   ½   ½   ½   ½   ½   ½   ½   ½   ½   ½   ½
1 → 6│ 7 │ 8 │ 9 │ 10│ 11│ 12│ 13│ 14│ 15│ 16│ 17│ 18│ 19│ 20│ 21│ 22│ 23│ 24│
           A   B       D   D   D   E G F G H
               C               E   F   G   I
                               F   G   H
                                       I
```

CREDENTIALS OR DOCUMENTATION

Secondary

A *Diploma de Conclusión de Ciclo Diversificado del Bachillerato en Ciencias, Letras, y Filosofía* (Diploma of Conclusion of the Diversified Cycle of the Baccalaureate in Science, Letters, and Philosophy): two-year academic secondary school program; admission based on completion of grade 9

B *Bachiller Técnico* (Technical Bachelor), *Técnico Medio* (Mid-Level Technician), *Enfermero Técnico Medio* (Mid-Level Technician-Nurse): three-year technical-vocational program; admission based on completion of grade 9

C *Maestro de Educación Primaria* (Teacher of Primary Education): three-year primary school teacher training program; admission based on completion of grade 9

Postsecondary

D Diploma of *Técnico Superior* (Higher Technician): two- or three-year programs in business, economics, engineering technology, marketing, and nursing; admission based on credential **A** or **B**

E *Título de Professor de Eucación Media* (Title of Secondary Education Teacher): four-year program offered at the *Universidad Nacional Autónoma de Nicaragua*; admission based on credential **A** or **C**

F Title of *Licenciado* (Licentiate): four- to five-year programs; admission based on credential **A** or **B**

G Title of *Arquitecto* (Architect) or *Ingeniero* (Engineer): five- to five and one-half-year programs; admission based on credential **A** or **B**

H *Doctor* (Doctor): six-year program in medicine; admission based on credential **A** or **B**

I *Maestría* (Master): two-year program beyond credential **F**

266

GRADING INFORMATION

Secondary

Ciclo Diversificado-see credential **A**:

Percentage	Description	Translation
91 - 100	*Excelente*	Excellent
71 - 90	*Muy Bueno*	Very Good
51 - 70	*Bueno*	Good
31 - 50	*Deficiente*	Deficient
0 - 30	*Muy Deficiente*	Very Deficient

Técnico Education-see credential **B**:

For Technical Subjects

Percentage	Description	Translation
91 - 100	*Excelente*	Excellent
71 - 90	*Muy Bueno*	Very Good
61 - 70	*Bueno*	Good
51 - 60	*Regular*	Pass
0 - 50	*Reprobado*	Fail

For Academic Subjects

Percentage	Description	Translation
90 - 100	*Excelente*	Excellent
80 - 89	*Muy Bueno*	Very Good
70 - 79	*Bueno*	Good
60 - 69	*Regular*	Pass
0 - 59	*Reprobado*	Fail

Higher Education

Percentage	Description	Translation
90 - 100	*Sobresaliente*	Outstanding
80 - 89	*Muy Bueno*	Very Good
70 - 79	*Bueno*	Good
60 - 69	*Regular*	Pass
0 - 59	*Reprobado*	Fail

- A 10-point scale is also used, with 10 being highest. The minimum pass is 6.

POSTSECONDARY INSTITUTION RECOGNITION BODIES

Asociación Nicaraguense de Instituciones de Educación Superior, Recinto universitario "Ruben Dario," Managua, Nicaragua. Tel: 505-311-2612.

Consejo Nacional de Universidades, Los Robles, 110 Carretera A. Masaya 2 cuadras al E., Media Cuadra al N., Managua, Nicaragua. Tel: 505-2-781053. Fax: 505-2-783385.

Ministerio de Educación Pública, P.O. Box Apartado 108, Complejo Civico, Modulo J, Managua, Nicaragua. Tel: 505-2-651451. Fax: 505-2-651695.

RESOURCES FOR ADDITIONAL INFORMATION

Aldrich-Langen, Caroline, and Kathleen Sellew, editors. 1987. *The Admission and Placement of Students from Central America: Belize, Costa Rica, El Salvador, Guatemala, Honduras, Nicaragua, Panama.* Annapolis Junction, MD: PIER.

Marcus, Jane E. 1996. *Central America Update. Special Report 1996.* Annapolis Junction, MD: PIER.

Internet Source:
UNESCO - World Academic Database: www.unesco.org/iau/educni.html

---

Compiler
Marybeth Mirzejewski
Evaluator
Educational Credential Evaluators, Inc., Milwaukee, WI

NIGER

YEARS OF EDUCATION →

```
     ½   ½   ½   ½   ½   ½   ½   ½   ½   ½   ½   ½   ½   ½   ½   ½   ½
1 → 6│ 7 │ 8 │ 9 │ 10 │ 11 │ 12 │ 13 │ 14 │ 15 │ 16 │ 17 │ 18 │ 19 │ 20 │ 21 │ 22 │ 23 │ 24 │
         A           B       E   H   I   L   N               Q-
                     C       F       J   M   O
                     D       G       K   N   P-
```

CREDENTIALS OR DOCUMENTATION

Secondary

A *Brevet d'Études du Premier Cycle/BEPC* (Certificate of First Level Studies)
B *Baccalauréat* (Baccalaureate): leads to postsecondary education
C *Baccalauréat Technique* (Technical Baccalaureate): leads to postsecondary education
D *Diplôme de Fin d'Études Nigeriens/DFEN* (Diploma of End of *Nigerien* Studies): for those who complete the three years of secondary school but who fail to qualify for credential **B** or **C**

Postsecondary

E *Diplôme Universitaire* (University Diploma)[1]
F *Diplôme d'Agronomie Générale/DAG* (Diploma of General Agronomy)
G *Diplôme d'Aptitude Pédagogique au Professorat des Collèges d'Enseignement Général/DAP/CEG* (Diploma of Pedagogical Aptitude in the Profession of Lower Secondary School Teaching)
H *Licence* (License)
I *Diplôme de Conseiller Pédagogique à l'Enseignement Primaire* (Diploma of Pedagogical Counselor in Primary Instruction)
J *Maîtrise* (Master)
K *Diplôme d'Ingénieur des Techniques de l'Agriculture/DITA* (Diploma of Engineer of Agriculture Techniques)
L *Diplôme d'Agronomie Approfondie* (Diploma of Advanced Agronomy)/*Diplôme d'Ingénieur Agronome* (Diploma of Engineer Agronomist)
M *Diplôme d'Études Supérieures Spécialisées* (Diploma of Higher Specialized Studies): requires credential **J** for admission
N *Diplôme d'Études Approfondies* (Diploma of Advanced Studies): requires credential **J** for admission (usually one year; sometimes two)
O *Doctorat en Médecine* (Doctorate in Medicine): six-year professional program beyond credential **B**
P *Doctorat de Troisième Cycle* (Third Cycle Doctorate): two or more years beyond credential **J**

Q   *Doctorat d'État* (State Doctorate): at least five years of study beyond credential **J**

[1]   *Diplôme Universitaire d'Études Littéraires/DUEL* (University Diploma of Literary Studies), *Diplôme Universitaire d'Études Scientifiques/DUES* (University Diploma of Scientific Studies), *Diplôme Universitaire d'Études Economiques/DUEE* (University Diploma of Economic Studies), *Diplôme d'Études Universitaires Générales/DEUG* (Diploma of General University Studies)

GRADING INFORMATION

Secondary and Postsecondary Education

Numeric	Description	Translation
16 - 20	*Très Bien*	Very Good
14 - 15	*Bien*	Good
12 - 13	*Assez Bien*	Good Enough
10 - 11	*Passable*	Pass
0 - 9	*Ajourné*	Fail

- A minimum overall grade of 10 is required to pass; however, individual subjects may be passed with grades lower than 10.

POSTSECONDARY INSTITUTION RECOGNITION BODY

Ministère de l'Enseignement Supérieur, de la Recherche et de la Technologie, BP 557, Niamey, Niger.

RESOURCES FOR ADDITIONAL INFORMATION

Mboungou-Mayenúe, D., ed. 1988. *Directory of African Universities.* 5th ed. Association of African Universities.

Internet Source:
UNESCO-World Academic Database: www.unesco.org/iau/educne.html

---

Compiler
Margaret L. Wenger
Senior Evaluator
Educational Credential Evaluators, Inc., Milwaukee, WI

NIGERIA

YEARS OF EDUCATION →

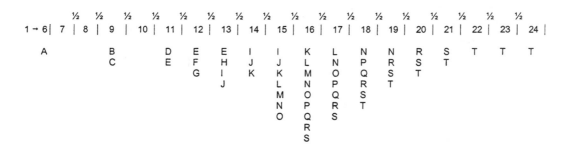

		½	½	½	½	½	½	½	½	½	½	½	½	½	½	½	½	½
1 → 6	7	8	9	10	11	12	13	14	15	16	17	18	19	20	21	22	23	24

```
1→6   7    8    9    10   11   12   13   14   15   16   17   18   19   20   21   22   23   24
 A         B         D    E    E    I    I    K    L    N    N    R    S    T    T    T
           C         E    F    H    J    J    L    N    P    R    S    T
                          G    I    K    K    M    O    Q    R    S
                          J         L    L    N    P    R    S    T
                                    M    N    O    Q    R    S
                                    N    O    P    Q    R    S
                                    O    P    Q    R    S
                                         Q    R    S
                                         R    S
                                         S
```

CREDENTIALS OR DOCUMENTATION

Secondary

A Primary School Certificate

B Junior School Certificate: started in 1980s

C Grade III Teachers Certificate: discontinued in 1960s

D School Certificate (also referred to as West African School Certificate); General Certificate of Education - Ordinary Level: phased out in 1980s

E Grade II Teachers Certificate: five years beyond credential **A**, three years beyond credential **B**, two years beyond credential **C**, or one to two years beyond credential **D**

F Senior School Certificate: implemented in 1982, with first graduates in 1988; three years beyond credential **B**

G Interim Joint Matriculation Examination: one year beyond credential **D**

H General Certificate of Education - Advanced Level: phased out in 1990s; two years beyond credential **D**

Postsecondary

I Grade I Teachers Certificate: discontinued in 1960s; two years beyond credential **D** or **E**

J National Diploma (also referred to as Ordinary National Diploma): two years beyond credential **D**, **E**, or **F**

K Nigerian Certificate of Education: three years beyond credential **D**, **E**, or **F**

L Higher National Diploma: two years beyond credential **J**

M Bachelor degrees in Arts and Sciences: four years beyond credential **D** or **F**, or three years beyond credential **G** or **H**

N Bachelor of Education: four years beyond credential **D** or **F**, or three years beyond credential **G** or **H**, or two to three years beyond credential **K**

O Bachelor degrees in Agriculture, Architecture, Engineering, Fine Arts, Laws, Nursing, and Technology: four to five years beyond credential **D** or **F**, or three to four years beyond credential **G** or **H**

271

P   Bachelor of Dental Science, and Bachelor of Medicine and Bachelor of Surgery (MBBS): five to six years beyond credential **D** or **F**, or four to five years beyond credential **G** or **H**

Q   Doctor of Veterinary Medicine: five to six years beyond credential **D** or **F**, or four to five years beyond credential **G** or **H**

R   Post Graduate Diploma: one year beyond credential **L**, **M**, **N**, **O**, **P**, or **Q**

S   Master degree: one to two years beyond credential **L**, **M**, **N**, **O**, **P**, or **Q**

T   Doctor of Philosophy: two to three years beyond credential **S**, or in some cases, three to five years beyond credential **M**, **N**, **O**, **P**, or **Q** [1]

[1]   The Doctor of Letters and the Doctor of Sciences may be also be awarded on the basis of a review of an individual's published research.

GRADING INFORMATION

Secondary

School Certificate and Senior School Certificate:

Numeric	Description
1	Excellent
2	Very Good
3	Good
4-6	Credit
7-8	Pass
9	Fail

Postsecondary Education

Numeric	Description
70-100	First Class Honours
60-69	Second Class Honours, Upper
50-59	Second Class Honours, Lower
45-49	Third Class Honours
40-44	Pass
0-39	Fail

- Variations in grading exist between and within universities, depending on the timeframe. Official transcripts usually provide information on grading procedures.

POSTSECONDARY INSTITUTION RECOGNITION BODIES

Ministry of Education, Ahmadu Bello Way, Victoria Island, Lagos. Tel: 234-1-616-943. Fax: 234-1-261-9904.

National Universities Commission, Aja Nwachukwu House, Plot 430, Aguiy, Ironsi Street, Maitama District, PMB 237, Garki GPO, Abuja. Tel: 234-9-523-3176. Fax: 234-9-523-3250.

RESOURCES FOR ADDITIONAL INFORMATION

Margolis, Alan M. 1977. *Nigeria: A Study of the Educational System of Nigeria and a Guide to the Academic Placement of Students in Educational Institutions in the United States*. Washington, D.C.: AACRAO.

National Office of Overseas Skills Recognition, et. al. 1993. *Country Education Profiles: Nigeria*. Canberra: Australian Government Publishing Service.

Internet Source:
UNESCO-World Academic Database: www.unesco.org/iau/educng.html

---

Compiler
James P. Meyers
Senior Evaluator
Educational Credential Evaluators, Inc., Milwaukee, WI

NORWAY

YEARS OF EDUCATION →

```
      ½   ½   ½   ½   ½   ½   ½   ½   ½   ½   ½   ½   ½   ½   ½   ½   ½   ½
1→6|  7 | 8 | 9 | 10| 11| 12| 13| 14| 15| 16| 17| 18| 19| 20| 21| 22| 23| 24|

         A              B     C  F  Q  J  k  n  w  z  6   4   15  4  25  25  26  26  26
                              D  G  L  l  o  x  1  7   7  24  25  26  26
                              E  H  P  m  p  y  2  11  9  25  26
                                 I  R        q  z  3  12  11  26
                                 J  S        r  1  4  13  13
                                 K  T        s     5  14  14
                                 L  U        t     6      15
                                 M  V        u     7      16
                                 N  W        v     8      17
                                 O  X           9      18
                                 P  Y           10     19
                                    Z              20
                                    a              21
                                    b              22
                                    c              23
                                    d
                                    e
                                    f
                                    g
                                    h
                                    i
                                    j
```

CREDENTIALS OR DOCUMENTATION

Secondary

A   *Vitnemål fra grunnskolen* (Certificate from Basic School): signifies completion of compulsory education

B   *Vitnemål fra den videregående skolen* (Certificate from Upper Secondary School): leads to postsecondary education

Postsecondary

C   *Bedriftsøkonomeksamen* (Business Economics Examination)

D   *Tolk* (Sign Language Interpreter)

E   *Yrkeslærer* (Vocational Subject Teacher): one-year program since 1993; the program was one semester through 1992

F   *Audiograf* (Audiographer)

G   *Datahøgskolekandidat* (Data College Candidate)

H   *Eiendomsmegler* (Real Estate Broker): one-year program following credential **C**

I   *Foretaksøkonom* (Enterprise Economics): one-year program following credential **C**

J   *Høgskolekandidat* (College Candidate): two- and three-year programs offered by colleges

K   *Husøkonom* (Accommodation Manager)

L   *Ingeniør* (Engineer): two- and three-year programs in engineering technology

M   *Kostøkonom* (Institutional Catering Manager)

N *Markedskandidat* (Market Candidate)
O *Tannpleier* (Dental Hygienist)
P *Vitnemål* (Certificate) awarded by music conservatories: two- and three-year programs
Q *Reseptar* (Prescriptionist)
R *Barnevernspedagog* (Child Welfare Worker)
S *Bibliotekar* (Librarian)
T *Bioengeniør* (Bioengineer)
U *Diplommarkedsøkonom* (Diploma in Marketing): one-year program following credential **N** or equivalent
V *Diplomøkonom* (Diploma in Business Administration): one-year program following credential **I** or two-year **J** program
W *Ergoterapeut* (Occupational Therapist)
X *Fysioterapeut* (Physical Therapist) or *Mensendieckutdanning* (Mensendieck Physical Therapy Education)
Y *Førskolelærer* (Preschool Teacher)
Z *Kommunalkandidat* (Local Government Administration Candidate)
a *Næringsmiddelteknolog* (Food Technologist)
b *Ortopediingeniør* (Orthopedic Engineer)
c *Radiograf* (Radiographer)
d *Revisor* (Auditor/Accountant): may include credential **C** and two-year credential **J** programs
e *Sosionom* (Social Worker)
f *Sykepleier* (Nurse): three-year programs which may be followed by one-semester or one-year advanced nurse training programs in specialized areas, such as geriatric, midwifery, or psychiatric nursing; see also credentials **q** and **s**
g *Vernepleier* (Social Educator)
h *Vitnemål* (Certificate) awarded by the Statens balletthøgskole (National College of Ballet and Dance): three-year programs in dance, dance teacher, or choreographer
i *Vitnemål* (Certificate) awarded by the Statens operahøgskole (National College of Operatic Art)
j *Vitnemål* (Certificate) awarded by the Statens teaterhøgskole (National College of Dramatic Art)
k *Candidatus/a magisterii/cand. mag.*: awarded by university faculties of mathematics and natural sciences
l *Diplomeksportøkonom* (Diploma in Export Marketing)
m *Examen oeconomiae/exam. oecon.*: awarded only by the Faculty of Social Sciences of the University of Oslo after three and one-half years of study
n *Allmennlærer* (General Subjects Teacher): four-year programs for teachers of grades one through nine; programs were three years through 1992
o *Candidatus/a magisterii/cand. mag.*: awarded by university faculties of arts and faculties of social sciences
p *Candidatus/a magisterii/cand. mag.*, also referred to as *regional cand.mag.*: awarded by a college, as opposed to a university, after a total of four years of study; may include one to three years of previous college or university study
q *Eldreomsorg* (Geriatric Nurse): one-year program following credential **f**
r *Handelsøkonom* (Business Administration)
s *Jordmor* (Midwife): one-year program following credential **f**
t *Kandidatsexamen* (Candidate Degree) awarded by the Norges Musikkhøgskole (Norwegian State Academy of Music)

u *Sivilmarkedsfører* (Marketing): one-year program based on credential **V**

v *Siviløkonom/siv. øk.*: four-year program in economics

w *Designkandidat* (Design Candidate): one and one-half-year program following three-year credential **J** program

x *Diplom* (Diploma) awarded by the Statens håndverks- og kunstindustriskole (National College of Art and Design): four and one-half-year program in industrial design

y *Kunstfagkandidat* (Art Candidate): one and one-half-year program following three-year credential **J** program

z *Praktisk-pedagogisk eksamen* (Practical-Pedagogical Examination): one-year teacher training program for those with credential **k**, **o**, **p**, or another postsecondary-level credential requiring at least four years of study; programs were one semester through 1992

1 *Sivilingeniør/siv.ing.*: four and one-half- to five-year programs in engineering, and five-year program in architecture

2 *Candidatus/a agriculturae/cand. agric.*: five-year program in agriculture

3 *Candidatus/a odontologiae/cand. odont.*: five-year program in dentistry

4 *Candidadus/a psychologiae/cand. psychol.*: five to seven-year program in psychology

5 *Candidatus/a pharmaciae/cand. pharm.*: five-year program in pharmacy

6 *Candidatus/a scientiarum/cand. scient.*: awarded by university faculties of mathematics and natural sciences; one and one-half years based on credential **k** or equivalent[1]

7 *Diplombibliotekar i informasjonskunnskap og EDB* (Diploma in Library and Information Science with Electronic Data Processing): two-year program based on credential **S**, **k**, **o**, or **p**

8 *Fiskerikandidat*: five-year program in fishery sciences

9 Master's degrees: one- to two-year programs with an international orientation; admission based on minimum of credential **k**, **o**, or **p**

10 *Sivilarkitekt/siv.ark.*: five-year program in architecture

11 *Canddidatus/a juris/cand. juris*: five- and one-half- to six-year program in law

12 *Candidatus/a oeconomiae/cand. oecon.*: two-year program in economics based on credential **m**

13 *Candidatus/a medicinae veterinariae/cand. med. vet.*: five- and one-half- to six-year program in veterinary medicine

14 *Licentiate/lic.*: awarded only by the University of Oslo after two years of study; based on minimum of credential **k**, **o**, or **p**

15 *Candidatus/a medicinae/cand. med.*: six- or six and one-half-year program in medicine

16 *Candidatus/a musicae/cand. musicae*: two-year program based on credential **o** or **p**

17 *Candidatus/a phililogiae/cand.philol.*: awarded by university faculties of arts; two years based on credential **o** or **p**

18 *Candidatus politicarum/cand. polit.*: awarded by university faculties of social sciences; two years based on credential **o** or **p**

19 *Candidatus/a sociologiae/cand. sociol.*: six-year program in sociology

20 *Candidatus/a theologiae/cand. theol.*: six-year program in theology

21 *Diplomeksamen* (Diploma) awarded by the Norges Musikkhøgskole (Norwegian State Academy of Music): two-year program based on credential **t**

22 *Idrettskandidat* (Physical Education and Sport Candidate): two-year program based on credential **o** or **p**

23 *Magister artium/mag.art.*: awarded by university faculties of arts and faculties of social sciences; two years based on credential **o** or **p**
24 *Candidatus/a paedagogiae/cand. paed.*: six and one-half-year program in education
25 *Candidatus/a paedagogiae specialis/cand. paed. spec.*: five-year program in special education based on completion of one and one-half to three years of previous postsecondary-level education
26 *Doctor* (Doctor): three-year university program based on any of credentials **r, u, v, x,** and **1** through **25**

---

[1] Any *cand. mag.* degree (credentials **k, o,** and **p**), awarded by a university or by a college, is considered equivalent in Norway.

GRADING INFORMATION

Secondary

Numeric		% of students	Norwegian Description	Translation
6	*seks*	2.1	*særdeles tilfredsstillende (s.tf.)*	Excellent
5	*fem*	13.6	*meget tilfredsstillende (m.tf.)*	Very Good
4	*fire*	24.3	*tilfredsstillende (tf.)*	Satisfactory
3	*tre*	27.3	*noenlunde tilfredsstillende (ng.tf.)*	Pass
2	*to*	20.2	*måtelig (måt.)*	Barely Passing
1	*ett*	9.6	*ikke tilfredsstillende (ik.tf.)*	Failure
0	*null*	2.9	-	-
-	-	-	*deltatt (delt.)*	Participated

Higher Education
Universities
Numeric scale of 1.0 through 6.0 is the most common, with 1.0 being highest and 6.0 being lowest. Grades of 4.1 to 6.0 do not appear on official transcripts. The minimum passing grade is 4.0 and is sufficient for graduation. It is theoretically sufficient for admission to advanced degree programs, although average grades of 2.5 to 2.7 are often required due to limited capacity.

Colleges
Numeric scale of 1.0 through 6.0 is the most common, with 1.0 being highest and 6.0 being lowest. Grades of 4.1 to 6.0 do not appear on official transcripts. The minimum passing grade is 4.0. Some colleges require an average of 3.5 for graduation.

• Variations from the above scales exist. For example, university law programs use a 1.00 (highest) through 6.00 (lowest) scale, having the minimum passing grade of 3.15. Programs in medicine and veterinary medicine may use a 12-point scale with 12.00 being highest and 6.00 as the minimum passing grade. Scales will often be described on transcripts.

Norges Handelshøyskole (Norwegian School of Economics and Business Administration)

Numeric	Description
7-9	Earned by approximately 5% of students; grades of 8 and 9 are rarely awarded
6	Earned by approximately the next 20% of students
4-5	Good
3	Average, Satisfactory
2	Below Satisfactory, Lowest Passing Grade
0-1	Failing

POSTSECONDARY INSTITUTION RECOGNITION BODIES

Ministry of Education, Research and Church Affairs. Postboks 8119 Dep., N-0032 Oslo. Tel: 47 22 24 90 90. Fax: 47 22 24 95 40.

The Ministry of Agriculture oversees the Agricultural University of Norway and the Norwegian College of Veterinary Medicine.

RESOURCES FOR ADDITIONAL INFORMATION

Feagles, Shelley M. and Karlene N. Dickey. 1994. *Norway. A Study of the Educational System of Norway and a Guide to the Academic Placement of Students in Educational Institutions in the United States.* Annapolis Junction, MD: PIER.

Higher Education in Norway. 1996. National Academic Information Centre, Oslo.

Internet Sources:
EURYDICE Eurybase: www.eurydice.org
Higher Education in the Nordic Countries: www.abo.fi/norden/welcom_e.htm
National Academic Information Centre (NAIC) of the Network Norway Council:
    www.nnr.no/NAIC/NAIC.html
Network Norway Council: www.nnr.no/English.html
Norwegian Council of Universities: www.uib.no/ur
UNESCO - World Academic Database: www.unesco.org/iau/educno.html

---

Compiler
Shelley M. Feagles
Senior Evaluator
Educational Credential Evaluators, Inc., Milwaukee, WI

OMAN

YEARS OF EDUCATION →

	½	½	½	½	½	½	½	½	½	½	½	½	½	½	½	½	½
1→6	7	8	9	10	11	12	13	14	15	16	17	18	19	20	21	22	23	24
						A	D	E	F	F	G	J		J	L		K
						B		E			H	L			M		
						C					I						

CREDENTIALS OR DOCUMENTATION

Secondary

A الشهادة الثانوية العامة (General Secondary Certificate): signifies completion of general secondary education and passing of national examination

B الشهادة الثانوية العامة والدراسات الإسلامية (General Secondary and Islamic Studies Certificate): awarded by the Secondary Islamic Institute upon successful completion of the secondary cycle and passing of national examination

C الشهادة الثانوية التجارية/الزراعية/الصناعية (Commercial/Agricultural/Industrial Secondary Certificate): awarded by technical secondary schools upon successful completion of secondary cycle and passing of national examination

Postsecondary

D شهادة في العلوم الإدارية (Certificate of Administrative Sciences or Business Certificate): one year of basic studies at the College of Administrative Sciences

E دبلوم متخصص (Specialized Diploma): one or one and one-half years in banking and finance fields (part-time programs)

F دبلوم (Diploma): two years in various business, banking and finance, and health fields; two and one-half years in pharmacy assistance; post-program internships required in health fields

G دبلوم عالي (Higher Diploma): three years in fields such as computer science, English translation, business administration, engineering, and educational technology

H دبلوم التمريض العام (Diploma in General Nursing): three years at the nursing institutes

I شهادة المؤهلات المهنية الوطنية العامة (General National Vocational Qualification Certificate): three years in electronics, engineering, and laboratory sciences at the Technical Industrial Colleges

J بكالوريوس (Bachelor's degree): four to five years, depending on the field of study

K بكالوريوس الطب والجراحة (Bachelor of Medicine and Surgery): three years of study plus a one-year internship after a five-year credential **J** in medical sciences

L دبلوم التأهيل (Qualification Diploma): one year of teacher training for those holding credential **J** in fields other than education

M دبلوم (Diploma): one year in the Faculty of Engineering and Science; requires five-year credential **J** for admission

279

GRADING INFORMATION

Secondary

Successful completion of each year requires a final grade not lower than the required minimum score in each subject. Minimum and maximum scores for the third year of general secondary education are listed below and are determined solely by final examination. Admission to many postsecondary programs requires a secondary certificate average of 60–65%, and at least 70% is required for university admission.

Subject	3rd-Year Lit Min	3rd-Year Lit Max	3rd-Year Science Min	3rd-Year Science Max
Islamic education	50	100	50	100
Arabic language	60	120	50	100
English language	40	100	40	100
Mathematics	16	40	64	160
Physics			40	100
Chemistry			40	100
Biology			40	100
Science	16	40		
History	40	100		
Geography	40	100		
Islamic civilization	40	100		

Higher Education

Sultan Qaboos University, Teacher Training Colleges

Grade	Percent	Grade Points
A	95–100	4.0
A-	90–95	3.7
B+	87–90	3.3
B	83–87	3.0
B-	80–83	2.7
C+	77–80	2.3
C	73–77	2.0
C-	70–73	1.7
D+	65–70	1.3
D	60–65	1.0
F	less than 60	0.0

- A minimum grade point average of 2.0 is required to remain in good standing.

Health and Nursing Institutes

Percent	Remark	Translation
85–100	ممتاز	Excellent
75–84	جيد جدا	Very Good
65–74	جيد	Good
50–64	مقبول	Pass
0–49	راسب	Fail

Institute of Public Administration

Percent	Remark
90–100	Excellent
80–89	Very Good
70–79	Good
60–69	Pass
0–59	Fail

POSTSECONDARY INSTITUTION RECOGNITION BODY

Ministry of Higher Education; PO Box 52, Ruwi, Postal Code 112, Sultanate of Oman. Tel: 968-693148 or 968-693149. Fax: 968-693469.

RESOURCES FOR ADDITIONAL INFORMATION

Internet Source:
UNESCO—World Academic Database: www.unesco.org/iau/educom.html

---

Compiler
Leslie S. Nucho
Vice President
AMIDEAST, Washington, D.C.

PAKISTAN

YEARS OF EDUCATION →

1→6	7	8	9	10	11	12	13	14	15	16	17		18	19	20	21	22	23	24
	½	½	½	½	½	½	½	½	½	½	½		½	½	½	½	½	½	
					A	B	F	J	M	O	W	X	j	X	q	x	dd	dd	ee	ee	qq→
						C	G	K	N	P		Y	k	i	s	y	ee	ee	ll	nn→
						D	H	L	O	Q		Z	l	m	u	z	gg	ii	mm	oo→
						E	I			R		a	m	n	v	cc	hh	jj		pp→
										S		b		o	w	dd		kk		
										T		c		p	x	ee				
										U		d		q	y	ff				
										V		e		r	z					
												f		s	aa					
												g		t	bb					
												h		u	cc					
												i		v	dd					
												x		w						
														x						

CREDENTIALS OR DOCUMENTATION

Secondary

A Secondary School Certificate awarded by the Boards of Intermediate and Secondary Education

B Certificate of Commerce: one-year program; requires credential **A** for admission

C Primary Teacher Certificate: one-year program; requires credential **A** for admission

D Diploma in Communications: one-year program; requires credential **A** for admission

E Diploma in Midwifery: awarded by the Pakistan Nursing Council; one-year program; requires credential **A** for admission

F Higher Secondary Certificate: awarded by the Boards of Intermediate and Secondary Education; two-year program; requires credential **A** for admission

G Intermediate Certificate awarded by the Boards of Intermediate and Secondary Education: two-year program; requires credential **A** for admission

H Lady's Health Visitor: awarded by the Pakistan Nursing Council; two-year program completed at public health schools; requires credential **A** for admission

I Diploma in Commerce: two-year program; requires credential **A** for admission

J Diploma of Associate Engineer in the fields of computer technology, engineering, and telecommunications: three-year program; requires credential **A** for admission

K Diploma in Nursing: awarded by the Pakistan Nursing Council; three-year hospital school of nursing program which is 40% theoretical and 60% practical; requires credential **A** for admission

Postsecondary

L   Certificate in Teaching: one-year program; requires credential **F** or **G** for admission

M   Bachelor of... Arts (Pass), Business Administration, Commerce (Pass), Home Economics, Laws in Shariah and Laws, Oriental Languages, Social Work, Science (Pass), and Science in the fields of medical technology, occupational therapy, and physical therapy: two-year programs; require credential **F** or **G** for admission

N   Bachelor of Science in Home Economics: four-year program; requires credential **A** for admission

O   Bachelor of Technology awarded by the University of Engineering and Technology, Lahore: three-year program requiring credential **F**, **G**, or **J** for admission; see also credential **i**

P   Bachelor of Technology awarded by Northwest Frontier Province University of Engineering and Technology: two-year program; requires credential **J** for admission

Q   Bachelor of... Arts (Honours), Business Administration, Commerce (Honours), Computer Science, Education (three-year program), Fine Arts, Science (Honours), Science in Applied Geology, and Social Work: requires credential **F** or **G** for admission; see also credentials **R**, **W**, and **Z**[1]

R   Bachelor of Education (one-year program): requires credential **M** for admission; see also credentials **Q** and **W**

S   Diploma in Library Science (only awarded by the University of the Punjab) and Bachelor of Library Science: one-year programs; require credential **M** for admission

T   Senior Diploma in Physical Education (only awarded by Gomal University) and Bachelor of Physical Education: one-year programs; require credential **M** for admission

U   Master of Oriental Languages: awarded by the University of the Punjab; one-year program; requires credential **M** for admission

V   Bachelor of Science in Nursing: two-year program; requires both credential **K** and **F**, or **G** for admission; see also credential **Z**

W   Bachelor of Education: one and one-half-year program offered by Allama Iqbal Open University; requires credential **M** for admission; see also credential **Q** and **R**

X   Bachelor of Laws: two- and three-year programs; requires credential **M** for admission

Y   Bachelor of Dental Surgery: four-year program; requires credential **F** or **G** for admission; see also credential **r**

Z   Bachelor's degrees in Arts (Honours), Science (Honours), and in the fields of agriculture, animal husbandry, ceramics, design, engineering, fine arts, nursing, and textile design: four-year programs; require credential **F** or **G** for admission; see also credential **Q** and **V**[1]

a   Bachelor of Pharmacy: four-year program; requires credential **F** or **G** for admission

b   Doctor of Veterinary Medicine: four-year program; requires credential **F** or **G** for admission

c   Master of Education: one-year program which requires credential **R** for admission; or two-year program which requires credential **M** for admission

d   Master of Library Science (and Information Systems): one-year program which requires credential **S** for admission; or two-year program which requires credential **M** for admission

e   Master of Science in Physical Education: awarded by Gomal University; one-year program; requires credential **T** for admission f   Master of...Arts, Business Administration, Commerce, Computer Science, Public Administration, Science, or Social Work: one-year programs which require credential **Q** for admission; or two-year programs which require credential **M** for admission; see also credential **t** and **y**

g   Master of Science in Home Economics: awarded by the University of the Punjab; two-year program; requires credential **N** for admission

h   Master of Science in Hematology: awarded by Baqai Medical University; two-year program; requires credential **M** for admission

i   Bachelor of Technology (Honours): awarded by the University of Engineering and Technology, Lahore; four-year program; requires credential **F**, **G**, or **J** for admission; see also credential **O**

j   Master of Science in Applied Geology, awarded by the University of the Punjab; one and one-half-year program; requires credential **Q** for admission

k   Master of Business Education: awarded by the University of the Punjab; one and one-half-year program; requires credential **Q** for admission

l   Master of Dental Surgery: awarded by the University of the Punjab; six-month program; requires credential **Y** for admission

m   Master of Educational Planning: awarded by Allama Iqbal Open University; two and one-half to three years of study following credential **M**

n   Bachelor of Architecture: five-year program; requires credential **F** or **G** for admission

o   Bachelor of Medicine and Bachelor of Surgery: five-year program; requires credential **F** or **G** for admission

p   Master of Science in Agriculture: one-year program; requires credential **Z** for admission

q   Master's degree in the field of computer science or engineering: one- or two-year programs which require credential **Z** for admission; see also credential **f** and **ff**

r   Bachelor of Dental Surgery: awarded by the University of Sindh; five-year program; requires credential **F** or **G** for admission; see also credential **Y**

s   Master of Pharmacy: one- and two-year programs requiring credential **a** for admission

t   Master of Business Administration: awarded by Allama Iqbal Open University; three-year program; requires credential **M** for admission; see also credential **f**

u   Master of Philosophy: one- and two-year programs; requires credential **d**, **e**, or **f** for admission

v   Master of Public Health: awarded by Baqai Medical University; one-year program; requires credential **Y** or **o** for admission

w   Diploma in Hematology: awarded by Baqai Medical University; one-year program; requires credential **Y** or **o** for admission

x   Master of Philosophy in Health Science: awarded by Baqai Medical University; one-year program; requires credential **V**, **Y**, **f**, or **o** for admission

y   Master of Arts awarded by International Islamic University: two- and three-year programs following credential **Z**; see also credential **f**

z   Master of Laws: two- or three-year programs following credential **X** or **Z**

aa Master of Science in Tropical Medicine: awarded by Baqai Medical University; one-year program; requires credential **o** for admission

bb Diploma in Cardiology: awarded by Ziauddin Medical University; one-year program; requires credential **o** for admission

cc Master of Science in Epidemiology: awarded by Aga Khan University; two-year program requiring credential **Z**, **f**, or **o** for admission

dd Doctor of Philosophy: two- to five-year program; requires credential **c**, **d**, **e**, or **f** for admission

ee Doctor of Medicine and Doctor of Surgery: two- to five-year program; requires credential **o** for admission

ff Master of Science in Computer Science awarded by International Islamic University, or Master of Science in Civil Engineering awarded by N.E.D. University of Engineering and Technology: three-year programs which require credential **Z** for admission; see also credentials **f** and **q**

gg Master of Philosophy in Hematology: awarded by Baqai Medical University; three-year program; requires credential **o** for admission

hh Doctor of Medicine Oncology: awarded by Ziauddin Medical University; three-year program; requires credential **o** for admission

ii Doctor of Philosophy: awarded by Quaid-I-Azam University; three-year program; requires a two-year credential **u** for admission

jj Doctor of Medicine Cardiology or Gastroenterology: awarded by Ziauddin Medical University; four-year program; requires credential **o** for admission

kk Master of Surgery Neuro Surgery: awarded by Ziauddin Medical University; four-year program; requires credential **o** for admission

ll Doctor of Medicine in the fields of internal medicine, nuclear medicine, microbiology, and radio-diagnosis: awarded by Ziauddin Medical University; five-year program; requires credential **o** for admission

mm Master of Surgery General Surgery: awarded by Ziauddin Medical University; five-year program; requires credential **o** for admission

nn Doctor of Oriental Languages: awarded by the University of the Punjab; five-year program; requires credential **dd** for admission

oo Doctor of Laws: awarded by the University of the Punjab; five-year program; requires credential **dd** for admission

pp Doctor of Literature and Doctor of Science: awarded by the University of Karachi; five-year program; requires credential **dd** for admission

qq Doctor of Literature: awarded by the University of the Punjab; six-year program; requires credential **dd** for admission

[1] Both three-year and four-year Bachelor of Arts (Honours) and Bachelor of Science (Honours) degrees are offered.

GRADING INFORMATION

Secondary

Division	Percentage
First	60 to 100
Second	40 to 59.9
Third	33 to 39.9
(Fail)	Below 33

Higher Education

Grade	Description
A	Excellent
B	Good
C	Satisfactory
D	Pass
F	Fail

Grade	Percentage
Distinction	85 to 100
High Pass	70 to 84
Pass	60 to 69
Marginal Pass	50 to 59
Fail	0 to 49

Baqai Medical University

Grade	Percentage
A	85 to 100
B	71 to 84
C	61 to 70
D	50 to 60
F	0 to 49

Institute of Business Administration

Grade	Percentage
A	87 to 100
B	72 to 86
C	60 to 71
F	0 to 59

National College of Arts

Division	Percentage
Distinction	85 to 100
First	60 to 84
Second	45 to 59
(Fail)	Below 45

NED University of Engineering

Grade	Percentage
A	85 to 100
B	70 to 84
C	60 to 69
D	50 to 59
F	0 to 49

University of Arid Agriculture: Graduate Programs

Grade	Percentage	Description
A	80 to 100	Excellent
B	65 to 79	Good
C	50 to 64	Satisfactory
D	40 to 49	Pass
F	0 to 39	Fail

POSTSECONDARY INSTITUTION RECOGNITION BODY

Ministry of Education: Block "D," Pakistani Secretariat, Islamabad. Tel: 92-51-212020. Fax: 92-51-822851.

Universities Grants Commission: Responsible for university funding; advises the Ministry of Education on issues of higher education. UGC, Sector H/9, Islamabad. Tel: 92-51-448371/74. Fax: 92-51-858018. E-mail: ugc%nahe@uunet.uu.net

RESOURCES FOR ADDITIONAL INFORMATION

The British Council. 1996. *International Guide to Qualifications in Education.* 4th ed. London: Mansell.

National Office of Overseas Skills Recognition. 1992. *Country Education Profiles: Pakistan.* Canberra: Australian Government Publishing Service.

Nursing in the World Editorial Committee. 1993. *Nursing in the World: The Facts, Needs, and Prospects.* 3rd ed. Tokyo: The International Nursing Foundation of Japan.

Internet Source
UNESCO-World Academic Database: www.unesco.org/iau/educpk.html

---

Compilers
Sonja Bhan, World Education Services, Inc., New York, NY
Bonnie Rosenthal, World Education Services, Inc., New York, NY

PALESTINIAN NATIONAL AUTHORITY

YEARS OF EDUCATION →

	½	½	½	½	½	½	½	½	½	½	½	½	½	½	½	½	½
1 → 6	7	8	9	10	11	12	13	14	15	16	17	18	19	20	21	22	23	24
						A		B	B	C	C	F	F					
											D	G	G					
											E		H					
											F							

CREDENTIALS OR DOCUMENTATION[1]

Secondary

A شهادة الدراسة الثانوية العامة (General Secondary Education Certificate, also known as the *tawjihi*): awarded after passing of national examination

Postsecondary

B دبلوم متوسط (Intermediate Diploma): two to three years, depending on field of study; requires credential **A** for admission

C بكالوريوس (Bachelor's degree): four to five years, depending on the field of study; requires credential **A** for admission

D دبلوم العالي في تأهيل التربوي (Teaching Diploma): one year of teacher training for holders of four-year credential **C** in scientific fields

E دبلوم عالي (Higher Diploma): one year, requiring four-year credential **C** for admission

F دبلوم عالي قي تربية (Higher Diploma in Education): one to two years, requiring credential **C** for admission

G ماجستير (Master's degree): two years, requiring credential **C** for admission

H بكالوريوس في الطب (Bachelor of Medicine): seven years, requiring credential **A** for admission

[1] Authority over Palestinian education was transferred from the Israelis to the Palestinians in September, 1994. Beginning with the 1995-96 academic year, the Palestinians unified the curriculum on the Jordanian model. Prior to that time, schools in the Gaza Strip followed the Egyptian system, and schools in the West Bank followed the Jordanian system.

GRADING INFORMATION

Secondary

Percent	Remark	Translation
90–100	ممتاز	Excellent
80–89	جيد جدا	Very Good
70–79	جيد	Good
60–69	مقبول	Acceptable
50–59	ضعيف	Poor
0–49	راسب	Fail

Higher Education

Most universities and colleges use the following grading scale:

Percent	Remark	Translation
90–100	ممتاز	Excellent
80–89	جيد جدا	Very Good
70–79	جيد	Good
60–69	مقبول	Satisfactory
50–59	ضعيف	Poor
0–49	راسب	Fail

- At Bethlehem University, the minimum passing score is 60.
- A grade of E designates a range considered minimally passing for individual courses, but failing as an average.

In graduate programs at Birzeit University, the following grading scale is used:

Percent	Remark	Letter Grade
90–100	Excellent	A
85–89	Very Good	B
80–84	Good	C
75–79	Satisfactory	D
70–74	Pass	E
Below 70	Fail	F

POSTSECONDARY INSTITUTION RECOGNITION BODY

Ministry of Higher Education; Ramallah, West Bank. Tel: 972-2-298-2610. Fax: 972-2-295-4518.

RESOURCES FOR ADDITIONAL INFORMATION

Franks, Lynne. 1987. *Israel and the Occupied Territories: A Study of the Educational Systems of Israel and the Occupied Territories and a Guide to the Academic Placement of Students in Educational Institutions of the United States.* Washington, D.C.: AACRAO.

Internet Source:
UNESCO—World Academic Database: www.unesco.org/iau/educxc.html

---

Compilers
Lina Rabadi
Educational Adviser
AMIDEAST, Jerusalem

Leslie Nucho
Vice President
AMIDEAST, Washington, D.C.

PANAMA

YEARS OF EDUCATION →

1→6	½ 7	½ 8	½ 9	½ 10	½ 11	½ 12	½ 13	½ 14	½ 15	½ 16	½ 17	½ 18	½ 19	½ 20	½ 21	½ 22	½ 23	24
			A		B	B C D		E	E F G	H	H I J	J K L	L M	M				

CREDENTIALS OR DOCUMENTATION

Secondary

A *Certificado de terminación de estudios correspondientes al primer ciclo de educación secundaria* (Certificate of completion of studies corresponding to the first cycle of secondary education): awarded after completion of the *ciclo básico* (basic cycle) or *ciclo comun* (common cycle)[1]

B *Bachiller agropecuario* (Agricultural Bachelor) and *Bachiller Industrial* (Industrial Bachelor): technical education lasting two to three years[1]

C *Bachiller* (Bachelor)...options in *ciencias* (sciences) and/or *letras* (arts), and *comerical* (commercial): academic education lasting three years[1]

D *Certificado de maestro normal maestro de enseñanza primaria* (Certificate of Primary Teacher): teacher training program lasting three years[1]

Postsecondary

E *Técnico* (Technician), *Secretario Ejecutive* (Executive Secretary), *Diploma de Enferma* (Diploma of Nurse): two and one-half to three years of study

F *Profesor en educación primaria* (Teacher of Primary Education): three-year program

G *Profesor en matemática* (Mathematics Teacher): three-year program

H *Licenciado/Licentiatura* (Licentiate): four- to five-year programs

I *Doctor de cirugía dental* (Doctor of Dental Surgeon): five-year program

J *Profesor de educación* (Teacher): one-year programs based on credential **H**

K *Doctor en medicina* (Doctor in Medicine): six-year program

L *Maestría* (Master): two-year programs based on credential **H** or equivalent

M *Doctor* (Doctoral degree): Three-year programs based on credential **H** or equivalent

[1] Secondary education begins after completion of six years of elementary education. *Ciclo comun* consists of the first three years of general secondary education. *Ciclo diversificado* (diversified cycle) consists of two years (rarely) or three years (usually) of specialized secondary education.

GRADING INFORMATION

Secondary

Numeric	Description
5	Highest Grade
4	
3	Minimum Pass
2	
1	Lowest Grade

Higher Education

Percentage	Description	Translation
91-100	*Sobresaliente*	Outstanding, Excellent
81-90	*Bueno*	Good
71-80	*Regular/Normal*	Average
61-70	*Minimo de Promoción*	Minimum Pass
0-60	*Fracasado*	Failure

POSTSECONDARY INSTITUTION RECOGNITION BODY

Ministerio de Educación, P.O. Box 2440, Panama, 3. Tel: 507-622671.
Fax: 507-629087.

RESOURCES FOR ADDITIONAL INFORMATION

Aldrich-Langen, Caroline, and Kathleen Sellew, editors. 1987. *The Admission and Placement of Students from Central America: Belize, Costa Rica, El Salvador, Guatemala, Honduras, Nicaragua, Panama.* Annapolis Junction, MD: PIER.

Centro Panameno Esatdouinidense (CentroPanUsa), Ave. Roosevelt, Balboa, Ancon, Al lado del McDonald's de la antigua Estación del Ferrocarril, Panama City, Panama. Tel: 507-232-6660. Fax: 507-232-7292. E-mail: panusa@sinfo.net

Foreign Educational Credentials Required for Consideration of Admission to Universities and Colleges in the United States. 1994. Washington, D.C.: AACRAO.

Internet Sources:
Consejo de Rectores de Panama: www.pa/consejo
Ministerio de Educación: www.educacion.gob.pa
UNESCO-World Academic Database: www.unesco.org/iau/educpa.html

---

Compiler
Judi Marino
Director of Admissions
Florida Institute of Technology, Melbourne

PAPUA NEW GUINEA

YEARS OF EDUCATION →

```
      ½   ½   ½   ½   ½   ½   ½  .  ½   ½   ½   ½   ½   ½   ½   ½   ½   ½
1 → 6| 7 | 8 | 9 | 10 | 11 | 12 | 13 | 14 | 15 | 16 | 17 | 18 | 19 | 20 | 21 | 22 | 23 | 24 |
                  A       B F  C    D    H        K    L         O    O         P    P
                            E  G    I              M
                            F       J              N
                            G
```

CREDENTIALS OR DOCUMENTATION

Secondary

A   School Certificate
B   Higher School Certificate from National High School: gives access to higher education

Postsecondary

Nonuniversity

C   Certificates from Technical College: one-year programs; prior admission requirement was grade 10[1]
D   Diplomas from Technical College: two-year programs; prior admission requirement was grade 10[1]
E   Diploma in forestry, diploma in nursing, and diploma in (secondary) teaching: three-year programs; prior admission requirement was grade 10; the diploma in teaching allowed access to credential J[1]

University

F   Certificate: one- and two-semester programs
G   Diplomas: one- and two-year programs
H   Diploma in architecture, electrical engineering, or surveying awarded by the University of Technology: three-year programs
I   Diploma in health science awarded by the University of Papua New Guinea (dental therapy, medical technology, radiography, and pharmacy): three-year programs
J   Bachelor's degree in education (in-service): two-year program which requires teaching experience and the diploma in (secondary) teaching (credential E) for admission
K   Bachelor's degree (including law): admission based on credential B
L   Bachelor's degree (honours): admission based on credential K
M   Bachelor's degree in architecture, building, forestry, or medicine: admission based on credential B
N   Graduate diploma: one-year program requiring credential K for admission

O Master's degree: two-year program (one year of coursework plus a thesis) officially requiring credential **K** for admission, but usually credential **L** is required

P Doctoral degree: earned after three to four years of research; this degree is on record, but there are very few recipients; admission based on credential **O**

[1] The nonuniversity postsecondary system of education is in transition. Although entrance requirements for technical colleges, teacher training colleges, and allied health fields now require grade 12 completion, prior admission requirements (no specific date, since it is being phased in) allowed for admission of grade 10 graduates. Universities have always required grade 12 completion for entrance.

GRADING INFORMATION

Secondary

Classification	Percentage of Students
Distinction	Top 5%
Credit	Next 20%
Upper Pass	Next 25%
Pass	Next 40%
Fail	Last 10%

In practical subjects, students are rated in comparison to other students within the school. For example, Agriculture 47/104 means that the students was 47th out of 104 students studying agriculture in that school. Practical subjects are graded in some schools on the basis of their percentage criteria achieved within the school. Results are then awarded as a grade as follows:

Description	Percentage
Excellent	90-100
Very Good	80-89
Good	70-79
Poor	60-69
Fail	0-59

Higher Education

Letter	Description	Letter	Description: Adult Matriculants Only
A	High Description	A	High Distinction
B	Distinction	B	Distinction
C	Credit	C	Credit
D	Pass		
E	Conceded Pass		
F	Fail		

POSTSECONDARY INSTITUTION RECOGNITION BODY

The Commission for Higher Education recognizes universities, teacher's colleges, technical colleges, schools of nursing, and agricultural colleges. In 1998 there were 34 institutions in this category.

Office of Higher Education, PO Box 5117, 1st Floor, Nambawan Finance Haus, Boroko NCD, Papua New Guinea. Tel: 675 301 2088. Fax: 675 325 8386.

Other agencies are responsible for recognition in the case of some specialized institutions.

RESOURCES FOR ADDITIONAL INFORMATION

Internet Source:
UNESCO - World Academic Database: www.unesco.org/iau/educpg.html

---

Compiler
Kathleen Sellew
Director, Papua New Guinea Higher Education Project
University of Minnesota

PERU

YEARS OF EDUCATION →

```
        ½   ½   ½   ½   ½   ½   ½   ½   ½   ½   ½   ½   ½   ½   ½   ½   ½
1 → 6|  7 | 8 | 9 | 10| 11| 12| 13| 14| 15| 16| 17| 18| 19| 20| 21| 22| 23| 24|

    A               B   D   E   F   F   F   I→  N→P→O→P→  P→  R→  R→
                    C       F   G   G   G   J→  O→Q→  Q→  R→
                            G   H   H   H   K
                            H                L
                                             M→
                                             N→
```

CREDENTIALS OR DOCUMENTATION

Secondary

Elementary and secondary education normally requires completion of a total of 11 years of schooling. It is usually preceded by one year of kindergarten, which is optional in a few instances.

A *Certificado Oficial de Educación Primaria* (Official Certificate of Primary Education)
B *Certificado de Técnico Operativo* (Certificate of Operative Technician), previously known as *Certificado de Auxiliar en Contabilidad* (Certificate of Assistant in Accounting): awarded upon completion of four years of technical secondary education
C *Certificado Oficial de Estudios de Secundaria* (Official Certificate of Secondary Studies): awarded upon completion of four years of secondary education[1]
D *Certificado Oficial de Estudios de Educación Secundaria Común* (Official Certificate of Studies in Common Secondary Education): awarded upon completion of five years of secondary education
E *Bachiller* (Bachelor): two-year program with admission based on credential **C**; expected to be awarded for the first time in 2001 or 2002[1]

Postsecondary

F *Certificado de Educación Superior en...* (Certificate of Higher Education in...): awarded upon completion of two, three, or four years of education at *Institutos Superiores Tecnológicos* (Higher Technological Institutes) and *Institutos Superiores Pedagógicos* (Higher Pedagogical Institutes); admission based on credential **C** or **D**
G *Diploma en ...* (Diploma in...): awarded upon completion of two, three, or four years of education at *Institutos Superiores Tecnológicos* (Higher Technological Institutes) and *Institutos Superiores Pedagógicos* (Higher Pedagogical Institutes); admission based on credential **C** or **D**
H *Técnico en...* (Technician in...): awarded upon completion of two, three, or four years of education at *Institutos Superiores Tecnológicos* (Higher Technological Institutes) and *Institutos Superiores Pedagógicos* (Higher Pedagogical Institutes); admission based on credential **C** or **D**

295

I *Grado Académico de Bachiller* (Academic Degree of Bachelor): awarded upon completion of at least five years of university study, variance depends upon regulations specific to the academic field and upon specific university requirements; admission based on credential D^2

J *Título de Licenciado* (Title of Licentiate), or *Título Profesional* (Professional Title): awarded upon completion of a credential I program plus additional requirements (examination, thesis, etc.); see also credentials **M, N,** and O^2

K *Título de Licenciado en Educación* (Title of Licentiate in Education) awarded by an *Instituto de Educación Superior Pedagógico* (Institute of Higher Pedagogical Education), and *Título Profesional de Licenciado en Educación* (Professional Title of Licentiate in Education) awarded by the *Instituto Pedagógico Nacional* (National Pegaogical Institute): five years of study with admission based on credential **D**

L *Título en Nombre de la Nación de Profesional en...* (Title in the Name of the Nation of Professional in...): awarded upon completion of five years of education at an *Escuela Superior* (Higher School), *Conservatorio* (Conservatory), or *Instituto* (Institute); admission based on credential **D**

M *Título de Abogado* (Title of Lawyer) or *Título Profesional de Abogado* (Professional Title of Lawyer): admission based on credentials **D** and **I**; professional requirement can be either a thesis or the oral defense of a civil case and a penal case[2]

N *Título de Cirujano-Dentista* (Title of Surgeon-Dentist) or *Título Profesional de Cirujano-Dentista* (Professional Title of Surgeon-Dentist): admission based on credentials **D** and **I**; curricula in the field of dentistry require at least five or six academic years[2]

O *Título de Médico-Cirujano* (Title of Physician-Surgeon) or *Título Profesional de Médico-Cirujano* (Professional Title of Physician-Surgeon): admission based on credentials **D** and **I**; curricula in the field of medicine require at least six or seven academic years[2]

P *Grado de Magister* (Degree of Master): awarded upon completion of one and one-half or two years of education beyond any I through **O**

Q *Especialista en...* (Specialist in...): awarded upon completion of one and one-half or two years of education beyond any credential I through **O**

R *Grado de Doctor* (Degree of Doctor): awarded upon completion of two years of education beyond credential **P**

[1] A change in the structure of secondary education beginning in 1999, to be implemented in stages, would require six years of primary education, followed by four years of secondary education, followed by two years of a *Bachillerto* (Baccalaureate) program. Successful completion of the *Bachillerato* would be necessary for admission to university. Although the terminology is the same, this is not the postsecondary-level credential listed as credential I.

[2] The award of *títulos* (titles) depends on the regulations and curriculum design of the specific university; length of study fluctuates between five and seven years. The time elapsing between completion of the requirements for the *grado académico de bachiller* (academic degree of bachelor) and the award of the *título* is dependent upon the swiftness of the student in completing the requirements for the *título* (an examination, a thesis, or other requirement). It is possible to earn the *grado académico de bachiller* and the *título* almost simultaneously.

GRADING INFORMATION
Secondary

Numerical	Significance
19-20	Rarely awarded
17-18	Outstanding
14-16	Excellent
13	Very Good
12	Good
11	Satisfactory
10	Fail
1-9	Not used

- Grades are usually lower in science: 14 and above may be considered excellent.
- Grades of 15 and above in social sciences may be considered excellent.

Postsecondary

Numerical	Significance
18-20	Rarely awarded
16-17	Outstanding
14-15	Excellent
12-13	Good
11	Pass
10	Pass at some universities; fail at others
1-9	Not used

- Grades are usually lower in science and engineering: 14 and above may be considered excellent.
- In social sciences, grades of 15 and above may be considered excellent.
- Grading varies among universities and among schools within universities. A certificate of rank or position is the most reliable indicator of achievement.

POSTSECONDARY INSTITUTION RECOGNITION BODY
Ministerio de Educación. Van de Velde 160, San Borja Norte, Lima, Peru.
Tel: 511-436-4990. Fax: 511-436-4992.

RESOURCES FOR ADDITIONAL INFORMATION
Fulbright Commission, Coronel Inclan 806, Miraflores, Lima 18, Peru.
Tel: 511-445-4746. Fax: 511-241-5319.

Gray, Collen. 1983. *Peru: A Study of the Educational System of Peru and a Guide to the Academic Placement of Students in Educational Institutions of the United States.* Washington, D.C.: AACRAO.

National Office of Overseas Skills Recognition, 1993. *Country Education Profiles: Peru.* Canberra: Australian Government Publishing Service.

Internet Source:
UNESCO - World Academic Database: www.unesco.org/iau/educpe.html

Compilers:
Judi Marino, Florida Institute of Technology, Melbourne
Illa Rocconi de Quintanilla, Educational Adviser, Fulbright Commission, Lima, Peru

PHILIPPINES

YEARS OF EDUCATION →

1 → 6 | 7 | 8 | 9 | 10 | 11 | 12 | 13 | 14 | 15 | 16 | 17 | 18 | 19 | 20 | 21 | 22 | 23 | 24 |
(½ marks appear between years 7 through 24)

10	11	12	13	14	15	16	17	18	19	20	21
A	B	C	C	C	C	J	K	K	O	O	R
B	C	D	D	F	J	K	L	L	P	P	S
	D	E	E	G	K	L	M	O	Q	Q	T
	E	F	F	H		M	N	P	R	R	U
		G	G	I		N	O	Q	S	S	V
		H	H	J		O			T	T	
		I	I						U	U	
									V	V	

CREDENTIALS OR DOCUMENTATION

Secondary

A Barangay High School Diploma: Barangay High Schools existed, primarily in rural areas, until the early 1990s. Since then, all Barangay High Schools were officially converted to regular high schools.

B High School Diploma: most commonly issued after 10 years of schooling, but may be issued after 11 (becoming more common, particularly in private schools) or 12 (extremely rare) years

Postsecondary

C *Sertipiko* or Certificate in any field, issued by a regular college or university: one to four years of study after completion of credential **A** or **B**

D Technical Education and Skills Development Authority (TESDA) National Certificate Level 1: one to two years of study beyond credential **A** or **B**

E TESDA National Certificate Level 2: one to two years of study beyond credential **A** or **B**

F TESDA National Certificate Level 3: two to three years of study beyond credential **A** or **B**

G TESDA National License: two to three years of study beyond credential **A** or **B**

H *Asoyado* or Associate degree: two to three years of study beyond credential **A** or **B**

I *Tapos sa Pagnanarses* or *Tapos sa Kurso ng Pagnanarses* or Graduate in Nursing (G.N.): two to three years of study beyond credential **A** or **B**; discontinued in 1984

J *Batsilyer sa mga Sining* or *Batsilyer sa Agham* or *Batsilyer* or Bachelor of Arts or Bachelor of Science or Bachelor, in any field except Law: four to five years of study beyond credential **A** or **B** (most commonly four years)

K *Diploma* or Post-Graduate Diploma or Post-Graduate Certificate: one to two years of study beyond credential **J**

L *Dalubhasa* or *Kadalubhasaan* or *Masterado* or Master degree in any field: two years of study beyond credential **J**

M Doctor of Dentistry (D.D.S.) or Doctor of Dental Medicine (D.D.M.) degree: six years of study beyond credential **A** or **B**

N Doctor of Optometry (O.D.) degree: six years of study beyond credential **A** or **B**

O   Doctor of Veterinary Medicine (D.V.M.) degree: six years of study beyond credential **A** or **B** (usually), or four years of study beyond credential **J** (occasionally)

P   *Batsilyer sa Batas* or *Batsilyer sa Pambabatas,* or Bachelor of Laws (LL.B.) degree: four years of study beyond credential **J**

Q   *Doktor sa Medisina* or Doctor of Medicine (M.D.) degree: four years of study beyond credential **J**

R   *Juris Doctor (J.D.)* degree: five years of study beyond credential **J**

S   Doctor of Business Administration (D.B.A.) or Doctor of Business Management (D.B.M.): three years of study beyond credential **L**

T   *Doktor sa Edukasyon* or Doctor of Education (Ed.D.), or Doctor of Education Management (D.E.M.), or Doctor of Mathematics Education (D.M.E.), or Doctor of Vocational Education (D.V.E.) degree: three years of study beyond credential **L**

U   *Doktor sa Pilosopiya* or Doctor of Philosophy (Ph.D.) degree: three years of study beyond credential **L**

V   Doctor of Public Administration (D.P.A.) or Doctor of Public Management (D.P.M.) degree: three years of study beyond credential **L**

- Most Philippine institutions award their credentials in English, but credentials in Pilipino are becoming more common.

GRADING INFORMATION

Secondary

Numeric			Letter	Description
1.00	5.00	98-100	A	Outstanding (O)
1.50	4.50	95-97	A-	Very Satisfactory (VS)
1.75	4.25	92-94	B+	Very Satisfactory (VS)
2.00	4.00	89-91	B	Satisfactory (S)
2.25	3.75	86-88	B-	Satisfactory (S)
2.50	3.50	83-85	C+	Moderately Satisfactory (MS)
3.00	3.00	80-82	C	Moderately Satisfactory (MS)
3.50	2.50	75-79	D	Provisionally Satisfactory (PS) or Needs Improvement (NI)
4.00	2.00		D-	Provisionally Failing (PF) or Needs Improvement (NI)
5.00	1.00	0-74	F	Failing (F) or Needs Improvement (NI)

Numeric	Description
75-100	*Paso* or Pass (P)
0-74	*Bagsak* (B) or Fail (F)

- Secondary schools that use the pass/fail grading scale rarely indicate the numeric grade, but instead mark all classes as P or B/F.

- Provisionally Satisfactory and Provisionally Failing are also written as Conditionally Satisfactory (CS) and Conditionally Failing (CF). These grades imply that the student will usually be able to receive a passing grade for the course by submitting extra work or passing an extra examination. This explanation also applies to the Conditional Failure (CF) grade below.

Higher Education

Numeric		Percentage			Letter Grade			Description
1.00	4.0	97.00-100	95-100	97-100	A	A	A	Excellent
1.25		94.25-96.99		94-96	A-		A-	Excellent
1.50		91.50-94.24	90-94	91-93	B+		B+	Very Good
1.75		88.75-91.49		88-90	B		B	Very Good
2.00	3.0	86.00-88.74	85-89	85-87	B-	B	B-	Good
2.25		83.25-85.99		83-84	C+		C+	Good
2.50		80.50-83.24	80-84	80-82	C		C	Satisfactory
2.75		77.75-80.49		75-79	C-		C-	Satisfactory
3.00	2.0	75.00-77.74		75-79	D	C		Pass
4.00	1.0	70.00-74.99	70-74	70-74	CF	D	D	Conditional Failure
5.00	0.0	0.00-69.99	0-69	0-69	F	F	F	Failure

- At some institutions, a 2.75 average is required to graduate, but often a 3.0 average is sufficient. At many universities, the colleges and schools within the institution will have different graduation requirements.

- Many schools employ slight variations on the above scales, but such variations will usually be explained on the transcript.

POSTSECONDARY INSTITUTION RECOGNITION BODIES

Commission on Higher Education (CHED), 3/F & 5/F Development Academy of the Philippines Building, San Miguel Avenue, Pasig City, Manila, Philippines. Tel: 2-633-5573. Fax: 2-633-1927. E-mail: ched@mnl.sequel.net

Technical Education and Skills Development Authority (TESDA), TESDA Complex, South Super Highway, Taguig, Manila, Philippines. Tel: 2-817-4000. Fax: 2-817-9040. (TESDA only recognizes postsecondary technical and vocational programs.)

ACCREDITING AGENCIES

- Accrediting agencies serve an important quality control purpose in the Philippines, and cooperate with the government in issuing Level IV accreditation, which is designed to identify "world-class" academic programs. All of these agencies are members of the Federation of Accrediting Agencies of the Philippines.

Accrediting Agency of Chartered Colleges and Universities of the Philippines, PUP Hasmin Hostel, Magsaysay Blvd., Santa Mesa, Manila, Philippines. Tel: 2-716-0944. Fax: 2-716-0944.

Association of Christian Schools and Colleges - Accrediting Agency, Inc., P.O. Box 71, Murphy District, Quezon City, Philippines. Tel: 2-911-5888.

Federation of Accrediting Agencies of the Philippines, 7/F Concorde Condominium, Benavides cor. Salcedo Streets, Legaspi Village, Makati, Manila, Philippines. Tel: 2-818-7553. Fax: 2-818-0013.

Philippine Accrediting Association of Schools, Colleges, and Universities, 10/F Aurora Towers, Cubao, Quezon City, Philippines. Tel: 2-911-2845. Fax: 2-911-0807.

Philippine Association of Colleges and Universities - Commission on Accreditation, Room 135, University of the Philippines Alumni Center, University of the Philippines, Diliman, Quezon City, Philippines.

RESOURCES FOR ADDITIONAL INFORMATION

Commission on Higher Education. 1997. *Directory of Higher Education Institutions in the Philippines.* Manila: Department of Education, Culture, and Sports.

Clemente, Alejandro. 1996. *Philippine Education into the 21st Century.* Quezon City, Philippines: Department of Education, Culture, and Sports.

Department of Education, Culture and Sports. 1997. *Facts and Figures on Philippine Education.* Manila: Department of Education, Culture, and Sports.

National Office of Overseas Skills Recognition. 1995. *Country Education Profiles: The Philippines.* Canberra: Australian National Government Publishing Service.

Southeast Asian Ministers of Education Organization. 1998. *Handbook on Diplomas, Degrees and Other Certificates in Higher Education in Asia and the Pacific.* Bangkok: Southeast Asian Ministers of Education Organization Regional Centre for Higher Education and Development.

Technical Education and Skills Development Authority. 1998. *Directory of Training Institutions in the Philippines.* Manila: Technical Education and Skills Development Authority.

Vorderstrasse, Jason, et.al. Unpublished, circa 1999. *The Philippines: A Workshop Report of the Educational System of the Philippines and a Guide to the Academic Placement of Students in Educational Institutions in the United States.* Contact PIER Publications (see Appendix A) for information about this book's availability.

Internet Sources:
Fund for Assistance to Private Education (FAPENET): www.fapenet.org
Technical Education and Skills Development Authority (TESDA): www.tesda.org
UNESCO-World Academic Database: www.unesco.org/iau/educph.html

---

Compiler
Jason Vorderstrasse
Attorney
United States Department of Labor, Office of the Solicitor
Los Angeles, CA

The information presented in this country profile is the result of independent research by the compiler, and does not necessarily represent the position of the United States Department of Labor or the United States government.

POLAND

YEARS OF EDUCATION →

```
    ½   ½   ½   ½   ½   ½   ½   ½   ½   ½   ½   ½   ½   ½   ½   ½   ½
1→6| 7 | 8 | 9 | 10| 11| 12| 13| 14| 15| 16| 17| 18| 19| 20| 21| 22| 23| 24|

    A           B   C   C   D   D H F H H I I K L              N→
                            E   E   G I I K J M→
                                F   H   J L
                                G   I
                                H
```

CREDENTIALS OR DOCUMENTATION

Secondary

A   *Świadectwo Ukończenia Szkoły Podstawowej* (Certificate of Completion of Elementary School): signifies completion of eight years of compulsory education

B   *Świadectwo Ukończenia Zasadniczej Szkoły Zawodowej* (Certificate of Completion of Basic Vocational School) [1]

C   *Świadectwo Dojrzałości* (Maturity Certificate), awarded in a variety of fields by a variety of institutions, including *Liceum Ogólnokształcące* (General Secondary School); *Liceum Medyczne* (Medical Secondary School); *Liceum Muzyczne* (Music Secondary School); *Liceum Pedagogiczne* (Pedagogical Secondary School); *Liceum Zawodowe* (Vocational Secondary School); and *Technikum Zawodowe* (Technical Secondary School): signifies completion of a four- or five-year program requiring credential **A** for admission [2]

D   *Dyplom Ukończenia Policealnego Studium Zawodowego* (Diploma of Completion of Post-Lyceum Vocational School): awarded in a variety of fields by a variety of institutions; signifies completion of a two-year program requiring credential **C** for admission

E   *Dyplom Ukończenia Studium Wychowania Przedszkolnego* (Diploma of Completion of Preschool Education School); or *Dyplom Ukończenia Studium Nauczycielskiego* (Diploma of Completion of Teacher Training School): signifies completion of a six-year program requiring credential **A** for admission or a two-year program requiring credential **C** for admission

Postsecondary

F   *Dyplom Ukończenia Wyższych Studiów Zawodowych* (Diploma of Completion of Higher Vocational Studies): signifies completion of a three-year program (or the part-time equivalent of a three-year, full-time program) requiring credential **C** for admission

G   *Dyplom* (Diploma) indicating the *Tytuł Inżynier* (Title of Engineer): requires credential **C** for admission [3]

H   *Dyplom* (Diploma) indicating the *Tytuł Licencjata* (Title of Licentiate): signifies completion of three to four years of study requiring credential **C** for admission

302

I   *Dyplom* (Diploma) indicating the *Tytuł Magister* (Title of Master): signifies completion of four to five years of study requiring credential **C** for admission [4]

J   *Dyplom* (Diploma) indicating the *Tytuł Dentysta* (Title of Dentist) or *Tytuł Stomatologa* (Title of Stomatologist): signifies completion of a five-year program requiring credential **C** for admission

K   *Dyplom* (Diploma) indicating the *Tytuł Lekarz Weterynarii* (Title of Veterinary Physician): signifies completion of a five and one-half-year program requiring credential **C** for admission

L   *Dyplom* (Diploma) indicating the *Tytuł Lekarz* (Title of Physician): signifies completion of a six-year program requiring credential **C** for admission

M   *Doktor Nauk* (Doctor of Science): signifies completion of a minimum three-year program requiring credential **I**, **J**, **K**, or **L** for admission

N   *Doktor Habilitowany* (Habilitated Doctor): signifies completion of a program requiring credential **M** for admission

[1]   Graduates are eligible for admission to a three-year program leading to credential **C** at a *Liceum Ogólnokształcące* (General Secondary School) or a *Technikum Zawodowe* (Technical Secondary School).

[2]   The *Świadectwo Dojrzałości* (Certificate of Maturity) is awarded to students who pass the maturity examination. It is required for admission to entry-level postsecondary programs. Students who do not take or pass the maturity examination receive a *Świadectwo Ukończenia* (Certificate of Completion).

[3]   This is a part-time program considered in Poland to represent the equivalent of three-years of full-time study. Graduates are eligible for a special two-year program leading to credential **I**.

[4]   Programs can sometimes be up to six years in length in the field of fine arts.

GRADING INFORMATION

Secondary

Prior to fall 1991:

Polish	Translation	Numeric
Bardzo Dobry	Very Good	5
Dobry	Good	4
Dostateczny	Satisfactory	3
Niedostateczny	Unsatisfactory	2

- The minimum passing grade is *Dostateczny* (3).

Since fall 1991:

Polish	Translation	Numeric
Celujący	Excellent	6
Bardzo Dobry	Very Good	5
Dobry	Good	4
Dostateczny	Satisfactory	3
Mierny	Poor	2
Niedostateczny	Unsatisfactory	1

- The minimum passing grade is *Mierny* (2).

Higher Education

Polish	Abbreviation	Translation	Numeric
Bardzo Dobry	*b.dob., b.db., b.d.*	Very Good	5
Dobry	*dob., db.*	Good	4
Dostateczny	*dost., dst., dt.*	Satisfactory	3
Niedostateczny	*n.dost., n.dst., n.dt., n.d.*	Unsatisfactory	2
Zaliczenie	*zal.*	Credit	-

- The minimum passing grade is *Dostateczny* (3).
- *Zaliczenie* is a passing grade on a pass/fail or satisfactory/unsatisfactory basis.
- Sometimes the words *ponad* (above) and *plus* (plus) are used to modify the grades *Dobry* and *Dostateczny*.
- Sometimes the word *dość* (enough) is used to modify the grade *Dobry*.
- Sometimes a plus symbol or decimal is used to modify the numeric grades "4" and "3" (e.g., "4+", "4.5", "3+", and "3.5").

POSTSECONDARY INSTITUTION RECOGNITION BODY

Ministerstwo Edukacji Narodowej (Ministry of National Education), Al. Szucha 25, 00-918 Warsaw, Poland. Tel/Fax: 48-22-628-93-29. Tel: 48-22-621-67-50.

RESOURCES FOR ADDITIONAL INFORMATION

Devlin, Edward, ed. 1992. *The Admission and Placement of Students from the Republic of Poland*. Annapolis Junction, MD: PIER.

Republic of Poland Ministry of National Education. 1997a. *Scientific and Academic Activities of Polish Universities: Agricultural Academies, Economical Academes, Teacher Education Schools*. Warsaw: Warsaw Agricultural University Press.

_____. 1997b. *Scientific and Academic Activities of Polish Universities: Technical Universities*. Warsaw: Warsaw Agricultural University Press.

_____. 1997c. *Scientific and Academic Activities of Polish Universities: Universities*. Warsaw: Warsaw Agricultural University Press.

Internet Sources:
Scientific and Academic Activities of Polish Universities: www.sggw.waw.pl/plusnew/
UNESCO - World Academic Database: www.unesco.org/iau/educpl.html

---

Compiler
Jason A. Wessel
Evaluator
Educational Credential Evaluators. Inc., Milwaukee, WI

PORTUGAL

YEARS OF EDUCATION →

```
      ½   ½   ½   ½   ½   ½   ½   ½   ½   ½   ½   ½   ½   ½   ½   ½   ½
1 → 6| 7 | 8 | 9 | 10 | 11 | 12 | 13 | 14 | 15 | 16 | 17 | 18 | 19 | 20 | 21 | 22 | 23 | 24 |
                        A               B   E   G   I    M→  N→  N→  N→  N→  N→
                                        C   F   H   L
                                        D       I   M→
                                                J
                                                K
```

CREDENTIALS OR DOCUMENTATION

Secondary

A *Certificado de Fim de Estudos Secundárias* (Certificate of Completion of Secondary Studies): leads to postsecondary education

Postsecondary

B *Bacharel* (Bachelor): three-year polytechnic program in administration, agriculture, cinema, dance, engineering and technology, forestry, management and accountancy, music, nursing, or theater

C *Bacharel* (Bachelor) in Education: three-year program[1]

D *Diploma do Ciclo Básico* (Diploma of the Basic Cycle): three-year university program in Fine Arts

E *Licenciado* (Licentiate): four-year university programs in arts or humanities

F *Licenciado* (Licentiate): four-year teacher training program requiring credential **A** for admission, or one-year program requiring credential **C** for admission[2]

G *Licenciado en Ensino* (Licentiate in Education): five-year program[3]

H *Licenciado* (Licentiate): five-year university program in the fields of agriculture and animal husbandry, environmental sciences, pharmacy, physical education, social sciences, and technology

I *Licenciado Ramo de Formação Educacional* (Licentiate in the Field of Educational Formation): five- or six-year university program[3]

J *Diploma do Ciclo Especial* (Diploma of the Special Cycle): two-year university program in fine arts requiring credential **D** for admission

K *Diploma de Estudos Superiores Especializados* (Diploma of Higher Specialized Studies): two-year polytechnic program in administration, agriculture, cinema, dance, engineering and technology, management and accountancy, music, or theater requiring credential **B** for admission

L *Licenciado* (Licentiate): six-year program in the fields of dentistry or medicine requiring credential **A** for admission; graduates are referred to as *doutor* (doctor) and use the initials "*dr*"

M *Mestre* (Master): requires a minimum of two years of coursework and a thesis; admission requires credential **E, F, G, H,** or **I**

N   *Doutor* (Doctor): no minimum study time required; usually three to four years after credential **H** or **M** in natural sciences or technology, five to six years after credential **E** or **H**, or **M** in other fields

[1]   Teachers for the first cycle of basic education (grades 1 to 4).

[2]   Teachers for the second cycle of basic education (grades 5 to 6).

[3]   Teachers for the third cycle of basic education (grades 7 to 9) and for secondary schools (grades 10 to 12).

GRADING INFORMATION

Secondary

Numeric	Description	Translation
18-20	*Muito Bom*	Very Good
14-17	*Bom*	Good
10-13	*Suficiente*	Sufficient
0-9	*Insuficiente*	Insufficient

- Grades in the 0-9 range are failing.

Higher Education

Numeric	Description	Translation
20	*Muito bom com distinção e louvar*	Very good with distinction and honors
18-19	*Muito bom com distinção*	Very good with distinction
16-17	*Bom com distinção*	Good with distinction
14-15	*Bom*	Good
10-13	*Suficiente*	Sufficient
5-9	*Mediocre*	Mediocre
0-4	*Mau*	Bad

- Grades in the 16-20 range are sometimes described by the term *muito bom* (very good).
- Grades in the 0-9 range are failing.

POSTSECONDARY INSTITUTION RECOGNITION BODY

Ministerio da Educação. Av. 5 de Outubro, 107-12. Lisboa 1050, Portugal.
Tel: 351-1-796-4915. Fax: 351-1-793-8206.

RESOURCES FOR ADDITIONAL INFORMATION

The British Council. 1996. *International Guide to Qualifications.* 4th ed. London: Mansell.

Internet Sources:
EURYDICE: Eurybase: www.eurydice.org
UNESCO - World Academic Database: www.unesco.org/iau/edupt.html

Compiler
James S. Frey
President
Educational Credential Evaluators, Inc., Milwaukee, WI

QATAR

YEARS OF EDUCATION →

```
        ½    ½    ½    ½    ½    ½    ½    ½    ½    ½    ½    ½    ½    ½    ½    ½    ½
1 → 6| 7 | 8 | 9 | 10 | 11 | 12 | 13 | 14 | 15 | 16 | 17 | 18 | 19 | 20 | 21 | 22 | 23 | 24 |
            A              B         G  I  J         L    M
                          C         H     K              N
                          D                             O
                          E                             P
                          F                             Q
                                                        R
```

CREDENTIALS OR DOCUMENTATION

Secondary

A General Preparatory Education Certificate
B *Thanawiya aam Qatari* (Qatari General Secondary Education Certificate): leads to postsecondary education
C *Thanawiya Fanni* (Diploma of Commerce)
D *Thanawiya Sina'ah* (Secondary School Technical [Trades] Certificate)
E Certificate of Secondary Institute for Islamic Studies
F Certificate in General Nursing

Postsecondary

G Air Traffic Control Officer Diploma, awarded by the Civil Aviation College
H Intermediate University Certificate in Primary Education, awarded by the Faculty of Education of the University of Qatar
I Aeronautical Meteorological Officer Diploma, awarded by the Civil Aviation College
J Technology Diploma, awarded by the College of Technology of the University of Qatar
K Aeronautical Radio Maintenance Engineering Officer Diploma, awarded by the Civil Aviation College
L Bachelor of... Administrative Sciences and Economics; Arts; Arts and Education; (Fine) Art Education; Education (Primary); Home Economics and Education; Islamic Studies and Education; Law and Shariah; Physical Education; Science; Science and Education; Science in Nursing; and Shariah and Islamic Studies: four-year programs
M Bachelor of... Chemical, Civil, Electrical, or Mechanical Engineering: five-year programs
N General Diploma in Education: lower primary teacher education program for holders of credential **L** in fields other than education
O General Diploma in Library Science and Information: one-year program based on credential **L**
P Higher Diploma in Urban Planning: one-year program based on credential **L**
Q Special Diploma in Education: upper primary teacher education program for holders of credential **L** in fields other than education
R Special Diploma in Counseling: one-year program based on credential **L**

GRADING INFORMATION

Secondary
Qatari Secondary Education Certificate:

Letter	Percent
A	85-100
B	70-84
C	55-69
D	40-54
F	0-39

Higher Education
Civil Aviation College:

Letter	Percent
A	90-100
B	80-89
C	70-79
D	60-69
F	0-59

- A minimum of 70% on a final examination is required to pass a course.

University of Qatar:

Letter	Points	Description
A	5	Excellent
B	4	Very Good
C	3	Good
D	2	Pass
F	0	Fail

- When a student repeats a previously failed course and passes it successfully, the student is given a grade of D even if a higher grade is earned the second time.

- The grade of D is considered acceptable, and represents the minimum average required for graduation.

POSTSECONDARY INSTITUTION RECOGNITION BODY

Ministry of Education, P.O. Box 80, Doha, State of Qatar. Tel: 974-413717.
Fax: 974-430437.

RESOURCES FOR ADDITIONAL INFORMATION

Al-Subaie, A. A. T. 1995. *International Encyclopedia of National Systems of Education.* 2nd ed. Ed. T Neville Postlethwaite. Tarrytown, New York: Elsevier Science Ltd.

Johnson, J. K., ed. 1984. *The Admissions and Academic Placement of Students from: Bahrain, Oman, Qatar, United Arab Emirates, Yemen Arab Republic.* Washington, D.C.: Joint Committee of Workshops.

Schmida, Leslie C., ed. 1983. *Education in the Middle East.* Washington, D.C.: AMIDEAST.

UNESCO. 1982. *World Guide to Higher Education.* Paris: Bowker.

Internet Source:
UNESCO - World Academic Database: www.unesco.org/iau/eduqa.html

---

Compiler
Brian Bates
Vice President for Student Affairs
Thunderbird, The American Graduate School of International Management
Glendale, AZ

ROMANIA

YEARS OF EDUCATION →

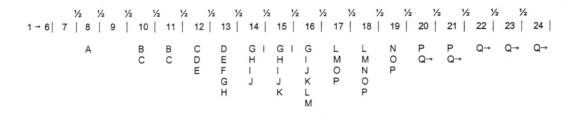

		½	½	½	½	½	½	½	½	½	½	½	½	½	½	½	½
1→6	7	8	9	10	11	12	13	14	15	16	17	18	19	20	21	22	23	24

```
         A        B    B    C    D    GI   GI   G    L    L    N    P    P    Q→  Q→  Q→
                  C    C    D    E    H    H    I    M    M    O    Q→  Q→
                            E    F    I    I    J    O    N    P
                                 G    J    J    K    P    O
                                 H         K    L         P
                                           M
```

CREDENTIALS OR DOCUMENTATION

Secondary

A   *Certificat/Diplomă de Absolvire a Gimnaziulu* (Certificate/Diploma of Graduation from Middle School) or *Certificat de Absolvire a Învăţămîntului de 8 Ani* (Certificate of Graduation from 8 Year Education): awarded upon completion of eight years of compulsory education

B   *Diplomă de Absolvire a Şcolii Complementare său de Ucenici* (Diploma of Graduation from Complementary or Apprentices' Schools): awarded upon completion of 10 or 11 years of vocational education; terminal credential or may lead to grade 10 in a *liceu* (secondary school); admission based on credential **A**

C   *Diplomă de Absolvire a Şcolii Profesionale* (Diploma of Graduation from Vocational Schools): awarded upon completion of 10 to 12 years of vocational education; terminal credential or may lead to grade 11 in a *liceu* (secondary school)

D   *Diplomă de Absolvire* (Diploma of Graduation) from a *liceu* (secondary school), *şcolă normal* (normal school), *or seminarul teologic* (theological seminary): four- to five-year program; admission based on credential **A**; terminal credential

E   *Diplomă de Bacalaureat* (Baccalaureate Diploma) from a *liceu* (secondary school), *şcolă normal (normal school), or seminarul teologic* (theological seminary): four- to five-year program based on credential **A**; gives access to further education

F   *Certificat de Calificare* (Certificate of Training): five-year vocational program representing completion of secondary education plus qualification for employment in a specific field; admission based on credential **A**

Postsecondary

G   *Diplomă de Absolvire a Şcolii Postliceale de Specialitate* (Diploma of Graduation from Post-Secondary Specialty Schools): one- to three-year, non-university specialized technical programs; requires credential **E** for admission

H   *Diplomă de Maiştru* (Diploma of Master), or *Diplomă de Absolvire a Şcolii Tehnice de Maistri* (Diploma of Graduation from a Master Technical School): one- to two-year non-university technical programs; requires credential **E** plus three years of work experience for admission

I   *Diplomă de Subinginer* (Diploma of Lower-Level Engineer): two-, two and one-half-, or three-year programs which may lead to the third or fourth year of credential **M** programs; requires credential **E** for admission

310

J   *Diplomă de Tehnician* (Diploma of Technician): two- to three-year technical programs; requires credential **E** for admission

K   *Diplomă de Conductor Arhitect* (Diploma of Assistant Architect): three-year program; requires credential **E** for admission

L   *Diplomă de Licentă* (Diploma of Licentiate): four-year program in most fields, or five years in fine arts, law, and pharmacy; requires credential **E** for admission

M   *Diplomă de Inginer* (Diploma of Engineer): five-year program, except in agriculture which can be four to five years; requires credential **E** for admission

N   *Diplomă de Arhitect* (Diploma of Architect): six-year program; requires credential **E** for admission

O   *Diplomă de Doctor-Medic* (Diploma of Doctor-Physician) six-year programs in dentistry and medicine, five or six-year program in veterinary medicine; requires credential **E** for admission

P   *Diplomă de Absolvire a Şcolii Postuniversitare* (Diploma of Graduation from Post-University Schools), *Certificat* (Certificate) for a *Cursul Postuniversitar* (Post-university Course), or *Diplomă de Studii Aprofundate* (Diploma of Advanced Studies): usually one- to two-year programs; requires credential **L, M, N,** or **O** for admission

Q   *Diplomă de Doctor* (Diploma of Doctor): at least three years of advanced education; requires credential **L** (from a five-year program), or credential **M, N, O,** or **P** for admission; those with credential **L** from a four-year program must complete an *anul 5 de specializarea* (5th year of specialization) in order to be eligible for admission

GRADING INFORMATION

All Levels of Education

Numeric	Description	Translation
10, *Zece*	*Excelent*	Excellent
9, *Nouă*	*Excelent*	Excellent
8, *Opt*	*Bun*	Good
7, *Sapte*	*Bun*	Good
6, *Şaşe*	*Suficient*	Sufficient
5, *Cinci*	*Suficient*	Sufficient
4, *Patru*	--	(Failing)
3, *Trei*	--	(Failing)
2, *Doi*	--	(Failing)
1, *Unu*	--	(Failing)

Description	Translation
Foarte Bien	Very Good
Bine	Good
Suficient	Sufficient

<u>Additional terms which may be used on transcripts</u>:

Admis	Admitted (implies satisfactory completion)
Scutit(ă)	Exempt
Promovat	Promoted (implies satisfactory completion, promoted to next year of program)
Repetent	Repeated (implies a failed year)
Echivalat	Equated (indicates that previous coursework has fulfilled that course requirement)
Examen Recunoscut	Exam Recognized (indicates that exam taken at a similar course is accepted)

POSTSECONDARY INSTITUTION RECOGNITION BODY

Connciliul National de Evaluare Academica şi Acreditave (National Council for Academic Evaluation and Accreditation): Strada Schitu Magureanu 1, Bucuresti 70626. Tel: 40-1-3127135.

RESOURCES FOR ADDITIONAL INFORMATION

Niesen, Karen, and Christine Y. Onaga. 1996. *1996 Supplement to the Wisconsin Directory of International Institutions.* Madison: The University of Wisconsin Press.

Internet Source:
UNESCO - World Academic Database: www.unesco.org/iau/educro.html

---

Compilers
Christopher Mickle
Assistant Director of Graduate Admissions
University at Albany, State University of New York

Majka D. Drewitz
Evaluator
Educational Credential Evaluators, Inc., Milwaukee, WI

RUSSIAN FEDERATION

YEARS OF EDUCATION →

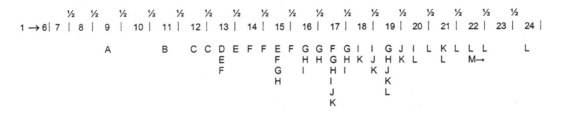

CREDENTIALS OR DOCUMENTATION

Secondary

A **Аттестат об основном общем образовании** [*Attestat ob osnovnom obshchem obrazovanii*] (Certificate of Basic General Education): Before 1992 this was called the **Свидетельство о неполном среднем образовании** [*Svidetel'stvo o nepolnom srednem obrazovanii*] (Certificate of Incomplete Secondary Education); awarded by **общеобразовательная школа** [*obshcheobrazovatelnaya schkola*] (General school); before 1984 this required eight years of school

B **Аттестат о среднем (полном) общем образовании** [*Attestat o srednem (polnom) obshchem obrazovanii*] (Certificate of Complete Secondary General Education): Before 1992 this was called the **Аттестат о среднем образовании** [*Attestat o srednem obrazovanii*] (Certificate of Secondary Education); awarded by **средняя общеобразовательная школа, гимназия, лицей** [*sredniaja obshcheobrazovatelnaya schkola, gimnasia, lycee*] (upper secondary schools), this represents completion of academic secondary education; before 1984 this required completion of ten years of school

C **Диплом о начальном профессиональном образовании с получением среднего (полного) общего образования** [*Diplom o nachalnom professionalnom obrazovanii s polucheniem srednego (polnogo) obshchego obrazovanija*] (Diploma of Vocational Education and Complete General Education): awarded by a **профессионально-технический лицей** [*professionalno-technicheskii lycee*] (vocational lyceum); three-year program following credential **A** or one to one and one-half years following credential **B**

Postsecondary

D **Диплом о среднем профессиональном образовании** [*Diplom o srednem professionalnom obrazovanii*] (Diploma of Non-University Level Higher Education): awarded by a **техникум** [*tekhnikum*] or **училище** [*uchilishche*]; requires credential **A** or **B** for entrance; for qualification as a technician, nurse, doctor's assistant, primary school teacher, etc.[1]

E **Диплом о среднем профессиональном образовании** [*Diplom o srednem professionalnom obrazovanii*] (Diploma of Non-University Level Higher Education): awarded by a **колледж** [*kolledzh*] (college); requires credential **A** or **B** for entrance; for qualification as higher level technician, junior engineer, senior pharmacist, specialized nurse, etc.[1]

313

F **Диплом о неполном высшем образовании** [*Diplom o nepolnom vischem obrazovanii*] (Diploma of Intermediate Higher Education): at least two years of higher education at **высшее учебное заведение: университет, академия, консерватория, институт** [*vischeje uchebnoe zavedenije: universitet, akademija, conservatorija, institut*] (university-level higher education institutions: university, academy, conservatory, institute); requires credential **B, C, D** or **E** for admission

G **Диплом бакалавра** [*Diplom bakalavra*] (*Bakalavr* Diploma): awarded by university-level institutions after a four-year program in various fields except medicine; not as specialized as credentials **H** and **I** below; requires credential **B, C, D,** or **E** for admission

H **Диплом специалиста** [*Diplom spetsialista*] (Diploma of Specialist): four-year program at university-level institutions, usually in Language or Teaching; a professional qualification corresponding to the specialty is awarded; requires credential **B, C, D,** or **E** for admission

I **Диплом специалиста** [*Diplom spetsialista*] (Diploma of Specialist): five-year program at university-level institutions (the majority of *diplom spetsialista* programs are this length, although some programs in science and technological fields provide deeper knowledge and skills and require a longer program); follows a specialized curriculum and culminates in defense of a diploma thesis/project; a professional qualification corresponding to the specialty is awarded; requires credential **B, C, D,** or **E** for admission

J **Диплом врача** [*Diplom vracha*] (Diploma of Medical Doctor): six-year program at university-level institutions in medicine; requires credential **B, C, D,** or **E** for admission

K **Диплом магистра** [*Diplom magistra*] (*Magistr* Diploma): two-year program at university-level institutions, includes coursework in addition to research for thesis or student teaching activity; requires credential **G** for admission

L **Кандидат наук** [*Kandidat nauk*] (Candidate of Sciences): three-year program requiring credential **I, J,** or **K** for admission; focuses on research for dissertation preparation and defense[2, 3]

M **Доктор наук** [*Doktor nauk*] (Doctor of Sciences): advanced research and dissertation that makes a significant contribution to the field of specialization; requires credential **L** for admission[3, 4]

1   Length of program will vary depending on basis of entry: For those with credential **A**, usually four years of study at a *tekhnikum/uchilishche* are required, or four and one-half years at a *kolledzh* (college). For those with credential **B**, two years of specialized study at a *tekhnikum/uchilishche* or four years of specialized study at a *kolledzh* are required.

2   Coursework is optional and examinations must be passed in philosophy, foreign language, and the specialty. Degree is awarded by the **Диссертационный совет** [*Dissertatsionnyi Soviet*] (Dissertation Council) of leading higher education institutions through the governmental **Высший аттестационный комитет** [*Visshij Attestatsionnyi Komitet*] (Supreme Certifying Committee). While it is possible for holders of the *magister* or *diplom spetsialista* to complete the degree in less than three years, in practice this rarely happens.

3   *Kandidat* and *Doktor nauk* diplomas are awarded in the same broad categories, including: **Кандидат/Доктор архитектуры** [*architectury*] (Architecture); **ветеринарных наук** [*veterinarnikh nauk*] (Veterinary Sciences); **искусствоведения** [*iskusstvovedeniya*] (Fine Arts); **медицинских наук** [*meditsinskikh nauk*] (Medical Sciences); **педагогических наук** [*pedagogicheskikh nauk*] (Pedagogical Sciences); **психологических наук** [*psychologycheskih nauk*] (Psychological Sciences); **сельскохозяйственных наук** [*selskohozyaistvenikh nauk*] (Agricultural Sciences); **социологических наук** [*sociologicheskih nauk*] (Social/Behavioural Sciences); **технических наук** [*tekhnicheskikh nauk*] (Technical Sciences); **физико-математических наук** [*physico-mathematicheskikh nauk*] (Physical-Mathematical Sciences); **филологичеких наук** [*filologicheskikh nauk*] (Philological Sciences); **экономических наук** [*economicheskikh nauk*] (Economic Sciences); **юридических наук** [*juridicheskikh nauk*] (Legal Sciences).

4   No coursework is involved for the Doctor of Sciences. The degree is awarded by the governmental **Высший аттестационный комитет** [*Visshij Attestatsionnyi Komitet*] (Supreme Certifying Committee).

GRADING INFORMATION

All Levels of Education

Russian	Transliteration	Numeric	Description
Отлично	*Otlichno*	5	Excellent
Хорошо	*Khorosho*	4	Good
Удовлетворительно	*Udovletvoritel'no*	3	Satisfactory
Зачет	*Zachet*	-	Passed
Неудовлетворительно	*Neudovletvoritel'no*	2	Unsatisfactory

- Courses graded as Passed (**Зачет**), also translated as "Credited" or "Tested," suggest that an examination was not taken, but all requirements were met.

- The grade of 2 is considered failing and is not shown on transcripts.

POSTSECONDARY INSTITUTION RECOGNITION BODY

Ministry for General and Professional Education of the Russian Federation; Department for Accreditation and Recognition; Chistoprudny bulv., 6, Center, Moscow 101856, Russian Federation. Tel: 7-095-925-6277, 7-095-925-4632, 7-095-923-1984.
Fax: 7-095-925-6277, 7-095-925-4632.

RESOURCES FOR ADDITIONAL INFORMATION

Popovych, Erika, and Brian Levin-Stankevich. 1992. *The Soviet System of Education.* Annapolis Junction, MD: PIER.

Internet Sources:
European Centre for Higher Education-CEPES, "The Doctorate in the Europe Region:"
    www.cepes.ro
Study Group on Education in Russia, the Independent States and Eastern Europe:
    www.kingston.ac.uk/~hs_s113/sgerisee
UNESCO - World Academic Database: www.unesco.org/iau/educru.html

---

Compiler
Gary Anderson, Evaluator
International Education Research Foundation, Inc., Los Angeles, CA

The compiler wishes to thank Prof. Yuri Akimov, head of the Department for Accreditation and Recognition, Russian Federation Ministry for General and Professional Education, for his generous assistance with this compilation.

SAUDI ARABIA

YEARS OF EDUCATION →

½	½	½	½	½	½	½	½	½	½	½	½	½	½	½	½	½	½
1 → 6	7	8	9	10	11	12	13	14	15	16	17	18	19	20	21	22	23	24

```
                          A       K  T  Q   Y   Y    Y   j    j    k    k
                          B       L  U  U       Z    b
                          C       M  V  V       a    g
                          D       N  W  W       c    h
                          E       O  X  X       d    i
                          F       P          e    j
                          G       Q          f
                          H       R          j
                          I       S
                          J
```

CREDENTIALS OR DOCUMENTATION

Secondary

A الشهادة الثانوية العامة/شهادة المرحلة الثانوية (General Secondary Certificate): awarded in science and literature tracks

B شهادة المدرسة التجارية/الزراعية (Commercial/Agricultural/Industrial Secondary School Certificate)

C الشهادة الثانوية العامة الشاملة/المطورة (Comprehensive Secondary Certificate): phased out in early 1990s

D الشهادة الثانوية العامة للمعاهد العلمية (General Secondary Certificate from the Religious Schools)

E الثانوية العامة لتحفيظ القرآن (Quranic Secondary School Certificate)

F الشهادة الثانوية العامة في التربية الفنية (General Secondary Certificate of Art Education)

G الشهادة الثانوية للتربية الرياضية (Secondary Physical Education Certificate)

H شهادة الدراسة الثانوية لمعاهد تدريب المعلمين (Secondary Teacher Training Institute Certificate): phased out in 1990s

I دبلوم المدارس الثانوية المهنية (Vocational Secondary School Diploma)

J دبلوم المعهد الصحي (Nursing Institute Diploma)

Postsecondary

K دبلوم مركز العلوم والرياضيات (Science and Mathematics Center Diploma): two years, requiring credential **A** for admission

L دبلوم الكلية المتوسطة لتدريب المعلمين (Junior College Teacher Training Diploma): two years, requiring credential **A** or **H** for admission

M دبلوم المعهد العالي في العلوم المالية والتجارية (Diploma of the Higher Institute for Financial and Commercial Sciences): two years, requiring credential **A** or **B** for admission

N دبلوم علم العرض (Earth Science Diploma): two years, requiring credential **A** for admission

O الشهادة الجامعية المتوسطة (Intermediate University Certificate): two years at the Intermediate/Junior Colleges of Technology; requires credential **A** or **I** for admission

P شهادة المعهد الفني العالي (Higher Technical Institute Certificate): two years, requiring credential **I** for admission (eliminated after 1983)

Q شهادة إتمام دورة معهد الإدارة العامة (Institute of Public Administration Certificate of Completion): two to three years, requiring credential **A** or **B** for admission

R شهادة الخدمة الاجتماعية (Certificate of Social Work): two years at Higher Institute of Social Work; requires credential **A** for admission

S شهادة تنبع جوي (Certificate in Meteorology): two years, requiring credential **A** for admission

T دبلوم متوسط في تقنية الحاسبات (Diploma of Computer Technology): two and one-half years, requiring credential **A** for admission

U دبلوم المعهد الفني العالي (Higher Technical Institute Diploma): one year, requiring credential **O** or **P** for admission

V كفاءة التدريس في المدارس المتوسطة (Intermediate School Teaching Qualification): one year at Science and Mathematics Centers; requires credential **K** for admission

W شهادة إتمام دورة مكثفة (Certificate of Completion, Intensive Program): one year of teacher training; requires credential **L** for admission

X بكالوريوس في العلوم العسكرية المتوسطة (Bachelor of Military Science/Naval Science/Aviation): three years, requiring credential **A** for admission

Y الإجازة العالية/إجازة البكالوريوس/بكالوريوس/لسانس (Bachelor's degree, licence): four to six years, requiring credential **A–J** (depending on field of study and secondary scores) for admission

Z دكتور في طب الأسنان (Doctor of Dental Medicine): five years, requiring credential **A** for admission

a بكالوريوس الزراعة والطب البيطري/بكالوريوس في طب وجراحة الحيوان (Bachelor of Agriculture and Veterinary Medicine, Bachelor of Veterinary Medicine and Surgery): five years, requiring credential **A** for admission

b دكتور في الطب البشري (Doctor of Medicine): six years, requiring credential **A** for admission

c الدبلوم الخاص/الدبلوم العام (Special Diploma/General Diploma, in education): one year, requiring credential **Y** for admission

d Marine Sciences Diploma: one year, requiring four-year credential **Y** for admission

e الدبلوم العالي (Higher Diploma): one year in education; requires four-year credential **Y** for admission

f شهادة التأهيل Certificate of Qualification): one year of teacher training; requires four-year credential **Y** for admission

g Advanced Diploma in legal studies: two years at the Institute of Public Administration; requires four-year credential **Y** for admission

h الدبلوم الخاص (Special diploma in translation): two years, requiring four-year credential **Y** for admission

i دبلوم الدراسات الدبلوماسية (Diplomacy Studies Diploma): two years, requiring four-year credential **Y** for admission

j ماجستير (Master's degree): two years, requiring credential **X** or **Y** for admission

l دكتوراه (Doctorate): three years, requiring credential **j** for admission

GRADING INFORMATION

Secondary

Percent	Remark	Translation
85–100	ممتاز	Excellent
75–84	جيد جداً	Very Good
65–74	جيد	Good
50–64	مقبول	Fair
0–49	راسب	Fail

Higher Education

Percent	Letter	5-point scale	4–point scale	Remark	Translation
90–100	A	4.0–5.0	3.6–4.0	ممتاز	Excellent
80–89	B	3.0–3.9	2.6–3.59	جيد جدا	Very Good
70–79	C	2.0–2.9	1.6–2.59	جيد	Good
60–69	D	1.0–1.9	1.0–1.59	مقبول/ضعيف	Pass, Weak
0–59	F	0.0–0.9	0.0–0.99	راسب	Fail

- Most transcripts list the grading scale used.
- In most cases, the remark is used for average scores, not individual course scores.
- In graduate programs, the minimum passing score is usually 70%.

POSTSECONDARY INSTITUTION RECOGNITION BODY

Ministry of Higher Education; Riyadh 11153, Saudi Arabia. Tel: 966-1-441-5555. Fax: 966-1-441-9004. E-mail: mohe@kfshhub.kfshrc.edu.sa.

RESOURCES FOR ADDITIONAL INFORMATION

National Office of Overseas Skills Recognition. 1992. *Saudi Arabia: A Comparative Study*. Canberra: Australian Government Publishing Service.

Oliver, E. Eugene. 1987. *Saudi Arabia: A Study of the Educational System of Saudi Arabia and a Guide to the Academic Placement of Students in Educational Institutions of the United States*. Washington, D.C.: AACRAO.

Al-Salloum, Hamad I. 1995. *Education in Saudi Arabia*. 2nd ed. Washington, D.C.: Saudi Arabian Cultural Mission to the United States.

Internet Sources:
Ministry of Higher Education (links to university websites):
www.mohe.gov.sa/univs/index.html

UNESCO—World Academic Database: www.unesco.org/iau/educsa.html

---

Compiler
Leslie S. Nucho
Vice President
AMIDEAST, Washington, D.C.

SENEGAL

YEARS OF EDUCATION →

```
         ½   ½   ½   ½   ½   ½   ½   ½   ½   ½   ½   ½   ½   ½   ½   ½   ½
1 → 6| 7 | 8 | 9 | 10| 11| 12| 13| 14| 15| 16| 17| 18| 19| 20| 21| 22| 23| 24|

    A         B   D   E   E       I   N   P   T   Z   a
              C               F   J   O   Q   U   a   b
                              G   K       R   V       c→
                              H   L       S   W
                                  M       Y   X
                                          Y
```

CREDENTIALS OR DOCUMENTATION

Primary and Secondary

A   *Certificat d' Études Primaires et Élémentaire/CEPE* (Certificate of Primary and Elementary Education)

B   *Certificat d'Aptitude Professionnelle/CAP* (Certificate of Professional Aptitude): three years of education at the lower secondary level at specialized vocational training centers

C   *Brevet d'Études du Premier Cycle/BEPC* (Certificate of First Cycle Studies): three years of general lower secondary education

D   *Diplôme d'Agent Technique de l'Agriculture/ATA* (Technical Diploma in Agriculture): four years of education at the lower secondary level at specialized vocational schools

E   *Brevet d'Agent Technique/Brevet de Technicien* (Technician Certificate): two or three years of education beyond credential **C**

F   *Certificat Élémentaire d'Aptitude Pédagogique/CEAP* (Elementary Certificate of Teaching Aptitude): three years of education beyond credential **C**

G   *Baccalauréat de l'Enseignement du Second Degré/Baccalauréat Technique* (Baccalaureate Diploma of Secondary Education/Technical Baccalaureate): three years of education beyond credential **B** or **C**

H   *Brevet Supérieur de Fin d'Études Normales* (Advanced Certificate of Completion of Teacher Training Studies): three years of teacher training education beyond credential **C**

Postsecondary

I   *Diplôme Universitaire d'Études Littéraires/DUEL* (University Diploma of Literary Studies): two-year program; admission based on credential **G**

J   *Diplôme Universitaire d'Études Scientifiques/DUES* (University Diploma of Scientific Studies): two-year program; admission based on credential **G**

K   *Diplôme d'Études Universitaire Générales/DEUG* (Diploma of General University Studies): two-year program; admission based on credential **G**

L   *Diplôme Universitaire de Technologie/DUT* (University Diploma of Technology): two-year program; admission based on credential **G**

319

M *Diplôme d'Études Juridique Générales/DEJG* (Diploma of General Legal Studies) or *Diplôme d'Études Economiques Générales/DEEG* (Diploma of General Economics Studies): two-year programs; admission based on credential **G**

N *Certificat d'Aptitude Pedagogique/CAP* (Certificate of Teaching Aptitude): three-year program; admission based on credential **G**

O *Licence* (Licentiate): one year of study beyond any of credentials **I, J, K,** or **L**

P *Certificat d'Aptitude a l'Enseignement Moyen* (Lower Secondary Proficiency Teaching Certificate): one year of study beyond credential **O**

Q *Maîtrise* (Master): one year of study beyond credential **O**, or two years beyond credential **M**

R *Maîtrise en Droit* (Master in Law): two years of study beyond credential **M**

S *Maîtrise ès Sciences Économiques* (Master in Economic Sciences): two years of study beyond credential **M**

T *Diplôme d'Ingénieur* (Diploma of Engineer): five years of study beyond credential **G**, or three years beyond credential **L**

U *Certificat d'Aptitude a l'Enseignement Secondaire* (Upper Secondary Proficiency Teaching Certificate): one year of study beyond credential **Q, R,** or **S**

V *Diplôme d'Études Approfondies/DEA* (Diploma of Advanced Studies): one year of study beyond credential **Q, R, S,** or **T**

W *Diplôme de Pharmacien* (Diploma of Pharmacist): five-year program; admission based on credential **G**

X *Certificat d'Études Supérieures* (Certificate of Higher Studies): offered in law or economics; one year of study beyond credential **R** or **S**

Y *Doctorat en Chirugie Dentaire* (Doctor of Dental Surgery): five-year program based on credential **G**

Z *Doctorat d'Etat en Médecine Vétérinaire* (State Doctor of Veterinary Medicine): six-year program based on credential **G**

a *Doctorat de Troisième Cycle* (Doctor of the Third Cycle): two years of study beyond credential **Q, R, S,** or **T**

b *Doctorat d'Etat en Médecine* (State Doctor of Medicine): seven-year program; admission based on credential **G**

c *Doctorat d'Etat* (State Doctor): admission based on credential **V**; requires at least two additional years of research

GRADING INFORMATION

All Levels of Education

Numeric	French	Translation
16-20	*Tres Bien*	Excellent
14-15	*Bien*	Very Good
12-13	*Assez Bien*	Good
10-11	*Passable*	Pass
9	---	
0-8	*Ajourné*	Fail

- Grades of 16 and above are rarely awarded. The passing grade for a single subject is usually 10, though a student is considered to have passed all subjects of an academic year, even for subjects graded below 10, when the combined average (*moyenne generale*) of all grades is 10 or above.

POSTSECONDARY INSTITUTION RECOGNITION BODY

Ministère de l'Éducation nationale, Direction de l'Enseignement superieur), Route de la Corniche Ouest, 5005 Dakar, Senegal. Tel: 221 225-730. Fax: 221 225-596.

RESOURCES FOR ADDITIONAL INFORMATION

AACRAO. 1994. *Foreign Educational Credentials Required for Consideration of Admission to Universities and Colleges in the United States.* 4th ed. Washington, D.C.: AACRAO.

The British Council. 1991. *International Guide to Qualifications in Education.* 3rd ed. London: Mansell.

Compiler
Jasmin Saidi
President
Academic Credentials Evaluation Institute, Inc., Beverly Hills, CA

SINGAPORE

YEARS OF EDUCATION →

	½	½	½	½	½	½	½	½	½	½	½	½	½	½	½	½
1 → 6| 7	8	9	10	11	12	13	14	15	16	17	18	19	20	21	22	23	24	

```
A              B       D   F   G   I   I   N   O   R→
               C       E       H   J   K   O
                                       L   P
                                       M   Q→
                                       N
```

CREDENTIALS OR DOCUMENTATION

Secondary

A   Primary School Leaving Examination/PSLE

B   *Sijil am Pelajaran Singapure-Cambridge* (Singapore-Cambridge General Certificate of Education), Normal (N) Level Examination: four-year academic and technical streams offered following credential **A**; students may opt to complete a fifth year of study in preparation for credential **C**

C   *Sijil am Pelajaran Singapure-Cambridge* (Singapore-Cambridge General Certificate of Education), Ordinary (O) Level Examination: four-year program following credential **A**

D   *Sijil am Pelajaran Singapure-Cambridge* (Singapore-Cambridge General Certificate of Education), Advanced (A) Level and Advanced Ordinary (AO) Level Examination: usually a two-year program following credential **C**

Postsecondary

E   Certificate awarded by the Institute of Technical Education: two-year program requiring credential **B** from the technical stream for admission

F   Diploma awarded by a polytechnic: three-year program requiring credential **C** for admission

G   Diploma awarded by a polytechnic: two-year program requiring credential **D** for admission

H   Diploma in Education or Diploma in Physical Education awarded by the National Institute of Education: two-year programs requiring credential **D** or equivalent for admission

I   Advanced Diploma awarded by a polytechnic: two-year, part-time program requiring credential **F** or **G** for admission

J   Bachelor's degree awarded by a university: three-year program in most fields of applied sciences, arts, business, and sciences; requires credential **D** for admission

K   Bachelor's degree (Honours) awarded by a university: one-year program requiring credential **J** for admission

L   Bachelor's degree awarded by a university: four-year program in building, dentistry, engineering, estate management, and law; requires credential **D** for admission

M   Bachelor of Arts or Science with Diploma in Education, including specialization in Physical Education, awarded by the National Institute of Education: four-year programs requiring credential **D** for admission

322

N   Postgraduate Diploma in Education awarded by the National Institute of Education: one-year program requiring credential **J**, **K**, or **L** for admission

O   Postgraduate Diploma in Education (Physical Education): two-year program requiring credential **J**, **K**, or **L** for admission

P   Bachelor's degree awarded by a university in the fields of architecture and medicine: five-year programs requiring credential **D** for admission

Q   Master's degree awarded by a university: a minimum of one year of study; requires credential **K** for admission

R   Doctor of Philosophy degree awarded by a university: a minimum of two years of study; requires credential **Q** for admission

GRADING INFORMATION

Secondary

General Certificate of Education, Normal Level: Graded on a numerical scale of 1-5, with 1 being highest and 5 being the lowest passing grade.

General Certificate of Education, Ordinary Level and Advanced Ordinary Level:

Numeric	Grade	Description
1-2	A	Highest passing grade
3-4	B	Pass
5-6	C	Pass
7	D	Below GCE O-Level Pass
8	E	Below GCE O-Level Pass
9	Ungraded	Fail, not recorded on the certificate

General Certificate of Education, Advanced Level: Graded on an alphabetical scale of A, B, C, D, E, O, and F, with A being highest and E being the lowest passing grade. Grade F will not be shown on the certificate. Grade O is awarded when the subject is failed at the advanced level, but is passed with at least the level of Grade C at the ordinary level.

Higher Education
Polytechnics:

Grade	Description
AD or Dist	Distinction
A	Excellent or Very Good
B	Very Good or Credit
C	Good or Good Pass
D	Pass
E	Subsidiary Pass
F	Fail
P	Ungraded Pass

Universities:

Grade	Description
Dist	Distinction
A	Excellent
B	Very Good
C	Good
D	Pass
E	Compensation Pass
F	Fail
P	Pass

POSTSECONDARY INSTITUTION RECOGNITION BODY

Ministry of Education, Higher Education Branch, 1 Kay Siang Road, Singapore 248922. Tel: 65-473-9111. Fax: 65-475-6128.

RESOURCES FOR ADDITIONAL INFORMATION

National Office of Overseas Skills Recognition. 1996. *Country Education Profiles: Singapore*. 2nd ed. Canberra: Australian Government Publishing Service.

Internet Sources:
UNESCO - World Academic Database: www.unesco.org/iau/educsg.html

---

Compiler
Cynthia Fish
CUNY Baruch College

SLOVAKIA

YEARS OF EDUCATION →

```
    ½   ½   ½   ½   ½   ½   ½   ½   ½   ½   ½   ½   ½   ½   ½   ½   ½
1→6| 7 | 8 | 9 | 10| 11| 12| 13| 14| 15| 16| 17| 18| 19| 20| 21| 22| 23| 24|
        A   B   C   D       E   G   H   J   L   P   P
                            F       I   K   M   Q   Q
                                    O   N
                                        O
```

CREDENTIALS OR DOCUMENTATION

Secondary

A *Vysvedčenie* (Report card): from Basic School, years 1 through 9; until 1998, the compulsory education was grade 8; effective with the 1998-99 school year students had to complete grade 9 in order to enter the secondary school; the length of the secondary schools remained the same

B *Výučný list* (Apprentice Certificate): two-year apprentice program

C *Výučný list* (Apprentice Certificate): three-year apprentice program

D *Vysvedčenie o Maturitnej Skúśke* (Certificate of Maturity Examination): awarded by a gymnasium, specialized secondary school, or specialized secondary pedagogical school; leads to further education

E *Vysvedčenie o Maturitnej Skúśke* (Certificate of Maturity Examination): awarded by an upper secondary specialized school; awarded to holders of credential **D** (usually from gymnasium) for specific professional training at the upper secondary level; leads to further education

Postsecondary

F *Absolventský Diplom* (Graduation Diploma): from a conservatory

G *Bakalár* (Bachelor's degree): the three-year *Bakalár* degree is the most common bachelor's degree

H *Bakalár* (Bachelor's degree): the four-year *Bakalár* degree is offered in a small number of programs

I *Magister* (Master's degree) and *Magister Umenia* (Master of Fine Arts): a first degree of a four-year duration in a relatively small number of programs; *Bakalár* is not necessarily a prerequisite

J *Magister* (Master's degree) and *Magister Umenia* (Master of Fine Arts): first or second degree totaling five years of university education; *Bakalár* is not necessarily a prerequisite

K *Inžinier* (Engineer): a five-year degree awarded to graduates in agriculture, economics, and engineering; *Bakalár* is not necessarily a prerequisite

L *Inžinier Architekt* (Architectural Engineer): awarded to graduates in architecture and city planning

M *Doktor Veterinárnej Medicíny* (Doctor of Veterinary Medicine)

N *Doktor Medicíny* (Doctor of Medicine): the same degree is awarded to both physicians and dentists

O *Doktor prírodních ved- RNDr.,* (Doctor of Natural Sciences); *Doktor farmacie-PharmDr.,* (Doctor of Pharmacy); *Doktor filozofie- PhDr.,* (Doctor of Philosophy); *Doktor pedagogiky- PaedDr.,* (Doctor of Pedagogy); *Doktor práv- JUDr.,* (Doctor of Law)[1]

P   *Philosophiae Doctor- PhD.*, (Doctor of Philosophy): the highest degree offered, minimum of three years after completion of *Magister* or *Inžinier* degrees

Q   *Artis Doctor- ArtD.*, (Doctor of Art): the highest degree offered, minimum of three years after completion of *Magister* degree

[1]   Graduates of the fields of study in which the academic degree of *Magister* is awarded, may take *examina rigorosa*, which also includes the defense of a thesis. There is no legal regulation for the duration of preparation for the *examina rigorosa*. Upon successful completion, higher education institutions award to students the academic degrees mentioned above.

GRADING INFORMATION

Secondary

Numeric	Description	Translation
1	*Výborný*	Excellent
2	*Chválitebný*	Very Good
3	*Dobrý*	Good
4	*Dostatočný*	Satisfactory
5	*Nedostatočný*	Unsatisfactory

Higher Education

Numeric	Description	Translation
1	*Výborný*	Excellent
2	*Velmi Dobrý*	Very Good
3	*Dobrý*	Good
5	*Nedostatočný*	Unsatisfactory
	Započitane	Credit or Pass

POSTSECONDARY INSTITUTION RECOGNITION BODY

Ministry of Education of the Slovak Republic (Ministerstvo Školstva Slovenskej Republiky), Stromovã 1, 813 30 Bratislava, Slovak Republic. Tel: 4217 372 695. Fax: 4217 374 368. E-mail: hrab@uip.sanet.sk

RESOURCES FOR ADDITIONAL INFORMATION

Alojz, Putala a kol. 1996. *Ako na vysokú školu, Informácia pre záujemcov o štúdium na vysokých školách v Slovenskej republike v školskom roku 1997/98.* Bratislava: Ministerstvo školstva Slovenskej republike, Bratislava.

Silny, Josef, Edward Devlin and Frederick Lockyear. 1992. *The Admission and Placement of Students from the Czech and Slovak Federal Republic.* Washington, D.C.: AACRAO and NAFSA.

Internet Source:
UNESCO - World Academic Database: www.unesco.org/iau/educsk
Universities and Schools in Slovakia:
www.sanet.sk/~ms/list/universities_and_schools.html

Compiler
Josef Silny, President
Josef Silny & Associates, Inc., International Education Consultants, Coral Gables, FL

SLOVENIA

YEARS OF EDUCATION →

```
        ½   ½   ½   ½   ½   ½   ½   ½   ½   ½   ½   ½   ½   ½   ½   ½   ½
1→6| 7 | 8 | 9 | 10| 11| 12| 13| 14| 15| 16| 17| 18| 19| 20| 21| 22| 23| 24|
        A           B   B   B   B           D   F   I   I   I       i       M   M   M
                            C               E   G   J   K
                                            H   L
```

CREDENTIALS OR DOCUMENTATION

Secondary

A *Spričevalo o koncani osnovni šoli* (Certificate of completion of compulsory school)

B *Spričevalo o zaključnem izpitu* (Certificate of final examinations from secondary school programs): awarded at end of two, three, four, or five years of study; two- or three-year programs are considered technical training; four- or five-year programs provide admission to short postsecondary technical and vocational programs (credentials **D** and **E**)

C *Maturiteno spričevalo* (Maturity Examinations Certificate): provides admission to all postsecondary programs

Postsecondary

D *Inženir* (Engineer)...with field, *Ekonomist* (Economist), *Organizator* (Manager), and other titles: awarded on completion of three-year specialized programs which permit professional employment in the field (until 1994 many programs were only two years in length); transfer to related university programs is rare and requires additional examinations

E *Višja medicinska sestra* (Nurse), *Višji delovni terapevt* (Occupational Therapist), *Višji fizioterapevt* (Physical therapist), and other paramedical credentials: three-year programs

F *Diplomirani* (Diplomate/Graduate)...with field, for example, *Diplomirani ekonomist*: four-year program

G *Professor* (Teacher, Secondary School)...with field, for example, *Professor matematike in Fisizke* (Teacher of mathematics and physics): four-year program,

H *Akademski* (Academician), awarded in Design, Fine Arts, Painting, and Sculpture, for example, *Akademski Glasbenik-Komposist* (Academy Musician-Composer): four-year program

I *Specialist* (Specialist) given in field of specialized study, for example, *Specialist klinićne psihologije* (Specialist in clinical psychology): one to two years of study beyond credential **F, G, H, J,** or **L**

J *Doktor veterinarske medicine* (Doctor of Veterinary Medicine): five years beyond credential **C**

K *Magister/Magistra* (Master): two years beyond credential **F, G,** or **H**

L *Doktor medicine* (Doctor of medicine), *Doktor stomatologije* (Doctor of Dentistry): six years beyond credential **C**

M   *Doktor znanosti* (Doctor of Science/Ph.D.): The field of study may be inserted in the title, for example, *Doktor tehniških znanosti* (Doctor of Technical Science): awarded after a minimum of four years and maximum of six years of study beyond credential **K**

[1]   Maturity Examinations Certificate is normally awarded after a four-year secondary school program, but a few five-year secondary school programs do exist, with the resulting credential being considered equivalent in Slovenia to the four-year programs.

GRADING INFORMATION

Secondary

Numeric[1]	Description[2]	Description[3]	Translation
5	*Odlično*	*Odličnim*	Excellent
4	*Prav Dobro*	*Prav Dobrim*	Very Good
3	*Dobro*	*Dobrim*	Good
2	*Zadostno*	*Zadostnim*	Pass
1	*Nezadostno*		Insufficient

Description[4]	Translation
Zelo Uspešno	Very Successful
Uspešno	Successful
Manj Uspešno	Less Successful

Description[5]	Translation
Vzorno	Exemplary
Primerno	Proper
Manj Primerno	Less Proper

- Slovenian has six declensions. The same word root has variable endings depending on how the word is used or what the word is modifying. Grading scale terms will vary, for example, *Odlično* and *Odličnim* both mean excellent; *Nezadostno* and *Nezadosten* both mean insufficient. Other grading scale terms may appear with slight variations on the endings.

[1] Used on annual grade reports.

[2] Used on certificate of completion of compulsory school (credential **A**) and on certificate of final examinations from secondary school (credential **B**) for required academic subjects and optional study in computer science and foreign languages.

[3] Used for overall result on credentials **A** and **B**. Note: Grade of *Nezadosten* (Insufficient) will not appear on records.

[4] Used for physical education, music education, art education, technical education, home economics, and non-compulsory subjects, with exception of optional study of computer science and foreign languages.

[5]   Used for behavior.

Higher Education

10 to 1, with 10 the highest and 6 passing. Grades of 5 or below are considered failing. Grades below 6 are used to determine a student's average grade. Failing grades are recorded internally and do not show on the student's record.

POSTSECONDARY INSTITUTION RECOGNITION BODY

Ministry of Education and Sport, Župančičeva 6, 61000 Ljubljana, Slovenia

RESOURCES FOR ADDITIONAL INFORMATION

Dickey, Karlene N. 1995. *Slovenia: A Study of the Educational Systerm of the Republic of Slovenia*. Annapolis Junction, MD: PIER.

Dickey, Karlene N. and Desmond C. Bevis. 1990. *The Admission and Placement of Students from Yugoslavia*. Annapolis Junction, MD: PIER.

Internet Sources:
Information on Slovenia and TEMPUS projects and description of vocational education and training: www.etf.eu.int/etfweb.nsf/pages/Slovenia
UNESCO - World Academic Database: www.unesco.org/iau/educsi.html

---

Compiler
Karlene N. Dickey
Associate Dean of Graduate Studies Emerita
Stanford University, Palo Alto, CA

SOUTH AFRICA

YEARS OF EDUCATION →

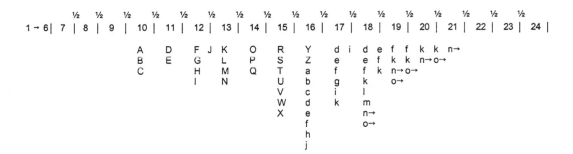

```
     ½   ½   ½   ½   ½   ½   ½   ½   ½   ½   ½   ½   ½   ½   ½   ½   ½
1→6| 7 | 8 | 9 | 10 | 11 | 12 | 13 | 14 | 15 | 16 | 17 | 18 | 19 | 20 | 21 | 22 | 23 | 24 |
                A   D   F J K   O   R   Y   d   i   d   e   f   f   k   k   n→
                B   E   G L     P   S   Z   e       e   f   k   k   k   n→o→
                C       H M     Q   T   a   f       f   k   n→o→
                        I N         U   b   g       k   o→
                                    V   c   i       l
                                    W   d   k       m
                                    X   e           n→
                                    f               o→
                                    h
                                    j
```

CREDENTIALS OR DOCUMENTATION

Secondary

A Standard Eight Certificate: awarded after ten years of compulsory education

B Nursing Assistant: representative of one year non-academic in-service training following credential **A**

C National N1 Certificate: awarded upon completion of one trimester vocational training after Standard Seven or Eight (nine to ten years of schooling)[1]

D National N2 Certificate: one trimester vocational training; admission based on credential **C**[1]

E National Intermediate Certificate: awarded upon completion of four N2 subjects together with courses in Business Afrikaans and Business English[1]

F National N3 Certificate: one trimester vocational training; admission based on credential **D**[1]

G National Senior Certificate: awarded upon completion of four N3 subjects together with courses in Business Afrikaans and Business English[1]

H Senior Certificate: twelve years of formal academic schooling

I Senior Certificate with Matriculation Endorsement: qualifies the holder for university admission for degree study

---

Legislation in respect of far-reaching educational reform in South Africa was passed during 1996/1997. The most prominent feature of this change is the establishment of the South African Qualifications Authority (SAQA), which will be responsible for the implementation of a National Qualifications Framework (NQF). The primary objective of the NQF is the integration of education and training to promote articulation and facilitate learner mobility. It allows for multiple pathways to the same learning ends, which will be expressed in terms of competencies and in this respect emphasizes the importance of recognition of all prior learning. According to NQF developments, pre-tertiary qualifications will be structured according to four levels of basic / general and further education: NQF Level 1: General Education Certificate (completion of nine years of formal academic schooling or its equivalent in adult basic education / vocational training; alternatively ten years of schooling if Grade 0, a reception year, is included); NQF Level 2: Further Education Certificate (ten years of schooling, or eleven including Grade 0); NQF Level 3: Further Education Certificate (eleven years of schooling, or twelve including Grade 0); and NQF Level 4: Further Education Certificate (twelve years of schooling, or thirteen including Grade 0) replacing the Senior Certificate.

Postsecondary

J   National N4 Certificate: one trimester vocational training following credential **F** or **H**

K   National N5 Certificate: one trimester vocational training following credential **J**

L   National Certificate: one year practice-oriented study at a technikon; admission requirement is credential **H**

M   Certificate in Agriculture: one year study at an agricultural college; admission requirement is credential **H**

N   National N6 Certificate: one semester non-academic vocational training following credential **K**

O   National Higher Certificate: two years practice-oriented study at a technikon; admission requirement is credential **H**

P   Higher Certificate in Agriculture: two years study at an agricultural college; admission requirement is credential **H**

Q   Enrolled Nurse: two years nursing training following credential **H**

R   National N Diploma: completion of credential **N** followed by two years supervised experiential learning in industry in a corresponding field

S   National Diploma: three years practice-oriented study at a technikon, including a period of supervised experiential learning (normally one year); admission requirement is credential **H**

T   General Nursing Diploma (before 1986): three years nursing training at a nursing college; admission requirement is credential **H**

U   Diploma in Agriculture: three years study at an agricultural college; admission requirement is credential **H**

V   Diploma in Education: three years teacher training at a college of education; admission requirement is credential **H**

W   Bachelor's degree, (General Arts, Science or Commerce): three years undergraduate study at a university; admission requirement is credential **I**

X   *Baccalaureus Technologiae* (Technological Baccalaureate), replacing the National Higher Diploma since the mid-nineties: four years applied degree study at a technikon, including one year of non-academic industrial attachment; admission requirement is credential **H**

Y   Higher Diploma in Education: one year advanced teacher training at a college of education, following credential **V,** or four years teacher training following credential **H**

Z   Further Diploma in Education: one year specialized teacher training at a college of education, following credential **V**

a   Post-basic Specialized Nursing Diplomas (before 1986): one year of further training following credential **T**

b   Nursing Diploma (after 1986): four years composite training in General Nursing and a specialization field (Midwifery, Psychiatric Nursing, or Community Health Nursing Science); admission requirement is credential **H**

c   Bachelor's degree, professional/career-oriented (e.g., in Engineering, Fine Art, Forestry, Music, and Quantity Surveying): four years study at a university; admission requirement is credential **I**

d   Post-Graduate University Diploma: one year study following credential **W, c,** or **i**

e   Honors Bachelor's Degree: one year study in one major subject; admission requirement is credential **W, c,** or **i**

f   Master of Business Administration: one year study in business administration after credential **W, c, i,** or **e**

331

g   Post-basic Advanced Specialized Nursing Diplomas: one year further specialized nursing training (Nursing Education or Nursing Administration) after credential **a** or **b**

h   *Magister Technologiae* (Technological Master) replacing the Master's Diploma in Technology (M.Dip.Tech) since the mid-nineties: one year applied study following credential **X**

i   Bachelor's Degree, career-oriented: five (Dentistry, Architecture) to five and one-half years (Veterinary Medicine); admission requirement is credential **I**

j   Second Bachelor's Degree: one year full-time or two years part-time study in a professional field such as Law (LLB), Education (BEd) or Divinity (BD); admission requirement is credential **W**

k   Master's degree: one to two years study (coursework and dissertation, or a dissertation following independent research); admission requirement is credential **c, e, i,** or **j**

l   Bachelor of Medicine and Bachelor of Surgery (MBChB): six years study in Medicine and Surgery, including a one-year internship; admission requirement is credential **I**

m   *Doctor Technologiae* (Technological Doctor), replacing the *Laureatus* in Technology since the mid-nineties: two years applied study; admission requirement is credential **h**

n   Doctor of Philosophy: a minimum of two years study (research and a thesis); admission requirement is credential **f** or **k**

o   Doctorate: signifies extensive independent research and publications

---

Higher educational qualifications will be categorized into four levels, 5 - 8, on the National Qualifications Framework (NQF). Level descriptors indicated the required outcomes at each level are yet to be finalized, but the most recent indications concerning the credit requirements at certain levels are as follows: NQF Level 5: Qualifications such as a National Certificate or equivalent consisting of at least 120 credits, as well as a National Diploma or equivalent, comprising at least 240 credits. NQF Level 6: Typically first degrees of at least 360 credits. NQF Level 7: Higher degrees and professional qualifications of at least 480 credits. NQF Level 8: Research degrees of at least 840 credits.

---

[1]   National N courses are vocationally oriented programs offered by technical colleges on a block release basis to make provision for a combination of theoretical and supervised practical training in industry. N1, N2, and N3 compare with Standard Eight, Standard Nine, and the Senior Certificate levels, respectively, but can only be deemed fully equivalent when two languages at the particular level are combined with the vocational subjects. The curricula for the National Intermediate Certificate (credential **E**) and the National Senior Certificate (credential **G**) include Business Communication in lieu of the academically oriented languages covered in the regular school.

GRADING INFORMATION
Secondary

Letter	Percentage	Description
A	80 - 100	Distinction
B	70 - 79	Very Good
C	60 - 69	Good
D	50 - 59	Average
E	40 - 49	Pass level for Higher Grade, except for second languages HG, where greater than 33% is required
F	33 - 39	Pass level for Standard Grade
G	20 - 32	Failure
H	0 - 19	Failure

- The minimum pass mark for all N courses offered at technical colleges is 40%.

Higher Education

The grading systems vary among universities and specific detail should best be obtained from individual institutions. The most commonly used systems are listed:

Percentage	Class/Division
75 - 100	1st Class
70 - 74	2nd Class Division 1
60 - 69	2nd Class Division 2
50 - 59	3rd Class
Below 50	Fail

Percentage	Description
75-100	Distinction
50-74	Pass
Below 50	Fail

- A general guideline is the following: highest on scale is 1st Class; minimum pass level is 3rd Class; lowest on scale is Fail.

- South African Qualifications Authority (SAQA) documentation which constitutes work in progress reflects the notion that Outcomes-based Education and Training (OBET) requires an alternative to norm-referenced marking, namely criterion-referenced marking. According to this learners are required to meet a set of stated (outcomes- or competency-based) criteria. If these criteria are met, the critical outcomes embedded in and specific outcomes stated in the qualification have been achieved. If not, the learner may attempt such achievement at a later stage. Grading as such is seen merely as a form of distinction among learners, but does not aim at the nomenclature of "passing" and "failing."

POSTSECONDARY INSTITUTION RECOGNITION BODIES

Certification Council for Technikon Education (Sertec) (also overseeing agricultural colleges), P.O. Box 74037, Lynnwood Ridge, Pretoria, 0040. Tel: 27 12 348 1406. Fax: 27 12 3486796.

Committee of Technikon Principals (CTP), Private Bag X680, Pretoria, 0001. Tel: 27 12 326 1065. Fax: 27 12 325 7387. E-mail: ctpwhyte@techpta.ac.za

Committee of Technical College Principals (CTCP), P.O. Box 8481, Pretoria, 0001. Tel: 27 12 323 0267. Fax: 27 12 323 0299. Democratic Nursing Association of South Africa (Denosa), P.O. Box 1280, Pretoria, 0001. Tel: 27 12 343 2315/6/7. Fax: 27 12 344 0750. E-mail: denosahq@cis.co.za

Department of Education, P.O. Box 895, Pretoria, 0001. Tel: 27 12 312 5999. Fax: 27 12 321 6770. E-mail: info@educ.pwv.gov.za. Webmaster@educ.pwv.gov.za

Registrar for Private Higher Education, Department of Education, Private Bag X8955, Pretoria. Tel: 27 12 312 5253. Fax: 27 12 328 6029. E-mail: beezhold@educ.pwv.gov.za

South African Vice Chancellor's Association (SAUVCA) (statutorily known as Committee of University Principals), P.O. Box 27392, Sunnyside, Pretoria, 0132. Tel: 27 12 429 3015: Fax 27 12 429 3071. E-mail: kotecp@alpha.unisa.ac.za

South African Qualifications Authority (SAQA), Private Bag X6, Waterkloof 0145. Tel: 27 12 346 5553. Fax: 27 12 346 5812. E-mail: gunthorp@mweb.co.za

RESOURCES FOR ADDITIONAL INFORMATION

Committee on Teacher Education Policy (COTEP). 1996. *Norms and Standards for Teacher Education*. Pretoria: COTEP.

Department of Education. 1997. *Formal Technikon College Instructional Programs. Report 151* (97/01). Pretoria: Department of Education.

Department of Education. 1995. *Formal Technical College Instructional Programs in the RSA. Report 191* (95/11). Pretoria: Department of Education.

Department of Education. 1996. *National Education Policy. General Policy for Technikon Instructional Programs. Report 150* (96/01). Pretoria: Department of Education.

De Villiers, H.C. 1995. "Free at last? Educational Reform in South Africa." *World Education News and Reviews* 8, 4:10-19.

Grobbelaar, J.W. and Brink, J.A. 1996. "The Universities of South Africa." *Commonwealth Universities Yearbook 1997-98*. Vol. II:1292-1296. New York: Grove's Dictionaries, Inc.

Human Sciences Research Council (HSRC). 1997. *Guide to Higher Education in South Africa.* Pretoria: Halfway House, Southern Directories.

South African Universities' Vice-Chancellors' Association (SAUVCA), 1998. "Update of Information for International Association of Universities." Circular 230/98 to Vice-Chancel.

Internet Sources:
Ministry of Education: education.pwv.gov.za
South African Qualifications Authority: www.saqa.org.za
UNESCO - World Academic Database: www.unesco.org/iau/educza.html

---

Compiler
Nadina Coetzee
Head, Centre for the Evaluation of Educational Qualifications
Human Sciences Research Council
Pretoria, South Africa

SOUTH PACIFIC REGION

This entry includes the countries of: Cook Islands, Fiji, Kiribati, Marshall Islands, Nauru, Solomon Islands, Tokelau, Tonga, Tuvalu, Vanuatu, and Western Samoa.

YEARS OF EDUCATION →

```
        ½   ½   ½   ½   ½   ½   ½   ½   ½   ½   ½   ½   ½   ½   ½   ½   ½
1 → 6| 7 | 8 | 9 | 10 | 11 | 12 | 13 | 14 | 15 | 16 | 17 | 18 | 19 | 20 | 21 | 22 | 23 | 24 |
            A   B   H   J   M   U   S   Y   Y   h   k   l   n-  n-
                C   I   K   O   T   a   g       i       m   o
                D   J   L   P   U   b           j
                E       M   Q   V   c
                F       N   R   W   d
                G           S   X   e
                            T   Y   f
                                Z
```

CREDENTIALS

Secondary

A   Form III Leaver's Certificate, Solomon Islands

B   Cook Islands School Certificate

C   Fiji Junior Certificate

D   Fiji Vocational Training Certificate: represents two years of study; admission used to require completion of grade eight (until about 1995) but now requires completion of grade ten

E   Higher Leaving Certificate, Tonga: until 1987

F   Kiribati Junior School Certificate

G   Year 10 Leaving Certificate, Vanuatu

H   Solomon Islands School Certificate

I   Tonga School Certificate: since 1987

J   Western Samoa School Certificate: awarded after a total of 11 or 12 years of education

K   Fiji School Leaving Certificate

L   Kiribati National Certificate

M   Pacific Senior Secondary Certificate (PSSC): administered by the South Pacific Board for Educational Assessment in Kiribati, the Solomon Islands, Tonga, Vanuatu and Western Samoa: awarded after a total of 12 or 13 years of education

N   University of the South Pacific Preliminary Year

O   Fiji Seventh Form Certificate

P   National University of Samoa Preparatory Year Course: requiring completion of Western Samoa grade 12 for admission

Q   University of the South Pacific Foundation Year Program: since about 1992 has been gradually phased out and is being replaced by credential O

Postsecondary

R   Certificate awarded by the Fiji Polytech (formerly known as the Fiji Institute of Technology): one year of study requiring credential K for admission

S   Certificate awarded by the Solomon Islands College of Higher Education: represents completion of two or three years of study requiring credential H, or Form III and a one-year foundation program for admission

335

T Diploma awarded by the Solomon Islands College of Higher Education: represents completion of two or three years of study requiring credential **H**, or Form III and a one-year foundation program for admission

U Certificate awarded by the University of the South Pacific: represents one half to one year of study requiring credential **O** or **Q** for admission

V Certificate in Agriculture awarded by the Hango Agricultural College: represents three years of study requiring credential **I** for admission

W Certificate in Nursing awarded by the Queen Salote School of Nursing, Tonga: represents completion of three years of study requiring credential **I** for admission

X Diploma awarded by the Fiji Polytech: represents completion of two years of study requiring credential **K** for admission

Y Diploma awarded by the University of the South Pacific: represents one, two, or three years of study usually requiring admission credential **O** or **Q** for admission

Z Diploma of Education awarded by the Western Samoa Teachers College: represents three years of study requiring credential **J** for admission

a Bachelor of Arts, Bachelor of Education, and Bachelor of Science awarded by the National University of Samoa represents two years of study requiring credential **P** for admission

b Certificate for Nursing awarded by the Tungaru Nurse Training School, Kiribati: represents three years of study requiring completion of 12 years of school for admission

c Diploma in Education awarded by the Fiji College of Advanced Education: represents two years of study requiring credential **O** for admission

d Diploma in Para-Veterinary Science awarded by the Hango Agricultural College, Tonga: represents one year of study requiring credential **V** for admission

e Diploma of Nursing awarded by the Fiji School of Nursing: represents completion of three years of study requiring credential **K** for admission

f Higher National Diploma awarded by the Fiji Polytech: represents completion of one year of study requiring credential **X** for admission

g Bachelor of Agriculture, Bachelor of Arts, Bachelor of Education, Bachelor of Science, and Bachelor of Technology awarded by the University of the South Pacific: represents three years of study requiring credential **O** for admission

h Bachelor of Laws awarded by the University of the South Pacific: represents one year of study requiring credential **g** for admission

i Master of Philosophy awarded by the University of the South Pacific: represents one year of study requiring credential **g** for admission

j Postgraduate Certificate in Education awarded by the University of the South Pacific: represents one year of study requiring credential **g** for admission

k Master of Business Administration awarded by the University of the South Pacific: represents approximately one and one-half years of study requiring credential **g** for admission

l Bachelor of Dental Science awarded by the University of the South Pacific: admission requires credential **O**; program consists of multiple steps, with various Certificates and Diplomas representing a total of five years of study awarded prior to the Bachelor of Dental Science degree

m Master of Arts and Master of Science awarded by the University of the South Pacific: represents two years of study requiring credential **g** for admission

n Doctor of Philosophy awarded by the University of the South Pacific: requires credential **g**, **h**, **i**, **k**, **l**, **m**, or **o** for admission

o Bachelor of Medicine and Bachelor of Surgery awarded by the University of the South Pacific: represents six years of study requiring credential **O** for admission

GRADING INFORMATION

Secondary

Letter	Numeric: Percentage	Numeric: Total points on FJCE	Numeric: Total points on FSLC
A	80-100	480-600	320-400
B	65-79	390-479	260-319
C	50-64	300-389	200-259

- FJCE refers to for Fiji Junior Certificate of Education
- FSLC refers to Fiji School Leaving Certificate

Kiribati National Certificate: Grades from 1 (highest) to 9 (lowest).

Solomon Islands School Certificate: Grades from A (highest) to E (lowest).

South Pacific Board for Educational Assessment:

Grade	Description
1	Excellent standard of achievement
2	Very high standard of achievement
3	High standard of achievement
4	Good standard of achievement
5	Satisfactory standard of achievement
6	Adequate standard of achievement
7	Some achievement
8	Lower level of achievement
9	Little level of achievement

- The South Pacific Board for Educational Assessment (SPBEA) was established in 1980 to provide an advisory service in educational evaluation to member countries and to the University of the South Pacific. Member countries include: the Cook Islands, Fiji, Kiribati, the Marshall Islands, the Solomon Islands, Tokelau, Tonga, Tuvalu, Vanuatu, and Western Samoa. In addition to advisory assistance with countries' existing and planned national examinations, the SPBEA became the examining and certifying body for the Pacific Senior Secondary Certificate. The PSSC is currently used by Kiribati, the Solomon Islands, Tonga, Vanuatu, and Western Samoa.

- Countries in this region have a history of offering foreign examinations, such as the New Zealand School Certificate Examination and the New Zealand University Entrance Examination. Some countries in the South Pacific still offer these examinations, however, local examinations, SPBEA examinations, and programs offered by the University of the South Pacific are replacing foreign examinations. Foreign examinations are not listed in this entry, but may be found under entries for the country which administers the examination.

Postsecondary

Form 7 Examination:

Letter	Percentage
A	80-100
B	65-79
C	50-64 (Minimum pass is 50%.)

Fiji College of Advanced Education:

Letter	Numeric	Description
A+	85-100	Distinction
A	80-84	Distinction
B+	75-79	Credit
B	65-74	Credit
C+	60-64	Pass
C	50-59	Pass
D	40-49	Fail
E	1-39	Fail
AG		Aegrotat Pass
GF		Grade Forfeited
N		Non-graded Fail
P		Non-graded Pass
RW		Results Withheld
SP		Supplementary Examination Required
X		Exemption Awarded

University of the South Pacific:

Letter	Description
A+, A	Pass With Distinction
B+, B	Pass With Credit
C+, C	Pass
R	Restricted Pass; a pass granted in a course in which a grade below the pass standard has been earned if high enough passes have been earned in other courses; limitations and regulations apply
Aeg	Aegrotat Pass; an ungraded pass granted to students who are prevented by legitimate illness or injury from appearing at the final examination and whose course work has been at the level of a B grade or better
Comp	Compassionate Pass; an ungraded pass granted to students who are prevented from taking the final examination due to circumstances beyond their control and whose course work has been at the level of a B grade or better
D	Work below the standard required for a pass
E	Very weak performance or failure to complete course requirements

- A number of non-university postsecondary institutions throughout the region offer vocational and technical programs in a variety of fields, such as business, fishery, marine studies, nursing, para-medical studies, tourism, and trades. Program lengths are normally one to three years. Admission requirements vary widely.

POSTSECONDARY INSTITUTION RECOGNITION BODY

Ministry of Education and Science and Technology, POB 2352, Govt Bldgs, Suva, Fiji. Tel: 312387. Fax: 303511.

RESOURCES FOR ADDITIONAL INFORMATION

Careers Section, Ministry of Education. 1989. *Careers Information 1990-1991.* Suva, Fiji: Careers Information Section, Ministry of Education.

Mangubhai, T. 1995. "Fiji." In *International Encyclopedia of National Systems of Education.* Ed. T. Neville Postlethwaite. Tarrytown, NY: Elsevier Science Ltd.

National Office of Overseas Skills Recognition. 1991. *Country Education Profiles: Fiji.* Canberra: Australian Government Publishing Service.

---. 1995. *Country Education Profiles: Fiji.* 2nd ed. Canberra: Australian Government Publishing Service.

---. 1997. *Country Education Profiles: Fiji.* 3rd ed. Canberra: Australian Government Publishing Service.

Internet Sources:
UNESCO - World Academic Database:
    Solomon Islands: www.unesco.org/iau/educsb.html
    Tonga: www.unesco.org/iau/educto.html
    Western Samao: www.unesco.org/iau/educws.html

_____

Compilers
Margit A. Schatzman
Vice President
Educational Credential Evaluators, Inc., Milwaukee, WI

Kristin M. Zanetti
Senior Evaluator
Educational Credential Evaluators, Inc., Milwaukee, WI

SPAIN

YEARS OF EDUCATION →

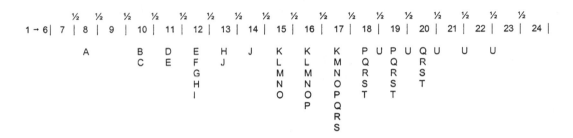

1→6	7	8	9	10	11	12	13	14	15	16	17	18	19	20	21	22	23	24
A			B C	D E	E F G H I	H J	J	K L M N O	K L M N O	K L M N O P Q R S	P Q R S T	U	P Q R S T	U	Q R S T	U		U

CREDENTIALS OR DOCUMENTATION

Secondary

A *Certificado de Estudios Primarios/Graduado Escolar* (Certificate of Primary Studies/School Graduate): signifies completion of compulsory education up to 1990 legislation

B *Título de Técnico Auxiliar* (Title of Assistant Technician)

C *Graduado en Educación Secundaria* (Graduate in Secondary Education): signifies completion of compulsory education starting with 1990 legislation (but implemented during 1990-2000)

D *Bachiller Unificado y Polivalente* (Unified and Multipurpose Bachelor)

E *Título de Técnico* (Title of Technician): one to two years beyond credential **C**

F *Curso de Orientación Universitaria* (University Orientation Course)

G *Bachillerato Experimental* (Experimental Baccalaureate)

H *Título de Técnico Especialista* (Title of Specialist Technician): two to three years beyond credential **B**

I *Título de Bachiller* (Title of Bachelor)

J *Título de Técnico Superior* (Title of Higher Technician): one to two years beyond credential **E**

Postsecondary

K *Diplomado* (Diploma Holder): three years beyond any credential **F** to **J**

L *Profesor de Educación General Básica* (General Basic Education Teacher) prior to 1990 legislation: three years beyond credential **F**, **G**, or **H**

M *Maestro* (Teacher) following 1990 legislation: three years beyond credential **I** or **J**

N *Arquitecto Técnico* (Technical Architect): three years beyond any credential **F** to **J**

O *Ingeniero Técnico* (Technical Engineer): three years beyond any credential **F** to **J**

P *Licenciado* (Licentiate): four or five years beyond any credential **F** to **J**

Q *Licenciado* (Licentiate) in Pharmacy and Veterinary Medicine: five or six years beyond any credential **F** to **J**

R *Arquitecto* (Architect): five or six years beyond any credential **F** to **J**

S *Ingeniero* (Engineer): five or six years beyond any credential **F** to **J**

T *Licenciado* (Licentiate) in Medicine: six years beyond any credential **F** to **J**

U *Doctor* (Doctor): two years of coursework plus dissertation (approximately one additional semester) beyond credential **P**, **Q**, **R**, or **S**

- The postsecondary credentials listed above represent "official" programs of study. There also exists another class of "unofficial" credentials referred to as *títulos propios* (university-specific titles). These use a variety of terms other than the terms used for the official ones, such as *Master* (Master), *Experto* (Expert), and *Graduado* (Graduate). Refer to the McCarty resource cited below for more information on these credentials.

GRADING INFORMATION: All Levels of Education

Spanish	Abbreviation	Translation	Numeric
Sobresaliente	SB	Outstanding	9-10
Notable	NT	Very Good	7-8
Bien	B	Good	6
Aprobado/Suficiente	AP	Passing/Sufficient	5
Suspenso/Insuficiente	S/I	Failed/Insufficient	0-4

- Five is the minimum passing grade and is sufficient for graduation. Most students receive grades of five or six.

Grade notations:

Spanish	Translation
Apto	Pass
No Apto	Fail
Convalidado	Transfer Credit Granted
Exento	Exempt
Pendiente	Incomplete
Anul	Cancel or Withdraw
Oyente (OY)	Audit
No Presentado (NP)	Did Not Sit for Examination

POSTSECONDARY INSTITUTION RECOGNITION BODY

Ministerio de Educación y Cultura (Ministry of Education and Culture), Sección Educación, C/ Alcalá 36, 28071 Madrid. Tel: 91-701-80-00. Website: www.mec.es

RESOURCES FOR ADDITIONAL INFORMATION

McCarty, Maxine R., et. al. 1997. *ECE Presents: The Educational System of Spain*. Milwaukee, Wisconsin: Educational Credential Evaluators, Inc.

Internet Sources:
EURYDICE Eurybase: www.eurydice.org/eurybase/files/dossier.htm
Ministerio de Educación y Cultura: www.mec.es/educ.html
UNESCO - World Academic Database: www.unesco.org/iau/educes.html

---

Compiler
James P. Meyers, Senior Evaluator
Educational Credential Evaluators, Inc., Milwaukee, WI

SWAZILAND

YEARS OF EDUCATION →

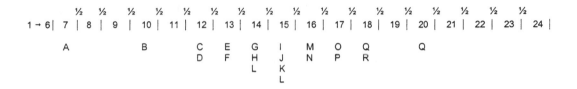

```
     ½   ½   ½    ½    ½    ½    ½    ½    ½    ½    ½    ½    ½    ½    ½    ½    ½
1→6|  7 |  8 |  9 |  10 | 11 | 12 | 13 | 14 | 15 | 16 | 17 | 18 | 19 | 20 | 21 | 22 | 23 | 24 |

     A           B         C    E    G    I    M    O    Q         Q
                           D    F    H    J    N    P    R
                                     L
                                     K
                                     L
```

CREDENTIALS OR DOCUMENTATION

Primary and Secondary

A   Swaziland Primary School Certificate: signifies completion of seven-year compulsory education
B   Junior Certificate
C   School Certificate, awarded by the University of Cambridge Local Examinations Syndicate
D   Primary Teachers' Certificate: two-year program requiring credential **B** for admission (to 1987)

Postsecondary

E   Certificate in Agriculture: one-year program requiring credential **C** for admission
F   Diploma in Management: one-year, part-time program requiring credential **C** for admission
G   Diploma in Accounting and Business Studies, Adult Education, Agricultural Education, Agriculture, Education, Home Economics, or Law: two-year program requiring credential **C** for admission
H   Secondary Teacher's Diploma: two-year program requiring credential **C** for admission (to 1987)
I   Diploma in Statistics: three-year, part-time program requiring credential **C** for admission
J   Primary Teacher's Diploma: three-year program requiring credential **C** for admission (since 1987)
K   Secondary Teacher's Diploma: three-year program requiring credential **C** for admission (since 1987)
L   State Registered Nurse: three-year program requiring credential **C** for admission, or a four-year program requiring credential **B** for admission
M   Bachelor's degree in Agriculture, Agricultural Education, Arts, Arts (Law), Commerce, Education, or Science: four-year program requiring credential **C** for admission[1]
N   Concurrent Diploma in Education: awarded with credential **M** (to 1987)
O   Postgraduate Diploma in Education: one-year program requiring credential **M** for admission

P   Master's degree in the fields of Arts and Science: one-year program requiring credential **M** for admission

Q   Bachelor of Laws: two-year program after Bachelor of Arts (Law), four years after any other Bachelor's degree; see credential **M**

R   Master of Education: two-year program requiring credential **M** for admission or one year beyond credential **O**

[1]   Part I: years one and two; Part II: years three and four

GRADING INFORMATION

Secondary

Numeric	Description
1-2	Very Good
3-6	Credit
7-8	Pass
9	Fail

Higher Education

Individual Subjects:

Letter	Percentage	Description
A	80-100	Excellent
B	70-79	Very Good
C	60-69	Good
D	50-59	Pass
E	40-49	Fail
F	0-39	Fail

Overall Results:

Class
1st Class
2nd Class, 1st Division
2nd Class, 2nd Division
Pass
Fail
Fail

- The grade of E is failing, but a supplementary examination may be taken.

POSTSECONDARY INSTITUTION RECOGNITION BODY

Ministry of Education: P.O. Box 39, Mbabane. Tel: 268-42491. Fax: 268-43880.

RESOURCES FOR ADDITIONAL INFORMATION

The British Council. 1996. *International Guide to Qualifications in Education.* 4th ed. London: Mansell.

Cameron, John, and Paul Hurst, eds. 1985. *International Handbook of Educational Systems.* Vol. II. Chichester, England: John Wiley and Sons.

Internet Source: UNESCO-World Academic Database: www.unesco/iau/educsz.html

---

Compiler
James S. Frey
President
Educational Credential Evaluators, Inc., Milwaukee, WI

SWEDEN

YEARS OF EDUCATION SINCE 1993 →

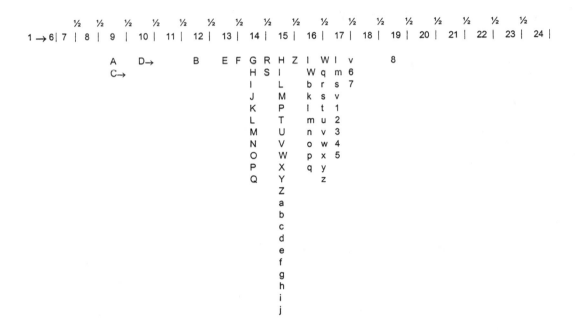

	½	½	½	½	½	½	½	½	½	½	½	½	½	½	½	½	½
1 → 6	7	8	9	10	11	12	13	14	15	16	17	18	19	20	21	22	23	24

```
              A    D→          B       E F G R H Z  I W l   v          8
              C→                       H S I       W q m 6
                                       I   L       b r s 7
                                       J   M       k s v
                                       K   P       l t 1
                                       L   T       m u 2
                                       M   U       n v 3
                                       N   V       o w 4
                                       O   W       p x 5
                                       P   X       q y
                                       Q   Y         z
                                           Z
                                           a
                                           b
                                           c
                                           d
                                           e
                                           f
                                           g
                                           h
                                           i
                                           j
```

CREDENTIALS OR DOCUMENTATION

Comprehensive changes occurred in the educational system in 1993. The terminology for credentials awarded prior to that time are not included here. See the PIER resource listed at the end of this entry for more information. Translations indicated are the official translations used at institutions throughout Sweden since 1993, rather than literal translations.

Secondary

A *Avgångsbetyg* (Leaving Certificate): nine years, awarded by a *grundskola* (compulsory school); signifies completion of compulsory school

B *Avgångsbetyg* (Leaving certificate): three years, awarded by a *gymnasieskola* (upper secondary school)[1]

C *Avgångsbetyg* (Leaving certificate): length varies, awarded by *Komvux* (Municipal Adult Education)[2]

D *Intyg om särskild behörighet* (Certificate of course completion), *Intyg om allmän behörighet* (Certificate of general program) awarded by *folkhögskola* (folk high schools): post-compulsory school programs of varying lengths; may lead to postsecondary education

Postsecondary

E *Flyglärarexamen* (University Diploma in Aviation Education): one-year program

F *Yrkesteknisk Högskoleutbildning/YTH - Högskoleexamen ...* (University Certificate in...: one and one-half years of vocational coursework

G *Högskoleexamen i/avseende grundläggande ...* (Diploma in ...): two-year program

H *Ingenjorsexamen* (University Diploma in Engineering/Lower Level): two- and three-year programs

I *Konstnärlig Högskoleexamen ...* (University Diploma in ...): two- to five-year programs, depending on the field of study

J *Landskapsingenjörsexamen* (University Diploma in Landscape Construction and Management): two-year program

K *Lantmästarexamen* (University Diploma in Agricultural and Rural Management): two-year program

L *Maskinteknikerexamen* (University Diploma in Marine Engineering/Lower Level): two- or three-year program

M *Receptarieexamen* (University Diploma in Dispensing Pharmacy) two- or three-year-program

N *Skogsteknikerexamen* (University Diploma in Forest Engineering): two-year program

O *Styrmansexamen* (University Diploma in Nautical Science/Mate Level): two-year program

P *Tandhygienistexamen* (University Diploma in Dental Hygiene): two- or three-year program

Q *Trädgårdsingenjörsexamen* (University Diploma in Horticultural Management): two-year program

R *Brandingenjörsexamen* (University Diploma in Fire Protection Engineering): two and one-half-year program

S *Social Omsorgsexamen* (University Diploma in Social Care): two and one-half-year program

T *Arbetsterapeutexamen* (University Diploma in Occupational Therapy): three-year program

U *Barn- och Ungdomspedagogisk examen* (University Diploma in Child and Youth Training): three-year program

V *Bildlärarexamen* (University Diploma in Art Education): three-year program

W *Grundskollärarexamen* (University Diploma in Education for Primary and Secondary School): three-, four-, or four and one-half-year program; or one-year program for those who have completed a three and one-half-year postsecondary program in another field; prepares for teaching of grades 1-7 or 4-9

X *Hushållslärarexamen* (University Diploma in Home Economics Education): three-year program

Y *Idrottslärarexamen* (University Diploma in Physical Education Teaching): three-year program

Z *Kandidatexamen...* (Bachelor of ...): three- or three and one-half-year programs; also awarded are the *Filosofie Kandidatexamen, Ekonomie Kandidatexamen, Teknologie Kandidatexamen* or *Politices Kandidatexamen*

a *Kandidatexamen i Hushållsvetenskap* (Bachelor of Home Economics [Dietetics/ Catering]): three-year program

b *Sjöingenjörsexamen* (University Diploma in Marine Engineering): three-year program; or one-year program requiring credential **L** for admission

c   *Sjökaptensexamen* (University Diploma in Nautical Science/Master Mariner Level): three-year program; or one-year program for those with credential **O**
d   *Sjukgymnastexamen* (University Diploma in Physiotherapy): three-year program
e   *Sjuksköterskeexamen* (University Diploma in Nursing): three-year program
f   *Skogsmästarexamen* (University Diploma in Forest Engineering): one-year program requiring credential **N** for admission
g   *Slöjdlärarexamen* (University Diploma in Craft Education): three-year program
h   *Socionomexamen* (University Diploma in Social Work): three-year program; see also credential **p**
i   *Studie- och Yrkesvägledarexamen* (University Diploma in Career Counselling): three-year program
j   *Civilekonomexamen* (Master of Business Administration and Economics): four-year program
k   *Folkhögskollärarexamen* (University Diploma in Folk High School Education): one-year program requiring either a university credential of at least three years, or three to five years of related work experience
l   *Logopedexamen* (University Diploma in Speech Pathology and Therapy): four-year program
m   *Magisterexamen* (Master of ...): four-year program; or one to two years requiring a university credential of at least three years for admission; also awarded are the *Filosofie Magisterexamen, Ekonomie Magisterexamen, Teknologie Magisterexamen, Farmacie Magisterexamen,* and *Politices Magisterexamen*
n   *Musiklärarexamen* (University Diploma in Music Education): four-year program
o   *Organistexamen* (University Diploma in Church Music): four-year program
p   *Social examen* (University Diploma in Social Work): four-year program including a half-year deacon program; see also credential **h**
q   *Specialpedagogexamen* (University Diploma in Special Education): one- or one and one-half-year-program requiring a university credential of at least three years for admission
r   *Barnmorskeexamen* (University Diploma in Midwifery): one and one-half-year program requiring credential **e** for admission
s   *Agronomexamen* (University Diploma in Agriculture): four and one-half- or five-year program
t   *Arkitektexamen* (University Diploma in Architecture, or Master of Science in Architecture): four and one-half-year program
u   *Civilingenjörsexamen ...* (University Diploma in ..., or Master of Science in ...): four and one-half-year program
v   *Gymnasielärarexamen* (University Diploma for Upper Secondary School): four and one-half -, five-, or five and one-half-year program; or one-year program requiring a university credential of at least three and one-half years
w   *Hortonomexamen* (University Diploma in Horticulture): four and one-half-year program
x   *Juris Kandidatexamen* (University Diploma in Laws): four and one-half-year program
y   *Psykoterapeutexamen* (University Diploma in Psychotherapy): one and one-half-year program completed over three years as a part-time student; admission requires a university credential of at least three years
z   *Tandläkarexamen* (University Diploma in Dentistry): four and one-half year program followed by one year of non-academic clinical practice
1   *Apotekarexamen* (University Diploma in Pharmacy): five-year program
2   *Jägmästarexamen* (University Diploma in Forestry): five-year program

3   *Landskapsarkitektexamen* (University Diploma in Landscape Architecture): five-year program

4   *Licentiatexamen ...* (Licentiate ...): two-year program requiring a university credential of at least three years for admission; also awarded are the *Filosofie Licentiatexamen* (Licentiate in Philosophy), *Teknisk Licentiatexamen* (Licentiate in Engineering); degree title can also include the field of study

5   *Psykologexamen* (University Diploma in Psychology): five-year program; or two years requiring a university credential of at least three years for admission

6   *Läkarexamen* (University Diploma in Medicine): five and one-half-year program followed by 21 months of internship for license to practice

7   *Veterinärexamen* (University Diploma in Veterinary Medicine [DVM]): five and one-half-year program

8   *Doktorsexamen ...* (Doctor of ...), *Filosofie Doktorsexamen* (Doctor of Philosophy), *Teknisk Doktorsexamen* (Doctor of Philosophy): four-year programs requiring a university credential of at least three years for admission; or two-year program beyond credential **4**; degree title can also include the field of study

- The number of years required to complete a program is based on the ratio of 40 *poäng* (points) equal to one year of full-time study. The actual length of enrollment may be longer than the points indicate, so, for example, a 160-point program might take longer to complete than the calculated four years.

1   Prior to 1992, two-, three-, and four-year lines were offered. In 1992 the number of programs in upper secondary school were reduced and all programs were converted to three years. They all now give general eligibility to postsecondary education.

2   Organized by subject courses identified by *etapp* (stage); *etapp 1* signifies completion of year 9 of compulsory school; *etapp 2* signifies completion of level 2 of upper secondary school; *etapp 3* signifies completion of level 3 of upper secondary school; *etapp 4* signifies advanced work in certain subjects in preparation for university admission.

GRADING INFORMATION

Secondary
Before 1994:

Numeric	Description
5	Highest
4	Above Average
3	Average
2	Below Average
1	Lowest

Since 1994:

Swedish	Translation
Mycket Väl Godkänd (MVG)	Pass With High Distinction
Väl Godkänd (VG)	Pass With Distinction
Godkänd (G)	Pass
Icke Godkänd	Fail

- Subjects with the grade of *Icke Godkänd* (Fail) will not be reported on transcripts.

Higher Education

Most programs use one of the following scales:
1) *Väl Godkänd (*Pass With Distinction); *Godkänd (*Pass); and *Underkänd* (Fail). *Väl Godkänd* is awarded less than 10% of the time.
2) *Godkänd (*Pass); and *Underkänd* (Fail).

Some engineering programs use the following scale: *fem,* 5, (highest); *fyra,* 4; and *tre,* 3 (lowest passing). Non-graded courses will be indicated with the grade of *Godkänd* (Pass).

Law programs use the following scale: *berömlig* (honours); *Med Utmärk Beröm Godkänd* (High Pass With Distinction); *Icke Utan Beröm Godkänd* (Pass With Distinction); *Godkänd (*Pass); and *Underkänd* (Fail).

Stockhom School of Economics: *Väl Godkänd* (Pass With Honour*),* 130-200; *Godkänd* (Pass), 100-129; and *Underkänd* (Fail), 0-99.

- Subjects with the grade of *Underkänd* (Fail) will not be reported on transcripts.

POSTSECONDARY INSTITUTION RECOGNITION BODY

The National Agency for Higher Education (*Verket för Högskoleservice/VHS)*, Birgerjarlsgatan 43, Stockholm, Box 7851, S-108 99 Stockholm. Tel: 46-8-453-50-00. Fax: 46-8-453-51-40.

RESOURCES FOR ADDITIONAL INFORMATION

Swedish NARIC. Hogskoleverket. Birger Jarlsgatan 43. Box 7851, S-103 99 Stockholm. Tel: 46-8-4537000. Fax: 46-8-4537050. E-Mail: info@hsv.se

Zanotti, Kathleen T., and Karlene N. Dickey. 1995. *Sweden: A Study of the Educational System of Sweden and Guide to the Academic Placement of Students in Educational Institutions in the United States.* Annapolis Junction, MD: PIER.

Internet Sources:
Higher Education in the Nordic Countries: www.abo.fi/norden/textvers/welcom_e.htm
Svenska Institutet: www.si.se/eng/eindex.html
UNESCO - World Academic Database: www.unesco.org/iau/educsw.html

---

Compiler
Kathleen T. Zanotti
Program Director
University of Illinois at Urbana-Champaign

SWITZERLAND

YEARS OF EDUCATION →

Because of the wide range of lengths of academic programs in Switzerland, the most common year the credential is awarded is represented on the ladder. See specific credential descriptions for more detailed information.

```
       ½   ½   ½   ½   ½   ½   ½   ½   ½   ½   ½   ½   ½   ½   ½   ½   ½
1 → 6| 7 | 8 | 9 | 10 | 11 | 12 | 13 | 14 | 15 | 16 | 17 | 18 | 19 | 20 | 21 | 22 | 23 | 24 |
            A       B   H   C   J   K   R   b   e   l       o       p
                            D   N   L   S   c   f   m
                            E       M   W   d   h   n
                            F       N   X   f   i
                            G       O   Y   g   j
                            H       P   Z   k   k
                            I       Q   a
                                    T
                                    U
                                    V
```

CREDENTIALS OR DOCUMENTATION

Secondary

A   *Certificat d'études* (Certificate of Studies) or *Certificat secondaire* (Secondary Certificate): only occasionally issued in the French-speaking section; no credential is regularly issued on completion of the nine-year compulsory education period, only annual grade reports; when credential **A** is referenced below, it refers to the end of compulsory education, not necessarily either of the two certificates listed here

B   *Diplom/Diplôme/Diploma* (Diploma) from a *Diplommittelschule* (Middle Diploma School) or *Ecole de culture générale/Scuola cultura generale* (School of General Culture): two to three years after credential **A**

C   *Fähigkeitszeugnis/Certificat de Capacité/Attestato di capacità* (Certificate of Competency): two to four years in a vocational training program after credential **A**

D   *Berufsmaturität/Maturité professionelle/Attestato di Maturità professionale* (Professional Maturity Certificate): four years of study in a vocational program, with substantial general education studies, following credential **A**

E   *Eidgenössisches Maturitätzeugnis/Certificat de maturité fédéral/Baccalauréat/ Attestato di Maturità federale* (Maturity Certificate [academic]): 12, 12½, or 13 total years of study; qualifies for university admission in all fields

F   *Eidgenössische anerkanntes kantonales Maturitätszeugnis/Certificat de maturité cantonal reconni par las Confédération/Attestato di maturità cantonale riconosciuto della Confederazione* (Federally Recognized Cantonal Maturity Certificates): 12, 12½, or 13 years of total study; qualifies for university admission in all fields[1]

G   *Kantonale Maturität/Maturité cantonale,Bachelier,Baccalauréate/Maturità Cantonale* (Cantonal Maturity/Bachelor, Baccalaureate): a total of 12, 12½, or 13 years of study; qualifies for university admission in certain fields

H *Diplom/Handelsdiplom/Diplôme de commerce/Diploma commerciale* (Commercial diploma); three- to four-year secondary commercial program following credential **A**

I *Handelsmaturität/Maturité commerciale/Maturità commercio* (Cantonal Commercial Maturity Certificate): four years of study beyond credential **A**; qualifies for university admission in certain fields

J *Primarlehrerpatent, Lehrerpatent, Fähigkeitszeugnisf für Elementarlehrer, Wahlfähigkeit als Lehrer, Lehrpatent/Certificat d'aptitude à l'enseignement primaire, Brevet d'enseignement primaire/Patente di Maestro di scuola elementare* (Primary School Teacher Certificate): four or five years of study in pedagogical upper secondary schools, following credential **A**; it gives university admission in all fields except medicine; for students with a Maturity Certificate, the program is one and one-half to three years of full-time training (in a teacher training institute)

Postsecondary[2]

K *Diplom Hotelier, Restaurateur HF (Hotel Fachschule)/Diplôme d'études supérieures... en restauration en hôtellerie /Diplôme de cadre en gestion hôtelière et en restauration* (Diploma of higher studies in hotel and restaurant management [Hotel Professional School]): one and one-half to three years of study beyond credential **C, D, E, F,** or **G,** or equivalent, plus practical experience

L *Diplom TS/Diplôme ET/Diploma ST* (Diploma from a Technical School): two years of advanced vocational study following credential **C,** plus a period of practical experience

M *Diplôme de langue et culture françaises* (Diploma in French Language and Culture): two years of study following credential **D, F, G, H, I,** or **J**

N *Diplôme pour l'enseignement du français en pays de langue étrangère* (Diploma for Teaching French in Non-French Speaking Country): two years of study after completion of any higher secondary program, in Switzerland or elsewhere; does not lead to further studies in Switzerland

O *Vordiplom I, II (Vordiplomprüfung), Ausweise (Prüfungen), Vorlizentiat, Zwischenexamen/Grundfächerprüfung/Candidatus ...,Propädeutisches Examen/Demi-license,Propédeutique I and II, Préexamen, Préliminaire I, II* (Intermediate Examination): certificate of examination results given upon completion of one to two and one-half years of foundation study, following credential **C, D, E, F, G, I, J**; sometimes given in two parts at the end of the first and second years of study

P *Eidgenössisches Turn- und Sportlehrer- diplom I/Diplôme fédéral I de maître d'éducation physique et de sport* (Federal Diploma of Teacher of Physical Education and Sport, Part I): two years of study after credential **C, D, E, F, G,** and **J**; see credential **g**

Q *Eidgenössisches Diplom für Instruktionsoffiziere* (Federal Diploma for Instruction of Officers-military): two years of study, plus one year of internship following credential **C, D, E, F, G,** and **J**; open only to Swiss citizens

R *Eidgenössisches diplomierter Hotelier/Restaurateur HF* [Federal Diploma of Hotel and Restaurant (Hotel Professional School)]: three years of study plus three years of practical experience; admission based on credential **C**

S *Akademisch-technischer Assistent, Assistentenprüfung,* (Academic-technical assistant in medical biology): three years of study beyond credential **C, D, E, F,** or **G**

T *Schwester (Krankenschwester) für...../Infirmière en.... /Infermiere..*(Nurse with....): three years of study after credential **B, C,** or **D**

U *Ergotherapeutin/Ergothérapeute* (Occupational Therapist): three years after credential **B, C,** or **D**

V *Physiotherapeutin/Physiothérapeute (*Physical Therapist): three years after credential **B, C,** or **D**

W *Ingenieur HTL/Ingénieur ETS/Ingegnere STS* (Engineer): three years of study beyond credential **C, D, E,** or **F** [3]

X *Architekt HTL, Architecte ETS,Architetto STS* (Architect): three years of study beyond credential **C, D, E,** or **F** [3]

Y *Chemiker HTL, Chimiste ETS* (Chemist): three years of study beyond credential **C, D, E,** or **F**[3]

Z *Betriebsökonom HWV/Economiste d'enterprise ESCEA/Economista aziendale SSQU* (Business Economist): three years of study beyond credential **C, D, E, F, G, H** and **I** [3]

a *Diplomierter Sozialarbeiter HFS/Diplôme d'assistant social* (Diploma of Social Worker): three years of study after **B, C, D, E, F, G, H, I,** or **J**

b *Diplom ...FH/Diplôme ...HES/Diploma ...* (Diploma, which will include field of study, e.g. *Diplom Ingenieur FH*): three to four years of study beyond credential **D**

c *Zertifikat of Nachdiplomstudium(NDS)/Diplom(NDS)/Certificat d'études/Certificat de la DIS* (Certificate of Postdiploma Studies): one to three years of full-time or part-time study after credential **W, X, Y,** and **Z**

d *Mittellehrerdiplom, Sekundarlehrerpatent/Fachpatent, Bezirkslehrerpatent, Oberschullehrerdiplom, Reallehrerdiplom/Brevet pour l'ensignement du degré secondaire inférieur* (Lower Secondary School Teacher's Certificate): three to four years of study following credential **E, F,** and **G**

e *Staatsexamen* (State Examination): five to six years of study after **E, F,** or **G**; a professional program giving access to doctoral study (credential **p**)

f *Lizentiat/License/Licenze* (Licentiate) or *Diplom* (Diploma): four to six years of study after credential **E, F, G,** or **J**

g *Eidgenössisches Turn- und Sportlehrer- diplom II/Diplôme fédéral II de maître d'éducation physique et de sport* (Federal Diploma of Teacher of Physical Education and Sport, Part II): two years of study after credential **P**

h *Eidgenössisches Zahnarztdiplom/Diplôme fédérale demédecin dentiste* (Federal Diploma of Dentist): open only to Swiss citizens; five years of study beyond credential **E** or **F**; the *Licence in médecine dentaire* (Licentiate in Dental Medicine), a five-year program, is open to non-Swiss citizens, and is an identical academic program

i *Eidgenössisches Apothekerdiplom/Diplôme fédérale pharmacien* (Federal Diploma of Pharmacy): open only to Swiss citizens; five years of study beyond credential **E** or **F**; the *Diplôme (universitaire) de pharmacien* (Diploma of Pharmacy), a five-year program, is open to non-Swiss citizens, and is an identical academic program

j *Eidgenössisches Tierärtzediplom* (Federal Diploma of Veterinarian): open only to Swiss citizens; five years beyond credential **E** or **F**

k Master of Advanced European Studies (MAES), Master of Health Administration, Master of Public Health, Master of Medical Education, Master of Public Administration, Master of Public Relations, Master of European and International Business, and other credentials referred to as "Master": one semester to two and one-half years beyond credential **f** or equivalent

l *Diplôme des études supérieures, Diplôme postgrades...* (Diploma of Advanced Studies): one to three years of study following credential **f**; provides access to doctoral studies (credential **p**); in the fields of business and management, also known in Switzerland as Master of....

m *Lehrkraft für Schulen der Sekundarstufe II, Oberlehrerdiplom/Diplôme de maître de gymnase, Certificat d'aptitude pédagogique* (Teaching Qualification for Academic Upper Secondary School): five to seven years of study after credential **E** or **F**

351

n *Eidgenössisches Arztdiplom/Diplôme fédérale de médecin* (Federal Diploma of Doctor): open only to Swiss citizens; six years of study beyond credential **E** or **F** (six and one-half years at the University of Lausanne); the *Certificat de fin d'études médicales* or *Diplôme de médecin de l'université,* six to seven-year program, is open to non-Swiss citizens, and is an identical academic program

o *Doktor der Medizin/Doctorat en médecine* (Doctor of Medicine): one and one-half to two years of study beyond credential **n**

p *Doktorat/Docteur/Dottorato* (Doctorate): three to five years of study after credential **f** or **I**

---

[1] In the canton of Valais, 14-year programs still exist for students preparing for the maturity exams in Greek, Latin, and Modern Languages.

[2] In addition to credentials listed there are a number of credentials offered for specialization in various subjects. Period of study ranges from one to four years. These are usually listed as Diplomas, Certificates, or Attestations. These credentials are not part of the standard track to higher degrees, but rather represent intensive study in a particular area.

[3] Programs are offered in *Höhere Technische Lehranstalt HTL, Ecole technique supérieure ETS, Scuola Tecnica Superiore STS* may be completed in three years of full-time study of four and one-half years of part-time study.

GRADING INFORMATION

Secondary

Numerical			German	French	Italian	Translation
10	6	1	Sehr Gut, Ausgezeichnet	Très Bien	Molto Bene	Very Good, Excellent
8	5	2	Gut	Bien	Bene	Good
6	4	3	Mittelmässig	Suffisant	Sufficiente	Sufficient
4	3	4	Unbefriedigend	Insuffisant	Insufficiente	Insufficient, Poor
2	2	5	Schlecht Schwach, Sehr Schwach	Mauvais	Molto Debollo	Very Bad, Failure

Higher Education

Scale A: 1-5, with 1 best, 3 passing:

Numerical	German	French	Italian	Translation
1	Sehr Gut	Très Bien	Molto Bene	Very Good
2	Gut	Bien	Bene	Good
3	Genügend	Suffisant	Sufficiente	Sufficient-Fair, Pass
4	Ungenügend	Insuffisant	Insufficiente	Insufficient-Poor, Fail
5	Schlecht	Mauvais	Molto Debole	Bad-Fail

Scale B: 4-0 with 4 best and 1 passing.

Scale C: 6-1, with 6 best and 4 passing. Several variations exist; some use a detailed point scale (e.g., 5.5, 5.8); some use Latin terms (e.g., summa cum laude); others use one of the three languages of Switzerland.

Scale D: 8 to 1, with 8 best and 4 passing.

Scale E: 10 to 1, with 10 best and 6 passing.

Scale F (Latin terms): 1-summa cum laude (outstanding); 2-insigni cum laude (excellent); 3-magna cum laude (very good); 4-cum laude (good); 5-rite (pass).

POSTSECONDARY INSTITUTION RECOGNITION BODIES

There is no central recognition body in Switzerland. All credentials issued by Swiss institutions at all levels have been certified by some recognition body. Certain fields are under the control of some agencies of the federal government; some are under cantonal control (26 cantons and half-cantons); others are under combined jurisdiction of the federal government and the cantons. And in a few areas, jurisdiction has been granted to an non-governmental agency, for example, the Swiss Red Cross (see below). The following paragraphs list the main recognition bodies.

1. Swiss Confederation (Confoederatio Helvetica {Latin},SchweizerischeEidgenössenschaft/ Confédération Suisse/Confederazione Svizzera). The federal government regulates education and training in the fields of medicine, dentistry, veterinary medicine, pharmacy, food chemistry, surveying, and physical education and sport, and the federal maturity examination.

    a. The two federal institutes, Federal Institute of Technology in Zurich and the Ecole Polytechnique de Lausanne, are under federal jurisdiction through the Board of the Swiss Federal Institutes of Technology (Rat der Eidgenössischen Technischen Hochschulen/Conseil des Ecoles polytechniques fédérales), ETH Zentrum, HAB, CH-8092 Zurich. Tel: 41 1 632 20 02. Fax: 41 1 632 11 90.

    b. The Federal Office for Public Health (Bundesamt für Gesundheit/Office fédéral de la santé publique/Ufficio federale della sanità publicca) is responsible for regulating and supervising education and training in the medical professions (medicine, dentistry, veterinary science, pharmacy) and for regulations for obtaining federal diplomas in these areas. Sektion Medizinalprüfungen, CH-3003 Bern. Tel. +41 31 322 94 83. Fax: 41 31 323 00 09. At present the organization and supervision of further/specialist education and training in the medical professions (including psychiatrists) is the responsibility of the Swiss professional associations; addresses can be obtained at the Swiss ENIC (see below).

2. Swiss Maturity Commission (Schweizerische Maturitätkommission SMK/Commission suisse de maturité) has jurisdiction over federal and cantonal maturity examinations recognized at the federal level. The office is located in the Bundesamt für Bildung und Wissenschaft/Office fédérale de l'éducation et de la science/Ufficio federale del l'educazione e della scienza (Federal Office of Education and Science), Hallwylstrasse 4, CH 3003 Bern. Tel: 41 31 322 9660. Fax: 41 31 322 7854.

3. The Federal Office for Professional Training and Technology (Bundesamt für Berufsbildung und Technologie/Office fédéral de la formation professionelle et de la technologie/Ufficio federale della formazione professionale e della tecnologia.) Effingerstrasse 27, CH-3003 Bern, Tel: 41 31 322 21 29. Fax: 41 31 324 96 15. This agency established and monitors vocational, professional, and technical education and training standards. The areas include crafts, industry, trade, banking, insurance, transport, catering (hotel and restaurant management), other services (including tourism), housekeeping, agriculture and dairy management, and information and documentation.

4. The Federal Board for the Fachhochschulen (Eidgenössische Fachhochschulkommission/ Commission fédérale de des hautes écoles spécialisées/Commissione federale delle scuole universitarie professionali) under the Federal Office for Professional Education and Technology, approved and supervises the newly created universities of applied sciences (schools of engineering, schools of economics, schools of applied arts, schools of agriculture) (Fachhochschulen FH/Haute Ècole spécialisée HES/Scuola universitaria professionale SUP) . Effingerstrasse 27, CH-3003 Bern, Tel. 41 31 322 55 52. Fax: 41 31 322 88 51.

5. a. Conference of the Cantonal Ministers of Education (Schweizerische Konferenz der kantonalen Erziehungsdirektoren/Conférence suisse des directeurs cantonaux de l'instruction publique) Zähringerstrasse 25, P.O. Box 5975, CH-3001. Bern. Tel: 41 31 309 51 11. Fax: 41 31 309 51 50. This is the coordinating agency for the 26 Swiss cantons and half-cantons. The cantons are responsible for compulsory education (nine years) and post-compulsory secondary academic programs, pedagogical education and training (including kindergarten), education and training in music, fine arts, performing arts, social work, translation and interpretation, and paramedical professions. The cantons may confer certain cantonal certificates, including the commercial maturity certificates for graduates of four-year commercial programs; certificates in teaching; and cantonal maturity certificates to indicate completion of an academic secondary program which does not have federal recognition. Cantons have the authority to grant official recognition to private schools with the canton (this recognition need not be accepted by the governments of any other canton or the federal government). Some cantons have jurisdiction over a university within their boundaries. The cantons issue vocational certificates of proficiency in accordance with federal requirements.

    b. Board for Fachhochschulen (Fachhochschulrat/Conseil des hautes écoles spécialisées/Scuola universitaria professionale), Fachhochschulrat, EDK, Zähringerstrasse 25, P.O. Box 5975, CH-3001 Bern. Tel: 41 31 309 51 25. Fax: +41 31 309 51 50. The cantonal Board established to approve and supervise the new universities of applied sciences (Fachhochschulen FH/Haute école spécialisée HES/Scuola universitaria professionale SUP) in the areas of music, theatre, health, teacher training, and social work (academies of music and theatre, schools of applied and fine arts, teacher training colleges, schools of social work, and schools of health). See footnote below.

6. Central Office of the Swiss Universities (Schweizerische Zentralstelle für Hochschulwesen; Office Central Universitaire Suisse), Sennweg 2, CH-3012 Bern. Tel: 41 31 306 60 45. Fax: 41 31 302 68 11. This office handles matters concerning the Swiss universities and the Federal Institute of Technology. It is also the office for the Conference of the Rectors of the Swiss Universities (Schweizerische Hochschulrektorenkonferens/Conférence des recteurs des universités suisses.), tel: 41 31 306 60 34, and the Recognition Information Center (Informationsstelle für Anerkennungsfragen), the Swiss ENIC (EuropeanNetwork of National Information Centres), the agency charged with academic recognition and mobility.

7. Swiss Red Cross (Schweizerisches Rotes Kreuz/Croix-Rouge Suisse/Croce Rossa Svizzera), Anerkennung Ausbildungsabschlsse, Werkstrasse 18, P.O. Box, CH-3084, Berne. Tel: 41 31 960 75 75. Fax 41 31 960 75 60. The Swiss Red Cross is responsible for regulating, supervising, and promoting education and training in the paramedical professions, including nursing and midwifery, technical nursing, laboratory technology, physical therapy and other therapies, and nutrition.

8. Swiss Hotel School Association (Association Suisse des Ecoles Hôtelières), P.O. Box 4943, CH-6002 Luzern. Tel: 41 79 402 77 77. Fax: 41 41 410 73 05. The association gives oversight to programs on hotel management in the private hotel schools. See also 3, hotel management schools.

RESOURCES FOR ADDITIONAL INFORMATION

The British Council, 1996. *International Qualifications Guide to Qualifications in Education.* 4th ed. London: Mansell.

Central Office of the Swiss Universities, Recognition Information Centre/Swiss ENIC. 1998. List of Qualifications Conferred by the Swiss Universities and Federal Institutes of Technology, Berne.

Dickey, Karlene N. 1981. *Switzerland: A Study of the Educational System of Switzerland.* Washington, D.C.: AACRAO.

Dickey, Karlene N. and Karen Lukas. 1991. *Swiss Higher Schools of Engineering and Swiss Higher Schools of Economics and Business Administration*. Washington, D.C.: AACRAO.

National Office of Overseas Skills Recognition. 1992. *Country Education Profiles: Switzerland*. Canberra: Australian Government Publishing Service.

Sirkka Pöyry, Philippa Bishop, Peter Jeffels and Françoise Côme, eds. 1997. *SEFI Guide on Engineering Education in Europe*. 4th ed. Belgium: SEFI.

Internet Sources:
Federal Council for Fachhochschulen: www.admin.ch/bbt/FH
Federal Office for Education and Science: www.admin.ch/bbw
Swiss European National Information Center (ENIC) szfhwww.unibe.ch
    E-mail: tremp@szfh.unibe.ch. Excellent source for specific questions.
Swiss Conference of Cantonal Ministers: edkwww.unibe.ch/e/default.html
Swiss Red Cross: www.redcross.ch; E-mail: info@redcross.ch
UNESCO-World Academic Database: www.unesco.org/iau/educch.html

---

Compiler
Karlene N. Dickey
Associate Dean of Graduate Studies Emerita
Stanford University, Palo Alto, CA

SYRIA

YEARS OF EDUCATION →

CREDENTIALS OR DOCUMENTATION

Secondary

A الشهادة الثانوية المهنية (Vocational Secondary Certificate): represents completion of two years of postpreparatory education

B الشهادة الثانوية العامة (General Secondary Certificate, also known as the Baccalaureate): awarded in science and literature tracks upon passing a national examination

C الشهادة الثانوية الفنية (Technical Secondary Certificate): awarded in industrial, commercial, agriculture, and home economics tracks upon passing a national examination

D الشهادة الثانوية الشرعية (Religious Secondary Certificate)

Postsecondary

E شهادة مساعد مجاز/شهادة دبلوم المعهد الصناعي/مساعد فني (Certificate of Licensed Assistant; Industrial Institute Diploma; Technical Assistant, and similar qualifications): two years at an intermediate institute, awarded in field of specialization; requires credential **B** or **C** for admission (religious intermediate institutes require credential **D** for admission)[1]

F شهادة أهلية التعليم الابتدائي (Teaching Certificate for Primary Education): two years at the Teacher Training Institute; requires credential **B** for admission

G دبلوم مدرس مساعد (Teacher Training Diploma): two years at the intermediate institutes; requires credential **B** for admission

H شهادة دبلوم التربية الرياضية (Physical Education Diploma): two years, requiring credential **B** for admission

I شهادة في تمريض (Nursing Certificate): three years, requiring credential **B** for admission

J إجازة (Bachelor's degree): four to six years, awarded in the field of specialization

K شهادة ممرضة اختصاصية توليد/عمليات/أطفال (Specialized Nursing Certificate in Midwifery/Surgery/Pediatrics): one to two years, requiring credential **I** for admission

L دبلوم التأهيل التربوي/دبلوم عام (Diploma of Educational Qualification/General Diploma): one year, requiring four-year credential **J** for admission

M دبلوم التأهيل والتخصيص/دبلوم خاص (Diploma of Qualification and Specialization/Special Diploma): one year, requiring credential **L** for admission

N دبلوم الدراسات العليا (Diploma of Higher Studies): one to two years (three to four years in medical specializations); requires credential **J** for admission

O ماجستير (Master's degree): one to three years, requiring credential **M** or **N** for admission

356

P دكتوراه (Doctorate): two or more years, requiring credential **O** for admission (the Faculty of Law requires two credential **N**s for admission to doctoral program)

[1] Frequently, graduates of the intermediate institutes receive a Graduation Certificate (مصدقة or وثيقة تخرج تخرج) rather than a separate diploma.

GRADING INFORMATION

Secondary

Minimum passing score for Arabic: 50%
Minimum passing score for other subjects: 40%

- Passing the general secondary examination requires a passing score in Arabic and in all but one of the other subjects, or a passing score in Arabic and all but two of the other subjects as long as the combined score for the failed subjects is at least 25%.
- The minimum passing total score is 102/240 (43%) in the literature track, and 104/260 (40%) in the science track.

Higher Education

Intermediate Institute Grading Scale
(for university-affiliated institutes)

Score	Remark	Translation
85–100	ممتاز	Excellent
75–84	جيد جداً	Very Good
65–74	جيد	Good
40/50–64	مقبول	Satisfactory

- Passing scores are 60% in applied or practical subjects, 50% in technical subjects, and 40% in theoretical subjects.
- Intermediate institutes not affiliated with a university use a grading scale similar to that used at the secondary level.

Undergraduate Grading Scale

Score	Remark	Translation
90–100	الشرف	Honors
80–89	الإمتياز	Distinction
70–79	جيد جداً	Very Good
60–69	جيد	Good
50–59	مقبول	Passing

- Grading is conservative, and often, the top students score in the high 60s.

Graduate Grading Scale

Score	Remark
95–100	Honors
85–94	Distinction
75–84	Very Good
65–74	Good
60–64	Passing

357

POSTSECONDARY INSTITUTION RECOGNITION BODY

Ministry of Higher Education; Damascus, Syria. Fax: 963-11-332-7719.

RESOURCES FOR ADDITIONAL INFORMATION

de Leeuw, Herman. 1996. "Intermediate Institutes in Syria." *World Education News and Reviews*, 9,4: 11–17.

National Office of Overseas Skills Recognition. 1992. *Syria: A Comparative Study*. Canberra: Australian Government Printing Service.

Internet Source:
UNESCO—World Academic Database: www.unesco.org/iau/educsy.html

---

Compiler
Leslie S. Nucho
Vice President
AMIDEAST, Washington, D.C.

TANZANIA

YEARS OF EDUCATION →

```
      ½   ½   ½   ½   ½   ½   ½   ½   ½   ½   ½   ½   ½   ½   ½   ½   ½
1 → 6| 7 | 8 | 9 | 10| 11| 12| 13| 14| 15| 16| 17| 18| 19| 20| 21| 22| 23| 24|

        A            B   C        D   J   P   Q   T   W   W   W   a   b→
                              E   K       R   U   X   Z   b→  b→
                              F   L       S   V   Y   b→
                              G   M           W
                              H   N
                              I   O
```

CREDENTIALS OR DOCUMENTATION

Primary and Secondary

A Primary Certificate: signifies completion of seven years of compulsory education
B Primary Teachers' Certificate, Grade C: three-year program requiring credential **A** for admission
C National Form IV Certificate or Certificate of Secondary Education
D National Form VI Certificate or Advanced Certificate of Secondary Education[1]

Postsecondary

E Certificate in Wildlife Management: two-year program requiring credential **C** for admission
F Primary Teachers' Certificate, Grade A: two-year program requiring credential **C** for admission
G Certificate in Agriculture, Applied Nutrition, or Food Science: two-year program requiring credential **C** for admission
H Lab Technician Certificate: two-year program requiring credential **C** for admission
I Certificate in Forestry or Veterinary Science: two-year program requiring credential **C** for admission
J Diploma in Education for lower secondary school teachers: one-year program requiring credential **F** for admission or two-year program requiring credential **D** for admission
K Diploma in Agriculture or Agricultural Education: one-year program requiring credential **G** for admission
L Full Technician Certificate: one-year program requiring credential **H** for admission or three-year program requiring credential **C** for admission
M Intermediate Certificate in Lab Technology: one-year program requiring credential **I** for admission
N Diploma in Forestry: one-year program requiring credential **I** for admission
O Motor Vehicle Maintenance Certificate: three-year program requiring credential **C** for admission
P Diploma in Fisheries Science or Wildlife Management: two-year program requiring credential **D** for admission

Q Diploma in Accountancy, Agriculture, Animal Production, Building Design, Building Economics, Crop Production, Engineering, Estate Management and Valuation, Home Economics, Land Surveying, Public Health Engineering, Transport Management, or Urban and Rural Planning: three-year program requiring credential **D** for admission

R Bachelor's degree in Agriculture, Arts, Commerce, Forestry, Law, Pharmacy, or Science: three-year program requiring credential **D** for admission

S Bachelor's degree in Arts or Science with an Education option for upper secondary school teachers: three-year program requiring credential **D** for admission

T Bachelor's degree in Engineering or Veterinary Science: four-year program requiring credential **D** for admission

U Postgraduate Diploma in Education, for upper secondary school teachers: one-year program requiring credential **R** for admission

V Postgraduate Diploma in Wildlife Management: two-year program requiring credential **P** for admission

W Master's degree: one- to three-year program requiring credential **R, S,** or **T** for admission

X Doctor of Dental Surgery: five-year program requiring credential **D** for admission

Y Doctor of Medicine: five-year program requiring credential **D** for admission

Z Diploma in Public Health: one-year program requiring credential **Y** for admission

a Master of Medicine: three-year program requiring credential **Y** for admission

b Doctor of Philosophy: at least a two-year research program requiring credential **W** for admission

GRADING INFORMATION

Secondary

National Form IV Certificate or Certificate of Secondary Education: Letter grades of A, B, C, D, and F are used.

National Form VI Certificate or Advanced Certificate of Secondary Education: Letter grades of A, B, C, D, E, S, and F are used. The grade of S signifies failure on the examination, but passing at the level of the National Form IV Certificate or Certificate of Secondary Education.

Higher Education

Individual Subjects:		Overall Results:
Letter	Description	Class
A	Excellent	1st Class
B+	Very Good	2nd Class, Upper Level
B	Good	2nd Class, Lower Level
C	Satisfactory	Pass
D	Fail	Fail
E	Fail	Fail

POSTSECONDARY INSTITUTION RECOGNITION BODY

Ministry of Science, Technology and Higher Education. P.O. Box 2645, Dar es Salaam. Tel: 255-51-46167. Fax: 255-51-44244.

RESOURCES FOR ADDITIONAL INFORMATION

The British Council. 1996. *International Guide to Qualifications in Education*. 4th ed. London: Mansell.

Internet Source:
UNESCO - World Academic Database: www.unesco.org/iau/eductz.html

---

Compiler
James S. Frey
President
Educational Credential Evaluators, Inc., Milwaukee, WI

THAILAND

YEARS OF EDUCATION →

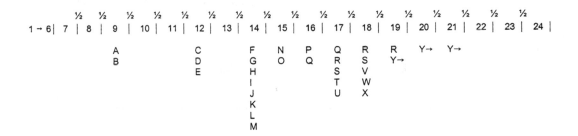

	½	½	½	½	½	½	½	½	½	½	½	½	½	½	½	½	½	
1 → 6	7	8	9	10	11	12	13	14	15	16	17	18	19	20	21	22	23	24

```
              A           C        F    N    P    Q    R    R    Y→   Y→
              B           D        G    O    Q    R    S    Y→
                          E        H              S    V
                                   I              T    W
                                   J              U    X
                                   K
                                   L
                                   M
```

CREDENTIALS OR DOCUMENTATION

Secondary

A *Matayom* (Secondary) III Certificate
B Certificate of Completion of Preliminary Course in Dramatic Arts
C *Matayom* (Secondary) VI Certificate
D Certificate of Completion of Intermediate Course in Dramatic/Fine Arts
E Certificate of Vocational Education

Postsecondary

F Diploma in Education
G Diploma in Technician Education
H Higher Vocational Diploma
I Associate Degree in ...
J Diploma in Medical Technology
K Certificate in Nursing and Midwifery
L Higher Diploma or Higher Certificate in Fine Arts
M Diploma in Vocational Education
N Diploma in Architecture
O Diploma in Fine Arts
P Higher Diploma in Technical Education: requires credential **M** for admission
Q Bachelor of ... four to five years; two years if admitted with credential **F** or **M**
R Master of ... one to three years; admission based on credential **Q**
S Graduate Diploma in... 1 year; admission based on credential **Q**
T Bachelor of Architecture
U Bachelor of Pharmacy
V Doctor of Veterinary Science
W Doctor of Dental Surgery
X Doctor of Medicine
Y Doctor of Philosophy: two years minimum; requires credential **R** for admission

GRADING INFORMATION

Secondary

Numeric	Percentage	Description
4	80-100	Excellent
3	70-79	Good
2	60-69	Fair
1	50-59	Pass
0	0-49	Fail

Higher Education

Grade	Point
A	4.0
B+	3.5
B	3.0
C+	2.5
C	2.0 (minimum pass for award of degree)
D+	1.5
D	1.0
F	0

Ramkhamhaeng University (an open university)

Grade/Numeric	Description
G (4.0)	Good
P (2.25)	Pass
F (0)	Failure

Sukhothani Thammathirat Open University

Grade	Description
H	Honours
S	Satisfactory
U	Unsatisfactory

POSTSECONDARY INSTITUTION RECOGNITION BODIES

Ministry of Education. Wang Chan Kasem, Thanon Ratchadamnoen, Bangkok 10300, Thailand. Tel: 66-2-628-5620. Fax: 66-2-281-1753. www.moe.go.th/nu/el.htm

Ministry of University Affairs. 328 Si Ayutthaya Road, Rachathewi, Bangkok 10400, Thailand. Tel: 66-2-246-0025. Fax: 66-2-245-8636. mis.mua.go.th/mua_info.htm

Other ministries are responsible for recognition in the case of some specialized institutions.

RESOURCES FOR ADDITIONAL INFORMATION

Tiger-Conquest, Faye and Nancy Katz. Unpublished, circa 1999. *The Educational System of Thailand.* Annapolis Junction, MD: PIER.

Internet Source: UNESCO - World Academic Database: www.unesco.org/iau/educth.html

---

Compiler
Nancy Katz
World Education Services - Midwest Office, Chicago, IL

TOGO

YEARS OF EDUCATION →

```
      ½   ½   ½   ½   ½   ½   ½   ½   ½   ½   ½   ½   ½   ½   ½   ½   ½
1 → 6|  7 |  8 |  9 | 10 | 11 | 12 | 13 | 14 | 15 | 16 | 17 | 18 | 19 | 20 | 21 | 22 | 23 | 24 |
              A               B       F   J   M   P           T   V
                              C       G   K   N   Q           U
                              D       H   L   O   R
                              E       I       S
```

CREDENTIALS OR DOCUMENTATION

Secondary

A   *Brevet d'Études du Premier Cycle* (Certificate of First Cycle Studies)

B   *Baccalauréat* (Baccalaureate)/*Diplôme de Bachelier de l'Enseignement du Second Degré* (Diploma of Bachelor of Secondary Education): leads to postsecondary education

C   *Baccalauréat Technicien* (Technician Baccalaureate): leads to postsecondary education

D   *Certificat de Fin d'Études Secondaires* (Certificate of Completion of Secondary Studies): for those who complete secondary school but do not qualify for credential **B** or **C**

E   *Certificat d'Aptitude Pédagogique* (Certificate of Pedagogic Aptitude)

Postsecondary

F   *Diplôme d'Études Universitaires Générales* (Diploma of General University Studies)

G   *Diplôme Universitaires d'Études Scientifiques* (University Diploma of Scientific Studies)

H   *Diplôme Universitaires d'Études Littéraires* (University Diploma of Literary Studies)

I   *Diplôme Universitaires de Techniques Juridiques* (University Diploma of Legal Studies)

J   *Licence* (License)

K   *Certificat d'Aptitude au Professorat de l'Enseignement du Second Degré/Secondaire* (Certificate of Aptitude in the Profession of Secondary Instruction)

L   *Ingénieur de Réalisation* (Practical Engineer)

M   *Maîtrise* (Master)

N   *Licence en Techniques de Commerce et Gestion* (License in Techniques of Business and Management)

O   *Licence en Techniques Economiques* (License in Economic Techniques)

P   *Diplôme d'Ingénieur* (Diploma of Engineer)

Q   *Ingénieur de Conception* (Design Engineer)

R   *Diplôme d'Études Approfondies* (Diploma of Advanced Studies): requires credential **M** for admission

S   *Diplôme d'Études Supérieures* (Diploma of Higher Studies): requires credential **M** for admission

T   *Docteur en Médecine* (Doctor of Medicine)

U   *Doctorat de Spécialité de Troisième Cycle* (Specialized Third Cycle Doctorate)
V   *Doctorat d'Ingénieur* (Doctorate of Engineer)

GRADING INFORMATION

Secondary and Postsecondary Education

Numeric	Description	Translation
16 - 20	*Très Bien*	Very Good
14 - 15	*Bien*	Good
12 - 13	*Assez Bien*	Good Enough
10 - 11	*Passable*	Pass
0 - 9	*Ajourné*	Fail

- A minimum overall grade of 10 is required to pass; however, individual subjects may be passed with grades lower than 10.

POSTSECONDARY INSTITUTION RECOGNITION BODY

Ministère de l'Éducation Nationale et de la Recherche Scientifque, BP 398, Lomé, Togo.

RESOURCES FOR ADDITIONAL INFORMATION

Mboungou-Mayengúe, D. ed. 1988. *Directory of African Universities*. 5th ed. Association of African Universities.

Internet Source:
UNESCO-World Academic Database: www.unesco.org/iau/eductg.html

---

Compiler
Margaret L. Wenger
Senior Evaluator
Educational Credential Evaluators, Inc., Milwaukee, WI

TUNISIA

YEARS OF EDUCATION →

	½	½	½	½	½	½	½	½	½	½	½	½	½	½	½	½	½
1 → 6	7	8	9	10	11	12	13	14	15	16	17	18	19	20	21	22	23	24

```
                 A                    B        E H H       L    N    S  U
                                      C        F I         M    O    T- V-
                                      D        G J              P
                                          K              Q
                                                        R
```

CREDENTIALS OR DOCUMENTATION

Secondary

A *Diplôme de Fin d'Études d'Enseignement de Base* (Diploma of Completion of Basic Education Studies)

B *Baccalauréat* (Baccalaureate)/*Diplôme de Bachelier de l'Enseignement du Second Degré* (Diploma of Bachelor of Secondary Education)

C *Brevet de Technicien* (Certificate of Technician)

D *Certificat de Fin d'Études Secondaires* (Certificate of End of Secondary Studies)

Postsecondary

E *Diplôme Universitaires d'Études Scientifiques* (University Diploma of Scientific Studies)

F *Diplôme Universitaires d'Études Littéraires* (University Diploma of Literary Studies)

G *Diplôme d'Educateur Polyvalent* (Diploma of General Educator)

H *Brevet de Technicien Supérieur* (Certificate of Higher Technician): can be five or six semesters

I *Certificat d'Aptitude au Journalisme* (Certificate of Aptitude in Journalism)

J *Certificat de Capacité en Droit* (Certificate of Ability in Law)/*Certificat de Capacité en Sciences Économiques* (Certificate of Ability in Economic Sciences)

K *Diplôme de Technicien Supérieur* (Diploma of Higher Technician)/*Diplôme de Technicien Supérieur de la Santé* (Diploma of Higher Health Technician)

L *Licence* (License)

M *Maîtrise* (Master)

N *Diplôme d'Ingénieur* (Diploma of Engineer)

O *Certificat d'Aptitude de Recherche* (Certificate of Aptitude in Research)

P *Diplôme d'Études Approfondies* (Diploma of Advanced Studies)

Q *Diplôme d'Études Supérieures Specialisées* (Diploma of Higher Specialized Studies)

R *Diplôme de Technicien Supérieur en Sciences Économiques et de Gestion* (Diploma of Higher Technician in Economic Sciences and Management)

S *Docteur en Médecine* (Doctor in Medicine)

T *Doctorat de Spécialité* (Doctorate of Specialty)

U *Diplôme de Recherches Approfondies* (Diploma of Advanced Research)

V *Doctorat d'État* (State Doctorate)

GRADING INFORMATION

Secondary and Postsecondary Education

Numeric	Description	Translation
16 - 20	*Très Bien*	Very Good
14 - 15	*Bien*	Good
12 - 13	*Assez Bien*	Good Enough
10 - 11	*Passable*	Pass
0 - 9	*Ajourné*	Fail

- An overall grade of 10 is required to pass; however, individual subjects may be passed with grades lower than 10.

POSTSECONDARY INSTITUTION RECOGNITION BODY

Ministère de l'Éducation Supérieur, BP 1030, rue Ouled Haffouz, Tunis, Tunisia.

RESOURCES FOR ADDITIONAL INFORMATION

Mboungou-Mayengúe, D., ed. 1988. *Directory of African Universities.* 5th ed. Association of African Universities.

Internet Source:
UNESCO-World Academic Database: www.unesco.org/iau/eductn.html

---

Compiler
Margaret L. Wenger
Senior Evaluator
Educational Credential Evaluators, Inc., Milwaukee, WI

TURKEY

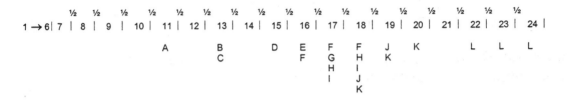

YEARS OF EDUCATION →

```
    ½   ½   ½   ½   ½   ½   ½   ½   ½   ½   ½   ½   ½   ½   ½   ½   ½
1 →6│7 │ 8 │ 9 │ 10│ 11│ 12│ 13│ 14│ 15│ 16│ 17│ 18│ 19│ 20│ 21│ 22│ 23│ 24│
              A       B       D   E   F   F   J   K       L   L   L
                      C               F   G   H   K
                                          H   I
                                          I   J
                                              K
```

CREDENTIALS OR DOCUMENTATION

Secondary

A *Lise Diploması* (Secondary School Diploma)

Postsecondary

B *Meslek Yüksek Okulu Diploması* (Vocational Higher School Diploma): two-year program based on credential **A**

C *Ön Lisans Derecesi* (Pre-Licentiate Degree): two-year program based on credential **A**

D *Lisans Diploması* (Licentiate Diploma) in fields other than Architecture, Dentistry, Medicine, Pharmacy, and Veterinary Science: four-year program based on credential **A**, or two-year program based on credential **C**[1]

E *Lisans Diploması* (Licentiate Diploma) in Architecture, Dentistry, Pharmacy, or Veterinary Science: five-year program based on credential **A**[1]

F *Yüksek Lisans Diploması* (Higher Licentiate Diploma): one- or two-year program requiring credential **D** or **E** for admission, or five-year program requiring credential **A** for admission[1]

G *Lisans Diploması* (Licentiate Diploma) in Medicine: six-year program based on credential **A**[1]

H *Bilim Uzmanlığı Diploması* (Science Specialist Diploma): two-year program requiring credential **D** or **E** for admission

I *Uzmanlık Belgesi* (Specialist Certificate): two-year program in Agriculture, Pharmacy, or Veterinary Science; requires credential **D** or **E** for admission

J *Güzel Sanatlar Ustalık Belgesi* (Fine Arts Mastery Certificate): three-year program requiring credential **D** for admission, or two-year program beyond credential **G**

K *Doktora Diploması* (Doctoral Diploma): two-year program requiring credential **F**, **H**, or **I** for admission, or three-year program requiring credential **D** or **E** for admission

L *Uzmanlık Belgesi* (Specialist Certificate) in Medicine: six-year program requiring credential **F** for admission; it is considered in Turkey to be the equivalent of credential **K**

---

[1] In professional fields such as Architecture, Dentistry, Engineering, Medicine, Nursing, Pharmacy, and Veterinary Science, graduates might receive an *ünvan* or *ünvanı* (title) instead of, or in addition to, credential **D**, **E**, **F**, or **G**.

GRADING INFORMATION

Secondary

Numeric	Letter	Description	Translation
5	A	Pek Iyi	Very Good
4	B	Iyi	Good
3	C	Orta	Average
2	D	Geçer	Passing
1	E	Geçmez	Failure

Higher Education

Percentage	Description	Translation
85-100	Pek Iyi	Very Good
65-84	Iyi	Good
50-64	Orta	Average
0-49	Geçmez	Failure

- There are more than 40 grading scales, including a wide variety of 0-100 scales. The scale listed above is used slightly more often than the others.

POSTSECONDARY INSTITUTION RECOGNITION BODY

Yükseköğretim Kurulu [YÖK] (Higher Education Council). 06539 Bilkent, Ankara, Turkey. Tel: 90-312-266-4731. Fax: 90-312-266-4759.

RESOURCES FOR ADDITIONAL INFORMATION

The British Council. 1996. *International Guide to Qualifications*. 4th ed. London: Mansell.

Frey, James S. 1992. *ECE Presents: The Educational System of Turkey*. Milwaukee: Educational Credential Evaluators, Inc.

Internet Source:
UNESCO - World Academic Database: www.unesco.org/iau/edutr.html

---

Compiler
James S. Frey
President
Educational Credential Evaluators, Inc., Milwaukee, WI

UKRAINE

	½	½	½	½	½	½	½	½	½	½	½	½	½	½	½	½	½
1 → 6	7	8	9	10	11	12	13	14	15	16	17	18	19	20	21	22	23	24

```
        A          B           C   C   E   F G F        H  H  H          I→ I→ I→
                               D   D       G G
```

CREDENTIALS OR DOCUMENTATION

After the Ukraine's independence from the Soviet Union in 1991, the Parliament of Ukraine adopted a "Law on Education" which, in part, introduced two new postsecondary credentials and four levels of accreditation of postsecondary institutions. It now regards all postsecondary education as "Higher Education."

Secondary

A **Свідоцтво про неповну загальну середню освіту** (Certificate of Incomplete General Secondary Education): represents completion of nine years of compulsory education

B **Атестат про повну загальну середню освіту** (Certificate of Completed Secondary Education): admission requires credential **A**; two-year program ending with a matriculation examination; permits access to universities and other higher education schools

C **Диплом** (Diploma): admission based on credential **B** for a two- or three-year program at a **технікум** (technical school) or **училище** (specialized vocational school); admission for a five-year program is based on credential **A**

Postsecondary

D **Диплом Молодшого Спеціаліста** (Junior Specialist Diploma): new credential awarded by a **технікум** (technical school) or college which transferred from the secondary sector to higher education level per the *Law on Education*; two- or three-year vocational programs with admission based on credential **B**

E **Диплом Бакалавра** (Diploma of Bachelor): new credential representing completion of a four-year program of study; admission based on credential **B**

F **Диплом Спеціаліста** (Specialist Diploma): five-year program, six years in the case of medicine; admission based on credential **B**

G **Диплом Магістра** (Master Diploma): new credential representing five- to six-year programs of study; admission based on credential **B**

H **Диплом кандидата наук** (Diploma of Candidate of Sciences): minimum of three years of study almost completely composed of independent research; admission based on credential **F** or **G**

I **Диплом доктора наук** (Diploma of Doctor of Sciences): at least three years of study beyond credential **H**; program is comprised of original published research

GRADING INFORMATION

Secondary and Postsecondary Education

Numeric	Ukrainian	Translation
5	відмінно	Excellent
4	добре	Good
3	задовільно	Satisfactory
2	незараховано	Fail
-	зараховано (зара.)	Credited, Passed

POSTSECONDARY INSTITUTION RECOGNITION BODY

Ministry of Education, 252135 Kyiv, Peremohy Pr. 10, Ukraine. Tel: 380-44-226-2661. Fax: 380-44-274-1049.

RESOURCES FOR ADDITIONAL INFORMATION

Ministry of Education of Ukraine. 1996. *Higher Education in Ukraine: Brief Directory 1996-1997*. Kyiv: Compass Publishing House.

Ministry of Education of Ukraine. 1997. *Law of Ukraine*. Kyiv: Genesa Publishing House.

Reuhl, Dr. G. and Prof. V. Pogrebnyak. 1996. *Study on the International Comparability of the System of Higher Education in the Ukraine*. Brussels: Trans-European Mobility Scheme for University Studies (TEMPUS).

Internet Source:
UNESCO - World Academic Database: www.unesco.org/iau/educua.html

___

Compiler
Marybeth Mirzejewski
Evaluator
Educational Credential Evaluators, Inc., Milwaukee, WI

UNITED KINGDOM

YEARS OF EDUCATION →

	½	½	½	½	½	½	½	½	½	½	½	½	½	½	½	½	½
1 → 6	7	8	9	10	11	12	13	14	15	16	17	18	19	20	21	22	23	24

```
                A   C   F   J   J   K   K   L   L   N→  N→
                B   D   G       K   L   L   M   M
                    E   H           M   M       N→
                    I   I
                        J
```

CREDENTIALS OR DOCUMENTATION

Secondary

A General Certificate of Secondary Education/GCSE and International General Certificate of Secondary Education/IGCSE: used internationally, as well as in England, Wales, and Northern Ireland upon completion of secondary education; replaces the General Certificate of Education-Ordinary Level/GCE-O and Certificate of Secondary Education/CSE qualifications that were in use prior to 1988

B General National Vocational Qualifications/GNVQ, and General Scottish Vocational Qualification (GSVQ), Foundation and Intermediate

C Scottish Certificate of Education/SCE: the "Standard Grade" replaced the "Ordinary Grade" in 1986

D Scottish Certificate of Education-Higher Grade/SCE-H: leads to higher education in Scotland

E Certificate of Sixth Year Studies/CSYS: any student who has passed a higher-grade subject (credential **D**) may attempt this on a subject basis

F General Certificate of Education-Advanced and Advanced Supplementary Levels (GCE-A and GCE-AS): leads to higher education in England, Wales, and Northern Ireland

G Advanced International Certificate of Secondary Education/AICE: international version of credential **F**

H General National Vocational Qualifications/GNVQ, and General Scottish Vocational Qualification (GSVQ), Advanced

Postsecondary

I Ordinary Certificate/OC and Ordinary Diploma/OD: vocational qualifications earned after two years of part-time study for the OC, and two years of full-time study for the OD; examinations externally administered by the Business and Technology Education Council (BTEC) or the Scottish Vocational Education Council (SCOTVEC); admission based on credential **A, B,** or **C**

J Higher National Certificate/HNC and Higher National Diploma/HND: vocational qualifications earned after two to three years of part-time study for the HNC, and two years of full-time study for the HND; examination externally administered by the Business and Technology Education Council (BTEC) or the Scottish Vocational Education Council (SCOTVEC); admission based on credential **D, E, F, G,** or **H**

K   Bachelor's degrees, Pass/Ordinary and Honours (Bachelor of Arts, Bachelor of Education, Bachelor of Engineering, Bachelor of Law, Bachelor of Science, etc.): three to four years following credential **D, E, F,** or **G**[1]

L   Postgraduate Certificates and Postgraduate Diplomas: vocational or professional qualifications; programs usually require one to two years of study; some convert to Master's degrees; admission generally based on credential **J** and in some cases, credential **K**

M   Master's degrees (Master of Arts, Master of Business Administration, Master of Philosophy, Master of Science, etc.): one to two years of study; may consist of pure research or a course of instruction including research; admission generally based on credential **K** (see also credential **L**)

N   Doctor of Philosophy, and other doctoral degrees: normally awarded after three to five years of supervised research following credential **M** or occasionally credential **K**[2]

[1]   Some professionally-oriented bachelor degree programs require a longer period of study than non-professionally oriented degree programs (BA, BSc., etc.). For example, the Bachelor of Dental Surgery, Bachelor of Veterinary Medicine, Bachelor of Medicine and Bachelor of Surgery (MB BChir) generally require five to six years of study.

[2]   Direct entry to doctoral degree programs is possible for graduates of Bachelor of Architecture, Bachelor of Divinity, and Bachelor of Philosophy degree programs. These three bachelor degree programs generally require five years of study following credential **D, E, F,** or **G**.

GRADING INFORMATION

Secondary
General Certificate of Secondary Education: Graded on an A through G basis, with A as the highest grade and G as the lowest grade. Ungraded performance (UG) is considered failing.

General Certificate of Education-Advanced and Advanced Supplementary Levels: Graded on an A through E basis with A as the highest grade and E as the lowest grade. The grades of N and O indicate a pass at the Ordinary level (but failure at the Advanced Level), and the grade of U indicates failure.

Scottish Certificate of Education-Standard Grade: Graded on an A through E basis, with A as the highest grade and E as the lowest grade. An "ungraded" examination represents failure.

Scottish Certificate of Education-Higher Grade, and Certificate of Sixth Year Studies: Graded on an A through E basis, with A as the highest grade and E as the lowest grade. The grade of O represents failing at the higher grade, but passing at the standard grade.

Postsecondary Education
Business and Technology Education Council:

Letter	Mark
A	Distinction
B, C	Merit
D	Pass
E	Marginal/Fail/Referral

Scottish Vocational Education Council:

Band or Grade	Percentage
7 - Distinction	70-100
6	60-69
5	50-59
1-4 - Failure	0-49

Bachelor's degrees:

Class or Division

I

II - Upper

II - Lower

III

- A Third Class (III) pass is acceptable for graduation.
- Honours degrees are usually classified according to divisions. Ordinary/Pass degrees are not classified.

POSTSECONDARY INSTITUTION RECOGNITION BODY

Universities are independent, self-governing bodies, empowered by a royal charter to create their own courses and award degrees. Standards are maintained by their use of external examiners.

RESOURCES FOR ADDITIONAL INFORMATION

The British Council. 1996. *International Guide to Qualifications in Education*. 4th ed. London: Mansell.

Internet Sources:
British Council Online: www.Britcoun.org
EURYDICE Eurybase-Scotland: www.eurydice.org
EURYDICE Eurybase-United Kingdom: www.eurydice.org
UNESCO - World Academic Database: www.unesco.org/iau/educgb.html

---

Compiler
Bella Anand
University of Wisconsin-Milwaukee

UNITED STATES OF AMERICA

YEARS OF EDUCATION →

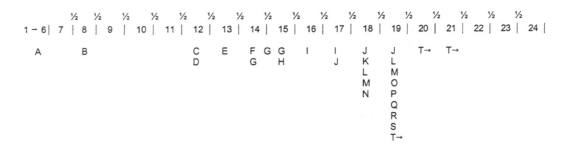

CREDENTIALS OR DOCUMENTATION

Secondary

Elementary and secondary education requires completion of a total of 12 years of schooling. It is usually preceded by one year of kindergarten which is optional in some school districts. Elementary (primary) education is most commonly comprised of five or six years of schooling; middle (or junior high school) is two or three years; and senior high school education is three or four years. A common pattern is presented below:

A   Completion of six years of elementary school: documentation consists of a school record or transcript; a graduation certificate may or may not be awarded

B   Completion of two years of middle school: documentation consists of a school record or transcript; a graduation certificate may or may not be awarded

C   High School Diploma: generally awarded by a senior high school

D   General Education Development: results are issued for performance on examinations; sufficient scores are considered to be a substitute for credential **C**

Postsecondary

E   Advanced Placement examinations: score results issued by the Educational Testing Service for performance on individual subject exams; grades of 4 to 5 are generally considered to certify completion of one year of postsecondary-level work in the subject, though exams are generally taken while in the last year of senior high school

F   Associate of Arts (A.A.) degree and Associate of Science (A.S.) degree: awarded by a community college, junior college, or other postsecondary institution; signifies completion of a two-year program requiring credential **C** or **D** for admission

G   Associate of Applied Science (A.A.S.) degree: awarded by a community college, junior college, or other postsecondary institution; signifies completion of usually a two-year program requiring credential **C** or **D** for admission; some two and one-half-year and three-year programs exist

H   Diploma in Nursing awarded by a hospital school of nursing: most programs require three years of study; admission based on credential **C** or **D**

I   Bachelor's degree: awarded by a college, university, or institute upon completion of a four-year program requiring credential **C** or **D** for admission; programs may require five years of study in some fields and at some institutions

J   Master's degree: awarded by a college, university, or institute upon completion of a one- to two-year program of study requiring credential I for admission; some programs in specialized fields require three years

K   Juris Doctor (J.D.) degree: three-year professional program in law based on completion of three years of pre-professional study; previously known as Bachelor of Laws (Ll.B.)[1]

L   Doctor of Chiropractic (D.C.): four- to five-year professional program based on completion of two years of pre-professional study[1]

M   Doctor of Dental Surgery (D.D.S.) or Doctor of Dental Medicine (D.M.D.): four-year professional program based on completion of two to three years of pre-professional study[1]

N   Doctor of Pharmacy (Pharm.D.): six-year professional program based on credential **C** or **D**, or two-year professional program based on credential **I**

O   Bachelor of Divinity (B.Div.) or Master of Divinity (B.Div.): three-year professional program in theology based on credential **I**

P   Doctor of Medicine (M.D.): four-year professional program based on completion of three years of pre-professional study[1]

Q   Doctor of Optometry (O.D.): four-year professional program based on completion of two to three years of pre-professional study[1]

R   Doctor of Osteopathy (D.O.): four-year professional program based on completion of three years of pre-professional study[1]

S   Doctor of Podiatric Medicine (D.P.M.): four-year professional program based on completion of three years of pre-professional study[1]

T   Doctor of Philosophy (Ph.D.), Doctor of Education (Ed.D.): advanced program of study, research, and writing of a dissertation requiring at least three years of study beyond credential **I** or at least two years of study beyond credential **J**

[1]   Minimum admission requirements include two or three years of study in a bachelor's degree program, as noted; however, often students complete a full bachelor's degree program prior to admission to the professional degree program.

GRADING INFORMATION: All Levels of Education

Letter	Percentage	Point	Description
A	90-100	4.00	Excellent
A-		3.67	
A/B		3.50	
B+		3.33	
B	80-89	3.00	Above Average
B-		2.67	
B/C		2.50	
C+		2.33	
C	70-79	2.00	Average
C-		1.67	
C/D		1.50	
D+		1.33	
D	60-69	1.00	Below Average
D-		0.67	
F	0-59	0.00	Failure

- The grading scale used by an institution is specified on transcripts/academic records.

POSTSECONDARY INSTITUTION RECOGNITION BODIES

Six regional commissions grant institutional accreditation. They are listed below. In addition, professional associations accredit programs in specified fields.

Middle States Association of Colleges and Schools: Delaware, District of Columbia, Maryland, New Jersey, New York, Pennsylvania, Puerto Rico, Virgin Islands

New England Association of Schools and Colleges: Connecticut, Maine, Massachusetts, New Hampshire, Rhode Island, Vermont

North Central Association of Colleges and Schools: Arizona, Arkansas, Colorado, Illinois, Indiana, Iowa, Kansas, Michigan, Minnesota, Missouri, Nebraska, New Mexico, North Dakota, Ohio, Oklahoma, South Dakota, West Virginia, Wisconsin, Wyoming

Northwest Association of Schools and Colleges: Alaska, Idaho, Montana, Nevada, Oregon, Utah, Washington

Southern Association of Colleges and Schools: Alabama, Florida, Georgia, Kentucky, Louisiana, Mississippi, North Carolina, South Carolina, Tennessee, Texas, Virginia

Western Association of Schools and Colleges: California, Hawaii, American Samoa, Guam, Commonwealth of the Northern Marianas, Trust Territory of the Pacific Islands

RESOURCES FOR ADDITIONAL INFORMATION

AACRAO. Published every two years. *Transfer Credit Practices of Designated Educational Institutions: An Information Exchange.* Washington, D.C.: AACRAO.

American Council of Education. Published annually. *American Universities and Colleges.* New York: Walter de Gruyter.

College Board. Published annually. *Index of Majors and Graduate Degrees.* New York: College Entrance Examination Board.

Higher Education Publications, Inc. Higher Education Publications, Inc. *Higher Education Directory.* Falls Church, Virginia: Higher Education Publications, Inc.

Compiler
Ann Fletcher
Assistant Provost
Stanford University, Palo Alto, CA

URUGUAY

YEARS OF EDUCATION →

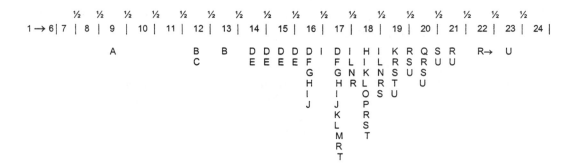

CREDENTIALS OR DOCUMENTATION

Secondary

A   Certificate of completion of the *Ciclo Básico Único* (Basic Unified Cycle):
encompasses the first three years of secondary education and is considered part of
the nine years of compulsory education

B   *Bachillarato Técnico* (Technical Baccalaureate): technical/vocational education track
consisting of the three years of the Basic Unified Cycle plus three or four additional
years depending on the program of study selected; courses are organized in
workshops with workshop experience considered fundamental to the programs;
programs are offered in agriculture, arts and crafts, industry training, and service
industry; at its highest levels, programs with a duration of six or seven years (totaling
12 or 13 years of education) afford access to university or teacher training
programs[1]

C   *Bachillarato Diversificado de Enseñanza Secundaria* (Diversified Baccalaureate of
Secondary Education): three-year program in the general secondary education
stream geared towards university preparation [1]

Postsecondary

D   *Títulos Intermedios* (Intermediate Titles) awarded by universities after two- to four-
year programs: some examples are *archivologo* (archivologist), three years;
analista/analista universitario (analyst/university analyst) or *técnico* (technician) in
business fields or computer programming, two to three years; *ayudante de ingeniero*
(engineering assistant), two years; *bachiller en química* (bachelor in chemistry),
three years; *técnico* (technician) in allied health professions, two and one-half to four
years; requires credential **B** or **C** for admission

E   *Traductor Público* (Public Translator): two- to two and one-half-year program;
admission requires credential **B** in a related area, or credential **C**

F   *Maestro(a) en Educación Primaria* (Primary Education Teacher) awarded by
institutos normales (normal institutes): four-year program; admission requires
credential **B** or **C**

G *Profesor(a)* (Secondary Education Teacher) awarded by *institutos de profesores* (teachers' institutes): four-year program comprising both theoretical and practical components; admission requires credential **B** or **C**

H *Trabajador(a) Social* (Social Worker): four- to five-year university program; admission requires credential **B** or **C**

I *Licenciatura/Licenciado(a)* (Licenciate): four- to five and one-half-year university programs; admission requires credential **B** in a related area, or credential **C**

J *Procurador en Derecho* (Legal Specialist): four- to five-year university program; admission requires credential **C**

K *Ingeniero* (Engineer): five- to six-year university program, depending on academic concentration; admission requires credential **B** in a related area, or credential **C**

L *Doctor en Odontologia* (Doctor in Dentistry): five- to five and one-half-year university program; admission requires credential **B** a related area, or credential **C**

M *Doctor en Derecho* (Doctor in Law): five-year university program; admission requires credential **C**

N *Escribano Público* (Notarial Law): five and one-half-year university program; admission requires credential **B** in a related area, or credential **C**

O *Arquitecto* (Architect): six-year university program; admission requires credential **C**

P *Doctor en Ciencias Veterinarias* (Doctor of Veterinary Sciences): six-year university program; admission requires credential **C**

Q *Doctor en Medicina* (Doctor in Medicine): eight-year university program; admission requires credential **C**

R *Posgrados y Especializaciones* (Postgraduate and Specialization Studies): one-year university program of specialization in a field; admission based on any credential **G** through **Q**; programs offered in the fields of communications, communications systems, and human resources and development; two- to six-year program of medical specialization exist for those with credential **Q**

S *Maestrias, Magister,* or *Master* programs: two-year university programs of specialization in a field; admission based on any credential **G** through **Q**; programs offered in the fields of administration, business administration (MBA), human resources, marketing, information systems and public policy; see also credential **T**

T *Magister en Química* (Master in Chemistry): five-year university program with admission requiring credential **B** in a related area, or credential **C**; or, two-year program following a *bachiller en química* (credential **D**); see also credential **S**

U *Doctorado* (Doctorate): usually three years of in-depth study and research, leading to the award of *Doctor en...* (Doctor in...) a specific field, not to be confused with credentials **L, M, P,** or **Q**; admission based on any credential **G** through **Q**

---

[1] Education in secondary schools encompasses six years of instruction divided into two 3-year cycles. Admission is based on completion of six years of primary education. The first or basic cycle is compulsory; the second cycle splits into either an academic track geared towards university preparation (credential **C**) or a technical/vocational track offered by public technical education schools (credential **B**). *The two systems are parallel in structure, and there is in actuality, little provision for transfer between the two, yet legally the provision exists for admission to a university with credential* **B**.

[2] Variation in *licenciado* curricula exist between universities, though programs in education, humanities, library science, and sciences tend to require four years of study; nursing tends to require four and one-half years; pharmacy and psychology tend to require five years; accounting and business fields require four to five and one-half years.

GRADING INFORMATION

Secondary and Postsecondary Education

Numeric	Definition	Translation	Abbreviation
12	*Sobresaliente*	Excellent	S.S.S.
11	*Sobresaliente Muy Sobresaliente*	Excellent -	S.S.MB.
10	*Muy Bueno Sobresaliente*	Very Good +	MB.MB.S.
9	*Muy Bueno*	Very Good	MB.MB.MB.
8	*Muy Bueno Bueno*	Very Good -	MB.MB.B.
7	*Bueno Muy Bueno*	Good +	B.B.MB.
6	*Bueno*	Good	B.B.B.
5	*Regular Bueno*	Good -	B.B.R.
4	*Regular Bueno*	Fair +	R.R.B.
3	*Regular*	Fair	R.R.R.
2	*Regular Deficiente*	Fail	R.R.D.
1	*Deficiente Regular*	Fail	D.D.R.
0	*Deficiente*	Fail	D.D.D.

* Grades of 12 and 11 are rarely used. A grading system using marks from 0-100 appears less frequently with notable variations on the minimum passing grade. Higher education institutions traditionally include grading information on transcripts.

* Lowest passing grade is 3, *Regular*.

POSTSECONDARY INSTITUTION RECOGNITION BODY

Ministerio de Educacion y Cultura, Dirección de Educación, Regulator, Reconquista 535, Montevideo. Tel: 598-2 96-1174. Fax: 598-2-96-5475.

RESOURCES FOR ADDITIONAL INFORMATION

Fulbright Commission for Educational Exchange Between Uruguay and the United States. Paraguay 1217, piso 1. Montevideo. Tel: 598-2-901-4160. Fax: 598-2-903-2031.

National Office of Overseas Skills Recognition. 1993. *Country Education Profiles: Uruguay.* Canberra: Australian Government Publishing Service.

Internet Sources:
Department of State Foreign Affairs Network/DOSFAN is a Great Cities cooperative initiative between the Office of Public Communication, Bureau of Public Affairs, and the Federal Depository Library at the University of Illinois at Chicago: www.state.gov/www/background_notes/
UNESCO – World Academic Database: www.unesco.org/iau/educuy.html
World Factbook prepared by the Central Intelligence Agency (CIA): www.odci.gov/cia/publications/factbook/

Compiler
Yvette Blanco
Assistant Director, Graduate Enrollment Services
Graduate School of Arts and Science
New York University

VATICAN CITY

Vatican City supervises two types of educational institutions: seminaries, which train priests; and ecclesiastical universities, which train church administrators, church officials, and faculty members for both seminaries and universities.

ROMAN CATHOLIC SEMINARIES

Roman Catholic seminaries are supervised jointly by the Congregation for Catholic Education in Rome and by the National Conference of Bishops in the country in which a seminary is located. Additions to the approved curricula can be made by the bishop of the diocese in which a diocesan seminary is located or by the superior of a religious order if the seminary is operated by a religious order (e.g., Dominican, Franciscan, Jesuit).

Primary and Secondary

Primary education is completed within the educational system of the country in which a seminary is located. Secondary education is completed either within the educational system of the country in which a seminary is located or in a *seminarium minus* (minor seminary). The curriculum of a minor seminary can encompass both lower and upper secondary education, or only upper secondary education, or upper secondary education plus one or two years of postsecondary education.

Postsecondary

Postsecondary education is completed in a *seminarium maius* (major seminary), in a program known as *sexennium philosophico-theologicum* (six-year philosophical-theological study), that is, two years of philosophy plus four years of theology leading to ordination as a priest.

In some countries, the philosophy portion of the major seminary curriculum, and (if applicable) the postsecondary portion of the minor seminary curriculum, can be completed at a university that is affiliated with the Roman Catholic church.

In many countries, no credential is awarded upon completion of the various stages of minor and major seminary curricula. In some countries, regular credentials are awarded. For example, in Italy students who complete a five-year minor seminary curriculum (upper secondary) or an eight-year minor seminary curriculum (lower and upper secondary) receive a *Testimonium Maturitatis e Lyceo* (Maturity Certificate from a Secondary School). In the United States, some seminaries award a Bachelor of Arts degree (with a major in Philosophy) to students who have completed the philosophy portion of the major seminary curriculum, and a Master of Divinity degree to students who have completed the theology portion.

Grading information for seminars is listed after the following section on ecclesiastical universities.

ECCLESIASTICAL UNIVERSITIES

Approximately 15 institutions in Vatican City or in Rome, and approximately 125 institutions in other countries, are governed by the Roman Catholic Apostolic Constitution 'Sapientia Christiana' of 15 April 1979 and the Norms of the Congregation for Catholic Education of 29 April 1979. Many of these "ecclesiastical universities" have the word *pontifical* in their name. They award degrees with authority granted by the Roman Catholic Church. In some cases, they also have received official degree-granting recognition from the authorities who supervise postsecondary education in the country in which the institution operates.

Most ecclesiastical universities award the credentials represented in this ladder:

YEARS OF POSTSECONDARY EDUCATION →

```
1 | 2 | 3 |  4  |  5  |  6  |  7  |  8  |  9  | 10 |

A   B   D    E     C           F     D     G→
                 G→    H→                  I→
```

A   *Baccalaureatus* (Baccalaureate) in Canon Law (Roman Catholic Church Law): one-year program requiring completion of upper secondary education for admission

B   *Baccalaureatus* (Baccalaureate) in philosophy: two-year program requiring completion of upper secondary education for admission

C   *Baccalaureatus* (Baccalaureate) in theology: five-year program requiring completion of upper secondary education for admission; or three-year program requiring credential **B** for admission

D   *Licentia* (Licentiate) in Canon Law: two-year program requiring credential **A** for admission, or completion of a major seminary curriculum[1]

E   *Licentia* (Licentiate) in philosophy: two-year program requiring credential **B** for admission[1]

F   *Licentia* (Licentiate) in theology: two-year program requiring credential **C** for admission[1]

G   *Doctoratus* (Doctorate) in Canon Law: research program at least one year in length requiring credential **D** for admission[2]

H   *Doctoratus* (Doctorate) in philosophy: research program at least one year in length requiring credential **E** for admission[2]

I   *Doctoratus* (Doctorate) in theology: research program at least one year in length requiring credential **F** for admission[2]

[1]   A *Licentia* qualifies one to teach at a major seminary.

[2]   A *Doctoratus* qualifies one to teach at a major seminary or at an ecclesiastical university.

GRADING INFORMATION

Some seminaries and ecclesiastical universities use the standard grading scale of the country in which they are located. Some use this scale:

Latin	Translation
Summa Cum Laude Probatus	Passed With Highest Praise
Magna Cum Laude Probatus	Passed With Great Praise
Cum Laude Probatus	Passed With Praise
Probatus	Passed
Non Probatus	Not Passed

- Some seminaries and ecclesiastical universities use a scale of 0 to 10 with 6 being the minimum passing grade.

POSTSECONDARY INSTITUTION RECOGNITION BODY

Congregazione per l'educazione cattolica (Congregation for Catholic Education), 3 Piazza Pio XII, Rome 00193, Italy. Tel: 39-50-698-4161. Fax: 39-6-698-4172.

RESOURCES FOR ADDITIONAL INFORMATION

The British Council. 1996. *International Guide to Qualifications in Education*. 4th ed. London: Mansell.

Capobianco, Joseph P. 1981. *Italy: A Study of the Educational System of Italy and a Guide to the Academic Placement of Students in Educational Institutions of the United States*. Washington D.C.: AACRAO.

Internet Source:
UNESCO - World Academic Database: www.unesco.org/iau/educva.html

---

Compiler
James S. Frey
President
Educational Credential Evaluators, Inc., Milwaukee, WI

VENEZUELA

YEARS OF EDUCATION →

```
    ½   ½   ½   ½   ½   ½   ½   ½   ½   ½   ½   ½   ½   ½   ½   ½   ½
1 → 6│7 │ 8 │ 9 │ 10 │ 11 │ 12 │ 13 │ 14 │ 15 │ 16 │ 17 │ 18 │ 19 │ 20 │ 21 │ 22 │ 23 │ 24 │
        A           B   C   E   E   E   F   G P Q O Q
                    D   D           F   G   J   R→  R→
                                    G   H   M   S→  T→
                                    H   I   P
                                        J   Q
                                        K   R→
                                        L   S→
                                        M
                                        N
                                        O
                                        Q
```

CREDENTIALS OR DOCUMENTATION

Secondary

A *Certificado de Educación Secundaria* (Certificate of Secondary Education): awarded upon completion of the three-year *Ciclo Básico Común* (Common Basic Cycle)

B *Bachiller en...Ciencias, Humanidades, Ciencias y Humanidades, en Comercio* (*Bachiller* in... Science, Humanities, Science and Humanities, Commerce): awarded after a two-year *Ciclo Diversificado* (Diversified Cycle); requires credential **A** for admission[1]

C *Bachiller...Agropecuario, Industrial, Asistencial, Mención Docencia* (*Bachiller* in... Agricultural and Animal Sciences, Industrial Studies, Social Services Areas, Specialization in Teaching): awarded after a three-year *Ciclo Diversificado* (Diversified Cycle); requires credential **A** for admission; leads to postsecondary education[1,2]

D *Técnico Medio* (IntermediateTechnician): two or three years of technical education; requires credential **A** for admission; may lead to credential **E** programs

Postsecondary

E *Técnico Superior/Tecnólogo* (Higher Technician/Technologist): two years (rarely), or three years of study (usually) requiring credential **B, C,** or **D** for admission

F *Licenciado* (Licentiate): four or five years, requiring credential **B** for admission[3]

G *Ingeniero* (Engineer): four years (rarely) or five years of study, requiring credential **B** in science, **C** in industrial studies, or **D** for admission

H *Profesor* (Teacher): four or five years of study, requiring credential **B** in appropriate specialty or **C** with *Mención Docencia* for admission; may be awarded as *Profesor en. . .* (specialization) or *Licenciado en Educación, Mención* (specialization)

I *Abogado* (Attorney): five years of study requiring credential **B** in humanities or sciences and humanities for admission

J *Arquitecto* (Architect): five years of study, or six years at *Universidad Central de Venezuela*; credential **B** in science required for admission

K *Contador Público* (Public Accountant): five years of study requiring credential **B** in commerce or science for admission

L *Farmaceútico* (Pharmacist): five years of study requiring credential **B** in science for admission

M *Médico Veterinario* (Veterinary Physician): five years of study requiring credential **B** in science or credential **C** in agricultural and animal sciences for admission

N *Odontólogo* (Dentist): five years of study requiring credential **B** in science for admission

O *Licenciado en Teología* (Licentiate in Theology): five years or seven and one-half years of study, requiring credential **B** in humanities or science and humanities for admission[4]

P *Médico Cirujano* (Physician-Surgeon): six years of study, or six and one-half years at *Universidad Central de Venezuela*; credential **B** in science required for admission

Q *Maestría* (Master): one or two years of study beyond any of credentials **F**, **G**, **H**, **K**, or **O**; the following terminology may be used--*magister en . . .* (specialization); *magister scientiae; magister scientarium; master en. . .* (specialization)

R *Doctor/Doctorado* (Doctor/Doctorate): two or more years of study beyond credentials **F**, **G**, **H**, or, in some cases, credential **Q**

S *Especialista* (Specialist) in non-medical areas: one or more years of study beyond related credentials **I**, **J**, **L**, **M**, and **N**

T *Especialista* (Specialist) in areas of medical science: two or more years of study beyond credential **P**

1 *Bachiller* is usually translated as "bachelor" in the English language. This term is used in Venezuela to denote an upper secondary school graduate, rather than a university graduate. To avoid confusion, it is not translated in the list of credentials or documentation.

2 All titles of *bachiller* are accepted for admission to postsecondary education; some postsecondary programs specify a required area of specialization.

3 Four-year *licenciado* programs are usually in the fields of *educación* (education) and *letras* (arts).

4 The theology curriculum at the Instituto Universitario Seminario Interdiocesano Santa Rosa de Lima consists of five years of study, while 15 semesters are required at the Instituto Universitario Salesiano Padre Ojeda.

GRADING INFORMATION

Secondary

A scale of 20 to 0 is used: *aprobado* (pass) grades range from 20 (highest) to 10 (lowest passing), and *aplazado* (failure) for grades 9 to 0.

Postsecondary Education

Technical Programs:
A scale of 9 to 0 is used mainly by *institutos universitarios* and some other technical institutions: *aprobado* (pass) grades range from 9 (highest) to 5 (lowest passing); however, a grade of 6 is required to continue to the next sequence or course. *Aplazado* (Failure) is represented by grades 4 to 0.

Traditional University Scale:
A scale of 20 to 0 is used by most universities. *Aprobado* (Pass) is represented by the grades 20 (highest) to 10 (lowest passing). *Aplazado* (Failure) is represented by grades 9 to 0. An average grade of 11 or 12 is often required for graduation.

Alternate University Scale:
A scale of 5 to 0 may be used, with 5 being highest and 3 being the lowest passing grade. Grades of 1 or 0 are rarely issued; rather the transcript may note the course as *aplazado* (failure) or *diferido* (deferred to next testing period).

385

POSTSECONDARY INSTITUTION RECOGNITION BODY

Ministerio de Educación, Consejo Nacional de Universidades. Mezzanina Esquina de Salas, Caracas, Venezuela. Tel: 58-2-562-9198 or 58-2-781-5584.

RESOURCES FOR ADDITIONAL INFORMATION

Consejo Nacional de Universidades. 1997. *Oportunidades de Estudio en las Instituciones de Educación Superior de Venezuela.* Caracas: Consejo Nacional de Universidades.

Division de Control y Evaluación del Ministerio de Educación. 1997.*Oportunidades de Estudio en la Educación Media de Venezuela.* Caracas: Ministerio de Educación.

Internet Source:
UNESCO – World Academic Database: www.unesco.org/iau/educve.html

---

Compiler
Sandra Dyson Rodríguez
SDR Educational Consultants
Foreign Educational Equivalencies, Houston, TX

VIETNAM

YEARS OF EDUCATION →

1 → 6	7	½ 8	½ 9	½ 10	½ 11	½ 12	½ 13	½ 14	½ 15	½ 16	½ 17	½ 18	½ 19	½ 20	½ 21	½ 22	½ 23	½ 24
			A			B	C D	C D E	C D	F G	F G	F G H→ I	H→ I	H→ I J→ K	J→ K	J→ K		

CREDENTIALS OR DOCUMENTATION

Secondary

A   Bang Tot Nghiep Pho Thong Co So (Diploma of Graduation from General School)
B   Bang Tot Nghiep Pho Thong Trung Hoc (Diploma of Graduation from General Secondary Education)

Postsecondary

C   Bang Tot Nghiep Cao Dang (Diploma of Graduation from Higher School) to 1995: one- to three-year vocationally oriented programs at a junior college
D   Bang Tot Nghiep Cu Nhan Cao Dang (Diploma of Graduation as Bachelor from Higher School) since 1995: one- to three-year vocationally oriented programs at a junior college
E   Chung Chi Dai Hoc Dai Cuong (Certificate of General University Education): two-year program requiring credential **B** for admission
F   Bang Tot Nghiep Dai Hoc (Diploma of Graduation from a University) to 1995: four-year programs in economics, humanities, natural sciences, and social sciences; five-year programs in agriculture, architecture, engineering, and pharmacy; six-year programs in dentistry and medicine; all required credential **B** for admission
G   Bang Tot Nghiep Cu Nhan (Diploma as Graduation as Bachelor) since 1995: two-year programs in economics, humanities, natural sciences, and social sciences; three-year programs in agriculture, architecture, engineering, and pharmacy; four-year programs in dentistry and medicine; all require credential **E** for admission
H   Bang Pho Tien Si (Diploma of Assistant Doctor, also translated as Diploma of Candidate) to 1990: minimum of two years beyond credential **F**
I   Bang Thac Si (Diploma of Worthy Scholar, also translated as Diploma of Master) since 1990: minimum of two years beyond credential **G**
J   Bang Tien Si Khoa Hoc (Diploma of Doctor of Science) to 1990: minimum of two years beyond credential **H**
K   Bang Tien Si (Diploma of Doctor) since 1990: two years beyond credential **I**

GRADING INFORMATION

Secondary and Postsecondary Education

Until 1993:

Numeric	Description	Translation
9-10	*Uu*	Excellent
7-8	*Binh*	Good
5-6	*Binh Thu*	Fairly Good
0-4	*Khong*	Not Good (failing)
---	*Dat*	Pass

Since 1993:

Numeric	Description	Translation
9-10	*Gíoi*	Excellent
7-8	*Kha*	Good
5-6	*Trung Binh*	Fair
0-4	*Kem*	Poor (failing)
----	*Dat*	Pass

POSTSECONDARY INSTITUTION RECOGNITION BODY

Higher Education Department, Ministry of Education and Training. 49 Dai Co Viet Street, Hanoi, Vietnam. Tel: 84-4-255-441. Fax: 84-4-259-205.

RESOURCES FOR ADDITIONAL INFORMATION

The British Council. 1996. *International Guide to Qualifications in Education*. 4th ed. London: Mansell.

Dean, Michael F. Unpublished, circa 1996. *Vietnam*. Contact PIER Publications (see Appendix A) for information on this book's availability.

Internet Source:
UNESCO - World Academic Database: www.unesco.org/iau/eduvn.html

---

Compiler
James S. Frey
President
Educational Credential Evaluators, Inc., Milwaukee, WI

YEMEN

YEARS OF EDUCATION →

		½	½	½	½	½	½	½	½	½	½	½	½	½	½	½	½	½
1 → 6	7	8	9	10	11	12	13	14	15	16	17	18	19	20	21	22	23	24

```
                    A       E  I  G   J   J   K           N
                    B       F         L   N
                    C       G         M
                    D       H
```

CREDENTIALS OR DOCUMENTATION

Secondary

A   شهادة الدراسات الثانوية العامة (General Secondary Certificate): awarded in science and arts (literature) tracks

B   شهادة الدراسات الثانوية للمعاهد العلمية (Islamic Secondary Certificate): awarded in science and arts (literature tracks)

C   شهادة الدراسات الثانوية التجارية/الزراعية/البيطرية (Commercial/Agricultural/Veterinary Secondary Certificate)

D   شهادة الدراسات الثانوية الفنية (Technical Secondary Certificate)

E   دبلوم طقني صناعي (Industrial Technical Diploma): represented five years of education after the intermediate level (grade 9); discontinued in 1994 (was considered equivalent to a secondary credential)

Postsecondary

F   دبلوم عالي في التربية (Higher Diploma in Education): two years of teacher training, requiring credential A for admission

G   دبلوم التمريض (Nursing Diploma): two to three years at health institutes, depending on field of study; requires credential A for admission[1]

H   دبلوم في... (Diploma in...): two years at the National Institute of Administrative Sciences; requires credential A or C for admission

I   الدبلوم العالي (Higher Diploma): two and one-half years at the Higher Technical Institute; requires credential D for admission

J   لسانس/بكالوريوس (Licence or Bachelor's degree): four to five years, depending on field of study (5 years for pharmacy and engineering); requires credential A, B, or C for admission

K   بكالوريوس في الطب (Bachelor of Medicine): six years; admission requires credential A

L   دبلوم الدراسات العليا (Higher Studies Diploma): one year, requiring four-year credential J for admission

M   دبلوم في... (Diploma in...): one year (four 12-week semesters) at National Institute of Administrative Sciences in management, accounting, or business administration; requires four-year credential J for admission

N   ماجستير (Master's degree): two years, requiring four-year credential J or K

[1] Prior to 1992 at the Sana'a Health Institute and several years earlier at the Higher Health Sciences Institute, admission required the General Preparatory School Certificate (completion of grade 9).

389

GRADING INFORMATION

Secondary

Percent	Remark	Translation
90–100	ممتاز	Excellent
80–89	جيد جدا	Very Good
70–79	جيد	Good
50–69	مقبول	Pass
0–49	راسب or ضعيف	Weak or Failing

Higher Education

Undergraduate grading scale

Percent	Remark	Translation
90–100	ممتاز	Excellent
80–89	جيد جدا	Very Good
65–79	جيد	Good
50–64	مقبول	Pass
0–49	راسب	Fail

Graduate grading scale

Percent	Remark	Translation
90–100	ممتاز	Excellent
80–89	جيد جدا	Very Good
70–79	جيد	Good
60–69	مقبول	Pass
0–59	راسب	Fail

- At the University of Aden, the minimum passing score at the graduate level is 65%.

POSTSECONDARY INSTITUTION RECOGNITION BODY

Ministry of Education; Sana'a, Republic of Yemen. Tel: 967-1-276432.
Fax: 967-1-274555.

RESOURCES FOR ADDITIONAL INFORMATION

Internet Source:
UNESCO—www.unesco.org/iau/educye.html

Compilers
Nasreen Murad
AMIDEAST, Yemen

Leslie Nucho
Vice President
AMIDEAST, Washington, D.C.

ZAMBIA

YEARS OF EDUCATION →

```
      ½   ½   ½   ½   ½   ½   ½   ½   ½   ½   ½   ½   ½   ½   ½   ½   ½
1 → 6│ 7 │ 8 │ 9 │ 10 │ 11 │ 12 │ 13 │ 14 │ 15 │ 16 │ 17 │ 18 │ 19 │ 20 │ 21 │ 22 │ 23 │ 24 │
       A       B           C   D   E   G   J   N   P R R R R R R W→W→W→W→ V
                                   F   H   K   O   Q   S   T W→U
                                       I   L                   W→
                                       L   M
```

CREDENTIALS OR DOCUMENTATION

Primary and Secondary

A   Primary School Leaving Certificate: signifies completion of compulsory education
B   Junior Secondary School Leaving Certificate
C   Certificate in General Agriculture: two-year program requiring credential **B** for admission
D   Zambian School Certificate

Postsecondary

E   State Enrolled Nurse: two-year program based on completion of grade 11
F   Certificate in Adult Education: one-year program requiring credential **D** for admission
G   Zambia Primary Teachers Certificate Education: two-year program requiring credential **D** for admission
H   Diploma in Junior Secondary Education: two-year program requiring credential **D** for admission
I   Diploma in Adult Education: two-year program requiring credential **D** for admission
J   Advanced Diploma in Junior Secondary Education: one-year program in mathematics and science requiring credential **H** for admission
K   State Registered Nurse: three-year program requiring credential **D** for admission
L   Diploma in Forestry: two-year program at Zambia Forest College, three-year program at Mwekera Forestry College; credential **D** required for admission
M   Diploma in the fields of accounting, agriculture, agricultural education, agricultural engineering, medical laboratory technology, nutrition, pharmacy, social work, and technology: three-year programs requiring credential **D** for admission
N   Certificate in Midwifery: one-year program requiring credential **K** for admission
O   Bachelor's degree in accounting, arts, arts with education, arts with library and information studies, business administration, human biology[1], law, nursing, science, science with education, social work, or special education: four-year program requiring credential **D** for admission
P   Bachelor of Education (Primary): three-year program requiring credential **G** or equivalent for admission
Q   Bachelor's degree in agriculture, architecture, engineering, and mineral sciences: five-year program requiring credential **D** for admission

R Master's degree: one and one-half- to three-year program requiring credential **O**, **P**, or **Q** for admission; see also credentials **U** and **V**

S Bachelor of Veterinary Science: six-year program requiring credential **D** for admission

T Bachelor of Medicine, Bachelor of Surgery: seven-year program requiring credential **D** for admission[1]

U Master of Veterinary Medicine: two-year program requiring credential **S** for admission

V Master of Medicine: four-year program requiring credential **T** for admission

W Doctor of Philosophy: minimum of two years after credential **R**

[1] The Bachelor of Human Biology is awarded at the end of the fourth year of the seven-year Bachelor of Medicine, Bachelor of Surgery program.

GRADING INFORMATION

Secondary

Numerical	Description
1-2	Distinction
3-4	Merit
5-6	Credit
7-8	Satisfactory
9	Unsatisfactory

Higher Education

Copperbelt University:

Percentage	Letter	Description
90-100	A+	Distinction
85-89	A	Distinction
80-84	B+	Meritorious
70-79	B	Very Satisfactory
60-69	C+	Definite Pass
50-59	C	Bare Pass
0-49	D	Fail

University of Zambia:

Percentage	Letter	Description
90-100	A+	Distinction
80-89	A	Distinction
70-79	B+	Meritorious
60-69	B	Very Satisfactory
50-59	C+	Definite Pass
40-49	C	Bare Pass
30-39	D+	Bare Fail
0-29	D	Definite Fail
–	S	Satisfactory pass in a practical course
–	P	Pass in supplementary examination
–	AG	Aggregate Pass
–	F	Fail in supplementary examination
–	U	Unsatisfactory on practical course
–	NE	No examination taken
–	WD	Withdrawn
–	LT	Left course during the year without permission
–	DQ	Disqualified in course by senate
–	DR	De-registered for failure to pay fees

POSTSECONDARY INSTITUTION RECOGNITION BODY

Ministry of Science and Technology, P.O. Box 50464, Lusaka, Zambia.
Tel: 260-1-252-053. Fax: 260-1-252-951.

RESOURCES FOR ADDITIONAL INFORMATION

The British Council. 1996. *International Guide to Qualifications in Education.* 4th ed. London: Mansell.

Internet Source:
UNESCO - World Academic Database: www.unesco.org/iau/educzm.html

---

Compiler
James S. Frey
President
Educational Credential Evaluators, Inc., Milwaukee, WI

ZIMBABWE

YEARS OF EDUCATION →

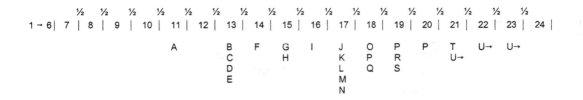

```
     ½   ½   ½   ½   ½   ½   ½   ½   ½   ½   ½   ½   ½   ½   ½   ½   ½
1→6| 7 | 8 | 9 | 10| 11| 12| 13| 14| 15| 16| 17| 18| 19| 20| 21| 22| 23| 24|
                  A       B   F   G   I   J   O   P   P   T   U→  U→
                          C       H       K   P   R       U→
                          D               L   Q   S
                          E               M
                                          N
```

CREDENTIALS OR DOCUMENTATION

Secondary

A   General Certificate of Education, Ordinary Level
B   General Certificate of Education, Advanced Level

Postsecondary

C   Diploma in Agriculture: two-year program requiring credential **A** for admission
D   National Technician's Diploma: two-year program requiring credential **A** for admission
E   National Technician's Certificate: two-year, part-time program requiring credential **A** for admission
F   Certificate in Education: three-year program (the middle year is supervised employment) requiring credential **A** for admission
G   National Higher Technician's Certificate: two-year, part-time program requiring credential **E** for admission
H   Diploma in Education: two-year program requiring credential **B** for admission
I   Bachelor: three-year programs in accountancy, agriculture, arts[1], business, law (B.L.), pharmacy, or science[1] requiring credential **B** for admission
J   Special Honours Bachelor's degree in accountancy, arts, education, or science: four-year programs requiring credential **B** for admission
K   Bachelor of Education in Adult Education: four-year program requiring credential **B** for admission
L   Bachelor of Science Honours in engineering: four-year program requiring credential **B** for admission
M   Bachelor of Laws (LL.B.): one-year program requiring credential **I** for admission
N   Certificate in Education: one-year program requiring credential **I** for admission
O   Bachelor of Veterinary Science: five-year program requiring credential **B** for admission
P   Master's degree in Arts or Science: two- or three-year program requiring credential **I, J, K, L**, or **M** for admission
Q   Master of Laws: one-year program after credential **M**, two years after credential **I**
R   Bachelor of Medicine, Bachelor of Surgery: six-year program requiring credential **B** for admission

S   Master of Education: two-year, part-time program after credential **J** or **K**
T   Doctor of Medicine, Master of Surgery: two-year program after credential **R**
U   Doctor of Philosophy: three to four years after credential **P**

[1] General degree or honours degree

GRADING INFORMATION

Secondary
General Certificate of Education, Ordinary Level:

Numeric	Letter	Description
1-2	A	Highest passing grade
3-4	B	
5-6	C	
7	D	
8	E	Lowest passing grade
9	U	Failing

General Certificate of Education, Advanced Level: Passing grades of A (highest) through E (lowest) are used. The grade of O indicates failure in the subject at the Advanced Level, but passing at the Ordinary Level.

Higher Education

Percentage	Description	Division
80-100	Distinction	First division
70-79	Merit	Second division, upper level
60-69	Credit	Second division, lower level
50-59	Pass	Third division
0-49	Fail	---

POSTSECONDARY INSTITUTION RECOGNITION BODY

Ministry of Higher Education. P.O. Box UA 275. Harare, Zimbabwe. Tel: 263-4-796-441. Fax: 263-4-728-730.

RESOURCES FOR ADDITIONAL INFORMATION

The British Council. 1996. *International Guide to Qualifications in Education*. 4th ed. London: Mansell.

Internet Source:
UNESCO - World Academic Database: www.unesco.org/iau/educzw.html

---

Compiler
James S. Frey
President
Educational Credential Evaluators, Inc., Milwaukee, WI

APPENDIX A

PART I: CONTACT INFORMATION OF PUBLISHERS AND DISTRIBUTORS OF RESOURCES ON FOREIGN EDUCATIONAL SYSTEMS

The International Admissions Bibliography prepared by the NAFSA: Association of International Educators Admissions Section (ADSEC) should be consulted for a comprehensive list of resources. At the time of this book's publication (September 1999) an updated edition of the bibliography was scheduled to appear in 1999.

American Association of Collegiate Registrars and Admissions Officers (AACRAO)
Office of International Education Services
One Dupont Circle, NW, Suite 520, Washington, D.C. 20036-1135. USA. Tel: 202.296.3359.
Fax: 202.872.8857. E-mail: oies@aacrao.nche.edu. Web site: www.aacrao.com

AMIDEAST
1730 M St., NW, Suite 1100, Washington, D.C. 20036-4505. Tel: 202.776.9600.
Fax: 202.822.6563. E-mail: inquiries@amideast.org. Web site: www.amideast.org

The British Council
10 Spring Gardens, London SW1A 2BN. United Kingdom. Tel: 44.0.171.389.4383.
Fax: 44.0.171.389.4292. E-mail: general.enquiries@britcoun.org. Web site: www.britcoun.org

College Board
Office of International Education
1233 20th Street, NW, Suite 600, Washington, D.C. 20036. Tel: 202.822.5900.
Fax: 202.822.5234. E-mail: internatl@collegeboard.org. Web site: www.collegeboard.org

Commonwealth Secretariat
Publications Unit, Information and Publications Division
Marlborough House, Pall Mall, London SW1Y 5HX, United Kingdom.
Tel: 44.0.1732.359387. Fax: 44.0.1732.770620. E-mail: books@commonwealth.int.
Web site: www.thecommonwealth.org

DAAD - German Academic Exchange
950 Third Ave., 19th Fl. New York, NY 10022. Tel: 212.758.3223. Fax: 212.755.5780.
E-mail: daadny@daad.org. Web site: www.daad.org

Educational Credential Evaluators, Inc.
PO Box 514070, Milwaukee, WI 53203-3470. Tel: 414.289.3400. Fax: 414.289.3411.
E-mail: eval@ece.org. Web site: www.ece.org

Institute of International Education
IIE Books, 809 United Nations Plaza, New York, NY 10017-3580. E-mail: iiebooks@pmds.org.
Web site: www.iiebooks.org

NAFSA Publications
To order publications:
P.O. Box 1020, Sewickley, PA 15143 Tel: 800.836.4994 or 412.741.1142. Fax: 412.741.0609.

Publisher's contact information:
1307 New York Ave., NW, 8th Fl., Washington D.C. 20005-4701. Tel: 202.737.3699.
Fax: 202.737.3657. E-mail: inbox@nafsa.org. Web site: www.nafsa.org

National Office of Overseas Skills Recognition
Government Publishing Service, GPO Box 84, Canberra, ACT 2601, Australia.
Fax: 61.06.295.4888. Web site: www.deetya.gov.au/noosr

Projects for International Education Research (PIER) Publications
PO Box 231, Annapolis Junction, MD 20701. Tel: 301.490.7651. Fax: 301.206.9789.
E-mail: pubs@aacrao.nche.edu. Web site: www.aacrao.com/pubs/catalog.html

UNESCO Publications
Bernan Associates, 4611-F Assembly Dr., Lanham, MD. Tel: 800.274.4447. Fax: 301.459.0056.
Toll free fax: 800.865.3450. Web sites: www.unesco.org; www.bernan.com

PART II: SPECIFIC MULTI-COUNTRY RESOURCES

The following publications were used as resources for many of the compilations in this publication.

Commonwealth Universities Yearbook
Compiled annually by the Association of Commonwealth Universities.
Grove's Dictionaries Inc. 345 Park Avenue South, New York NY 10010-1707.
Tel: 800.221.2123 or 212.689.9200. Fax: 212.689.9711. E-mail: grove@grovereference.com.
Web site: www.grovereference.com/

International Handbook of Universities
Compiled triennially by the International Association of Universities.
Order from Grove's Dictionaries, see above.

World List of Universities and Other Institutions of Higher Education
Compiled biennially by the International Association of Universities.
Order from Grove's Dictionaries, see above.

A Guide to
Educational
Systems
Around the World

Edited by Shelley M. Feagles

NAFSA

**Association of
International Educators**

NAFSA: Association of International Educators promotes the exchange of students and scholars to and from the United States. The association sets and upholds standards of good practice and provides professional education and training that strengthen institutional programs and services related to international educational exchange. NAFSA provides a forum for discussion of issues and a network for sharing information as it seeks to increase awareness of and support for international education in higher education, in government, and in the community.

International Standard Book Number: 0-912207-83-3

Library of Congress Cataloging-in-Publication Data

A guide to educational systems around the world / edited by Shelley M. Feagles.
    p. cm.
  Includes bibliographical references.
  ISBN 0-912207-83-3
  1. School grade placement--Handbooks, manuals, etc. 2. School
credits--Evaluation--Handbooks, manuals, etc. 3. Degrees, Academic--Handbooks,
manuals, etc. 4. Foreign study--Handbooks, manuals, etc. I. Feagles, Shelley M. II.
NAFSA: Association of International Educators (Washington, D.C.)

LB3061.5 .G85 1999
371.21'8
                                        99-046085